LOCAL AREA NETWORKS
THE NEXT GENERATION

LOCAL AREA NETWORKS
THE NEXT GENERATION
SECOND EDITION

Thomas W. Madron

WILEY

John Wiley & Sons, Inc.
New York • Chichester • Brisbane • Toronto • Singapore

For Beverly

The first edition of this book, *Local Area Networks: The Second Generation* by Thomas W. Madron was published by John Wiley & Sons, Inc., New York, in 1988.

Library of Congress Cataloging-in-Publication Data

Madron, Thomas William, 1937-
   Local area networks: the next generation / Thomas W. Madron. --
2nd ed.
    p. cm.
   Includes bibliographical references.
   ISBN 0-471-52250-3
   1. Local area networks (Computer networks) I. Title.
TK5105.7.M333 1990
004.6'8--dc20   90-30057
                                                 CIP

Printed in the United States of America

90 91 10 9 8 7 6 5 4 3 2 1

PREFACE

Local Area Networks: The Next Generation, Second Edition, not only provides up-to-date material on the state of local area networks (LANs), it also conveys the concepts needed in order to understand what LANs can do for you. Unlike many of the other LAN books available today, this one is concerned, as was its first edition, with the use of LANs conceived more broadly than as a means to provide some connectivity for personal computers. Although there are few hard statistics available, it is likely that more LANs are installed in large organizations than in small ones. This means that most LANs will exist in the framework of larger networks with the requisite need for bridges, gateways, and routers. A primary focus of this book is, therefore, to describe the role and function of LANs in a distributed networking environment. This focus is carried forward from the first edition and reflects the growing perspective of a large number of the LANs being manufactured and marketed today.

As LANs have become more important in large organizations, the issue of standards has become more important. The managers of small standalone LANs not intended to be connected to any larger computer or information network can probably ignore the standards issues or at least place them at a lower level of priority in the decision-making process. The managers of large networking systems and computer environments must, on the other hand, take standards into account if they want departmental LANs to communicate in an integrated fashion with other networking elements. This book, therefore, unlike many others, contains a considerable amount of material on contemporary national and international standards and the way they are developing. The secondary objectives of the book include not only a discussion of standards, but also explanations of the more important LAN technologies currently available, management issues, and the need for connectivity.

Some changes from the first edition have been made to virtually every chapter in the book. A major additional chapter has been added, Chapter 5, entitled, "LANs: Network Operating Systems," and Chapter 4 (originally Chapter 5), formerly entitled "LANs in the Micro–to–Mainframe Link," has not only undergone a name change to "Linking LANs," but has been completely rewritten from a new perspective. Chapter 4 still contains material concerning the micro–to–mainframe link, but it goes beyond that more restrictive issue. In the new Chapter 5, I have attempted to demonstrate what network operating systems (NOSs) are, and to describe a few of the major players including Banyan, IBM, Novell, and 3COM and their strategies for the 1990s. An important major element of the strategies of these manufacturers for the 1990s is the support being demonstrated for national and international standards—a rather significant change from the period in which the first edition was written.

As both a consultant and a manager of large-scale computing and communications facilities, I have not only had the opportunity to study LANs as an observer, but have also been responsible for the design, acquisition, and implementation of both departmental LANs based on microcomputers and general-purpose LANs connecting well over a thousand devices including micros, minis, and mainframes. The consequence of this blend of experiences is, I hope, a sensitivity to technical, organizational, and practical issues confronting the successful implementation of LANs.

The "next generation" of LANs will be characterized by adherence to national and international standards and by increasing bandwidth measured in transmission speed. Connected to those LANs will be not only the traditional devices, such as personal computers and high-performance workstations, but also control devices, factory tools, FAXs, and a larger number of other machines that are computer controlled with the capacity for an interface to the LAN. Appropriate networking will make possible truly intelligent buildings regardless of whether those buildings are homes, offices, or manufacturing plants. In the next ten years those intelligent buildings will become linked to regional, national, and international networks.

Neither the first edition nor this edition was written in a vacuum. A variety of people have assisted me as I have worked through these manuscripts. I must note that a number of former staff members of mine have, over the years, helped me refine my concepts and ideas. Dr. Gregory Stone reviewed both the original edition and this revision, making a number of thoughtful suggestions. In the preparation of Chapter 5, early drafts of the chapter were reviewed by staff people at Banyan, IBM, and Novell, and their assistance was very helpful. Most of the suggestions I incorporated into the manuscript, some I did not. As always, my wife Beverly was forced to listen to my thoughts and ideas concerning LANs. Notwithstanding the assistance received from all and sundry, I, of course, bear the responsibility for the veracity of the material contained herein.

Thomas W. Madron
Somerset, New Jersey
January 1990

CONTENTS

CHAPTER 1

LOCAL AREA NETWORKS: THE NEXT GENERATION

The growth of local area networks (LANs) in the mid-1980s helped shift our thinking from computers *qua* computers to the way in which we communicate among computers, and why. LANs are particularly important in that it is a LAN that will be connected to many workstations as the first stage in a larger distributed networking and computing environment. LANs are also important to many smaller organizations because they are the route to a distributed, multiuser computing environment capable of starting in modest manner, but expandable as the organization's needs grow. One reviewer of the first edition of this book commented that I may have waxed too freely with the concept of a "second generation" of LANs. Be that as it may, it is clear that in the two years since its publication, LAN development has moved along at a remarkable pace and a good many of the promises of LANs can now be fulfilled, although more are in the offing. It is appropriate, therefore, to renew the claim that the widespread use of LANs has contributed to generating a second generation. As we will note, one of the most profound influences on LAN development has been the adoption of national and international standards—standards that even the giants of the industry are finding it impossible to ignore.

Information networks can be organized in a variety of ways, and some of these are described in later pages. By the early 1980s it was possible to distinguish between what have been called "local" networks and what I shall refer to as "global" networks (solely to distinguish them from "local" networks). In many local networks all the nodes are microcomputers, although there is noth-

1

ing inherent in the technology that requires such a condition, albeit the existence of large numbers of microcomputers have probably been a major factor in the development of LANs.

Increasingly mini and mainframe computers are an integrated part of local networks. Perhaps the most pervasive and important network development of the 1980s was the recognition that computer driven devices are now the peripherals of the network, rather than the network being the peripheral of a computer. Note also that I used the term "computer driven devices," since we must now think about attaching intelligent tools on a manufacturing floor, imaging devices including FAX machines, and other devices to LANs as well as the traditional micros, minis, and mainframes. Certainly the term "computer network" is now outmoded and even the term "data communications network" may be too restrictive in an era when not only character data but also graphics, images of all sorts, and voice and video fragments must also be recognized as information with which networks must deal. *Information* processing requires *information* networks which provide services beyond those characterized by traditional voice and data transmissions.

Local networks are to be distinguished from global networks (sometimes called "Wide Area Networks" or WANs) in that global networks typically have at least one or more computer nodes central to the operation of the network. The central node is at least a time-sharing minicomputer and is frequently a large mainframe computer. In a global network microcomputers are often used as intelligent terminals within the network. While such WANs still exist and will continue to do so for the foreseeable future, it is also true that as very large global networks are being reengineered, they often no longer are focused on specific machines but are built around global connectivity issues. This is certainly true of the concept of networking as it has developed in the Open Systems Interconnection (OSI) Model (see Chapter 2) and the standards based on that model. By way of contrast, LANs were invented with a focus on connectivity. Local networks may serve on local users, may be attached to one another, or may themselves be nodes in a global network. Local area networks can have radii which range from a few hundred meters to about 50 kilometers. Global networks can be extended worldwide, if needed.

LANs and WANs do not meet all networking needs, however. There is a need for a high-speed network that will extend beyond the area covered by a LAN, but is not restricted to the normal methods of wide area networking. The Institute of Electrical and Electronics Engineers (IEEE) 802.6 Committee has adopted standards for a Metropolitan Area Network (MAN) and the American National Standards Institute (ANSI) has developed the FDDI and FDDI-II standards to expand the concept of local networking to include an area from a maximum radius of about 7 kilometers to a radius of about 50 kilometers. A MAN is defined as a network with a diameter of not more than 50 kilometers. Such a network clearly meets a need for an intermediate size information communication system that could have benefits beyond those offered by either LANs or WANs.

From the early to mid-1980s anarchy reigned among local area network makers. Not even IBM's entry into the market imposed order, partly because IBM introduced two major LANs based on different physical technologies and preannounced others. IBM's Token-Ring LAN has clearly been marked as its primary strategic LAN implementation, however. Notwithstanding IBM's entry into the LAN market, new LANs are being introduced, and the debate concerning the "best" one continues. Some order has started to become evident, however, as the IEEE/ANSI and OSI standards are being translated into products. If we listen carefully to the heated debates still taking place among the manufacturers and vendors of LANs it would appear that the battles are technical in nature, although a closer look may convince us otherwise. Ostensibly the battlelines were drawn over four major issues:

1. Access methods [Carrier Sense Multiple Access/Collision Detection (CSMA/CD), token passing, or neither]

2. Bandwidth (how fast or how much data can I pass)

3. Broadband vs. baseband (with telephony as a slow-starting third)

4. Physical medium or cable plant (coaxial or twisted pair, as a starting oversimplification)

Today the battle has moved, at least in part, to the user interface and the ease of use of the LAN, regardless of the base technology. A large part of the reason for this movement is the widespread acceptance of networking standards, both national and international. There has also been a recognition that there is a need for some variety in base technologies in the marketplace. Many of the old battles can still be seen and heard when discussions of appropriate "backbone" technologies for a campus environment take place, however.

LOCAL AREA NETWORKS— WHAT ARE THEY?

Local area networks are sometimes described as those that "cover a limited geographical area...," where every "node on the network can communicate with every other node, and...requires no central node or processor."[1] A supplementary definition, such as that given by Lee A. Bertman, suggests that a local area network "is a communications network capable of providing an intrafacility internal exchange of voice, computer data, word processing, facsimile, video conferencing, video broadcasting, telemetry, and other forms of electronic messag-

messaging."[2] A more restrictive definition frequently seen has been repeated by Robert Bowerman: LANs "are designed for sharing data between single-user workstations."[3] A local area network must be *local* in geographic scope, although the term "local" might mean anything from a single office or a large building to a multibuilding educational or industrial campus. One clear attribute of a LAN is connectivity—the ability for any given point (node, connection) to communicate with any other point. Part of the power of a LAN is the capacity to integrate multimedia electronic communications (data, video, voice, etc.).

From this effort to distinguish a local area network, it is clear that we are far from achieving a precise and commonly accepted definition. One good summary attempt to describe LANs was provided by the IEEE 802 Standards Committee in 1982.[4] The IEEE characterization of a local area network was conveniently summarized in the widely quoted Datapro *EDP Solutions*.[5] The attempt to define the meaning of "local area network" closely follows Datapro's summary, although some modifications have been made. According to the IEEE 802 Committee, "A Local Network is a data communications system that allows a number of independent devices to communicate with each other." A LAN can be further characterized as:

▼ Intra-institutional, privately owned, user-administered, and not subject to FCC regulation: Excluded from this are common carrier facilities including both public telephone systems and commercial cable television systems.

▼ Integrated through interconnection by a continuous structural medium: Multiple services may operate on a single set of cables.

▼ Capable of providing full connectivity

▼ Supportive of both low-speed and high-speed data communications: LANs are not subject to speed limitations imposed by traditional common carrier facilities and can be designed to support devices ranging in speed from 75 b/s (bits per second) based on almost any technology to about 140 Mb/s [Mega (million) bits per second] for commercially available fiber-optic LANs.

▼ Commercially available (off-the-shelf): The LAN market is still volatile, notwithstanding IBM's LAN offerings, and many systems are still custom-designed. Even announced products may still be in beta-test. Since LAN is more a concept than a product, the term "commercially available" should be taken to mean that the LAN components which provide device connections to a physical medium such as a cable television (CATV) system are commercially available.

These are the characteristics which make local area networks attractive to organizations both large and small. For large organizations the realization that much computing takes place close to the source of computing power was an important but not necessarily overwhelming reason for LANs. Xerox, an early leader in LAN development (and the inventors of Ethernet), found in one study that as much as 80 percent of all data processing requirements take place within 200 feet of the host computer and an additional 10 percent are satisfied by resources within a half mile.[6] While that finding was and is widely reported, it is useful primarily as marketing information rather than being the driving force behind the deployment of LANs, even in large organizations, and, of course, not at all where LANs provide the only information processing environment in small organizations.

DISTRIBUTED NETWORKS— WHAT ARE THEY?

Both local and global networks may be distributed networks, but they perform somewhat different functions for an organization. It is widely acknowledged that in recent years the cost per processing unit (mips, memory, whatever) of computing hardware has been declining. Even more recently this same phenomenon has become true of data communications equipment. As these artifacts of the marketplace have happened, the relative expenditures for computing equipment has been declining, while the relative expenditures for networking equipment has been increasing as percentages of the total information management budget. Part of this restructuring of expenditures was a mere reflection of the fact that while many organizations had sophisticated computing, they had primitive data communications. In any event, these budgetary changes have led some industry analysts to incorrectly "sense that the traditional concept of linking many company locations into a common network to utilize centralized facilities was waning in its desirability."[7] It is clear that the "'gurus of the future' are correct when they forecast a pivotal role for networking in future information distribution solutions."[8] The networks of the 1990s will tend to be decentralized because data processing and data bases will become increasingly distributed. The organizational implications of such a situation are manifold, but one major implication is the decentralization of responsibility (within the organization) for the maintenance and function of the networks. On a global scale, networks may be established when needed instead of being hardwired (with leased telephone lines, for example).

While global networks may or may not be distributed networks, local networks almost always distribute processing among many intelligent nodes, usually (though not necessarily) hardwired together. Such a local network can then become an intelligent node of a global network. The local network can participate in what Paul Truax, of Truax & Associates Inc., calls the "four corporate information disciplines." These four "disciplines" are office automation, data processing, database administration, and telecommunications.[9]

At several points we have spoken of centralized and distributed processing as if the two concepts in networks were at opposite ends of some continuum, although this is not the case. Nor can distributed processing be thought of simply as decentralized computing. One definition, suggested by Data 100, states that distributed computing places "a substantial part of the pre- and post-processing of data, and access to data at the places where the data originates and is used...while maintaining central control of the network."[10] It is not uncommon for networks which start as simple centralized systems to migrate to distributed systems without conscious design of systems analysts. Historically, a typical batch terminal in a network was replaced with a mini- or microprocessor-based device providing local file storage and processing capabilities as well as the capacity to generate batch jobs (or interactive jobs, for that matter).

WHY LOCAL AREA NETWORKS?

Local area networks are unique because they simplify social processes. Global networks are implemented to make more cost-effective use of expensive mainframe computers. Local area networks are implemented to make more cost-effective use of people. Connectivity is the driving concept behind local area networks in a manner unknown to global ones. LANs are a recognition of the need for people to use data and, as a by-product, to pass data from one person to another.

One key to the interest in local area networks is that those who govern large organizations have recognized that "organization" implies social interaction. Computers do not run organizations, people do. Computers do not make decisions, people do. Computers, no matter how smart, only assist people in the running of organizations. Since an organization is primarily a social process, it will operate most efficiently when decision-assisting tools are available to the people who populate it. This means that the people using computing in organizations do not do so in isolation, but rather as social beings engaged in commerce and conversation.

Into the organizational milieu many different computing facilities have been introduced: microcomputers, terminals, intelligent copiers, and large and small computers. Yet an empty computer is like an empty mind—of little or no use to anyone, including its owner. If each computer facility must be filled anew, and by hand, then work is made less—not more—efficient. In the developing information age, it is important that technology assist people to reduce the amount of information to manageable levels and to improve the quality of that information. In an organizational context networks provide the means for allowing the available computing power to be used to its most complete extent. Other issues have also been important in generating interest in LANs, including the desire for independence in computing, the need for departmental computing, and the economy of LANs.

The Desire for Independence in Computing

The desire for independence in computing predates the invention and growth of LANs. In 1983 I wrote that one factor in the growth in the use of microcomputers was the desire by computer users to gain independence from a central computing staff.[11] That was certainly not a unique observation on my part as many others had identified similar concerns. It was early noted by many users that large systems are not necessary for the kind of problems for which they might use computers.

Two classes of software appeared in the late 1970s and early 1980s that generated significant interest in micros: word processors and spreadsheets. These developments, along with micro-based database management systems, were major factors in the unprecedented growth in the use of micros in all kinds of organizations, from small to large. The difficulty with central computing facilities was that applications that many users wanted were thought by central systems staff to be "trivial," or else the software was simply too expensive at the time to be cost-effective.

It quickly became evident, however, that there needed to be an almost instant "recentralization" of computing, in that people were wasting a good deal of time reentering data already in machine-readable form, or that many people needed to be accessing (and perhaps updating) the same data. These are both issues that have traditionally been met by large central computer systems. It was also recognized that in larger organizations much of the required data already existed in corporate databases and should have been able to be downloaded to the micro. The consequence of the recognition of these issues brought on the demand for LANs and for micro–to–mainframe links with substantially more intelligence than simply using a micro as a terminal. A departmental database, or a portion of a corporate database relevant to the work of a department, could be loaded on a "file server" and accessed by many people linked together in a local area network. Thus, LANs became a logical extension of the original motives behind the acquisition of microcomputers.

The Need for Departmental Computing

At the same time that there was a growing desire by computer users to achieve greater independence from central computing facilities, there was a growing movement in both the public and private sectors for greater accountability on the part of constituent units of organizations of all sizes. In addition, there was a reassessment of the desirability of centralization in large organizations, and a recognition of the need for acquiring and maintaining a competitive advantage in all organizations. The practical impact of these movements was that work groups and departments in large organizations, and small organizations of all kinds discovered the need to be masters of their own fates, especially with regard to computing.

Because of the growing use of micros during the early 1980s, along with a growth in computer literacy, it became clear that "departments" needed to have computing power at their disposal. From a cost perspective it was clear that micros were the answer to computing power, and that LANs were the method to be used to attach the micros to one another. In the early 1980s high-performance multiuser systems were still too expensive for the use of departments or small organizations, and there were questions concerning the need for such systems when large numbers of cheap micros were already available. By the end of the decade, however, the cost of high-performance micros was no longer a detriment to their use as file servers.

LANs vs. Multiuser Systems

During the latter half of the 1980s, a spirited competition developed between vendors of small multiuser systems and LANs. The reason for this is that competition for small multiuser systems by LAN manufacturers, along with newly developed low-cost, high-performance multiuser computer systems brought the price down to a point where multiuser systems could be considered by even small organizations. During the late 1970s and early 1980s, a small multiuser system, such as IBM's System/36, could be purchased for around $100,000 with a few workstations. Today a much improved successor to the System/36/38, the AS400, has a starting price less than those of its predecessors. The drop in price must, in part, be attributed to Digital Equipment Corporation's introduction of the MicroVAX, a small multiuser system with starting prices at about $10,000. Other large manufacturers, such as AT&T, have also introduced small, relatively inexpensive multiuser systems. I won't attempt to list all those currently on the market, but there are many. These prices, by the mid-1980s, were almost competitive with micro-based LANs.

Alternatively, however, LAN development has also been taking place at a rapid rate. The LAN board that must be placed in a micro to attach it to a LAN started in the early 1980s at about $800. By the mid-1980s the price had dropped to about $400 and by the end of the decade to about $200. By using selected technologies it was possible to buy boards for less than $100. Likewise, the price of micros was also dropping rapidly. A $4,000 machine in the early 1980s was down to about $500 at this writing and high-performance systems available for not much more than $5,000. Rapid drops in the price of peripheral equipment, especially hard disk drives, also contributed to growing interest in micros and micro-based LANs. The prices given here should be taken prudentially since they will probably have changed by the time you read this book. However, the trends are important to note. Also by the end of the 1980s, it was possible to directly attach a variety of devices extending far beyond micros to LANs, including mainframes, control devices, and imaging systems.

So how do we make a choice? Why LANs over a departmental multiuser system? From the standpoint of a department or other small organization, both LANs and multiuser systems have some disadvantages that cannot be overlooked. First, when either are acquired they force the department to recognize what large central computer system organizations have always understood—that there is a considerable amount of management overhead necessary to keep such a system running properly. Second, there is also a certain amount of operational overhead that must be taken into consideration. If a department does not want to hire additional personnel, or if existing personnel cannot be reassigned, or, if a central organization cannot take management responsibility for the local systems, then departmental computing may not be appropriate. After all, once several people are dependent on a system, then that system must have user identification codes assigned, passwords protected, and backups made of important data—all time-consuming chores that on a large central system are standard operating procedures. With the advantages of departmental computing come the disadvantages.

Some of the advantages of multiuser systems over LANs are as follows:

▼ High-performance large capacity disk drives allow the maintenance and manipulation of very large files.

▼ Processing speed is often much better, although this is rapidly changing.

▼ Inexpensive "dumb" terminals can be used for access to the system. With the rapid drop in price of micros and the perceived value of a micro as a performance enhancement tool, the slight cost advantage of dumb terminals is often dismissed, however.

▼ Operational procedures, such as backup, can often be managed better than with a network of micros.

Some disadvantages are:

▼ When the system is down, everybody is down.

▼ Maintenance costs are often higher than for micro-based systems.

▼ The number of users is often more limited than with LANs. At the low-cost end the typical limit is 16 users, and the practical limit is often 10 or 12 on a 16-user system in order to provide good response time.

▼ Many users may already be utilizing micros that could perform many functions of the multiuser system.

In contrast, some of the advantages of micro-based LANs are:

▼ Since virtually all processing is distributed out to micro-based work-stations, one component down will not disrupt other users, except in the case of the file server. Redundant file servers, using a fault-tolerant technology, can, however, almost eliminate this problem.

▼ The cost of a micro is almost as inexpensive as buying a "dumb terminal."

▼ New users can be added with marginal cost.

▼ The number of users can grow quite large without major and costly upgrades. Typical networks allow for up to 64 or more users without incurring any additional "central" costs other than additional microcomputers equipped with an appropriate network interface card.

There are some disadvantages, however:

▼ Performance in accessing data file servers is, in large part, a function of the performance of the disk drives available and these are often inferior to those in multiuser systems (but not always).

▼ Disk capacity is often inferior to potential capacity in multiuser systems, although in both the price of large capacity disk drives increases the cost of the systems.

▼ The time required to do processing on micros may be excessive when compared to a multiuser system (and both may be excessive when compared to a central mainframe system).

▼ At least some operational procedures—such as backup—may be at the mercy of the end user, which means it will probably be spotty.

When balancing these advantages and disadvantages, I most frequently come down on the side of LANs (but not always). Since this is a book on local area networks, it should not be surprising that this is the case. It should be noted, however, that some of these technologies are starting to merge. It is now possible to use a high-performance "multiuser" system, such as a MicroVAX- or an 80386- (or 80486-) based micro, as a file server on a LAN. This could give the performance of a multiuser system with all the advantages of a micro-based LAN. While this approach may increase the cost of the LAN, such increases are becoming marginal. Likewise, multiple servers can be used providing additional disk storage on the LAN. Read/Write Optical disk storage is also apt to have a major impact on LAN configurations, as well, even though such devices tend to be somewhat slower than magnetic media. Recent advances in magneto-optical storage technology is certainly improving the access times of such devices, however. It should be possible to acquire fast, very high capacity storage devices at reasonable prices in the early 1990s.

LANs vs. Standard Terminals

Notwithstanding the desire to be independent of large central computer systems, it will still be necessary in many organizations for users to communicate with the central mainframe. There must be, therefore, a means by which that communication takes place. One (expensive) way to do the job is to put both a terminal and a micro on everyone's desk. With many modern mainframe computer systems, terminals are linked to the mainframe through a terminal control unit. Several terminals are connected to the controller and a single line links the controller to the computer. With the acquisition of a communications server for the LAN, however, the LAN itself can act as if it were a terminal controller and be linked to the central system. This approach has the immediate advantage of precluding the need for multiple devices on a single desk. In a sense this provides the best of both worlds. The disadvantages of this approach may include some performance degradation in mainframe access as well as some reduction in the cost- effectiveness of the micro–to–mainframe link.

LANs vs. Telephony

Contemporary Electronic Private Automatic Branch Exchange (EPABX) technology is sometimes offered as an alternative to local area networks. There are both cost and performance problems to this approach, however. An EPABX can certainly be an alternative to a general LAN if the LAN is to operate only at terminal speeds (typically in the 9.6 Kb/s to 19.2 Kb/s range). This is in contrast to 1, 2, 4, or even 10 *million* bits per second realized by LANs. There can be limits to the total growth of such a system, however, without any of the attendant advantages of the LAN. Small systems may not be able to be engineered in any cost-effective manner. The cost of an EPABX can exceed the cost of the LAN before any computing equipment is even acquired. For the purposes of discussion in this book, therefore, telephony is not seen or presented as a viable technical alternative to local area networks.

THE NEED FOR CONNECTIVITY

Connectivity is a central concept in local area networks, meaning that any device on the LAN may be addressed as an individual connection. For a large computer with many ports, each port is a connection, whereas a single-user terminal or microcomputer is also a connection. *Sessions* take place when a circuit is established between or among connections. Some LANs have the capacity to allow multicast or broadcast sessions—transmissions to a subset of all connections or to all connections. Network *nodes* are intelligent devices on a network and may support one or more connections. Networks of similar or different characteristics may be connected to each other through gateways, which, in principle, allow a user/connection on one network to communicate with a user/connection on another. Over the next few years many of the newer communications devices, such as FAX, voice and video services, image distribution, and perhaps cellular telephones, will become important ingredients of LANs. It will also become increasingly important for LAN vendors to provide appropriate interfaces to Integrated Services Digital Networks (ISDN) since this technology will shortly allow telephone systems to carry packetized voice, compressed full motion realtime video, and other information transfers requiring high speed and bandwidth. Although initial ISDN implementations will support lower speed standards, those speeds are substantially greater than the older technologies used for telephony. Moreover, very high-speed standards for ISDN enhancement are in process. ISDN services are likely to become one of the major technologies for linking LANs remote from one another as the ISDN services become widely available in the early 1990s.

NETWORK TOPOLOGIES

There are a variety of ways in which networks might be organized, and most networks are in a constant state of change and growth. If the computer network has only a main-site or host computer doing all data processing from one or more remotes, it is a centralized network. If there are remote computers processing jobs for end-users, as well as a main-site computer (that is itself optional), then we may have the beginnings of a distributed network. A distributed network can be either centralized or dispersed, but a network that does not involve distributed processing can only be centralized, since all data processing is done on a main-site computer.

It is possible for a single communications system to provide communications for two or more concurrently operating computer networks. We will review several characteristic (although oversimplified) network configurations: point–to–point; multipoint; star (centralized); ring (distributed); bus structure (distributed); and hierarchical (distributed); with more on local area networks. Figure 1.1 contains diagrammatic representations of the various network configurations or topologies.

Point–to–Point

A point–to–point network is undoubtedly the simplest network, for it has only a computer, a communications line (direct or through the telephone system), and one terminal at the other end of the wire. The terminal can be either a remote batch terminal (RBT) or interactive. This was the earliest form of network, and many networks still begin in this fashion, gradually developing into more complex entities. In such a system the central computer need not be large. A

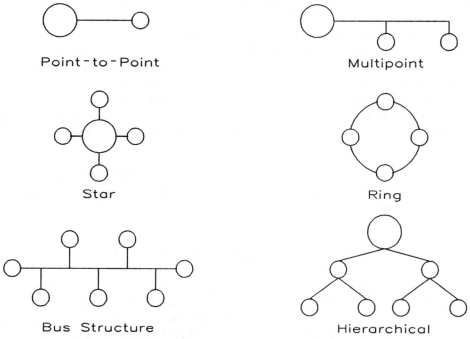

Figure 1.1   Network Topologies

microcomputer can act as a host computer for one or more terminals. Normally, however, such systems have a large computer as the host system.

Multipoint Networks

Multipoint networks originally constituted a straightforward extension of point–to–point systems in that instead of a single remote station, there are multiple remote stations. Those remote stations were either RBTs or interactive or both. The remote stations may be connected via independent communications lines to the computer or may be multiplexed over a single line. In either a point–to–point or a multipoint system, the characteristics of the remote workstations are a function of the work to be accomplished at the remote site. Local networks in some of their manifestations are expansions of the multipoint concept. In its original context, a multipoint system contained only one node with "intelligence"—with only one computer on the system. A local network will normally have intelligence at all or most points on the system without the necessity for any central system.

Centralized (Star) Networks

To reiterate, a centralized network is one in which primary computing is accomplished at a single site with all remote stations feeding into that site. Often such a system is thought of as a star network with each remote site entering the central system via a single communications line, although point–to–point and the classical multipoint systems were also centralized networks. Typically, however, a multipoint network did not have distributed processing capabilities, although a star network may have other computers out at the end of its communications lines. The computer that supported a traditional multipoint network might, itself, have been linked into a star network. Electronic Private Automatic Branch Exchange systems, based on telephone technology, is the local area network technology using a star topology where the switch constitutes the central node.

Ring (Distributed) Networks

A ring network is organized by connecting network nodes in a closed loop with each node linked to those adjacent on the right and left. The advantage of a ring network is that it can be run at high speeds, and the mechanisms for avoiding collisions are simple. As Saal has noted, the "ring topology does not have the flexibility that bus structures (see below have, yet it forces more regularity into the system...."[12] Ring networks sometimes use *token passing* schemes to determine which node may have access to the communications system.

Bus Structures (Distributed)

The bus network depicted in Figure 1.1 is configured, at least logically, with taps (arms branches, etc.) extending off a central backbone. As a signal traverses the bus—normally a coaxial, fiber-optic, or twisted pair cable—every connection listens for the signal that carries an address designation. Bus systems, such as Ethernet or most broadband (cable television) systems, employ either a bi-directional single cable with forward and return paths over the same medium, or employ a dual cable system to achieve bi-directionality. With systems based on cable television, a signal processor exists at the *headend* that takes a low incoming signal from a device on the bus and up- converts it for retransmission on a higher-frequency channel.

Hierarchical (Distributed) Networks

A hierarchical network represents a fully distributed network in which computers feed into computers that in turn feed into computers. The computers used for remote devices may have independent processing capabilities and draw upon the resources at higher or lower levels as information or other resources are required. A hierarchical network is one form of a completely distributed network. The classical model of a hierarchical distributed network is that used by Texas Instruments, in which there are several IBM 3090s at the top and IBM 4341s or similar machines in the mid-range, fed by a combination of minis (such as the TI990), micros, and other machines at the bottom. The TI990s may function as a third level and the micros (or intelligent terminals) at a fourth level.

LANS FOR ORGANIZATIONAL NEEDS

In the first edition of this book there was a distinction made between *General Purpose or Micro-based LANs,* and another discussion of *Hybrid LANs.* Those characterizations are no longer truly necessary although the issues they posed still need clarification. The original dichotomy was established between those LANs that supported thousands of connections, provided low-speed (asynchronous, RS-232-C support) access as well as high-speed access, and those that were designed primarily to connect micros. Even today, to the uninitiated, "local area network" means only those networks that link microcomputers. Yet, as is implied in Figure 1.2, LAN technology has gone far beyond these simple distinctions.

"General purpose" LANs were originally conceived as those produced by manufacturers such as Sytek, Inc., Ungermann-Bass, Bridge Communications, and others that provide local area networks using several different media but consisting primarily of terminal servers to which devices are attached for asynchronous, RS-232-C communications. This approach, that was almost the only viable one in the early 1980s, allows a variety of dumb terminals and micros to communicate primarily (although not exclusively since any node can address any other node) with a multiuser system. If that multiuser system is an IBM-type mainframe, then it was also necessary to have an asynchronous communications front-end processor attached to the computer as is still necessary for an SNA network (see Figure 1.2). All of this was costly, to say the least; but coupled with a general purpose communications medium, such as a broadband CATV system, it provided a level of connectivity previously unattainable. It is still frequently useful to be able to communicate over a LAN with asynchronous devices, but the options have grown immensely. The disadvantage of such an approach is that data communication is typically limited to 9.6 Kb/s or

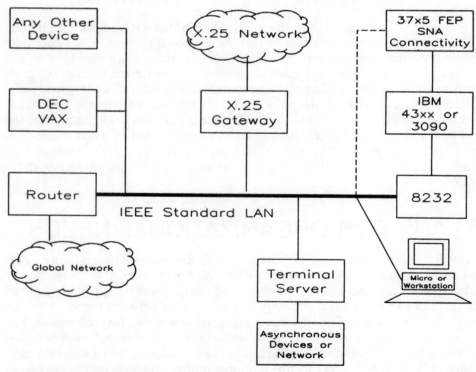

Figure 1.2   LAN Connectivity

19.2 Kb/s and they do not support most of the sophisticated end-user services that are a desirable feature of micro-based LANs. On the other hand, almost any device can be made to communicate asynchronously; with the ability to do so, a communication system will be fully connective.

The earlier manifestations of the micro-based LANs, by way of contrast, were not designed to provide connectivity except to a file server and to other micros on the network. This approach early became a problem in large organizations, although that is still the configuration found in small organizations. Several manufacturers, especially DEC, Wang (although Wang was an early manufacturer of broadband-based LANs), and others quickly saw the need for attaching more than micros to their larger systems and DEC, in particular, became a strong advocate of Ethernet. Essentially, however, micro-based LANs were conceived as work-group or departmental systems. As is easily seen from Figure 1.2, the possibilities have become much broader.

IBM mainframes still have to be "front-ended" with something since they do not directly communicate with anything except through "channels." We will not get into a discussion of what an S/370 channel configuration is, but suffice it to say that it is a relatively high-speed path (1.5 Mbyte/s, 3 Mbyte/s, or possibly 5 Mbyte/s or 6 Mbyte/s) to get data into or out of the computer. A 37xx FEP (or its cloned equivalent) is an expensive machine and has never been an ideal means for communicating with the mainframe except for SNA connectivity, with 3270 display systems and related communications. In 1988 IBM introduced the 8232 LAN controller which is an industrial strength 80286 microcomputer with a mainframe channel interface. Any of IBM's microcomputer LAN boards or selected third-party Ethernet boards can be inserted into the 8232. The cost of an 8232 is a fraction of the cost of an FEP. Combined with software running under VM or MVS (IBM mainframe operating systems) this connection provides high-speed access as directly as possible to a LAN.

Terminal servers also continue to play a role and will continue to do so until asynchronous devices disappear—a possibility that was predicted a few years ago, but which in recent years has proven to be false. Although, in principle, any IEEE standard LAN can function in such an environment, products were most widely available for 802.3 (Ethernet). In Figure 1.2 the router implies connectivity with OSI or Transport Control Protocol/Internet Protocol (TCP/IP) global networks, as does the X.25 gateway. A number of other possibilities exist for routing, gatewaying, or bridging to other networks as well. A VAX can be plugged (with an appropriate interface board) directly into the Ethernet as can a number of other devices. In other words, it is now possible to use a LAN as a front-end to a variety of devices and at the same time, use it as a micro-based system with micros and their associated servers. In other words, the technologies of the general-purpose and the micro-based LANs are rapidly converging and for a number of purposes have already done so.

The "gotcha" in all this is the paucity of good, reliable network operating environment software to make everything work smoothly and effectively. In order to have everything depicted in Figure 1.2 communicate with one another as late as 1989, it was necessary to run TCP/IP (see Chapters 3 and 4) protocols over the LAN to provide a "real" system. The reason for this is that DEC wants their customers to run DECnet, IBM wants to use proprietary software, and the micro-based network operating systems (NOSs) were, at the end of 1989, just coming to recognize the need to support protocols beyond what they had produced to link micros to one another. While the entire environment can and will come together using TCP/IP, it leaves something to be desired from the standpoint of user interaction. Moreover, at this writing terminal server mechanisms familiar to users of micro-based LANs were not readily available, although as we shall note later (see Chapter 5), this is being remedied even as I write.

SERVICES AND SERVERS

A service is often delivered through a *server*. The term "server" has been widely used and accepted in the context of LANs, although it is an appropriate concept in any network environment. A server contains the hardware, and at least part of the software, necessary to produce the service. Whether talking about print servers, file servers, communication servers, or others, servers usually operate at some point remote from the end-user and are designed for multi-user access to expensive, complicated, or infrequently used services. Services might also include processes, software, or hardware other than servers, such as support for specialized terminal emulations in a LAN to a mainframe link.

File and Print Servers

File and print servers were among the original enticements of local area networks. The servers allowed multiple users to access expensive peripherals and to maintain common databases. Outgrowths of file serving were added value services, such as electronic mail. Electronic mail, however, can be implemented in a completely distributed environment, although it is often accomplished in a more straightforward fashion if common file servers are available. As the cost of high capacity, hard disks and quality printers have declined, however, the emphasis has moved to the issue of common database systems and more exotic or expensive peripherals, such as large plotters, or other devices. What is true of local area networks is even truer of the capabilities available on large mainframe computers.

In one sense mainframe and large minicomputers constitute the ultimate in high-performance file and printer servers. High-speed high-quality laser printing is frequently available and the corporate database is accessible. If the organization's network is a large one, then a corporate-wide electronic mail system may be possible only through the central computer. In these contexts, the mainframe acts as a big peripheral to the micro. File servers on either a LAN or a WAN can also be used as archival devices for micros and when used in this manner are, indeed, microcomputer peripherals. On the other hand, micros as target nodes on a large network provide distribution points for reports or other information the organization deems necessary for its proper operation. Because data can be extracted from the corporate database, however, we must confront the issue of the integrity of the data being transferred.

An important distinction between LANs and multiuser computer systems that must be clearly understood is that in a micro-based LAN actual processing is distributed out to users' workstations. In a multiuser computer environment, however, processing is centralized at the multiuser system. This is a very important distinction for reasons already cited. It is also an important distinction because of the increasing power of file servers. When micro-based LANs were introduced in the early 1980s, a file server was typically just another machine of the same variety as the workstation. This meant that there was a major road block to increasing the performance of the LAN. Almost from the beginning the data rates of even the slowest LAN technology were faster than the access rates of the hard disk drives supported by the servers. Moreover, micros designed as single user devices were pressed into multiuser service, a fact that also degraded performance.

The problems just noted have resulted in a search for better, faster computers to be used as file servers. Because of the relatively high cost of even small minicomputers, the search has usually been directed toward improving micro technology, machines based on Intel's 80386 or 80486 processor. That approach is changing, however, as a by-product of major computer manufacturers, such as DEC, IBM, Hewlett-Packard, and others, recognizing the market demand for LANs as a method for delivering multiuser services at low cost, and developing relatively inexpensive multiuser minicomputers.

Virtually all the major minicomputer manufacturers, plus IBM, now support Ethernet and several support IBM's Token Ring. As we have noted, there were some holdouts with respect to Ethernet and there are some concerning Token Ring. For a manufacturer to continue selling its wares, it will have to support the major LAN systems and the basic LAN technology specified by the various standards organizations: IEEE in the United States and the International Organization for Standardization (ISO) in Europe. In both cases this means that IEEE 802 LAN standards are used.

Getting 802.3/Ethernet or Token Ring cards for a few micros does not make a network, however. We have already discussed the concept and realities of servers and their necessity. An additional item of software is also required: a Network Operating System. It is the NOS that brings the LAN environment together so that it can actually be useful. Suffice it to say at this point that the NOSs commercially available are becoming better all the time and somewhat lower-level (or more primitive, depending on one's point of view) network operating environments, such as TCP/IP-based software, is available.

Communication Servers—Gateways and Bridges

Because most LANs operate within the context of larger networks, and because in large organizations several or many departmental LANs may have to communicate with one another, gateways and bridges have been manufactured. While these devices will be discussed more extensively in Chapter 4 and elsewhere in this book, it is important that you understand the function gateways and bridges perform early in our discussion. Unfortunately these two terms are used with great imprecision in many trade journals and computer magazines. It has become reasonably common, however, to distinguish between the two, and the definitions that follow will be used consistently in this book. A "gateway" consists of the hardware and software necessary for two technologically *different* networks to communicate with one another.

In contrast to a gateway, a "bridge" is used to link two technologically *similar* networks to one another. Two Ethernets, for example, would be linked with a bridge rather than a gateway. Both gateways and bridges are necessary to expand connectivity and to allow people to communicate with one another or with network resources not located on the LAN of which one is a primary member. If all networks being linked use the same network operating system, such as Novell's Netware, the use of gateways and bridges may be quite simple—at least from the perspective of the end-user. If different NOSs are being used, or if different network architectures are being used, the bridges or gateways may become complicated both from a technical standpoint and from a user's perspective.

After making the neat distinction between gateways and bridges, let me hasten to introduce several caveats. First, the issue of what is technologically "similar" or "different" is more apparent than real. Part of the reason for this lies in the fact that networks, as has been implied previously, but will now be made explicit, can be defined in terms of hardware or software or a combination of the two. In Chapter 2 we will discuss the OSI protocol stack which is a "layered" network architecture. Regardless of hardware differences among several networks, and regardless of the base protocols of those networks (Ethernet and X.25, for example), if those networks both or all use the same layered protocol stack it is possible to have bridging between the same layer on two electrically and mechanically dissimilar networks. Likewise, the IEEE 802 Committee has defined a "MAC layer bridge" where the Media Access Control (MAC) sublayer of the OSI Data Link Control layer is the point at which bridging can take place between or among IEEE standard networks. In such an instance, a Token Ring could be *bridged,* not *gatewayed,* to an 802.3 (CSMA/CD, Ethernet) network, thus obviating a statement to the contrary made in the previous paragraph.

In other words, in a network premised on a layered architecture, if control for the bridging mechanism takes place in layer *n,* then lower layers need not be the same or similar in the networks being bridged. Bridging at the electro/mechanical level requires electro/mechanical equivalence; bridging at the MAC sublayer requires MAC equivalence; bridging at the OSI Network layer requires Network layer equivalence, otherwise gateways will be required since in gateways, *protocol conversion* takes place. It is possible that in the future fully adaptive networks will be developed that will modify or eliminate the need for the bridges and gateways just described. The conceptual advantage of an adaptive network is that it would improve the transparency of that network to the end-user. However, such networks will require devices with a degree of intelligence not currently available.

LAN FUTURES

During the 1980s local area networks became an important and integral part of a wide range of information processing systems. Particularly in the areas of office automation and distributed processing they play a major role. But local area networks are not limited to systems like Ethernet or Token Ring. They can be expansive and form the basic networking approach for a multibuilding campus-like institution whether in the public or private sector. The technology which, in the early to mid-1980s, offered the most generalized approach to local area networking was broadband cable television. By 1990 many of the installation and engineering problems that made fiber-optic cable expensive had been solved or were close to a solution and it had become the medium of choice for backbone construction in many institutions. Yet broadband is alive and well as evidenced by the fact that several of the IEEE LAN standards provide broadband options as well as fiber. During the 1990s it is likely that fiber will begin to replace coaxial cable as the medium for broadband systems thus reducing the contention between those opting for broadband coaxial systems and some networks using fiber optics.

There are physical layer technologies used for networking—and for LANs—other than those described in this book. It is possible that technologies such as satellite, packet radio, and cellular phone will provide the base for wireless LANs. Such systems could be useful in mobile applications and in organizational situations where office or manufacturing locations change frequently. It is not difficult to imagine military needs for such systems. Packet radio is, in fact, the foundation for mobile LANs used by IBM, Federal Express, and other corporations. The idea for the use of radio technology for such purposes is not new. Dr. Edwin Armstrong, in the 1930s, for example, simultaneously transmitted music on a main FM channel and facsimile pictures on a subcarrier. Unfortunately, the vacuum tube technology of the time was unstable, unreliable, and expensive. The use of the FM or television band subcarriers has the disadvantage of being a simplex (one-way) communications system, but there are many applications when this is appropriate. Even the possibility of distributing some publications—also an idea from the 1930s—electronically has been recently revived. Unlike the use of subcarriers, satellites, packet radios, and cellular telephones can all be used in multiway communications. When these systems are used in a LAN-like network some form of carrier sense multiple access (see Chapters 2 and 7) often provides the protocol base necessary for appropriate multiway communication. The potential for these new or revived technologies for information dissemination is the topic for another book, however.

How can we talk about the "next" generation of LANs? Certainly with the broad acceptance of LAN standards, continuing development of LAN technology (IBM's Token Ring, for example) and the application of improved Very Large Scale Integrated (VLSI) circuits technology to LAN interfaces, the hardware, software, and organization of LANs has progressed immensely since the early 1980s. The most important change, brought on by the developments just noted, is the dramatic reduction in cost of establishing a LAN, particularly micro-based systems. This has meant, in turn, that practical LAN availability has undergone a dramatic shift to the point where organizations and groups that could not afford LANs in 1980 or 1981 can now own several. In fact, LANs and PCs are sufficiently affordable so that applications can now be contemplated—such as intelligent homes—that only a short time in the past were not thought to be feasible. In these contexts, then, we can talk about Local Area Networks: The Next Generation.

REFERENCES

1. H. J. Saal, "Local-Area Networks," *Byte,* October 1981 (6, 10), pp. 96–97.

2. L. A. Bertman, "Exploring the Capabilities of Local Area Networks," *The Office,* May 1983, p. 55.

3. Robert Bowerman, "Choosing a Local Area Network," *Interface Age,* July 1983, p. 55.

4. IEEE Project 802, "Local Network Standards: Introduction," Draft C, May 17, 1982.

5. Datapro Research Corporation, *EDP Solutions,* December 1982, pp. CS10-650-101 and CS10-650-102.

6. The study by Xerox has been widely quoted. See Linda B. Drumheller and Nicholas A. Lombardo, "LANs: Here to Stay?," *Small Systems World,* May 1983, pp. 25–29.

7. Dale G. Mullen, "Is Your Telecommunications Network Obsolete?," *Telematics,* Vol. 1, No. 4, September 1981, pp. 17–19.

8. See Mullen, Ref. 7, p. 18.

9. From an address to the 1980 DPMA International Conference, as quoted by Wayne L. Rhodes, Jr., "Office of the Future: Light Years Away?," *Infosystems,* Vol. 28, No. 3, March 1981, pp. 40–50.

10. As reported by John M. Lusa et al., "Distributed processing: Alive and Well," *Infosystems,* November 1976, pp. 35–41.

11. Thomas W. Madron, *Microcomputers in Large Organizations* (Englewood Cliffs, NJ: Prentice-Hall, 1983), Chapter 1.

12. Harry Saal, "Local Area Networks: An Update on Microcomputers in the Office," *Byte,* May 1983, p. 62.

LOCAL AREA NETWORK STANDARDS

Standards benefit the consumers of computer and communications products, but force manufacturers to consider quality rather than gimmicks. Standards discussions have never been embraced with enthusiasm by manufacturers—especially large corporations—since they lose control over customers. As a by-product of standards, many different manufacturers can produce compatible and complementary equipment thus reducing the possibility that one or a few companies can monopolize a niche of the industry. Because many manufacturers can produce compatible equipment where standards exist, marketing is forced to emphasize quality and value-added services rather than particular protocol differences. This leads to competition and lower prices for consumers of the products.

In this chapter we will consider the state of standards discussions and adoptions and introduce a few of those most important for local area networking. In particular, the International Organization for Standardization's (ISO) Open Systems Interconnection (OSI) Model provides a general reference framework for LAN standards, while The Institute of Electrical and Electronics Engineers 802 Committee is attempting to provide standards that can be used to guide the manufacture of LAN components and software. In subsequent chapters we will consider several specific standards that are of the utmost importance when considering LANs and the way they work.

THE NATURE AND CHARACTER OF STANDARDS

Lest we wax too enthusiastic concerning the standards movement, let me hasten to add that standards will not and should not end debate over what is "best" concerning some specific technology. Standards committees are typically composed of computer scientists from universities and representatives of manufacturers with special interests concerning the technology being considered. A final draft of a standard is likely to be a compromise among a variety of special interests, therefore, mediated by the need for technical definitions that make some sense. Contemporary standards are not designed to be chiseled in stone. Rather, they are designed to be enlarged and modified so that new technologies can coexist with older devices.

The standards with which we are concerned are those that deal with LAN media, access, and data transmission. A secondary concern will be for those future standards that define gateways and bridges. Part of the IEEE 802 project is the attempt to standardize the first two layers (physical and link) of the Open System Interconnection Model. Of the several sublayers (logical link control, media access control, physical, and medium), three communications access methods were the first elements to be endorsed: CSMA/CD, token bus, and Token Ring.[1]

NETWORKS IN THE CONTEXT OF THE OSI/ISO MODEL

To understand some of the issues involved in network planning and to lend credibility to the project itself, it is useful to take a quick look at some of the relevant standards available. There are several standards organizations in North America and Europe that seek to rationalize electronic systems. Among those organizations are the International Standards Organization and The Institute of Electrical and Electronics Engineers. Standards of any kind for networks are of recent origin, a situation which has led to an almost chaotic array of network products.

In 1977 the ISO chartered a committee to study the compatibility of network equipment, a development that eventually led to the publication of the Open System Interconnection Reference Model. In this context, "open system" refers to a network model open to equipment from competing manufacturers. As Frank Derfler and William Stallings have noted, the OSI "reference model is useful for anyone involved in purchasing or managing a local network because it provides a theoretical framework..." by which networking problems and op-

ISO/OSI Reference Model

Open System Interconnection

Layer	Function
Layer 7 Application	End-user and end-application functions such as file transfer (FTAM), virtual terminal service (VTP), and electronic mail (X.400).
Layer 6 Presentation	Data translation for use by Layer 7 such as protocol conversion, data unpacking, encryption, and expansion of graphics commands.
Layer 5 Session	Provides for the establishing of a session connection between two presentation entities to support orderly data exchange.
Layer 4 Transport	Transparent transfer of data between session entities relieving the session layer of concerns for data reliability and integrity.
Layer 3 Network	Provides the means to establish, maintain, and terminate network connections among open systems, particularly routing functions across multiple networks.
Layer 2 Data Link	Defines the access strategy for sharing the physical medium, including data link and media access issues.
Layer 1 Physical	Definition of the electrical and mechanical characteristics of the Network.

Figure 2.1   Open System Interconnection Model
NOTE: This model is an attempt to define functional tasks in a network, althrough several layers may be combined in a single piece of equipment or software.

portunities may be understood.[2] The OSI model divides networking issues into functions or layers. These layers are depicted in Figure 2.1.

Overview of OSI

The Reference Model was devised to allow "standardized procedures to be defined enabling the interconnection and subsequent effective exchange of information between users."[3] "Users," in this sense, means systems consisting of one or more computers, associated software, peripherals, terminals, human operators, physical processes, information transfer mechanisms and related elements. These elements together must be capable of "performing information processing and/or information transfer."[3] Standards developed from the Reference Model will permit various networks of the same or different types to easily communicate with one another as if they constituted a single network.

At the outset it is important to keep in mind that conformance with the Reference Model does not imply any particular implementation or technology. It does not, in other words, specify a medium (such as fiber-optic cable, twisted pair, or coax), nor a specific set of recommendations such as the IEEE 802.3, 802.4, or 802.5 networks in the United States. The Reference Model is designed to support standardized information exchange procedures, but provides neither details nor definitions or interconnection protocols.[4] The Reference Model, therefore, is a frame of reference for open systems with implementation details being left to other standards. Because the Reference Model is a frame of reference, it provides the framework for the definition of services and protocols which fit within the boundaries established.

Scope and Field of Application

The development of the OSI Model has been led by the CCITT and those recommendations have been adopted by ISO. The scope of the Reference Model is relatively broad and may be summarized in the following five points:[5]

1. To specify a universally applicable logical structure encompassing broad communications applications, especially those of CCITT;

2. To act as a reference during the development of new communications services;

3. To enable different users to communicate with each other by encouraging the compatible implementation of communication features;

4. To enable the steady evolution of communications applications, particularly those of the CCITT, by allowing sufficient flexibility so that advancements in technology and the evolving needs of users can be accommodated;

5. To allow new user requirements to be satisfied in a manner compatible with existing services consistent with OSI.

The Reference Model is designed to be applied in the development of interconnection protocols for communications services as follows:

1. A new requirement is first expressed in user oriented terms, then analyzed to allow the requirement to be grouped into appropriate functional subsets;

2. A formal description technique (FDT) may be required for the specification of a requirement although narrative text will also be used for clarification;

3. A set of service definitions and protocol specifications is evolving for each of the seven layers, thus extending the application of OSI;

4. New functions will be incorporated into the Reference Model to enhance future applicability;

5. For new uses and applications of OSI where no appropriate protocol is contained in the Recommendations, new protocols, particularly for the application layer, will be needed—and, we might add, are in the process of being written.

Open Systems Interconnection Environment

It is important to understand that OSI is concerned with the exchange of information among open systems—not with the internal functioning of each individual "real" open system. This concept is depicted in Figure 2.2. A "real system" in this context is one that complies with the requirements of the OSI Model in its communications with other "real systems." A real system is, therefore, a set of "one or more computers, associated software, peripherals, termi-

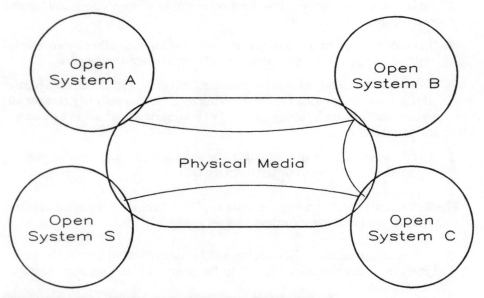

Figure 2.2   Open Systems Connected by Physical Media
SOURCE: International Telegraph and Telephone Consultative Committee (CCITT), Recommendation X.200, Reference Model of Open Systems Interconnection for CCITT Applications, Fascicle VIII.5–Rec. X.200 (1984), p. 5.

nals, human operators, physical processes, information transfer means, etc., that forms an autonomous whole capable of performing information processing and/or information transfer."[6] Within an open system an application process performs the information processing for a particular application.

Aspects of systems not related to interconnection are outside the scope of OSI. This still leaves broad scope for OSI for it is concerned not only with the transfer of information among systems, but also with their ability to interwork to achieve a common or distributed task. This is implied by the expression, "systems interconnection." The fundamental objective of OSI is to define a set of Recommendations to enable open systems to cooperate. Cooperation involves a broad range of activities:

1. Interprocess communication: the exchange of information and the synchronization of activity among OSI application processes;

2. Concern with all aspects of the creation and maintenance of data descriptions and data transformations for reformatting data exchanged among open systems;

3. Concern with storage media and file and database systems for managing and providing access to data stored on the media;

4. Process and resource management by which OSI application processes are declared, initiated and controlled, and the means by which they acquire OSI resources;

5. Integrity and security of data during the operation of open systems; and

6. Program support for comprehensive access to the programs executed by OSI application processes.

Since some of these activities may imply exchange of information among the interconnected open systems, they may be of concern to OSI.

Concepts of a Layered Architecture

In a layered architecture each open system is viewed as logically composed of an ordered set of subsystems.[7] The seven subsystem layers of OSI have been depicted in Figure 2.1. Subsystems that are adjacent to one another in the vertical hierarchy communicate through their common boundary. Within each subsystem or layer are *entities*. Entities in the same layer, but in different open systems, are termed *peer-entities*. Some conventional definitions have been developed to refer to the components of the layered architecture:

(N)-Subsystem:. An element in a hierarchical division of an open system that interacts directly only with elements in the next higher division or the next lower division of that open system

(N)-Layer: A subdivision of the OSI architecture, constituted by subsystems of the same rank (N)

(N)-Entity: An active element within an (N)-subsystem

Peer-entities: Entities within the same layer

Sublayer: A subdivision within a layer

(N)-Service: A capability of the (N)-layer and the layers beneath it, which is provided to (N + 1)-entities at the boundary between the (N)-layer and the (N + 1)-layer

(N)-Facility: A part of the (N)-service

(N)-Function: A part of the activity of (N)-entities

(N)-Service-access-point: The point at which (N)-services are provided by an (N)-entity to an (N + 1)-entity

(N)-Protocol: A set of rules and formats (semantic and syntactic) which determines the communication behavior of (N)-entities in the performance of (N)-functions

Layering and the method for referring to each layer (N, N + 1, N − 1, etc.) are depicted in Figure 2.3. The highest layer does not have an (N + 1)-layer above it and the lowest layer does not have an (N − 1)-layer below it. The physical medium is not a part of the layered architecture.

When an entity communicates, it does so with a peer at the same layer at another open system. Not all peer (N)-entities need or even can communicate, however. Conditions that prevent such communication includes the possibility that they are not in interconnected open systems or that they do not support the same protocol subsets. A distinction is made between the *type* of some object and an *instance* of that object. A type is a description of a class of objects while an instance of this type is any object that conforms to this description. The instances of the same type constitute a class. A computer program, for example, is a type of something and each copy of that program (running perhaps on different machines or concurrently on the same

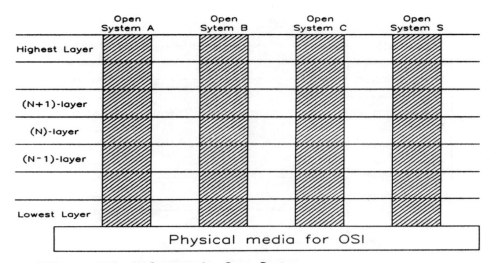

Figure 2.3 Layering in Cooperating Open Systems
SOURCE: International Telegraph and Telephone Consultative Committee (CCITT), Recommendation X.200, Reference Model of Open Systems Interconnection for CCITT Applications, Fascicle VIII.5–Rec. X.200 (1984), p. 8.

machine) are instances of the type. In the OSI model communication occurs only between (N)-entity instances at all layers. Connections are always made to specific (N)-entity instances.

As we noted above, a layer may have sublayers. Sublayers are small substructures which extends the layering technique to cover other dimensions of OSI. A sublayer, therefore, is a grouping of functions in a layer which may be bypassed, although the bypassing of *all* the sublayers of a layer is not allowed. A sublayer uses the entities and connections of its layer. We will later look at such sublayering in a discussion of the IEEE 802 standard, particularly the Logical Link Control and Media Access Control which are sublayers of the OSI Data Link Layer (Layer 2). Except for the highest layer, each (N)-layer provides (N + 1)-entities in the (N + 1)-layer with (N)-services. The highest layer represents all possible uses of the services which are provided by the lower layers.

It is important to understand that an open system can be OSI compatible without providing the initial source or final destination of data. In other words, an open system need not contain the higher layers of the architecture. The IEEE 802 standard, for example, applies only to the lowest two layers: Data Link and Physical. This is often the source of significant confusion since when we talk of 802.3 (commonly called Ethernet) or 802.5 (token ring) the discussion sometimes proceeds to commentaries on TCP/IP or XNS or some other "protocol." TCP/IP and

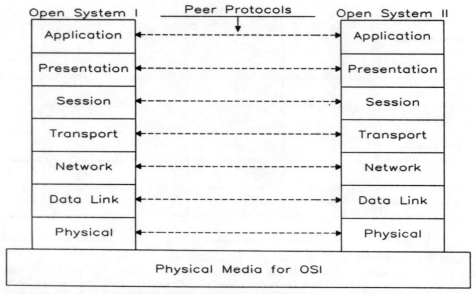

Figure 2.4   Seven-Layer Reference Model and Peer Protocols
SOURCE: International Telegraph and Telephone Consultative Committee (CCITT), Rec-
ommendation X.200, Reference Model of Open Systems Interconnection for
CCITT Applications, Fascicle VIII.5–Rec. X.200 (1984), p. 8.

XNS exist at layers beyond the Physical and Data Link (although TCP/IP and XNS
are not OSI standard protocols). Peer entities communicate through peer protocols at the appropriate layer of the OSI architecture as seen in Figure 2.4.

A commonly misunderstood issue relates to error detection and notification. In a fully elaborated set of interconnected open systems, using a number
of peer protocols at some or all of the layers of the Reference Model, each (N)-
protocol may require its own error detection and notification functions to provide a higher probability of both protocol-data-unit error detection and data
corruption detection than is provided by the (N − 1)-service. Thus we may have
multiple levels of error detection and notification. Error detection itself is a
management function of which there are three major categories: (i) application
management; (ii) systems management; and (iii) layer management.

Not all open systems provide the initial source or final destination of
data. The physical media for OSI may not link all open systems directly.
Some open systems, therefore, may act only a relay open systems, passing
data to other open systems. A related concept is *routing*. A routing function
within the (N)-layer enables communication to be relayed by a chain of (N)-

entities. Neither lower nor upper layers know that a communication is being routed by an intermediate (N)-entity. An (N)-entity participating in a routing function may have a routing table. The functions and protocols that support the forwarding of data are provided in the lower layers: Physical, Data Link, and Network. This forwarding function is illustrated in Figure 2.5.

A number of layered data communications architectures exist, but others than OSI are often proprietary and not designed to promote the inter-operability of networks. The two best known examples are IBM's SNA and DEC's DNA. It is possible, therefore, to formulate alternative layering strategies. In the construction of the OSI Model, however, some general principles were developed to guide the process. In closing this section it may be useful to review those principles:

1. Do not create too many layers since excessive numbers lead to excessive complexity;

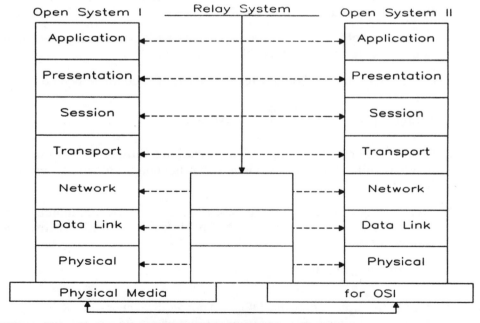

Figure 2.5   Communication Involving Relay Open Systems
SOURCE: International Telegraph and Telephone Consultative Committee (CCITT), Rec-
ommendation X.200, Reference Model of Open Systems Interconnection for
CCITT Applications, Fascicle VIII.5–Rec. X.200 (1984), p. 8.

2. Create a boundary between layers at a point where the description of services can be small and the number of cross-boundary interactions are minimized;

3. Create separate layers to handle functions that are manifestly different;

4. Collect similar functions in the same layer;

5. Select boundaries at a point which past experience has demonstrated to be successful;

6. Each layer should contain easily localized functions so that the layer could be easily redesigned to take advantage of new technologies without changing the expected services from and provided to the adjacent layers;

7. Create a boundary where it may be useful at some point in time to have the corresponding interface standardized;

8. Create a layer where there is a need for a different level of abstraction in the handling of data;

9. All changes of functions or protocols to be made within a layer without affecting other layers (refer back to number 6);

10. Create for each layer boundaries with its upper and lower layer only.

Three additional principles apply to sublayering:

11. Create further subgrouping and organization of functions for form sublayers within a layer in cases where distinct communications services need it;

12. Create, where needed, two or more sublayers with a common, and therefore minimal functionality to allow interface operation with adjacent layers; and

13. All bypassing of sublayers.

With respect to principle 7, note that OSI does not require interfaces within open systems to be standardized. There was, when that principle was written, some disagreement over the usefulness of standards for internal interfaces. Moreover, even when standards for such interfaces are defined, the Recommendation is clear in rejecting adherence to such a standard as a condition of openness.

The Seven Layers of OSI

Following the principles enunciated above, the OSI seven-layer model has evolved. It might be useful to review Figure 2.1. Layers 1–6, together with the physical media for OSI provide a step-by-step enhancement of communication services. In the OSI model Layer 1 is the hardware base for the network but does not include the physical communication media. Layers 2 through 7 are implemented in software. In Table 2.1, I have attempted to list some of the standards either adopted or in the process of development by layer. Several of those standards—the LAN standards emanating from IEEE—are the primary focus of this book and will be explored in detail. They represent much of the work that has been done for Layers 1 and 2. Other illustrations will be given in this chapter.

Throughout the set of standards discussed in this book two concepts recur and need to be defined here: *connectionless* and *connection-oriented* services. These are also sometimes referred to as *datagram* and *virtual circuit* services, respectively. Generally, a datagram may be defined as a finite length packet with sufficient information to be independently routed from source to destination without reliance on previous transmissions. Datagram transmission typically does not involve end-to-end session establishment and may or may not entail delivery confirmation acknowledgment. A connection-oriented service establishes a virtual connection that gives the appearance to the user of an actual end-to-end circuit. The virtual connection contrasts with a physical circuit in that it is a dynamically variable connection where sequential user data packets may be routed differently during the course of a virtual connection. A connectionless service does not set up a virtual or logical connection between hosts and does not guarantee that all data units will be delivered or that they will be delivered in the proper order. The advantages of connectionless service are flexibility, robustness, and connectionless application support. Connectionless applications are those that require routing services but do not require connection-oriented services.

A datagram service, such as that provided by the U.S. Department of Defense (DOD) Internet Protocol [(IP) see Chapter 10], is a connectionless service. Likewise, in the context of OSI, some protocols provide connection-oriented services while others provide connectionless services. Moreover, both these services can exist at several levels. The ISO 8473 standard, for example, is a connectionless protocol for the Network Layer and functions similarly to IP, while ISO 8073 is a connection-oriented protocol at the Transport Layer. As will be seen in Chapter 4, the IEEE Std 802.2 (ISO 8802/2) Logical Link Control standard can be implemented as either a connectionless or connection-oriented service in the Data Link Layer. Typically, if a network is configured to handle connection-oriented

Table 2.1 OSI Intra-Layer Standards

Layer	Standard Name	Number
Application	Office Document Architecture (ODA)	ISO 8613
	File Transfer, Access, & Mgt. (FTAM)	ISO 8571
	Virtual Terminal	ISO 9040
	Network Management	ISO 9595/96
	Manufacturing Message Spec.	ISO 9506
	Distributed Transaction Proc.	ISO 10026
	Document Filing & Retrieval	SC 18N 1264/5
	Remote Database Access Protocol	ISO 9576
	Job Transfer & Manipulation	ISO 8832/33
	Document Transfer, Access, and	
	Manipulation Protocol	CCITT T.431/433
	The Directory	CCITT X.500, ISO 9594
	Message Handling Service	CCITT X.400, ISO 10020/21
	Common Service Elements:	
	Association Control Service	
	Elements (ACSE)	ISO 8649/50
	Reliable Transfer Service Elements (RTSE)	ISO 9066
	Remote Operations Service Elements (ROSE)	ISO 9072
Presentation	Connection-oriented Presentation Protocol	ISO 8823
	Connectionless Protocol	ISO 9576
Session	Connection-oriented Session Protocol	ISO 8237
	Connectionless Protocol	ISO 9548
Transport	Connection-oriented Transport Protocol	ISO 8073
	Connectionless Protocol	ISO 8602
Network	Connectionless Protocol	ISO 8473
	X.25	ISO 8208
	End System to Intermediate System	
	Exchange Protocol	ISO 9542
	Proposal on how to use ISDN in OSI	
	and OSI in ISDN	ISO 9574

(Continued)

Table 2.1 (*Continued*)

Layer	Standard Name	Number
Data Link	Logical Link Control	IEEE 802.2, ISO 8802/2
	Media Access Control:	
	CSMA/CD	IEEE 802.3, ISO 8802/3
	Token Bus	IEEE 802.4, ISO 8802/4
	Token Ring	IEEE 802.5, ISO 8802/5
	Fiber Distributed Data Interface	ISO 9314
Physical	CSMA/CD	IEEE 802.3, ISO 8802/3
	Token Bus	IEEE 802.4, ISO 8802/4
	Token Ring	IEEE 802.5, ISO 8802/5
	Fiber Distributed Data Interface	ISO 9314
	Slotted Ring	ISO 8802/7
OSI Model Related		
	Application Layer Structure	ISO 9545
	Procedures for OSI Registration Authorities	ISO 9834
	Security Architecture	ISO 7498-2
	Naming and Addressing	ISO 7498-3
	Management Framework	ISO 7498-4

NOTE: While several of these standards are completed, many were still under development at the time of writing, although completion was anticipated during 1988 or 1989. Enhancements were also being made to existing standards (such as the 8802 LAN standards and to modem standards) and these are not listed separately.

services at say, the Transport Layer, the protocols at the Network and Data Link Layers would likely be implemented as connectionless services.

Mentioned above was the U.S. Department of Defense's Internet Protocol standard. DOD also has defined TCP: Transmission Control Protocol. At least in the United States significant literature is developing concerning the relationship between TCP/IP and OSI. The reason for this is that a great deal of internetworking in the United States is currently being accomplished through the use of TCP/IP. The DOD, along with the U.S. Government generally, has committed itself to moving from TCP/IP to OSI. That movement will likely continue into the 21st century to accomplish but it requires that the relationship of TCP/IP to OSI be well understood. To describe completely the OSI structure, standards at every level from the Network layer through the Application layer would have to be described thus providing sufficient material for an entire book. Some parallel comment on OSI and TCP/IP standards is necessary because already networks in the United States, including both those of the Department of Defense and the National Science Foundation, explicitly project migration from TCP/IP to OSI. It is important, therefore, to understand where parallel protocols fit and how we get from one standard to the other.

Compared with TCP and IP, OSI standards provide equivalent or superior functionality. X.400, the international message transfer standard, provides significantly greater capability than the Simple Mail Transfer Protocol (SMTP). A standard since 1984, X.400 is gaining significantly in vendor support. The international standards corresponding to TCP/IP's File Transfer Protocol (FTP) and virtual terminal services (Telnet) are FTAM and VTP, respectively. These were not yet widely available at this writing, but will provide much greater capability when implemented. A report issued in 1985 by the National Research Council (NRC, U.S.) detailed many of the reasons for migration from TCP/IP to OSI.[8] With respect to the U.S. Department of Defense the NRC study produced three findings[9]:

1. DOD objectives can be met by international standards.

2. TCP and OSI transport are functionally equivalent.

3. There are significant benefits for DOD in using standard commercial products.

In the long run the cost of OSI products should be lower than corresponding TCP/IP products. There are, however, some functional benefits in addition to lower cost:

1. The variety of commercial products integrated with OSI-related standards will continue to grow and expand.

2. OSI counterparts to FTP, SMTP, and Telnet do not suffer from the same limitations.

3. OSI-related standards extend far beyond the DOD standards in areas such as document architecture, network management, and transaction processing.

During the period of transition it will be necessary for many TCP/IP networks to operate in parallel with OSI networks, using application layers gateways that map between TCP/IP and OSI applications. As networking becomes more global and as TCP/IP runs out of addresses, OSI will become the dominant internetworking standard. With these notes in mind, we will now turn to a discussion of the seven layers of the OSI Reference Model.

Layer Functions

Each layer in the OSI reference model defines a layer or level of function. Compatibility of equipment can be defined within a layer, or lower-level implementations can be hidden to achieve compatibility at some higher level. The dual purposes of the model are to ensure information flow among systems and at the same time permit variation in basic communications technology. Moreover, in any given organization, it might be possible to have one network take care of the lower levels and another network the higher levels, using gateways among the networks.

In the ISO model, Layer 1 is the hardware base for the network. Layers 2 through 7 are implemented in software. The Application Layer (Layer 7) provides services for network users. The responsibility for the initiation and reliability of data transfers takes place in Layer 7. General network access, flow control, and error recovery are, in part, a function of this layer. Tasks are performed at the Layer 7 level and all lower levels are designed to support the applications. Electronic message systems, terminal emulation capabilities, and file transfer programs are illustrative of the software operating at Layer 7.

Translation of information for use by Layer 7 is accomplished in the Presentation Layer (Layer 6). Such services as protocol conversion, data unpacking, translation, encryption, character set changes or conversions, and the expansion of graphics commands take place in Layer 6.

Of particular importance to local area networks is Layer 5 (the Session Layer). Recall that one major reason for implementing a LAN is connectivity—the ability for any two or more devices to connect with one another. When a link is made between two devices, a session is established. In a somewhat more technical sense, the Session Layer provides for the establishment and termination of streams of data from two or more LAN connections or nodes. When a network maps network addresses on specific connections a Level 5 function is taking place.

The purpose of the Transport Layer (Layer 4) is to provide an additional, yet lower level, of connection than the Session Layer. Within the transport layer issues dealing with a fundamental level of reliability in data transfer are confronted. These issues include flow control, error handling, and problems involved with the transmission and reception of packets. We will return to a more detailed discussion of packets in a later chapter, so suffice it to say that a packet is composed of user originated data plus information the network needs to transport user data from one network node to another.

In many local area networks, a functional Layer 3 (Network Layer) is not needed. Networks that require routing mechanisms among nodes require Layer 3. LANs, however, in some implementation, have data broadcast to every node, and a particular connection collects those packets properly addressed to it. Baseband LANs, such as Ethernet, typically broadcast on only a single "channel" and require no routing. Broadband systems, however, are frequently designed with frequency agility (the ability to use more than a single "channel") and, therefore, require some bridging mechanism—that mechanism requires some routing technique.[10] When LANs are connected via gateways to one another, however, a functional Layer 3 is required.

The Data Link Layer (Layer 2) defines the access strategy for sharing the physical medium (the cable of whatever variety). We will discuss such access strategies at greater length later, but common LAN techniques include Carrier Sense Multiple Access/Collision Detection and token passing schemes. Techniques for network specific information in data packets, such as a node address, are functions of Layer 2.

Layer 1 is the Physical Layer—the layer that defines the electrical and mechanical characteristics of the network. Modulation techniques, frequencies at which the network operates, and the voltages employed are all characteristic of Layer 1. Because all networks must implement Layers 1 and 2, they have received the most attention from network vendors. If the attention paid to these layers results in compatible components, then we will know if the concept of standards has been useful. Standards are often less a technical accomplishment than they are the illustration of some vendors' ability to lobby a standard to success.

The development and implementation of OSI standards promises to make new and expanding networks easier and less expensive to operate in multi-vendor environments. With increasing frequency OSI is the model being followed by manufacturers, and by requirements of governments and user organizations worldwide. In the United States OSI standards have been incorporated into the National Bureau of Standards' (NBS) "Federal Information Processing Standards." OSI is a key factor in the development of the Manufacturing Automation Protocol (MAP), developed by General Motors. And the U.S. Department of Defense has reviewed OSI protocols for suitability for its requirements, although it supports its own Transport Control Protocol. Other standards, such as those of the IEEE are integrated into the OSI scheme.[11]

THE COMPLEXITY OF STANDARDS

The task of establishing standards is complex and not easily achieved. In fact, part of the problem is political rather than technical, since for any given technology there may be one or more special interests that may have a great deal to lose, depending on the adopted standards. This problem is reflected in the IEEE 802 Committee's decision to support both bus and ring topologies and two media (baseband and broadband). The committee decided to standardize virtually all serious proposals rather than just one. This was likely a compromise based on the recognition of the need for broad acceptance of the standards if they were to make a difference.

The complexity issue can be illustrated by comparing the IEEE "local network reference model" to the OSI model. Three (sub)layers comprise the local network model[12]:

▼ Physical. This deals with the nature of the transmission medium, electrical signaling, and device attachment.

▼ Medium access control. Since many devices share a single medium, some method for regulating access to that medium is necessary.

▼ Logical link control. This defines the establishment, maintenance, and termination of the logical link between devices.

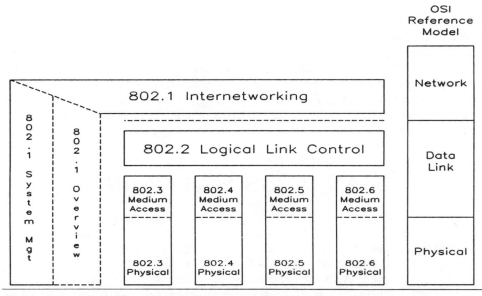

Figure 2.6   Relationship of IEEE Standards and the OSI Reference Model
SOURCE: Based on IEEE P802.1, Draft E, July 1, 1987, Overview, Internetworking, and Systems Management, unapproved draft published for comment only, by permission of the IEEE. All rights reserved by The Institute of Electrical and Electronics Engineers, Inc., p. 7.

The relationship between the OSI and local network models is depicted in Figure 2.6. The long-term advantage of acceptable standards is that many different manufacturers will be able to produce compatible devices and this will, in the long run, be a boon to purchasers of such systems.

The strategy being pursued by the IEEE's 802 Committee is to provide a flexible framework for LANs. At least part of the reason for this approach has likely been the inability to impose single standards on a wide range of special interests. In addition, however, there is an implicit recognition that needs of users differ as well as demands of LAN manufacturers. The 802 Standards Committee is actually producing a family of standards for local area networks. Those most frequently discussed as of this writing were the following:

1. ANSI/IEEE Std 802.3 (ISO DIS 8802/3), a bus using CSMA/CD (see below) as the access method.

2. ANSI/IEEE Std 802.4 (ISO DIS 8802/4), a bus using token passing (see below) as the access method.

3. ANSI/IEEE Std 802.5, a ring using token passing as the access method.

ANSI/IEEE Std 802.2 (ISO DIS 8802/2) specifies the IEEE Standard Logical Link Control protocol and is used in conjunction with the medium access standards. The relationship among these standards and their relationship to the ISO Open System Interconnection Reference Model is specified in greater detail in a document entitled IEEE 802.1. Other access methods were under investigation or recently adopted as of this writing, particularly, 802.6 (Metropolitan Area Networks).

STANDARDS FOR MEDIA

Perhaps the best example of the flexible approach to standards is the development of the 802.3 (Ethernet) standard. The 802.3 Subcommittee earlier adopted a CSMA/CD access method, and since Ethernet was already being manufactured using a 50 Ohm baseband coaxial cable, a similar cabling system (medium) was adopted. Although the 802.3 standard was adopted in 1983, the committee continues to develop the standard, especially with regard to alternative media definitions (broadband coax, twisted pair, fiber optic, etc.).

By 1984 it was apparent that the IEEE's 802 Committee on local-network standards was considering several additional standards recommendations.[13] The 802.3 Subcommittee was trying to standardize a number of possible combinations of transmission media and data rates that might use CSMA/CD. By 1986, standards were adopted or ready for adoption using twisted pair and fiber-optic cable as well as coaxial cable. Because the 802.3 Subcommittee was also working on a broadband Ethernet standard as well as the original baseband standard, traditional CATV coaxial cable (75 Ohms) was also available as a medium. This same development can be seen with the 802.4 and 802.5 standards as well.

Many media are used to provide LAN services. The most common are twisted pair copper cables and coaxial cables (for either baseband or broadband). As the engineering problems involved in using fiber optics disappear, this technology will become more important, possibly overtaking coax sometime in the 1990s. Also used for some LAN applications are flat multiconductor "ribbon" cables, infrared light transmitters and receivers, and microwave systems.

Twisted Pair

For many years electrical and electronic communications were accomplished using paired copper wires, hence the term "twisted pair." Although modern telephone systems use many different forms of media today, telephone technology is still logically based on the twisted pair (usually two pair), and the cabling within buildings for telephone systems always uses two pair of copper wires. Because electrical characteristics of copper wire introduce distortion that increases with speed and distance, copper wire has some limitations for data transmissions over distances of any magnitude. At high-speed, bandwidth is also a problem.

Coaxial Cable

For broadband systems and many baseband systems, the practical alternative to twisted pair is coaxial cable. Coax has a single center conductor, surrounded by an insulator, surrounded by a wire-mesh shield. Coax can handle much greater bandwidth and, in particular, can handle electrical signals running at radio frequencies. The center conductor and the wire-mesh shield share the same common geometric axis and are, therefore, "coaxial" to one another. Coax comes in a number of standard sizes up to about .75 inches, with the larger sizes handling more like pipe than like wire.

Coaxial cable is classed not only by its physical size, but also by its impedance (measured in Ohms), and coax of different impedance is used for different purposes. For example, IBM 3270-type terminals are connected to their controllers by coax that has an impedance of 90 Ohms, while CATV systems use coax with an impedance of 75 Ohms. While coax is not noise-free, it can operate in electrically noisy environments that would defeat twisted pair. The

CATV industry has popularized the use of coax and created specialized contractors capable of designing and installing systems. Many new buildings, at least for large organizations, are prewired for CATV just as they are prewired for telephone. Hardware is readily available for making splices and taps for the distribution of information via CATV coaxial systems.

Fiber-Optic Cable

By 1990 fiber-optic cable provided a feasible alternative to twisted pair and coax for many applications. While twisted pair and coax must be placed in locations free of overt environmental problems (either physical or electrical), fiber-optic cable does not have that drawback. It cannot be accidentally grounded, it is not troubled by electrical noise, nor does submersion in water bother it. Fiber-optic cables are made of nonconducting glass and information is transmitted via optical techniques. Many of the problems inherent in twisted pair and coax are avoided with fiber optics, although the optical properties of the cable can be affected by kinks or similar damage. The potential transmission speed of fiber-optic cable is higher than coax and coax is higher than twisted pair.

In the mid-1980s the primary problem with fiber optics was that devices for splicing and tapping the cable were expensive and difficult to use. This meant that while fiber-optic cables could be used for point–to–point high-speed communications with considerable success or for limited connection LANs, it was not yet possible to use it for extended distribution wiring. Many estimates suggested that the engineering problems with the use of fiber optics in a LAN would be overcome by the late 1980s or early 1990s and these estimates have proven to be quite accurate. Certainly fiber optics can be used for heavy-use short-run requirements or long-haul applications. Also unlike the use of coax, connecting devices have not been standardized for fiber-optic cable. The lasers used for the transmission of information still have relatively high prices although they are falling.[14] The ability to use fiber economically was changing rapidly by the end of the 1980s. This is perhaps best illustrated in the use of fiber by telephone companies as a *home* wiring technology. As early as 1986 Southern Bell experimented with the use of fiber for wiring homes. By 1988 a few more telephone companies had also started to experiment. By 1989, however, this movement seemed to mushroom. In late 1989 one forcast estimated that in the United States from a low number in 1989 of close to zero, some 225,000 homes would be wired with fiber by 1992.[15] Even 225,000 homes is still a long way from covering the 60 or 70 million homes in the U.S., but considering the potential cost of replacing the existing copper wire, this seems like an enormous and very fast leap.

There is no one "best" transmission medium. The selection of a medium is dependent on the use to which it is put. If we decide to build a CATV system, for example, economics may still dictate the use of coax although this is rapidly changing. It is quite likely that during the 1990s fiber will replace coax for many of the applications for which coax was once used. In a similar vein, a flat copper ribbon cable might be most appropriate for a given application rather than coax, as might twisted pair. The fundamental question is not, "What medium shall I use?," but "what do I want to accomplish?" In a practical sense, the question of medium is not usually, even for a large organization, an open option. If we want a PBX, then we get an abundance of twisted pair; if we want CATV or baseband, then we expect a large amount of coax.

Standards for Data Transmission

Up to this point I have written glibly of baseband and broadband with little attention to explaining these concepts. They relate primarily to the way in which data are transmitted on a medium. With baseband systems signals are transmitted at their original frequencies (i.e., unmodulated). In contrast, broadband—often used to characterize communications based on CATV technology—is characterized by a large bandwidth resulting in the capacity for very high data rates. Broadband systems are modulated and in their CATV context, are analog systems. Another way of thinking about data transmission is either as digital or analog. With analog systems the signal consists of a continuously varying physical quantity, such as voltage, which reflects variations in some quantity, such as sound. A digital signal, by way of contrast, is a discrete or discontinuous signal where various states are discrete intervals apart.

The classic analog signaling system is telephony. From the time of its U.S. development, by Alexander Graham Bell to the present, the telephone system has been analog, although current technology is gradually changing that. The simplest voice connection consists of two wires, a filtered direct current (DC) of relatively low voltage, a carbon microphone to modulate the current, and an earphone composed of an electromagnet against which rests a thin magnetic membrane (in the early systems, simply a thin piece of sheet iron or steel) that will reverberate as the DC current is changed by the microphone. The microphone is constructed by using a container filled with carbon granules that are, in turn, connected to two copper wires.

As words are spoken into the microphone, the carbon granules move and change the resistance of the circuit through the microphone, thereby changing (modulating) the actual level of the DC current. On the listening end, the strength of the electromagnet changes in time with the changes in the strength of the DC current, thus making the membrane move back and forth, producing or reproducing sound. The way in which telephone modems used for data transmission across analog telephone lines work is that a circuit is constructed that takes digital data [sometimes encoded as a negative DC current (0) or a positive current (1)] and translates the binary states into frequencies of known duration in the range of human sound, one frequency for 1, another for 0. At the receiving end the modem retranslates the analog signals (demodulates them) into more appropriate discrete DC voltage levels for further use by a terminal or other computer. These frequencies, by the way, are standardized—at least up to a point. Radio-based systems, such as microwave or CATV systems, work in analogous ways. In radio systems a radio signal at a specified frequency (a carrier signal) is modulated and demodulated to provide digital information, although digital radio (and television, of course) is coming into greater use. The reason for modulated systems is that much of the Earth's public communications system is still analog. There is considerable overhead with such systems and they are prone to "noise" or error.

As we saw previously, a digital signal can be encoded by making two different DC voltage levels mean the discrete binary digits, 1 or 0. There are several ways of doing this. Sometimes either a positive or negative voltage signifies a 1, while the absence of voltage signifies a 0. Alternatively, a positive voltage might be used to mean a 1 and a negative voltage a 0. The latter technique is referred to a Non-Return to Zero (NRZ). The primary advantage of these techniques is that they are easy to use and it is easy to construct circuits to generate them. There are a number of disadvantages, however. First, it is sometimes difficult to determine where one bit ends and another begins. The transmitter and receiver must be clocked or synchronized. It is also more difficult to isolate the electrical components of the data communications devices and the other components of a larger device.

For baseband LANs, the IEEE standards recommend alternative methods of data transmission: Manchester or Differential Manchester encoding. With the Manchester code there is a transition at the middle of the bit period. A bit period is the length of time a signal takes to define a data bit. In Figure 2.7 the difference between NRZ encoding and Manchester encoding can be clearly seen. The mid-bit transition serves as both a clock and data. A high-to-low transition signifies a 1, while a low-to-high transition signifies a 0. When Differential Manchester encoding is used, the mid-bit transition only provides clocking. The encoding of a 0 or 1 is represented by the presence or absence of a transition at the beginning of a bit period. Because the clock and data are included in a single serial data stream, Manchester coding is considered to be self-clocking. For Manchester coding, polarity of the voltages is irrelevant, since data are encoded as the presence or absence of a transition in either direction. Both forms of Manchester coding are used in the 802 standards. Note,

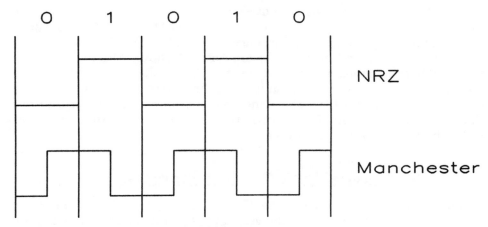

Figure 2.7   Digital Signaling Techniques

however, that these are essentially baseband techniques and when used on broadband systems must go through a defined modulation system.[16]

As we already pointed out, standards are not static. Additions to the IEEE 802 standard and products based on those expanded standards allow users of Ethernet local area networks, for example, to change between baseband and broadband channels easily through a device that allows Ethernet controllers to access broadband media. A radio-frequency transceiver that modulates the Ethernet signals and puts them on one channel of a multichannel network was added to the IEEE 802.3 specification, providing an easy upgrade for users of baseband Ethernet networks. The expansion of the 802.3 standard to include Ethernet on broadband provides a more generalized means for building a large Ethernet backbone system encompassing an industrial complex or university campus.[17]

IEEE LAN STANDARDS OVERVIEW

Throughout this chapter we have blithely discussed bits and pieces of various IEEE LAN standards without describing those standards. In Chapters 7, 8, and 9 we will treat those most important to this book in significant detail: 802.3, 802.4, and 802.5. At this juncture, however, it is important to introduce you to the broad outlines of those standards for reference in subsequent chapters. It may be helpful to look again at Figure 2.6 and the manner in which the IEEE standards fit into the OSI model. The overview and internetworking issues are treated in 802.1, while 802.2 deals with the Logical Link Control (LLC, see below). 802.3 deals with Carrier Sense Multiple Access with Collision Detection, a token passing bus standard is described by the 802.4 standard, and 802.5 defines a token ring system. The primary issues of 802.3, 802.4, and 802.5 revolve around the definition of the Media Access Control. Although it will be described in this chapter, we will not devote an entire chapter to the Metropolitan Area Network standard adopted in 802.6. For further information on 802.6 and further detail on all the 802 standards, you may find it helpful to read Thomas W. Madron, *LANS: Applications of IEEE/ANSI 802 Standards* (New York: John Wiley & Sons, Inc., 1989).

Logical Link Control Standards

As can be seen in Figure 2.6, with the IEEE 802 standards the Logical Link Control and Media Access Control sublayers correspond to the Data Link Layer of the OSI model while the physical layer of 802 corresponds roughly to the physical layers of the OSI. LLC is that part of a data station that supports the logical link functions of one or more logical links. The LLC generates command packets or frames (called "protocol data units" or PDUs) or interprets such PDUs. In particular, the responsibilities assigned to a LLC include[18]:

1. Initiation of control signal interchange;

2. Organization of data flow;

3. Interpretation of received command PDUs and generation of appropriate response PDUs;

4. Error control and recovery functions in the LLC.

In addition to the basic functions just noted, two primary services are specified: unacknowledged connectionless service and connection-oriented services. The first is a datagram-style that allows the sending and receiving of LLC frames with no acknowledgment for assured delivery.[19] All forms of connection, point–to–point, multipoint, broadcast, and multiplexed, are supported.

In contrast to unacknowledged service is the connection-oriented service. The latter provides a virtual circuit form of connection between service access points. In other words, this service provides the means by which a network node (entity), in the words of the IEEE 802.2 standard, "can request, or be notified of, the establishment of Data Link Layer connections." The result of this service is that sequencing, flow control, and error recovery can be provided for the Data Link Layer. In order to reset a session, a reset service is provided by which established connections can be returned to the initial state. We can summarize the connection-oriented services as follows:

1. Connection establishment. This is defined as the means by which a network entity can request or be notified of the establishment of Data Link Layer connections.

2. Connection reset. This is a return to the initial state of an established connection.

3. Connection termination. The request or notification of the termination of Data Link Layer connection.

4. Connection flow control. The means to control the flow of data across the Network Layer/Data Link Layer interface for a specified connection.

Standards for Media Access Control

Standards for media access control in LANs deal with the methods for allowing a particular node to transmit on the data transmission channel available to it. Common sense dictates that if LAN manufacturers were left to develop media access control systems they would likely be proprietary and would not communicate from one to another. This is not to say that a single preferred standard will develop in the near future, but with the promulgation of the IEEE 802.3 (CSMA/CD), 802.4 (Token Bus), and 802.5 (Token Ring) standards, the proliferation of techniques was limited. Furthermore, since the standards are public, all possible manufacturers can build to those specifications. This means that there is the likelihood that hardware from different manufacturers may be mixed in a single network, providing competitive pricing for the consumer. Even with multiple standards, the developments are "starting to bring the industry closer together."[20]

With a LAN configured with either a bus or a ring topology a single cable, or perhaps two (one for forward, the other for reverse signals), will carry all messages. This means that on a well-used system more than one node will be attempting to get a message on the cable at any one time. The manner in which access to the cable is gained then becomes important for the LAN. Two primary methods are used to control access: Carrier Sense Multiple Access/Collision Detection and token passing. The IEEE 802 Committee (Local Area Networks) has proposed standards for both access methods. The 802.3 standard addresses CSMA/CD, while 802.4 deals with token passing.[21] The 802.3 standard is almost identical with Ethernet although 802.4 uses a token passing scheme.

CSMA/CD (802.3)

The first of the 802 standards dealing with media access control was CSMA/CD. The original baseband version of this technique was developed by Xerox[22] as part of its Ethernet local network.[23] During the mid-to-late 1970s, as Xerox was working on Ethernet, MITRE was developing a broadband-based system also based on CSMA/CD. By 1980 other companies were busily at work on other CSMA/CD systems. Although the 802.3 standard is often referred to in the industry as "Ethernet," the standard as it was adopted did not follow precisely the Xerox definitions, although there was great similarity. Most of the 802.3 compatible hardware being produced will not work on older Ethernet systems, although some manufacturers support both. The broadband 802.3 standard attempted to define the rules for placing the earlier baseband protocols on broadband. It should be noted that there are some LANs on the market that use CSMA without collision detection, although these will likely pass by the wayside as buyers insist on 802.3 compatible equipment.

With a CSMA/CD system, collisions are assumed to be a normal operational occurrence. The most frequently used analogy is the comparison of a CSMA/CD-based LAN to a group discussion. In such a discussion each member of the group listens for an opportunity to be heard. On some occasions, however, two or more members will attempt to speak at the same time. In such a situation other members will hear only partial messages. In a LAN each network device listens all the time but defers transmission if the cable is in use.

In a highly loaded CSMA/CD network, the periods of silence may be very short. The consequence of short periods of silence is that several devices may attempt to transmit at the same time resulting in collisions. Large numbers of collisions will result in lower network throughput, since many retransmissions will have to take place. In baseband systems, such as Ethernet, collisions are detected by adding a direct current bias to the signal and having all stations look for a DC level greater than that of a single transmitter. On a broadband system (since it cannot pass DC signals), when the transmitter receives the reflection of what was sent (a result of full duplex mode), a bit-by-bit comparison is accomplished and any discrepancy is assumed to be the result of a collision and the signal is retransmitted. Broadband examples using CSMA/CD are LocalNet 20 from Sytek, Inc. and Net/One by Ungermann-Bass. Systems that implement Ethernet on broadband, such as those manufactured by DEC, Chipcom, and others, are also examples of broadband CSMA/CD systems.

Any CSMA system must deal with collision and the manner in which collisions are handled will determine other characteristics of the network. Without collision detection the typical approach is to transmit when the medium is idle, then if the medium is busy, wait an amount of time determined by a probability distribution and try again. This is called a *non-persistent* protocol. Modifications to this approach include 1-persistent and p-persistent protocols. Collisions are determined by a lack of acknowledgment from the receiving station. The objective is to reduce the likelihood of collisions to the bare minimum. With CSMA, however, there will be collisions, especially as traffic increases and the various wait states associated with busy detection will decrease throughput of the network. Consequently, it is necessary for a system of any substantial size to provide collision detection.

In the IEEE CSMA/CD specification, the persistence algorithm used is 1-persistence. Therefore, for any given node, if the medium is idle, transmit; if the medium is busy, continue to listen until the channel is sensed idle, then transmit immediately; if there is a collision, wait a random amount of time and start over. Collision detection, in general, is accomplished by having the node continue to listen to the medium during transmission. For packets of the correct length, a collision can be detected before the entire packet is sent. In that case, the transmitting node stops transmitting immediately and sends a short jamming signal to alert all stations that a collision has occurred. Following the jamming signal the node waits a random amount of time and then attempts to transmit again. Wasted bandwidth is now reduced to the amount of time it takes to detect a collision.

How long does it take to detect a collision? Generally, on a baseband system, the delay is twice the propagation delay. The propagation delay is the amount of time necessary for a signal to travel from one point on a circuit to another. In a broadband system the delay is four times the propagation delay due to the fact that if two nodes were in the same room, with a session between them, the signal would have to move from one node to the headend and then back an equal distance. On a baseband system, the signal only has to travel half the distance. The result of these facts is that in a baseband system the frame or packet length must be at least twice the propagation delay and with broadband systems at least four times the propagation delay. This also means that there is a limit on the end-to-end length of a CSMA/CD network—if the cable is too long collisions will never be detected properly.

Token Passing (802.4 and 802.5)

Token passing, which was used largely for ring topologies, in 1983 became commercially available on systems using bus structures. A "token" simply designates the location "of the poll on a distributed polling list."[24] Each network device must be polled and, as that polling is done, each station has an opportunity to transmit. Consequently, there can be no collisions, and token passing is, in fact, a collision avoidance technology. Polling need not take place in a centralized fashion, for each station can pass the "token" on following a transmission. Because there is no collision detection (and no collisions) the capacity of a token passing system may be accurately calculated, although a token passing scheme relies on all devices being serially polled, which implies its own set of problems.

3M, in early 1983, announced a broadband bus topology LAN using token passing as did Token/Net from Concord Data Systems. The 3M (now Allen-Bradley) used a chip set incorporating ARCnet, the oldest token passing bus system, developed during the 1970s by Datapoint. The IEEE 802.5 standard defines a token ring, while the 802.4 standard defines a token bus. IBM's Token Ring generally follows the 802.5 standard. Just as CSMA/CD can result in lower throughput under conditions where large numbers of collisions occur, so too a token passing scheme can degenerate under heavy loads measured in terms of the number of connections on the system, since the token must pass every node before returning to any given connection.

Without getting involved in excessively technical details, suffice it to say that there has been a rather heated controversy between supporters of CSMA/CD and token passing systems. Both have advantages and disadvantages. For the potential consumer of LAN products, however, the issue between the two schemes is used in marketing efforts. With appropriate network management techniques, either system will provide adequate access. Until 1983 it was not even possible to obtain token passing on broadband systems and even then the offerings were limited. From a managerial perspective—and this will not be a universally accepted statement—the issue is not so much whether CSMA/CD is better or worse than token passing, but whether the overall design philosophy of the LAN vendor meets the system needs of the buyer. At this writing it was not evident that either system was clearly superior to the other, although proponents of the two systems would deny that fact.

Manufacturers can, of course, produce products that implement only a part of any given set of standards. In 1985, for example, the Microprocessor Products Group of Motorola Inc. introduced a single-chip token-bus local-area-network controller that is compatible with the standards set by General Motors Corporation's Manufacturing Automation Protocol. The MC 68824 token-bus controller uses a chip that implements the IEEE 802.4 Committee's Media Access Control sublayer of the International Standards Organization Open Systems Interconnection Data Link Layer. Sold through OEMs, the MC 68824 was available for shipment in the second quarter of 1986.[25]

Token Bus (802.4)[26]

Although the nodes on a token bus may be physically connected in a bus—as on a broadband CATV system, for example—they form a *logical* ring. Each node is assigned logical positions in an ordered sequence, with the last member of the sequence followed by the first. Each station must know the identity of the nodes preceding and following it. The physical configuration of the bus is irrelevant and independent of the logical ordering. The "token" in a token bus system is a control frame or packet that regulates the right of access to the medium. Among other things, the token frame contains a destination address. The target station, when the token has been received, is granted control of the medium for a specified length of time.

During the time a station has control over the medium, it may transmit one or more frames and may poll stations and receive responses. When the time expires, or when the node has completed its transmissions, it passes the token to the next logical station. Transmissions, therefore, consist of alternating token and data transfer sequences. A token bust may also allow non-token using stations that can respond only to polls or requests for acknowledgment. Management functions are more extensive for a token bus than for a CSMA/CD LAN. One or more stations must perform *ring initialization, additions to the ring, deletions from the ring,* and *error recovery.*

Ring initialization is the procedure used to determine which node goes first, second, and so forth. When the logical ring is started, or after it has broken down, it must be reinitialized. There must be some method available to add either new or non-participating nodes to the ring. Similarly, there must be a method for a node to be removed from the ring, either arbitrarily or voluntarily. If two or more stations try to transmit at the same time, it means that there are duplicate ring addresses and an error condition occurs. Similarly, when no station thinks it can transmit, the ring has been broken and an error condition also occurs. There must, therefore, be an error recovery mechanism available.

Under 802.4 specifications, the physical connections use 75 Ohm CATV coaxial cable and analog [radio frequency (RF)] signaling. There are actually three forms of physical connection specified. Two of the three use "single-channel" signaling, which means that the transmitters do not have a tight bandwidth, and frequency division multiplexing—like that used for cable television systems—cannot be used. In other words, this is intended essentially for a cable system dedicated only to the LAN, not as part of a general broadband installation that might use the cable system for multiple purposes, including video. The third option uses a full commercial quality broadband system that can carry multiple data and video channels. The simplest, most restricted, and cheapest option operates at 1 Mb/s. The second option operates at 5 Mb/s or 10 Mb/s, and, unlike the first option allows the use of splitters to achieve a tree topology. The full broadband option provides three data rates: 1 Mb/s occupying a 1.5 MHz channel; 5 Mb/s using a standard CATV 6 MHz channel; and 10 Mb/s absorbing a 12 MHz channel. Note that in the full broadband system, two data paths are required (to and from the headend translator), and the full bandwidth needed is actually twice the figures quoted (3, 12, and 24 MHz, respectively).

Token Ring (802.5)

Although the token bus must ultimately run over a logical ring, the token ring is a physical ring. It consists of a set of stations serially connected by a transmission medium. Information is transferred sequentially, bit by bit, from one active node to the next. Each node or station serves as the means for attaching one or more devices (such as terminals and workstations) to the ring. Each station regenerates and repeats each bit. The station that has access to the medium transfers information onto the ring thereby allowing it to be read by subsequent stations, and those stations addressed, in turn, copy the information as it passes. The originator of the information finally removes the data from the ring.[27]

The token is defined by a unique signaling sequence that circulates on the medium following each information transfer. After detection, any station may capture the token by modifying it. There are two basic formats in token rings: tokens and frames. The token consists of three eight-bit sequences or "octets." The first octet is the starting delimiter (SD), the second is the access control (AC), and the third is the ending delimiter (ED). When the token is captured, the station modifies it to a start-of-frame sequence and appends additional fields making it a complete frame. When the information transfer is complete, the sending station generates a new token.

The token ring was originally proposed in 1969[28] and was known as the Newhall ring, named after one of its developers. The 802.5 standard was an outgrowth of research conducted by IBM.[29] IBM's Token Ring Network, as developed by Texas Instruments, is an implementation of the standard. In IBM's implementation of the Token Ring Network for PCs, the token ring logic and medium access control is contained on a board inserted into the micro. The connection on the board is then wired (using shielded twisted pair) to a wiring concentrator. Multiple concentrators can be daisy-chained in a ring to provide access for a fairly large number of stations. Although IBM's Token Ring Network uses a ring topology, the ring itself is contained in the wiring concentrator(s). Consequently, the physical wiring of a Token Ring Network is actually done as a star. More will be said about this in later chapters.

Metropolitan Area Networks (802.6)

In recognition of the need for standards beyond the LAN, yet less than standard wide area networks, the Metropolitan Area Network Working Group IEEE

802.6 was established in 1981. Unlike LANs, which are designed for data transmission, the emerging MAN standards support data, voice, and video transmissions. Since MANs are designed for networks spanning distances greater than five kilometers and are viewed as integrated information networks, LAN access methods have serious deficiencies. Consequently, the 802.6 working group early moved toward a time-division multiple-access (TDMA) protocol.[30] One way to think about a MAN is as a network of LANs. While the emerging MAN standards are not limited to linking LANs, it is certainly one major possibility. Although standards for networks less than wide area networks, but more than LANs, are desirable, it remains to be seen whether this effort by the IEEE will prove successful. We should note that the term "metropolitan" is used somewhat generically to include areas up to city size, but can also mean large campus environments, as well. As a general purpose high speed information communications utility, however, a MAN could have wide use, particularly if the protocol could utilize existing transmission media, such as CATV systems and existing twisted pair or fiber-optic telephone lines.

EMERGING STANDARDS

It is clear that standards are emerging as strong determinants of the products manufacturers will produce. The use of products conforming to the standards, provided one is careful in the selection process, may mean that products from a variety of manufacturers will be able to work well together. This is most evident in the development of products for the 802.3 (Ethernet) standards. In a real networking situation, it is very likely that a single vendor solution will prove untenable. With 802.3 conforming products, it is already possible to design and construct an integrated Ethernet network with products from many vendors. This availability of products has price and performance implications and provides real choices for the network designer. As standards continue to mature, these user benefits are bound to grow and improve. In subsequent chapters we will consider the 802.3, 802.4, and 802.5 standards in much greater detail.

REFERENCES

1. Anon, "IEEE Committee Addresses LANs," *Computer Design,* Vol. 24, No. 2, February 1985, p. 146.

2. Frank Derfler, Jr. and William Stallings, *A Manager's Guide of Local Networks* (Englewood Cliffs, NJ: Prentice-Hall, 1983), p. 79.

3. The actual text of standards are sometimes difficult to obtain. An easily accessible compilation of many of the more important standards can be found in Harold C. Folts, Ed., *McGraw-Hill's Compilation of Data Communications Standards,* Edition III (New York: McGraw-Hill, 1986), 3 volumes. The ISO 7498 standard (OSI) was adopted from the CCITT Recommendation X.200, which has been used as the basis for the discussion in this chapter and references are made to that document, designated as *Fascicle VIII.5–Rec. X.200*. In references following the identification of the actual standard, volume and page references to the standard as found in *McGraw-Hill's Compilation of Data Communications Standards. Fascicle VIII.5–Rec. X.200*, p. 3 (Vol. 2, p. 2235).

4. Reference 3, p. 3 (Vol. 2, p. 2235).

5. Reference 3. Both the listing which designates the scope of OSI as well as the listing of points concerning the application of the Reference Model following either identically or very closely the wording in the Introduction to the standard.

6. Reference 3, p. 4 (Vol. 2, p. 2236).

7. The concepts of a layered architecture are given in Ref. 3, p. 40, pp. 6ff (Vol. 2, p. 2238ff), Section 5.

8. National Research Council, *Transport Protocols for Department of Defense Data Networks,* February 1985.

9. As summarized in "Department of Defense (DOD) Protocol Standards," in William Stallings et al., *Handbook of Computer-Communications Standards* (New York: Macmillan Publishing Company, 1988), Vol. 3, p. 22.

10. Note Gregory Ennis, "Routing Tables Locate Resources in Bridged Broadband Networks," *Systems & Software,* March 1983.

11. The state of OSI development can be followed in various places. See, for example, Jean Bartik, "OSI: From Model to Prototype as Commerce Tries to Keep Pace," *Data Communications,* March 1984, pp. 307–319; Jerrold S. Foley, "The Status and Direction of Open Systems Interconnection," *Data Communications,* February 1985, pp. 177–193; Sunil Joshi and Venkatraman Iyer, "New Standards for Local Networks Push Upper Limits for Lightwave Data," *Data Communications,* July 1984, pp. 127–138; and Kevin L. Mills, "Testing OSI Protocols: NBS Advances the State of the Art," *Data Communications,* March 1984, pp. 277–285.

12. William Stallings, "A Tutorial on the IEEE 802 Local Network Standard,"

in Raymond L. Pickholtz, Ed., *Local Area & Multiple Access Networks* (Rockville, MD: Computer Science Press, Inc., 1986), pp. 2–3.

13. E. E. Mier, "Proliferating Permutations of the Ethernet 'Standard,'" *Data Communications,* Vol. 13, No. 14, December 1984, pp. 48 and 50+.

14. Charles L. Howe, "Still Only a Glimmer: Optical Fiber in U.S. LANs," *Data Communications,* Vol. 16, No. 1, January 1987, pp. 66, 68, and 70.

15. John Markoff, "Here Comes the Fiber-Optic Home," *The New York Times,* Section 3 (Business), November 5, 1989, pp. 1 and 15.

16. For more detail on Differential Manchester encoding see IEEE Standards Board, *IEEE Standards for Local Area Networks: CSMA* (New York: The Institute of Electrical and Electronics Engineers, Inc., 1985), pp. 80 and 81; Stallings, Ref. 13, pp. 28 and 29; William Stallings, "Digital Signaling Techniques," *IEEE Communications Magazine,* December 1984; and William Stallings, *Data and Computer Communications* (New York: Macmillan Publishing Company, 1985).

17. Note the comments by Menachem E. Abraham, "Running Ethernet Modems over Broadband Cable," *Data Communications,* Vol. 15, No. 5, pp. 199ff (8 pages).

18. IEEE Standards Board, *IEEE Standards for Local Area Networks: Logical Link Control,* ANSI/IEEE Std 802.2–1985 (New York: The Institute of the Electrical and Electronics Engineers, Inc., 1984), pp. 20 and 21.

19. Stallings, Ref. 12, p. 7.

20. M. Edwards, "Standards Chart Direction of Local-Area Network Advances," *Communications News,* Vol. 22, No. 10, October 1985, pp. 60–64 and 66.

21. IEEE Standards Board, *IEEE Standards for Local Area Networks: Carrier Sense Multiple Access with Collision Detection (CSMA/CD)* (New York: The Institute of Electrical and Electronics Engineers, Inc., 1985); IEEE Standards Board, *IEEE Standards for Local Area Networks: Token-Passing Bus Access Method and Physical Layer Specifications* (New York: The Institute of Electrical and Electronics Engineers, Inc., 1985).

22. See, for example, the following: R. Metcalfe, D. Boggs, C. Thacher, and B. Lampon, "Multipoint Data Communication System with Collision Detection," U.S. Patent No. 4,063,220, 1977; R. Metcalfe and D. Boggs, "Ethernet: Distributed Packet Switching for Local Computer Networks," *Communications of the ACM,* July 1976; and J. Shoch, Y. Dala, and D.

Redell, "Evolution of the Ethernet Local Computer Network," *Computer,* August 1982.

23. G. Hopkins and P. Wagner, "Multiple Access Digital Communications System," U.S. Patent No. 4,210,780, 1980; and G. Hopkins, "Multimode Communications on the MITRENET," *Proceedings of the Local Area Communications Network Symposium,* May 1979.

24. C. Kenneth Miller and Robert H. Douglas, "Local Area Networks: A Comparison of Standard Bus Access Methods," *Digital Design,* June 1983, pp. 125–128.

25. L. N. Rowe, "Motorola Adds LAN Controller," *Computer Systems News,* October 14, 1985, p. 23.

26. IEEE Standards Board, *IEEE Standards for Local Area Networks: Token-Passing Bus Access Method and Physical Layer Specifications* (New York: The Institute of Electrical and Electronics Engineers, Inc., 1985).

27. IEEE Standards Board, *IEEE Standards for Local Area Networks: Token Ring Access Method and Physical Layer Specifications* (New York: The Institute of Electrical and Electronics Engineers, Inc., 1985), p. 23.

28. W. Farmer and E. Newhall, "An Experimental Distributed Switching System to Handle Bursty Computer Traffic," *Proceedings of the ACM Symposium on Problems in the Optimization of Data Communications,* 1969.

29. N. Strole, "A Local Communications Network Based on Interconnected Token Access Rings: A Tutorial," *IBM Journal of Research and Development,* Vol. 27, September 1983; and R. Dixon, N. Strole, and J. Markov, "A Token-Ring Network for Local Data Communications," *IBM Systems Journal,* Vol. 22, No. 1, June 1983, pp. 47–62.

30. William E. Bracker, Benn R. Konsynski III, and Timothy W. Smith, "Metropolitan Area Networking: Past, Present, and Future," *Data Communications,* Vol. 16, No. 1, January 1987, pp. 151–159. See also, IEEE 802.6 Working Group on Metropolitan Area Networks, *Draft IEEE Standard 802.6: Metropolitan Area Network* (New York: The Institute of Electrical and Electronics Engineers, Inc., 1986).

LANS AS NODES IN LARGER NETWORKS

If you are not part of an organization large enough to have computing facilities beyond your own working environment, you may want to skip this chapter. On the other hand, some of the problems and opportunities discussed here may give you insights into issues faced by colleagues in larger organizations. For the rest of you, however, read on, so that there will be a common ground for understanding some of the issues faced when implementing a microcomputer-based LAN in the context of a larger network. As an aside, you should be aware of the "fact" that some of the wider network concepts and issues may apply to you even if you have no regular or formal external network. When it comes to contemporary computing, networking stands as perhaps the most critical single issue affecting access to computing power.

DISTRIBUTED PROCESSING AND LOCAL AREA NETWORKS

There are, according to James Martin, two main reasons why we might wish to perform a transaction on a distant machine.[1] First, our local equipment may have insufficient power to perform the task at hand. Second, the data needed by our transaction may be stored elsewhere. The first reason is often seen in scientific and research institutions where sheer number-crunching power is required. The second is often seen in commercial or governmental environments where the *corporate database* is kept and maintained. The two functions are not mutually exclusive, of course. A large, powerful database management system may need additional computing power in order to meet response time objectives, or it may be desirable to maintain large amounts of data subject to extensive scientific analysis to be available to multiple researchers.

Even when we access a remote computer, we may not be engaging in distributed processing. Computer networks consisting of a central computer and a number of terminals linked by a data communications system have been around for a long time. For distributed processing to take place, the "system" must consist of more than one processor. A by-product of the generality of this definition is that a very large number of configurations are possible. Some constraints can be placed on the generality of these statements by insisting that the processors be in different locations, be linked by communications systems, serve one organization, serve a coherent set of objectives, and/or that the processors are linked in an integrated fashion. These, and other possible constraints serve to help us think about distributed processing, but they are probably violated more often than observed in any real organization. Moreover, with the advent of the wide distribution of microcomputers, a distributed processing environment may grow without the explicit knowledge or acquiescence of the owners of the parent machines.

Distributed Computing

There are other terms and concepts helpful in the understanding of distributed processing. Two concepts are particularly useful: distributed data processing (DDP) and distributed intelligence. A distributed data-processing system is one that employs more than one geographically separate processors linked by telecommunications. Distributed intelligence involves the use of processors in terminals, controllers, or peripheral machines to execute functions that individually do not perform the complete processing of a transaction. In the latter half of the 1980s, LANs became important elements in distributed processing environments. A very simplified diagram of LANs in a distributed processing system may be found in Figure 3.1.

Among the various network topologies discussed in Chapter 1 and graphically depicted in Figure 1.1 was a hierarchical system. When a LAN—which may be a bus, a ring, or a star—is a node in a distributed system, a hierarchical structure is at least implicitly established. As shown in Figure 3.1, the mainframe is tied to the LAN through a data communications line of some sort—we'll discuss the options for that line later—in one of several ways: through a gateway or communications server on the LAN, or through a more direct attachment such as a board in a VAX or an 8232 channel attached LAN controller

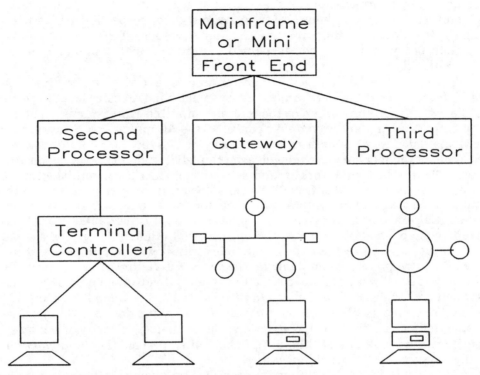

Figure 3.1   LANs in a Traditional Distributed System

for an IBM mainframe. A file server may be attached to either LAN. A specific example may be helpful.

In a university, for example, a central file of alumni is likely maintained for access by several departments including an Alumni Office, the Athletics Department, the President's Office, and perhaps the Registrar's Office, as well as individual academic departments. The Alumni Office produces many mailings during the year, both of a general nature and to specific subsets of the complete alumni file. Each year specific class reunions are organized for 5-, 10-, and 20-year intervals. In 1990, therefore, there will be reunions for the classes of 1985, 1980, and 1970.

The staff members of the Alumni Office are bound together in a PC-based LAN as depicted in Figure 3.1, which also has several laser printers attached to the file server. Transactions are generated that access the mainframe's database system to separately subset and download the alumni for the classes of 1970, 1980, and 1985 to the file server. Three different staff members might be assigned as project managers for the three class reunions, so each of those people, from their own workstations, write "personalized" letters of invitation to the alumni for the years individually assigned, merge the respective mailing lists now on the file server, and print the letters and envelopes. There will be follow-up mailings, of course, so they keep the files until the 1990s round of reunions is completed.

The process just described has many advantages and virtually no disadvantages from the standpoint of project management. First, to complete the entire project no direct intervention by the central computing center staff is needed—the projects are under the complete control of the Alumni Office. Second, only a single database of alumni is kept, thereby conserving computer resources whether at the local or central level, even though it is shared by many departments. Third, the actual work of processing the projects is accomplished at the most convenient (and user friendly) level of the computing environment without placing stress on the central mainframe for doing what is, in reality, trivial computer processing. In essence, all processing on this particular project has been accomplished at the most appropriate level of computing. The several project managers have maintained complete control over their projects and are, therefore, completely accountable for the success or failure of the projects. By the mid-1980s it was possible to structure systems that worked precisely as described, although I will hasten to add that few worked as smoothly as implied even though most failures could probably be laid at the doorstep of organizational, rather than technical, constraints. Unfortunately, in many, if not most, organizations intra-organizational "glitches" often prevent the deployment of truly integrated distributed processing.

Bear in mind that I have, thus far, described only one possible network environment out of many available. In a smaller organization without a central mainframe, there might be a network of LANs, for example, with each LAN being the peer of all others. Likewise, there might be a network of multiple mainframes or super-minis, some of which might have local hierarchical structures, others of which might be organized as equal peers in a high-speed LAN. Then, too, the mainframe or super-mini might be tightly integrated into the LAN to directly serve as the LAN's file server. The precise details of a particular configuration will depend on a number of technical, political, and other organizational factors, but cost-effective technology is available to make such distributed processing available. The point is that increasingly we will see LANs being placed as nodes in a distributed system rather than terminal controllers with dumb terminals (or PCs acting as dumb terminals) at the end of the line.

In this section I have attempted to demonstrate the viability of LANs as nodes in a larger, distributed network. To that end I have tried to keep the discussion at a functional level apart from any discussion of vendors. In most real situations, however, it will not be possible to simply start from scratch and devise the "best" solution. For the majority of installations it will be necessary to integrate LANs into an existing network of some kind. Two of the most important network architectures—sponsored by large computer manufacturers—are IBM's System Network Architecture (SNA) and DEC's Digital Network Architecture (DNA). In addition, because of the potential future impact of Metropolitan Area Networks (MANs), we will look at how LANs will be integrated into that environment. LAN Network Operating Systems (NOSs) also constitute network architectures and these will be considered in a later chapter. At that point it will be important to understand how LANs fit into the overall OSI scheme of things, and that will be illustrated by reference to MAP, the Manufacturing Automation Protocol. Finally, in this chapter, we look at LANs in the context of the Internet, the TCP/IP national network in the United States important to the public sector, but with growing importance for the private sector as well.

Three of the networks discussed in the following pages are full-fledged network architectures: TCP/IP, SNA, and DNA. They are all layered architectures although none is OSI standard. MAP, by way of contrast, is a self-contained NOS since MAP assumes a LAN as the primary Physical and Data Link Layer communications medium: an IEEE 802.4 token bus system. The other architectures can and do use a wide variety physical media and are not linked to IEEE's Media Access Control (MAC) standards. In each subsequent section we will explicitly compare the architectures with the OSI model in an effort to demonstrate selected architectural details. Do not be mislead by this method of presentation, however. SNA, DNA, and TCP/IP are not OSI standard. Clearly both SNA and DNA are proprietary standards adopted by IBM and DEC, respectively. Even TCP/IP, although usually thought of as a standard, was devised by the U.S. Department of Defense for its own proprietary use. The brief comments on MANs point up the differences between fully elaborated network architectures and the IEEE standard in that the IEEE 802.6 (MAN) standard, like its LAN standards, deal only with the Physical and Data Link Layers of the OSI model. In order to have a fully functional network, the other elements of a complete architecture are necessary.

LANS AND MANS

Although the IEEE has adopted a MAN standard, there are only a relatively few examples of what might be called MANs available and these do not conform to the proposed IEEE standard. Those networks that do exist are largely based on CATV and are often called Institutional Networks, or I-Nets. For several years I-Nets have been part of the franchising requirements of many community cable systems, but most cable companies have yet to fulfill the promises of the franchises. Moreover, recent legislation by Congress has reduced the role of local government in the governing and regulation of cable companies leading to a further decrease in implementation of I-Nets. Finally, cities themselves have been remiss in not actually following up on franchise requirements. These failures, coupled with somewhat confused legal relationships between services reserved to telephone companies and cable systems has meant that companies, local governments, school systems, and the like, have continued to build their own networks based on leased telephone lines, private short-haul microwave, and occasionally on cable systems.

Cable operators, when they have attempted to provide data communications services, have had very mixed results at best. Part of the problem has been that they have marketed such services in inappropriate ways. Sammons Cable, Warner Communications, and others, have attempted to market consumer-based data services that include the distribution of data of various sorts as well as videotex systems. Market studies over the past 15 years have indicated that in the United States (unlike Europe) consumers are not yet ready to pay for videotex services. On the other hand, in markets where clear data communications services are needed, cable companies have been rather myopic in their evaluation of the need. In almost any University community, for example, there are hundreds or thousands of people (students, faculty, and staff) that need high-speed access to University computer facilities. Typically that access is through dial-up telephone service that has been mediocre at best and relatively slow (300 b/s or 1200 b/s).

With the development of higher-speed (2400 b/s and 9600 b/s) reasonably priced telephone modems this situation is changing. Because analog telephone service is electronically noisy, however, the extensive error correction techniques necessary for high-speed dial access service results in an unpredictable service which may not have throughput greater than 300 b/s or 1200 b/s. Cable companies, by way of contrast, could offer high-quality high-speed (9600 b/s or 19,200 b/s) services for user to central system in a cost effective manner without having to support any computer facilities of their own. For a cost approaching that of added value consumer services, such as pay TV (HBO, Cinemax, Showtime, and similar services), cable companies could provide good quality data communications services. Yet cable companies have failed to take advantage of these possibilities. Owing to recent decisions of the Federal Communications Commission (FCC), the Bell Operating Companies (BOCs) may be able to compete with the CATV systems using the BOC's fiber plant and ISDN is only a few years off.

In Figure 3.2 some possible options may be seen for LAN to MAN connectivity. Early in the work of 802.6 it considered a slotted ring proposal put forth by Burroughs, Plessey, and National Semiconductor. Although 802.6 dropped consideration of the earlier slotted ring that topology has continued to be developed in Japan. In November 1987, 802.6 adopted Queued Packet and Synchronous Exchange (QPSX) as the sole MAN standard—at least for the present. Almost immediately the name of the QPSX was changed to the Distributed Queue Double Bus (DQDB) because the Australian group that pro-

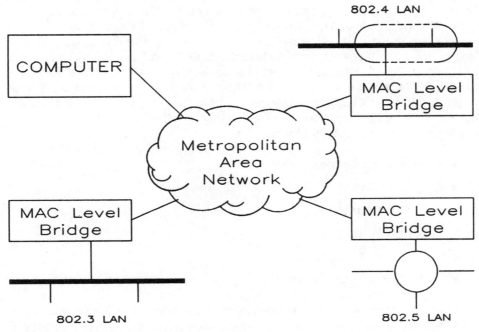

Figure 3.2   MAN to Other Connectivity

moted the standard set up a firm with the QPSX name to sell products. The competing proposal, the multiplexed slot and token ring (MST), was withdrawn as a draft standard and is being sold as a proprietary network.[2] The MAN, at least in its 802.6 manifestation, is depicted as a cloud since at this writing it was still possible that the MST proposal could be resurrected. MST may, in fact, be the bridge to FDDI-II (see below) since both are based on the same FDDI technology.

The metropolitan area network, an evolutionary step beyond the local area network, promises high-speed communications at distances greater than any LAN can handle. But in another sense, the MAN is what standards groups will make it. Just what standards will define a MAN is being hammered out by the 802.6 Committee of The Institute of Electrical and Electronics Engineers. The committee outlines several goals for a MAN standard: it should accommodate fast and robust signaling schemes; it should guarantee security and privacy and permit establishment of virtual private networks within MANs; it must ensure high network reliability, availability, and maintainability; and it should promote efficient for MANs regardless of their size. The Distributed Queue Double Bus dual bus MAN proposal sponsored by Telecom Australia was adopted because it meets or exceeds those requirements.[3] The DQDB architecture is illustrated in Figure 3.3. It is conceived as a system that will likely run on either a broadband CATV system or on fiber optic cable at 150 Mb/s or greater.

The difficulty in describing MAN standards is that the standards are still in the process of being developed. As John L. Hullett and Peter Evans have noted, however, a "good standard is crucial to MAN development, since interoperability between computer and telecommunications networks is a prerequisite to a successful launch of the new technology."[4] Unlike the 802 LANs, a MAN is expected to carry voice and video information in addition to data. Typical MAN traffic is expected to include[5]:

▼ LAN interconnection

▼ Graphics and digital images

▼ Bulk data transfer

▼ Digitized Voice

▼ Compressed Digitized Video

▼ Conventional terminal traffic

Because of the requirements for voice and video, a mode of communications somewhat different than either asynchronous or synchronous transmis-

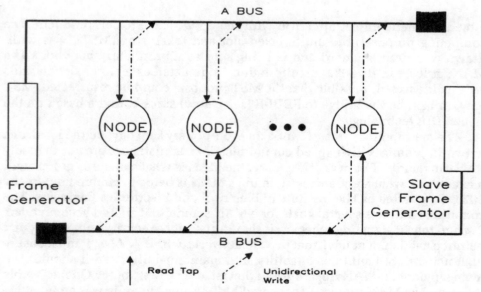

Figure 3.3   Dual Bus Architecture

sion is needed. As a result, the term "isochronous" transmission has been added to the better known concepts of asynchronous and synchronous transmission. With asynchronous communications the time intervals between units of transmission (bytes, octets, etc.) may be of unequal length. Timing signals generated at the transmitting and receiving stations control the synchronization of units of transmission for synchronous communications. Isochronous communications go a step beyond synchronous, in that the transmission of units are equally timed, thus providing evenly spaced transmission of bytes. The latter is important for voice and video because this allows the data communications network to operate much like a standard speech digitizer would generate voice signals thereby eliminating the need for buffering mechanisms. These developments might be summarized by simply noting the important trend toward the use of packetized data and the services required for the delivery of those data.

The way in which LANs will be connected to MANs is through a MAC Layer Bridge (see Chapter 6 for more detail). Bridges can operate several different layers of the OSI model, although typically they will exist in either the Data Link Layer or in the Network Layer. In the IEEE LAN standard interoperability is typically achieved through a device that contains a MAC layer specific for the LAN technology of the two networks being bridged. As you will see in subsequent chapters, the output of the MAC sublayers are consistent with one another. Consequently, data moving in and out of the MAC sublayer is standardized in order to work with Logical Link Control (LLC).

LANS AND THE INTERNET: TCP/IP

Both TCP/IP and OSI are, of course, layered protocol stacks. The TCP/IP protocol set consists of four layers that might be labeled as Physical, Routing, Service, and Application.[6] OSI is, of course, structured around the seven-layer OSI Reference Model. The physical layer is not actually specified by TCP/IP. The user is free to use any physical transmission including wide-, metropolitan-, and local-area-based networks. The most common networking systems at this writing were X.25 and IEEE 802.3 (Ethernet), both of which are explicit parts of the OSI framework. Remember in the discussions of the IEEE 802.x networks the 802 specifications dealt only with the OSI Physical and Data Link Layers, with the Logical Link Control (LLC) sublayer providing a standardized access to the Network Layer. It is at the rough equivalent of the OSI Network Layer where TCP/IP begins.

The TCP/IP Internet Protocol (IP) is more or less equivalent to the Network Layer of the OSI Model, while TCP corresponds to, at least, the Transport Layer and in some ways to the Transport (4) through the Presentation (6) Layers. The comparable international protocols are the Connectionless-Mode Network Service (OSI 8473) for the Network Layer and the Connection Oriented Transport Protocol Specification (OSI 8073) for the Transport Layer. The other TCP/IP related protocols are related to the Application Layer and include the File Transfer Protocol (FTP), the Simple Mail Transfer Protocol (SMTP), and the Terminal Emulation protocols (Telnet). Approximately equivalent international standards include File Transfer, Access and Management (FTAM, OSI DIS 8571), the Message Handling System (X.400), and the Virtual Terminal Protocol (VTP, OSI DIS 9041). In general the OSI protocols are richer than those of TCP/IP. Moreover, related international protocols exist in the layers between Transport and Application that support a wide variety of services.

The Relationship of TCP/IP and OSI

Before going further with the discussion of the relationship of OSI and TCP/IP, we should clarify the use of the abbreviation "OSI," which is sometimes used to refer to the Open Systems Interconnection Reference Model, described in Chapter 2. It is also used to designate a more-detailed set of protocols to be used as guidelines for configuring a real OSI network. It is in the latter sense that we will use it in this chapter. When we use "OSI" to mean the Reference Model it will be modified appropriately. Figure 3.4 is an attempt to display the relationship among the layers of TCP/IP, the OSI Reference Model, and the actual component standards for guiding the development of real systems.[7]

The right-hand side of Figure 3.4 is a display of the seven layer names of the OSI Model. Within the boxes are ISO standard names or numbers of some of the standards for each layer. It may be helpful to refer back to Chapter 2, Table 2.1 for a more comprehensive listing of OSI standards. On the left-hand side of Figure 3.4 are some layer names for the four levels of TCP/IP and in the boxes the names of the TCP/IP components at those levels. The TCP/IP protocol stack has been equated to the appropriate layers of the OSI Model, but bear in mind that it is easier to draw such figures than to actually make such components equivalent. In general, the OSI standards are much richer both in number and in functionality than the TCP/IP standards. One of the challenges for users of TCP/IP networks over the next few years will be the need to migrate to OSI standards.

Migration from TCP/IP to OSI

The purpose of both TCP/IP and OSI is to provide a set of communications protocols that are manufacturer independent. The motive of the U.S. Department of Defense when it started developing TCP/IP in the late 1970s was to broaden the base of hardware and software from which they had to choose for purposes of competitive bidding, rather than be stuck with a proprietary networking sys-

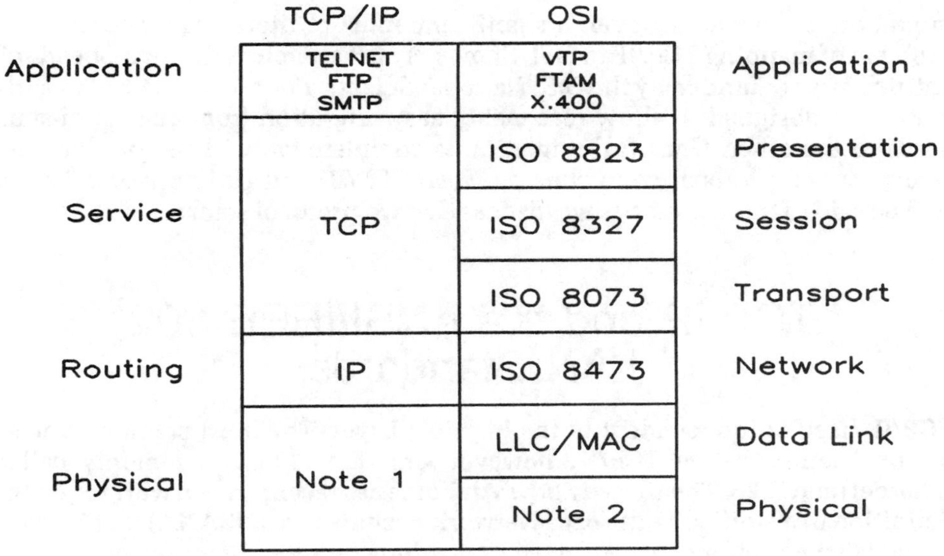

TCP/IP		OSI	
Application	TELNET FTP SMTP	VTP FTAM X.400	**Application**
Service	TCP	ISO 8823	**Presentation**
		ISO 8327	**Session**
		ISO 8073	**Transport**
Routing	IP	ISO 8473	**Network**
Physical	Note 1	LLC/MAC	**Data Link**
		Note 2	**Physical**

Figure 3.4   TCP/IP –OSI Architectures

NOTES: 1. Some writers suggest that "Ethernet" and "X.25" are the normal standards for TCP/IP. X.25 actually exists at the Network Layer while using HDLC as a Data Link protocol. X.25 and 802.3, therefore, are used only to deliver TCP/IP packets to IP (routing).
2. The Physical Layer in OSI parlance includes various modum standards, IEEE 802.x LANs, and the 8802/7 slotted ring standard.
3. X.400, message handling service; ISO 8823, connection-oriented presentation protocol; ISO 8327, connection-oriented session protocol; ISO 8073, connection-oriented transport protocol; ISO 8473, connectionless protocol; LLC, logical link control; MAC, media access control.

tem such as IBM's SNA. With the development of international standards, however, it has become clear that over the decade of the 1990s far greater numbers of manufacturers will support international standards than TCP/IP as the major approach internetworking. International standards also have the support of most of the governments of Western Europe as well as the support of standards organizations. These factors, coupled with the richer functionality and more extensive protocol stack of the international standards, has led U.S. governmental organizations, including the Department of Defense, to announce that they too will move to OSI over the next decade.

In the interim, however, at this writing, more products were available for TCP/IP than for OSI. Moreover, the installed base of TCP/IP networks was far greater than for OSI standard networks. All this means is that the migration from TCP/IP-based networks to OSI-based networks will take several years and for some purposes there may be room for both. A consequence of the need for migration has been, however, a significant spurt of literature discussing the problem of mapping TCP/IP to OSI. Some networks, such as the high-speed scientific network funded by the U.S. National Science Foundation (NSF) in early 1987, was designed to allow reasonably easy migration from one set of standards to the other. Until full migration is complete we will see products for gateways and protocol converters between TCP/IP and OSI networks.[8] More will be said of these issues as we discuss the two protocol stacks.

TCP/IP and the ANSI/IEEE 802 LAN Standards

TCP/IP itself is independent of the Physical Layer. The most commonly used protocol suites below TCP/IP, however, are IEEE 802.3 (commonly called Ethernet) and X.25. The United States Air Force has recently been working on the definition of a Unified Local Area Network Architecture (ULANA) that seeks to formalize the relationship between the two protocol suites for the purpose of providing user transparent communications, especially for linking dedicated workstations and shared database capabilities.[9] ULANA is, therefore, one specification of the way in which TCP/IP and IEEE 802.3 can work together. In the ULANA scheme the IEEE MAC sublayer and the IEEE Physical Layer underlie the Internet Protocol without making use of the IEEE Logical Link Control. IP, of course, feeds TCP and TCP, and in turn, supplies services to TELNET, FTP, and SMTP. This formal use of IEEE standards will, ultimately, enhance the ability of the Air Force to migrate to OSI standards.

An Introduction to TCP/IP

It is unfortunate that in their writings some authors occasionally mislead the unwary into the belief that there is some automatic relationship among certain standard protocol stacks. This is especially apparent in discussions of LANs. I will, therefore, reiterate again, that although TCP/IP has been frequently implemented on 802.3 standard LANs, TCP/IP is a set of protocols unrelated to the Physical and Data Link layers as described in the OSI Reference Model. TCP/IP can be implemented on top of virtually any physical data communications medium and related Physical and Data Link layer protocols.

One other caveat should be noted. The classification of TCP and IP into different network layers is not accidental. TCP can reside on a single integrated network and not require IP. That is, if node A on network Y wishes to communicate with Node B on network Y, routing functions that exist within IP are typically not required. If network Y is an IEEE 802.3 LAN, for example, the 802.3

standard implementation will take care of getting a frame from node A to node B. If, however, node A on network Y wishes to send a message to node C on network X, and network X is, perhaps, an X.25 network, then IP is required. TCP provides the packet sequencing, error control, and other services required to provide reliable end-to-end communications, while IP will take the packet from TCP, pass it through whatever gateways are needed, for delivery to the remote TCP layer through the remote IP layer.[10] Some networks, in fact, may use IP, but not TCP, preferring instead to use some alternative protocol at the transport layer.

Although we have been using, and will continue to use, the hybrid term "TCP/IP" to refer to several different protocols, the set of protocols is often termed the "Internet protocol suite" or the "Internet protocol stack." At this writing the term "protocol stack" seemed to be the catch-term of choice by the data communications industry and we will continue to use it here. The internet stack consists, as we implied above, not only of TCP and IP, but also of some application layer protocols. We will also continue to use "TCP/IP" to refer to the entire internet stack.[11]

Much of the impetus for the development of TCP/IP was the need for inter-networking services—the ability of an end-user to communicate through a local machine to some remote machine or remote end user. The "traditional" TCP/IP services are supported by the appropriate protocols which are described in this chapter. Those protocols are:

▼ The File Transfer Protocol (FTP) which allows the transfer of files from one computer on the "Internet" to any other computer on the Internet;

▼ The Network Terminal Protocol (Telnet) provides a means for allowing a user on the Internet to log on to any other computer on the network;

▼ Simple Mail Transfer Protocol (SMTP) allows users to send messages to one another on the Internet.

Each of the services implied by these protocols should generally be present in any implementation of TCP/IP, although SMTP is not always supported by microcomputer-based systems.

TCP/IP was originally designed before the widespread deployment of microcomputers and high-performance workstations. It was conceived in an era when users communicated through minicomputers and mainframes. With the changing nature of both computer technology and data communications technology, however, a need has developed for some computers on the Internet to perform specialized services, leading to a "server/client" model for the delivery of services. A server system provides specific services for network users, while a client system is a user of those services. Server and client may be on the same or different computers. Additional services provided within the scope of TCP/IP are[12]:

▼ Network file systems;

▼ Remote printing;

▼ Remote execution;

▼ Name servers;

▼ Terminal servers; and

▼ Network-oriented window systems.

Not all the protocols that support these services, however, are a part of the official TCP/IP protocol stack.

The way in which information is transferred from one node to another in an TCP/IP network is illustrated in Figure 3.5. TCP communicates with applications through specific "ports" and each port has its own local number or address. If a process on node A, associated with port 1, must send a message to port 2, node B, that process transmits the message to its own Service Layer TCP with appropriate instructions to get it to its intended destination (node and port). TCP hands the message to IP with instructions to get it to the appropriate node. IP, in turn, transmits to the Physical layer with instructions to get the message to the gateway, which is the first *hop* to node B. This sequence of events is regulated by adding control information to user data at the various layers:

Application ———————————————— >User Data

User Data + TCP Header ———————— >TCP *segment*

TCP *segment* + IP Header ——————— >IP *datagram*

IP *datagram* + NAP Header ——————— >*packet*

TCP segments user data into manageable units, then appends a TCP header which includes the *destination port, segment sequence number,* and *checksum* to test for errors in transmission. This unit is called a *TCP segment*.

Once the TCP segment has been assembled, it is passed to IP where an IP header is appended. A major item stored in the IP header is the destination Host/Node address. The resulting unit is an *IP datagram*. Generally, a datagram may be defined as a finite length packet with sufficient information to be independently routed from source to destination without reliance on previous transmissions. Datagram transmission typically does not involve end-to-end session establishment and may or may not entail delivery confirmation acknowledgment. The IP datagram is then given to the Physical Layer where the network access protocol appends its own control information, thus creating a *packet*. The packet is then sent out on the physical medium. The packet header contains sufficient information to get the entire packet from node A to at least the gateway and perhaps beyond. In the case of an IEEE 802.3 network, for example, the packet would be an 802.3 frame which encapsulates the TCP/IP data and control information. Note that error correction is likely to take place at several levels. We will see in Chapters 7, 8, and 9 that the 802.3, 802.4, and 802.5 protocols do their own error correction. The IP header also contains a checksum, as does the TCP header. At the receiving end, the reverse process takes place.

In Figure 3.5 the "layer" labeled "Physical" is intended to contain both the functions of the OSI Data Link and Physical Layers. All nodes of a TCP/IP network might reside on a single LAN, such as an Ethernet. In such a case, TCP/IP would be operating as a LAN NOS. The original concept behind TCP/IP was, however, that it would provide a common standard for linking many remote ma-

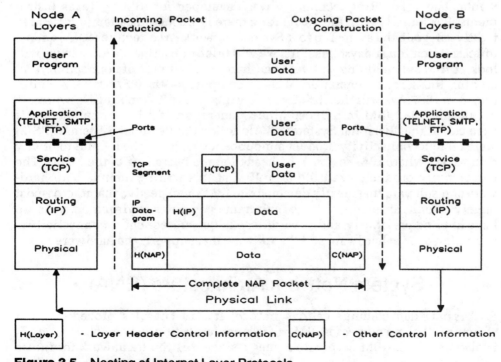

Figure 3.5   Nesting of Internet Layer Protocols
NOTES: H(Layer) denotes Layer Header Control Information [H(TCP), H(IP), H(NAP)];
         C(NAP) denotes Other Control Information.

chines, and more recently, many remote networks, together. Consequently, some sort of system of router/gateway/bridge must be used.

LANS IN THE CONTEXT OF IBM'S SNA NETWORKS*

At this writing IBM was marketing two primary LAN architectures: the IBM PC Network, implemented originally as a CATV-based broadband system and later supplemented with a baseband version, and the Token Ring Network. It has announced future support for at least one additional LAN, a token bus system for manufacturing. It has also announced LAN support for users of 3270 Display System devices through future modifications of 3274 cluster controllers. Each of these LANs was originally based on a common software interface called NETBIOS. As we will see, IBM now supports several other software interfaces, as well. Primary strategic support has been placed on the Token Ring Network, although IBM's primary impetus seems to be to give the market whatever it wants. The Token Ring technology was developed for IBM by Texas Instruments. Particularly with the Token Ring there is an ongoing attempt by IBM to tightly integrate the system in to it System Network Architecture (SNA) and its office automation subsystems. First we will briefly describe SNA. Then we will look at IBM's developing software and hardware support of connectivity, including the second generation of microcomputers—the PS/2 family—introduced in 1987. We will then briefly review the PC and Token Ring Networks.

In mid-1987 IBM introduced a new generation of microcomputers—this time called the "Personal System/2." Alongside the Personal System/2 (PS/2) were related connectivity product announcements. It may be helpful to briefly summarize where IBM seems to be headed at the beginning of the 1990s. The connectivity products available from IBM at this writing include both hardware and software that clearly demonstrate IBM's perspective that micros exist largely as enhancements to large mainframe computer environments. As we have implied previously, and as we will consider subsequently, connectivity is a function of both hardware and the software that supports the hardware.

System Network Architecture (SNA)

SNA *is not* a data communications protocol. It is a set of rules, procedures, and structures that encompasses IBM's data communications design philosophy. It is also part of an IBM corporate strategy, since it is the framework for future

*This section has been largely reproduced with permission of the Publisher, Howard W. Sams & Co., *Micro-Mainframe Connections* by Thomas Madron, ©1987.

IBM data communications development. New IBM products will have the SNA guidelines imposed on them.

The scope of SNA is broad, and as a result, none of IBM's products implement the entire architecture. Conversely, IBM's individual products implement only those elements of SNA that pertain to the function of the specific product. SNA is often confused with various explicit or implicit components of the architecture. SNA *is not* a Data Link control system such as SDLC, although SDLC is the most common protocol used; it is not a communications access method (not VTAM); and it is not a standard like X.25. Because of IBM's market position, however, it might be called a *de facto* communications architecture standard.[13] From a competitive perspective, it is certainly true that DEC and others have had to come to terms with SNA.

SNA is a layered architecture similar to the International Standards Organization's Open Systems Interconnection model, described in Chapter 2. In Figure 3.6 the relationship of the scope of OSI, SNA, SDLC, and BSC models is seen. Figure 3.6 is neater than the reality of the situation, but the effort is nevertheless useful. SNA proper is divided into only five (not seven) layers—"End-User"

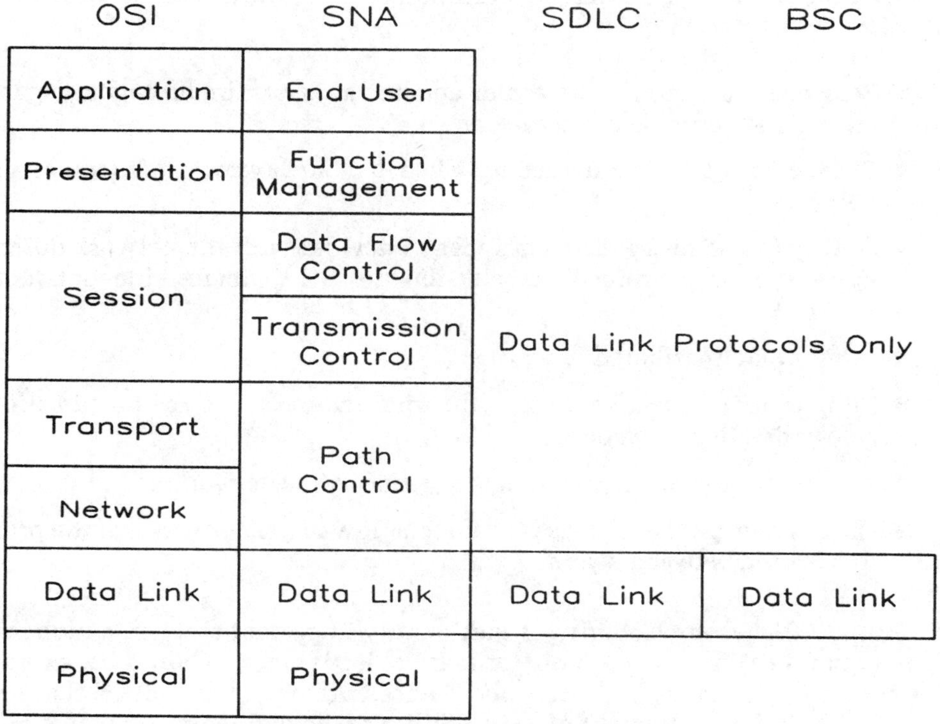

OSI	SNA	SDLC	BSC
Application	End-User		
Presentation	Function Management		
Session	Data Flow Control		
	Transmission Control	Data Link Protocols Only	
Transport	Path Control		
Network			
Data Link	Data Link	Data Link	Data Link
Physical	Physical		

Figure 3.6   Scope of OSI, SNA, SDLC, and BSC Models

and "Physical" are not part of the formal scope of SNA. The "Data Link" layer is marginal to SNA. The remaining four do not neatly fit the OSI model. On the other hand, the OSI model is the standard, not SNA, and IBM and others have found the relationship of the two helpful.[14] Clearly, SDLC and BSC are concerned only with data link control and have limited scope. SDLC is clearly the data link control method most frequently used with SNA.

A major difference between OSI and SNA is that although OSI provides only a functional model, SNA defines not only functions but also protocols that are to be used within the single-vendor IBM environment. Compatibility with SNA clearly involves more than consistency with the data link control layer. Nor is SNA merely a replacement for BSC networks, since SNA is a network *architecture*. In contrast, BSC is only a method for Data Link control.

This book is not the place for a full-scale discussion of SNA, but some discussion of SNA concepts is necessary in order to have a firm understanding of the context in which LANs exist in an IBM network. Much of IBM's office automation emphasis for the next few years will be based on SNA as will methods used to integrate PCs into that environment. SNA is also a dynamic and growing concept within IBM itself. The fundamental design objectives and features for SNA were and are similar to other data communications networks as follows:

▼ Easy communication between or among end-users, including transparency of the network to those users;

▼ Separation of function accomplished by the layered architecture of SNA;

▼ Ability to use many different types of devices with the network doing any necessary protocol conversion to SNA device independent protocols;

▼ Support for distributed functions;

▼ Support for resource sharing by allowing end-users to dynamically allocate or de-allocate resources;

▼ Ability to dynamically reconfigure or modify the network;

▼ Clearly defines the formats for data that flow in the network and the protocols used between layers.

Support for resource sharing is particularly important since in a modern data communications network one primary objective is, or should be, extensive connectivity among end-users and devices. Among other things, that resource sharing can be thought of as the ability of the end-user to switch from one application to another from a single terminal—a feature not usually available in a BSC network. "Application" in the sense used here means from one teleprocessing monitor to another, including the possibility of moving from one IBM host to another through a Front End Processor (FEP).

Here are some SNA terms and concepts that will prove useful in later discussions:

▼ A *domain* consists of all the physical and logical components controlled by one common point in the network.

▼ The *Systems Services Control Point (SSCP)* is the common control point.

▼ A *node* is a logical grouping of network components that have uniquely defined characteristics.

Each node contains a *Physical Unit (PU)*, which is the resource controller for the node.

Nodes normally contain *Logical Units (LUs)* to interface end-users to the network, including a network address.

An LU or a PU is addressed through a logical entity assigned a unique network address called the *Network Addressable Unit (NAU)*. NAUs defined by SNA include PUs, LUs, SSCPs, and data links.

SNA Node Summary:

Node	PU-Type	IBM Hardware*	Software
Host	PU-T5	309x, 43xx	VTAM
Com. Ctrl.	PU-T4	37x5	NCP
Cluster Ctrl.	PU-T2.1	PC. Off. Automa.	...
Cluster Ctrl.	PU-T2.0	3174, 3274, 3276, 3790	...

*NOTE: Many manufacturers produce compatible equipment, and boards are available allowing PCs to emulate 3x78 and 3x79 terminals. This summary is not complete and includes only the most commonly used PU types.

PU-T2.1 has only been recently defined (1983) and is designed for Peer-to-Peer (for PCs, for example) coupling or subarea (see below) routing. The former is, in principle, non-mediated—that is, it is not necessary for routing through VTAM or NCO, although two PCs communicating with one another through different SNA cluster controller will likely have to pass through the Communications FEP (the boundary area indicated in Figure 3.7.

▼ An SNA *subarea* is either a Host subarea or a Communications Controller subarea producing a higher level grouping of nodes.

A *network address* is 16 bits long and contains both a subarea address and an element address (individual NAU).

In some segments of the network only short, local addresses are desirable and the translation between local and network addressing is through the *boundary function* that resides in either the Host or Communications Controller.

A diagram of a complete SNA network may be seen in Figure 3.7. Microcomputers, as will be seen below, can replace the 3x74 (or 3x76) and/or the 3x78/79 terminals in an SNA network. Logical Unit (LU) 2.2 was designed to provide the basic services necessary to have consistent data transfer among LUs. Remember than an LU exists within a PU.

Software Connectivity Products

For purposes of discussion the IBM software products that affect the connectivity among micros and the relationship of micros in a wider SNA network are:

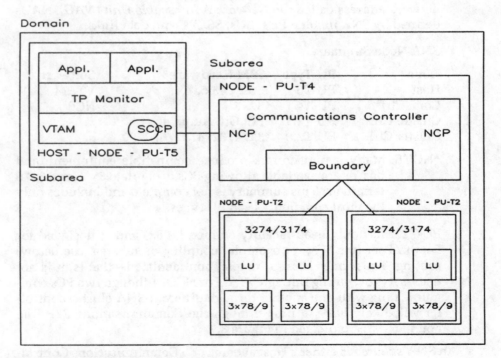

Figure 3.7   Example of an SNA Network

▼ NETBIOS on the micro specifically designed to be used in conjunction
with IBM's LAN hardware: Because NETBIOS was developed for use with
IBM's network operating system, it will be discussed in Chapter 5;

▼ Enhanced Connectivity Facilities (ECF) which provide virtual disk and
file services for a microcomputer connected either through a Token Ring
LAN gatewayed to an SNA network or through a 3270 display station
emulation card connected through a 3174 (or the old 3274) cluster controller: Conceived primarily as micro–to–mainframe link software, ECF
will be discussed in Chapter 4;

▼ APPC and LU 6.2 for the micro, mini, and mainframe for application–
to–application communication at the highest layers of network
architecture;

▼ *Systems Application Architecture (SAA)* that provides a framework for
the development of "consistent application across the future offerings of
the major IBM computing environments—System 370, System/3x and
Personal Computer" (Announcement 287-088, March 17, 1987).

Advanced Program-to-Program Communication (APPC) and LU 6.2

Of particular importance to the micro–to–mainframe connection is IBM's development of APPC and Logical Unit (LU) 6.2 that was designed to provide enhanced SNA support for distributed processing.[15] The express purpose of
APPC is to provide a single strategic LU type for all IBM products that support
distributed processing. Although SNA supports several different types of sessions, LU-to-LU sessions are among the most important but they can be established only between or among LUs of the same type. LU Type 6.2 is the architectural base for APPC. A *distributed transaction* within SNA consists of user
application processing executed cooperatively on multiple systems. APPC and
LU 6.2 provide the structure for making that cooperative execution possible.

LU 6.2, therefore, specifies a consistent set of functions, formats, and protocols for conversations (sessions) between programs on separate processors.
Those processors may be mainframes, minis, or micros, although appropriate
software implementing LU 6.2 must be available. Technically, "processor" in
this context means an execution environment supplied by a Logical Unit. Facilities are furnished for LU-to-LU and LU-to-SSCP conversations. An LU-to-
LU session may not include access to any central processor, a significant departure for IBM, although in an SNA network, it is likely that peer-to-peer
communications from a micro-to-micro would still take a tour through the
Front End Processor.

LU 6.2 provides protocols primarily for session management at the upper layers of SNA. Error recovery within LU 6.2, for example, is at a much higher layer than error recovery with SDLC. In an LU 6.2 transaction, errors can occur in program logic where the transaction program is responsible for error recovery, in synchronization processing, or in the session itself. In the latter case the transaction is informed of the error by a return code indicating conversation failure. Action can then be taken to de-allocate the conversation, which releases the dead session. This is somewhat similar to automatic logoff when a line drops, a condition that many applications written for IBM mainframe environments do not handle well. Systems that do not handle this condition properly create both technical and security problems. "Synchronization," in this instance, means the synchronization of linked transaction processes rather than anything having to do with a data link protocol.

The importance of all this for a microcomputer user is that in an SNA environment APPC/LU 6.2 provides the support for the transparent interchange of data stored consistently with Document Content Architecture (DCA), organized and addressed according to Document Interchange Architecture (DIA), and distributed by System Network Architecture's Distribution Services (SNADS), responding to a request by an application program somewhere on the network. SNADS operates at the "Function Management" layer of SNA (see Figure 3.2), higher than APPC/LU 6.2.[16]

There has been considerable confusion evidenced in industry literature concerning the future software environment for IBM networks resulting at least in part from IBM's integration efforts. One report suggested that IBM confused software developers at the Communications Networks '87 show held in February 1987 in Washington, D.C. with an announcement concerning protocols. Since late 1985, IBM had encouraged developers to support Advanced Program-to-Program Communication (APPC) protocols in their communications software. A senior market support representative from IBM, Robert D. Dill, seemed to suggest that developers should not use NETBIOS, but should instead use the Enhanced Connectivity Facility (ECF). Dill said that ECF is advantageous both in creating peer-to-peer networks between mainframes and personal computers and in the personal computer environment itself. Dill described the move away from NETBIOS and toward ECF as "strategic."[17]

Although NETBIOS, APPC, and ECF may seem to overlap, they were designed to meet somewhat different needs. Parenthetically, we must note that IBM has started issuing "support for" statements concerning IEEE 802.2 (LLC) software interfaces, as well, into its literature. NETBIOS extends the operating environment of the PC to allow applications to communicate with the Network Interface Card (NIC), and, therefore, the network, whether that be the PC Network, Token Ring, or something else. APPC is a subsidiary architecture within the context of SNA that provides the set of rules necessary for interapplication communications. ECF is designed to allow IBM host operating environments (MVS/TSO and VM/CMS) to operate as servers for PCs communicating in a variety of ways. Furthermore, none of these software structures have anything to do with the LAN protocols (CSMA/CD, Token Ring, etc.) at all. ECF is irrelevant if there is no micro–to–mainframe connection, and it is unlikely that APPC would be implemented without that same connection.[18] APPC requires specific implementations and the cost of ECF is high. This also assumes, of course, that you have a central IBM system operating under MVS with TSO or VM/CMS. In other words, it is unlikely that either software written to APPC standards, or ECF, will replace NETBIOS at any time in the near future.

Systems Application Architecture

The Systems Application Architecture seems to be a recognition by IBM that it has been in the process of developing a set of almost mutually exclusive computer and connectivity products that must now be brought together. The elements of SAA are:

▼ Common User Access

▼ Common Programming Interface

▼ Common Communications Support

The third element is of greatest importance for the subject of this book, although the common programming interface will have impact on how software development takes place. The most important feature of the common programming interface is IBM's re-endorsement of COBOL and FORTRAN as the primary programming languages, along with C. Common versions of these languages will be supplied for all computer products from micros to mainframes, thus allowing the easy porting of applications from one system to another. The endorsement of C is also of great importance because this will provide a common systems programming language (which heretofore has been the local Assembler languages) across all computer systems regardless of hardware architecture.

Common Communications Support is designed to interconnect SAA applications, systems, networks, and devices. This connectivity will come about through designated communications architectures for each SAA environment. These are the building blocks for IBM's approach to distributed processing. The SAA is a combination of SNA and international standards and the announcement "reaffirms" IBM's commitment to openness. Considering the amount of speculation and fear expressed in the trade press concerning the possibility of IBM closing down its previous openness, this is likely to be an important announcement over the long term. The original 1987 announcement included support for several functional elements and, by 1989, SAA products were becoming available.

Data Streams.   Data stream support includes the 3270 display system, Document Content Architecture, and Intelligent Printer Data Stream. The 3270 display system continues to be important in IBM's strategy. SAA support for the 3270 data stream consists of user-provided data and commands, as well as control information that governs the way data is handled. Likewise, the System/3x family will continue to support the 5250 data stream. Document Content Architecture (DCA) defines the rules for specifying the form and meaning of a text document. Within an SNA network, it provides for uniform interchange of textual information in the office environment and consists of format elements optimized for document revision. Other manufacturers, such as DEC and Wang, are beginning to provide translation systems from DCA into their own document processing systems. Intelligent Printer Data Stream (IPDS) is a high function data stream intended for use with all points addressable page printers.

Application Services.   Application services include support for SNA Distribution Services (SNADS), Document Interchange Architecture (DIA), and the SNA Network Management Architecture. SNADS provides *asynchronous* distribution capability in an SNA network, thereby avoiding the need for active sessions between the end points. As IBM has become more open, and as it has come to recognize that national and international standards are important, it has also come to provide greater support for communications techniques that have received short shrift in the past, particularly asynchronous support. DIA provides a set of protocols that define several common office functions performed cooperatively by IBM products. IBM's approach to managing networks is described by the SNA Network Management Architecture, which provides a set of protocols for monitoring network operations from a central location.

Session Services.   The only session service protocol family supported in the initial announcement is LU 6.2. As we have noted elsewhere, LU 6.2 is a program-to-program communication protocol. LU 6.2 is a set of interprogram communication services, including a base subset and optional supplementary services. The objective is to provide compatibility of communication functions across systems. At the microcomputer level this may suggest some replacement for functions currently supported by NETBIOS, although this is far from clear.

Network.   Two types of network support are encompassed within SAA: A SNA low-entry networking node (Type 2.1 node) and X.25. The former supports peer-to-peer communication through a common set of protocols that allow multiple and parallel SNA sessions to be established between Type 2.1 nodes that are directly attached to one another. X.25 support illustrates the bending of IBM to international standards and defines a packet-mode interface for attaching data terminal equipment (DTE) to packet-switched networks. DTEs may include host computers, communication controllers, and terminals.

Data Link Controls.   Although SNA has never supported a single Data Link control, the emphasis has been on SDLC, and this emphasis is reaffirmed in SAA. SDLC, you will remember, is a discipline for managing synchronous code-transparent serial-by-bit information transfer between nodes that are joined by telecommunication links. Added to SDLC for Data Link control is the system used by the IBM Token Ring Network. An important omission in SAA is the lack of support for the Ethernet Data Link protocol. Even though IBM is coming to recognize the importance of Ethernet, and the fact that it will not go away, SAA in 1987 contained no recognition of its importance. This is surprising because more-or-less concurrent announcements from IBM reaffirmed support of the PC Network in both its broadband and baseband versions. The Data Link protocol used by PC Network is a CSMA/CD system similar to IEEE 802.3, and the baseband version is very like StarLan which served as the basis for the low-speed twisted pair 802.3 standard (see the discussions on IEEE Std. 802.3 in Chapter 7). IBM's literature only claims 802.2 (LLC) conformance for the PC Network. Regardless of explicit products, however, support for the 802.3 Data Link control standard will likely be added to SAA at some point.

Microcomputer Hardware/Software Connectivity Products

Perhaps the best way to describe IBM's 1987 announcement of the Personal System/2 family of microcomputers is to suggest that they seem to be viewed strategically as connectivity products themselves. The PS/2 microcomputers are clearly products that are directed toward placement in large organizations and large networking environments. The IBM LANs were also enhanced to take advantage of the new PS/2 microcomputers. Continued support for NETBIOS was illustrated with an enhanced version of the PC Network Program and PS/2 versions of all LAN interface cards were announced including the Token Ring, PC Network (broadband), and PC Network (baseband). This allows older PCs to be connected in a common network with PS/2 machines. Although most existing PC software should work on the new systems, applications written specifically for the new machines under OS/2 will not work on the older systems. One software enhancement, the LAN Manager, enhances the network management capability of the Token Ring and provides network management capability to the broadband IBM PC Network.

Although the old IBM Local Area Network Support Program had many limitations, cost was one of its strengths. Some of the enhancements made in the PC

LAN Program V.1.3 has resulted in improved performance. The important enhancements include support for the new PS/2 boards for Token Ring and PC Network (both broadband and baseband). Of most importance, it extends supports not only for NETBIOS, but also for an IEEE 802.2 interface. In addition, support for APPC/PC is provided for both Token Ring and PC Network. Although the PC Network (LAN) Support Program contains considerable improvements, both the old network interface cards as well as newly enhanced NICs are supported. The important point of all this is that applications written for IEEE 802.2/LLC, NETBIOS, or APPC/PC application interfaces can be run on *all* IBM LANs, thus providing portability across LAN technology. Novell, in particular, and other manufacturers of generic network operating systems now provide support to IEEE and APPC/PC interfaces as well as to their own and to NETBIOS.

The key elements of IBM's connectivity products for microcomputers are LANs and terminal emulation capabilities. The terminal emulations are focused on the 3270 display system for System/370 users, and on 5250 Display Station emulation for S/34, S/36, S/38 and their successor, the AS400 minicomputers. The Token Ring, while the primary strategic LAN product, does not seem to have obliterated the PC Network in either the broadband or baseband versions. The broadband version, particularly, is being enhanced for what IBM regards as a specialized niche in the market: those users that require combining their LAN with other services such as video, voice, security, and/or additional data channels on a common broadband medium. All LANs can be used to meet the requirements of small businesses and individual work groups, of course.

Trying to follow what IBM is doing is always complicated. Part of the problem is that IBM has been around a long time and has an impact in most parts of the information processing industry. They have, consequently, produced a large number of connectivity products over the years and must now attempt to bring some order out of their own somewhat chaotic product inventory. At the same time they have to avoid alienating large customers that have a major impact on IBM sales. An IBM networking environment will, therefore, always be a compromise among what is best, what is new, and what is installed. Moreover, even within IBM these compromises are not entirely driven by technology. Different divisions of IBM engineer and manufacture different connectivity products. Consequently, there will be the inevitable jockeying for position and prestige within IBM's organization. The competitive tools for the contending groups are the old and new products they produce. As a result of such conflicts, there must be political as well as technical compromises. The concept of an overarching connectivity architecture such as SAA is one approach to managing these compromises. One clearly evident, if not explicitly stated, IBM strategy in managing outside competition is to co-opt popular technology. This is evidenced by a growing number of products supporting Ethernet and connectivity to asynchronous computers (always referencing the Series/1, but often informally acknowledged to support DEC's VAX family and similar systems).

LANS IN A DIGITAL DNA ENVIRONMENT

In sharp contrast to IBM's LAN strategies—that seem to regard LANs as unavoidable peripherals brought on by market demand—DEC has adopted LAN technology as central to its network philosophy. DEC, along with Xerox, became an early partner in the development of Ethernet and later a leader in the development of the IEEE 802.3 standard. Today it is almost impossible to buy a large DEC VAX computer without also buying at least one small Ethernet system. DEC has developed DNA as a response to the need for an integrated approach to networking that includes both WANs and LANs. The Digital Network Architecture is the framework for all DEC's communications products.

Whereas the broad outline of IBM's SNA have remained relatively constant for many years, DEC's DNA has undergone several major changes starting with Phase I in 1978 through Phase V announced in 1987. The current installed base is an amalgam of Phase IV and Phase V protocols. The important element of Phase V is a major move to a largely OSI compliant network architecture. At the three upper layers (Application, Presentation, and Session), Phase V retains older Phase IV elements in support of existing products. OSI compliant software products are added in parallel to the older products. At the lower four layers, Phase V moves almost entirely to OSI compliant protocols although it does retain DDCMP at the Data Link Layer. For an overview of this evolution, see Figure 3.8.

Within the framework of DNA, network managers can configure either WANs or LANs. Of particular importance to this book's discussions are the Network Application and Data Link Layers. The Network Application Layer may contain both user- and DEC-supplied modules. It defines network functions used by the User and Network Management layers. Included as a function of the Network Application Layer is access to other networks, including X.25 and IBM's SNA. So ubiquitous is IBM's influence in the information-processing industry that virtually all other manufacturers must supply links into IBM systems. The Data Link Layer is important because it supports DEC's Digital Data Communications Message Protocol (DDCMP), X.25 protocol, and Ethernet protocol. DNA software and hardware modules within layers are linked by protocols between layers. The result of a DNA structured network is DECnet.[19]

As was implied with IBM's synchronous data link control within SNA, DDCMP, X.25, and Ethernet are, among other things, protocols for organizing the data bit stream on the appropriate medium. Data are, therefore, organized in packets (or blocks) that are rigidly defined. This is true not only of those already mentioned, but also for Token Ring and PC Networks, as well. Standards typically allow each manufacturer some flexibility in the use of the protocols so that even when media access and physical layer conditions are identical, two Ethernets on the same physical cable may not be able to communicate with one

OSI	DNA Phase IV	DNA Phase V	
Application	User	User	FTAM, X.400 Others
	Network Mangement	Network Management	
Presentation	Network Application	Network Application	OSI Presentation
Session	DECnet Session Control	DECnet Session Control	OSI Session
Transport	End-to-End Communication DECnet Transport (NSP)	Common Transport Interface	
		DECnet Transport (NSP)	OSI Transport
Network	DECnet Routing (Adaptive Routing)	ISO Connectionless Service ISO Connection-Oriented Service ISO ES-IS Routing Protocol IS-IS Routing Protocol	
		X.25	
Data Link	Ethernet DDCMP X.25	DDCMP Ethernet/802.2 LLC/802.3 MAC HDLC	
Physical	Physical	802.3 Physical Others as necessary	

Figure 3.8   Scope of OSI and DNA Models

another. In addition, overlayed on the data link control structure may be a file transfer protocol of some form or another, which may be folded within, say, an Ethernet packet. In Chapter 7 we will take up Ethernet (802.3) in detail. DEC's implementation of Ethernet is sufficiently important to its view of networking, however, that it is desirable to mention some highlights at this point. For that reason we will take a closer look at DEC's implementation of Ethernet even though the discussion may make more sense once you have read Chapter 7.

DEC Ethernet Messages

Ethernet (IEEE 802.3) is a standard that lies at OSI Layers 1 (Physical) and 2 (Data Link). The part of the standard that falls in the Data Link Layer consists of the Media Access Control sublayer and Logical Link Control, rather than encompassing a full data transmission protocol. The MAC services for Ethernet include CSMA/CD and the basic frame format (see Chapter 7). There is flexibility within the frame format, particularly with respect to source and destination addresses that may be either 16 or 48 bits in length. Manufacturers are free to use either the 16- or 48-bit format, or to support both (although this is not required by the standard). Developers are also free to link the frame to higher level protocols, which is what DEC does. This results in many manufacturers using the same equipment, possibly over the same cable, without the ability for devices on networks defined by protocol to communicate with one another.

The Ethernet Data Link has one type of message or frame. The construction and processing of frames is the result of the data encapsulation function of the Data Link Layer. The sub-functions of framing include addressing and error detection. No explicit framing information is required with Ethernet because the access method (CSMA/CD) provides the necessary framing cues. Two addresses—for source and destination stations—are provided. Error detection is accomplished with a Frame Check Sequence (FCS)—a 32-bit CRC. In a DNA (Phase IV) network environment composed of DDCMP media, Ethernets, and X.25 systems, every node has a unique address. This requires the use of the 48-bit address field. The Ethernet Data Link Frame format, as used by DEC, may be seen in Figure 3.9.

The implementation flexibility provided within the 802.3 standard is clearest in the definition of the source and destination addresses. As noted above, the address fields may be either 16 or 48 bits. The 48-bit field allows a specific Ethernet node to have a unique address across all interconnected

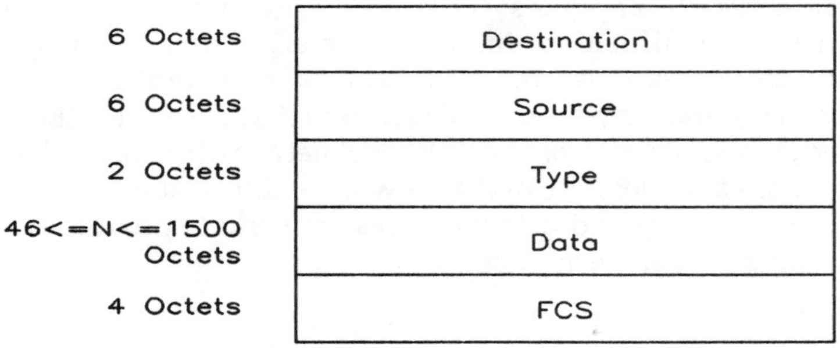

6 Octets	Destination
6 Octets	Source
2 Octets	Type
$46 <= N <= 1500$ Octets	Data
4 Octets	FCS

Figure 3.9   DEC Ethernet Data Link Frame Format

NOTES: Destination: The destination data link address is one of three types: physical, multicast, or broadcast.
Source: The source data link address always contains the physical address of the station transmitting a frame.
Type: The type field is reserved for use by higher-layer protocols to identify the higher-level protocol associated with a frame.
Data: The data field contains higher-level protocol data with full transparency. The minimum length of the data field ensures that all frames occupy the channel long enough for reliable collision detection.
FCS: The frame check sequence contains the CRC-32 polynomial check on the rest of the frame.

SOURCE: *DECnet: Digital Network Architecture, General Description*, Document No. AA-N149-TC (Maynard,MA: Digital Equipment Corporation, 1982), p. 2.12.

Ethernets or other networks. In DNA (Phase IV), each Ethernet node has a 16-bit node address. If that node is also a DNA node, then the 16-bit address is prefixed by a 32-bit address assigned to DNA nodes. DNA addresses are, therefore, unique over a single DNA network, which may include multiple Ethernets and DDCMP and X.25 links. Associated with this capability is the Type field, which identifies any higher level protocols associated with the frame. Type values are assigned to the DNA routing protocol and to DNA Maintenance Operation protocols. In the 802.3 standard, the field that DEC labels "Type" is actually defined as a length field stipulating the length of the data field. We should also note that for DEC the error control functions necessary for reliable communications are provided by the Network Services Protocol (NSP) in a DNA environment.

DECnet Summary

Both SNA and DNA are network architectures designed to absorb new and increasingly efficient communications technologies. Communications technology is among the fastest changing within the information-processing industry. Consequently, a network architecture must be capable of change and adaptation. Moreover, a network architecture can also specify common communication mechanisms and user interfaces that allow the intercommunication of many different kinds of computer systems. In the absence of such networking standards, it would be difficult or impossible to effect data exchange and resource sharing among various operating systems, communications devices, and computer hardware. A by-product of all this is that a user in a DECnet environment can make use of a number of high-level network functions thus allowing better and more complete use of the network and its resources. Also, wide area networks can be integrated with local area networks to provide the correct level of networking for a given application.

LANS AND OFFICE AUTOMATION

Office Automation refers to efforts to provide automation for common office tasks, including word processing, filing, and record keeping. In 1982, when researching a book entitled *Microcomputers in Large Organizations.*[20] I surveyed the members of the Dallas Chapter of the Data Processing Management Association concerning the use of micros at that time. Even though 103 uses were mentioned, the median number of micros per represented corporation was quite small. In fact, in 1982 in Dallas, only 54 percent of the sample reported that their employers had one or more micros, and the median number of micros across all the organizations represented in the sample was only 3.5 per organization. Conversely, in a survey conducted on behalf of the entire Data Processing Management Association in 1986, a large majority (77.5 percent) reported that they used PC-based workstations. Clearly, times are changing.

In an effort to find out how microcomputers were being used, even as early as 1982, as well as to further refine the meaning of "office automation," respondents were asked to list the uses their organizations made of micros. The resulting master list included (but was not restricted to) the following:

Account inquiry

Auditing

Balance of accounts

Budgeting

Database inquiry system

Data collection of various kinds

Dealer support

Distributed processing

Education (computer-based training)

Engineering applications

Finance (forecasting)

Finance (petty cash)

Financial analysis of various kinds

Graphics

Insurance proposals

Intelligent desk calculators

Intelligent terminals

Inventory control

Manager's workstations

Operations research

Organizational maintenance (organization charts, lists, etc.)

Personnel programs

Plotting

Policy ratings

Production planning models

Project control

Purchase order status

Run costs history

Sales and marketing

Scheduling (staff)

Shipping records

Statistics

Stock balance

Tax computations

Training

Word processing

By contemporary standards this is not a surprising list. On the other hand, it helps provide a more detailed understanding of the concept of "office automation." All of these activities are those carried on in normal office environments. Yet, with few exceptions, in a normal office or department, more than one person will have to access the same information, and almost all of the applications listed could involve more than one person.

Even though efficient, cost-effective LANs were unavailable in 1982; it rapidly became apparent that the growing number of micros in use in offices needed to communicate with one another and with the corporation's mainframe or minicomputer systems. The rapid acceptance and deployment of micros in the period from 1982 through 1986 probably did more than any other single thing to sensitize people to the need for networking, especially in office automation applications. The need for micro-based LANs is clear even when the respondents had access to large onsite or remote computing facilities.

Not everyone, of course, had access to LANs even at this writing. Only 25.7 percent of the respondents in the 1986 DPMA general survey reported having access to such systems, but LANs were among the most active markets in the industry. Considering much of the publicity surrounding LANs, one might think that the primary target might be smaller businesses or organizations without access to large mainframe systems. This does not seem to be the case, however. Of those with some kind of mainframe access, 30.1 percent also used micro-based LANs. Conversely, of those with no mainframe access, only 17.3 percent reported using microcomputer-based LANs. The point is that departmental or micro-based LANs are becoming important in the midst of main-frame-oriented users. Mainframes simply do not seem to be accepted by people as appropriate for office automation, yet the need is clear for shared resources in departments attempting to automate. It is for this reason that LANs are becoming increasingly important components of office automation systems.

LANS AS THE FOCUS OF A LARGER NETWORK

To this point we have discussed LANs as if they were always at the end of a distributed network, rather than in the center of it. Rather than having a large super-minicomputer or a mainframe as the focus of a larger network, it may be, especially with the growing speed and power of the computers used as servers on LANs, that the LAN itself will become the center of a broader network. This possibility has already been recognized to some extent by manufacturers, such as Novell, that are providing asynchronous gateways, thus allowing access by modem or by other devices running at speeds lower than those of the typical LAN.

REFERENCES

1. James Martin, *Design and Strategy of Distributed Data Processing* (Englewood Cliffs, NJ: Prentice-Hall, 1981), pp. 10 and 11.

2. Paul R. Strauss, "The Standards Deluge: A Sound Foundation or a Tower of Babel?," *Data Communications,* September 1988, Vol. 17, No. 10, p. 160.

3. (a) John L. Hullett and Peter Evans, "New Proposal Extends the Reach of Metro Area Networks (Dual Bus Scheme)," *Data Communications (USA),* February 1988, Vol. 17, No. 2, pp. 139–140, 143–144 and 147. Much of the information regarding QPSX is taken from this article. (b) See also, R. M. Newman, Z. L. Budrikis, J. L. Hulett, "The QPSX MAN," *IEEE Commun. Mag. (USA),* April 1988, Vol. 26, No. 4, pp. 20–28.

4. See Ref. 3(a), p. 139.

5. Mollenauer, p. 119.

6. (a) Alan Reinhold, "TCP/IP," *Communications Systems Bulletin* (Raleigh, NC: IBM Telecommunications Marketing Center, February 1988), p. 7. Other authors have named these layers somewhat differently, e.g., (b) William Stallings et al., "Department of Defense (DOD) Protocol Stan-

dards," *Handbook of Computer-Communications Standards* (New York: Macmillan Publishing Company, 1988), Vol. 3, p. 21. The formal definitions for the TCP/IP standards are found in the U.S. Military standards documents and in Requests-for-Comments (RFCs) available over the Internet or from the DDN Network Information Center, SRI International, 333 Ravenswood Avenue, Menlo Park, CA 94025.

7. Stallings et al., Ref. 6(b), p. 21, have compared TCP/IP (DOD) and OSI Reference layering somewhat differently and have named the four layers as Process, Host-to-Host, Internet, and Network Access. RFC: 793 (1981), which is one of the formal documents detailing TCP, labels the layers as Application, Host, Gateway, and Network. My labeling is a modification of that found in Reinhold, Ref. 6(a), p. 33. For a recent overview of TCP/IP see William Stallings, "Tuning into TCP/IP," *Telecommunications,* September 1988, Vol. 22, No. 9, pp. 23ff. Note also, Michael Hurwicz, "TCP/IP: Temporary Glue or Long-term Alternative?," *ComputerWorld,* September 26, 1988, pp. 73ff.

8. H. Kim Lew and Cyndi Jung, "Getting There from Here: Mapping From TCP/IP to OSI," *Data Communications,* August 1988, Vol. 17, No. 8, pp. 161ff.

9. Jerry Cashin, "ULANA: New Name in Networking," *Software Magazine,* October 1988, Vol. 8, No. 12, pp. 91–94.

10. For a brief description, see Bill Hancock, "TCP/IP for Network Services," *DEC Professional,* July 1988, pp. 102ff.

11. (a) Defense Communications Agency, *Military Standard Transmission Control Protocol,* MIL-STD-1780, May 10, 1984. It is also reprinted in (b) Defense Communications Agency, *DDN Protocol Handbook* (Menlo Park, CA: DDN Network Information Center, SRI International, December 1985). See also (c) RFC: 793 (1981), "Transmission Control Protocol." One introduction to TCP/IP is (d) Charles L. Hedrick, "Introduction to the Internet Protocols," Computer Science Facilities Group, Rutgers, the State University of New Jersey, Center for Computers and Information Services, Laboratory for Computer Science Research, September 22, 1988, unpublished paper.

12. Hedrick, Ref. 11(d), pp. 2–3.

13. "Introduction to Systems Network Architecture," a report from the *Data Communications Technology Series* (Cupertino, CA: Communications Solutions, Inc., 1980).

14. (a) Ibid., pp. 5–7; (b) F. P. Corr and D. H. Neal, "SNA and Emerging International Standards," *IBM Systems Journal,* Vol. 18, No. 2, 1979, and (c)

Art Krumrey, "SNA Strategies," *PC Tech Journal,* Vol. 3, No. 7, July 1985, pp. 40ff.

15. This discussion of APPC and LU 6.2 is based on Gerard Joseph, *An Intro-duction to Advanced Program-to-Program Communication (APPC)* (Research Triangle Park, NC: International Business Machines, 1983), document No.GG24-1584-0.

16. For further information see Krumrey, Ref. 14(c); Robert J. Sundstrom, "Program-to-Program Communications—A Growing Trend," *Data Communications,* February 1984, pp. 87–92; L. David Passmore, "Coming: A New SNA," *Datamation,* Vol. 31, No. 22, November 15, 1985, pp. 102–112; and John W. Verity, "The Shifting Shape of SNA," *Datamation,* Vol. 31, No. 22, November 15, 1985, pp. 93–98.

17. Laurie Flynn, "IBM Changes Its Strategy on Protocols," *InfoWorld,* Vol. 9, No. 7, February 16, 1987, p. 1(2).

18. ECF is described in IBM's program announcement of March 17, 1987 (287-084) and related documents. Some of the misunderstanding about the relationships of the various products, protocols, and architectures continues to be found in the trade literature. See, for example, two articles by Mike Hurwicz: "Not a Standard: When NETBIOS means network bias," *LAN: The Local Area Network Magazine,* January 1987, pp. 60–61; and "APPC Is Coming: LAN Standard of the Future?," *LAN: The Local Area Network Magazine,* March 1987, pp. 50–54. A somewhat better description of NETBIOS is given by Jamie Lewis, "NETBIOS: Going Beyond Interrupt 5C," *LAN: The Local Area Network Magazine,* December 1986, pp. 23–24.

19. For more detailed discussions of both SNA and DECnet, see Thomas Wm. Madron, *Micro Mainframe Connection* (Indianapolis, IN: Howard W. Sams, 1987), Chapters 6 and 8. For a good and reasonably detailed discussion of DNA, see Anon., *Digital's Networks: An Architecture with a Future* (Maynard, MA: Digital Equipment Corporation, 1984).

20. Thomas W. Madron, *Microcomputers in Large Organizations* (Englewood Cliffs, NJ: Prentice-Hall, 1983), pp. 132–135.

C H A P T E R   4

LINKING LANS

In many organizations LANs cannot stand by themselves. They must be linked either with other LANs, to a Wide Area Network (WAN), or to a centralized computing facility (a large minicomputer or mainframe). LANs are rapidly becoming the interface of choice between human users and broader, more encompasing needs for information exchange. Clearly our ideas about the role and usefulness of LANs is constantly changing and growing. The growth of local area networks in the mid-1980s helped shift our thinking from computers *qua* computers to the way in which we communicate with computers, and why. By the late 1980s vendors were clearly promoting the use of LANs as a major link in the micro–to–mainframe connection, although some components were still missing.

Digital Equipment Corporation, for example, was presenting an integrated approach to its organization of computing linked by Ethernet. To an Ethernet backbone it was possible to attach a large VAX or a small personal computer and have them communicate with one another. It was also possible to attach bridges and gateways that would allow access to a broader DECnet environment or even to an IBM SNA network. The principal difficulty with all this was that it was and is necessary to adopt DEC's view of the way a network should be structured rather than providing an empirically (as distinct from a theoretically) open architecture. IBM, too, was providing similar services originally through the use of its Token Ring Network and PC Network, and more recently to 802.3/Ethernet, attachable to newly announced controllers and computers.

There are many different kinds of LANs having different implications for interoperability and the micro–to–mainframe connection. LANs are of particular importance because it is to a LAN that many workstations will be connected as the first stage in a distributed networking and computing environment. It is frequently the case that a micro-based LAN is seen as a means for enhancing the productivity of a department or work-group. Especially in large organizations, however, LANs can rarely exist independently of larger networks. A small organization or business rarely has this particular problem and can structure a LAN to handle most, if not all, its networking needs. When a LAN is itself a node of a large distributed processing network it becomes clear that part of increased productivity is (or should be) the ability to transfer data from one place or user to another without having to spend the time and money necessary to re-enter those data.

Many different computing facilities have been introduced into the organizational milieu: microcomputers, terminals, intelligent copiers, large computers, small computers. Yet an empty computer is like an empty mind—of little or no use to anyone, including its owner. If each computer facility must be filled anew, and by hand, then work is made less, not more efficient. In the developing information age it is important that the technology assist people to reduce the amount of information to manageable levels and to improve the quality of that information. In an organizational context networks provide the means for allowing the computing power available to be used to its most complete extent.

LANS AS THE USER-INTERFACE IN A DISTRIBUTED NETWORK

We discussed in Chapter 1 some of the motives end-users have in requesting (demanding?) micro-based LANs. During the mid-1980s we frequently observed the not very cost-effective situation of an employee having more than one terminal-like device on his or her desk: a microcomputer and a standard terminal. The micro may be connected to a departmental LAN, while the terminal may be connected to a large corporate network. This was, of course, a short-term interim solution in many organizations and should probably not occur in any situation. Perhaps even more common is to have both a LAN board in the micro as well as a terminal emulation board providing IBM 3x78 emulation. The LAN board is connected to the departmental LAN and the 3178/3x78 board to a 3x74 cluster controller. This is still not a cost-effective solution.

The appropriate solution is to have only the connection to the LAN with the LAN gatewayed to the larger network and providing the appropriate terminal emulation. Certainly this situation is becoming more common and is the way of future developments. The primary problem with this approach is that response time on the corporate network may be longer when running over a LAN gateway as with an emulation board. One typical method for providing 3178/3x78 emulation over a LAN is to equip a communications server on the LAN with a device that allows it to emulate a 3174/3274 cluster controller. Software is also provided to the workstation so that it can act as a simple terminal when in a session with the communications server. In that mode the PC is often emulating a standard asynchronous terminal—usually a DEC VT100. What this often means to the user is that response time is sluggish or that it appears to be sluggish because of the methods for screen handling. Moreover, many of the products did not have appropriate file transfer capabilities and could not be used with many standard micro–to–mainframe software packages that provide expanded use of the mainframe by micros. There were also differences in approach between general purpose LANs and micro-based LANs.

General Purpose LANs

General purpose LANs are those that are designed to provide high levels of connectivity among diverse hardware. Examples are the asynchronous, RS-232-C based networks like System 2000 from Sytek, Inc., and Net/One from Ungermann-Bass. The advantage of such systems is that any device can communicate with any other device on the network without going through some central processor or communications controller. The disadvantage is that those systems provide only a connective transport system lacking the user services implied by Layer 7 (Application) of the OSI model. Organizations that buy such systems typically must provide their own server mechanisms for anything but the most rudimentary services. Reliance is placed on the end-user to make appropriate connections, much like the use of the telephone. Both the networks mentioned are primarily broadband systems and their power lies in their ability to provide a common communications medium among a large numbers (several thousand connections) of diverse equipment.

Today it is possible to use a wide variety of topologies, cable plants, and transmission techniques with large-scale LANs. Note the comparisons in Table 4.1. General purpose LANs can and are being used to replace older star networks based on a variety of point-to-point links. The disorder inherent in the management of star networks can be restored through the use of a LAN for general purpose data communications. Moreover, it can often allow the interconnection of a wide variety of devices in a multivendor computing environment not previously possible. Particularly in a distributed computing environment a LAN can often be of far more help than any other form of networking because it can serve as the backbone for an orderly hierarchy of computing functions from micro to mainframe.

Table 4.1 Comparison of Transmission Media

	Twisted Pair Wire	Baseband Coax	Broadband Coax	Fiber Optic Cable
Topologies	Ring, star, bus, tree	Bus, tree, ring	Bus, tree	Ring, star, tree
Max Nodes[a]	<=1,024	<=1,024	<=25,000	<=1,024
Max Length[b]	<=3 km	<=10 km	<=50 km	<=10 km
Bandwidth[c]	<=10 Mb/s[e]	<=10 Mb/s	<=400 MHz	>50 Mb/s
Signal:				
Channels[b]	1	1	54	1
Direction	Uni	Bi	Uni	Bi/Uni
Duplex[d]	Half/Full	Half	Half/Full	Half/Full
Type	Analog or Digital	Digital	RF Analog	?
Application	Data Voice	Data	Data Voice Video	Data Voice Video
Noise Immunity	Low	Medium	High	Highest

[a] These estimates are approximate and some manufacturers claim a larger number of nodes with a given medium.

[b] Again, these estimates are approximate and may be exceeded with some systems, or be significantly lower for others.

[c] With the current state of technology, about the best use of broadband is .83 Mb/s per 1 MHz, although the theoretical maximum is much greater. The maximum aggregate bandwidth in Mb/s is, therefore, about 333 Mb/s.

[d] With broadband two channels must be used to achieve full duplex.

[e] 10 Mb/s on twisted pair tends to be retricted to relatively short distances.

Micro-based LANs

In contrast to general purpose LANs are microcomputer-based LANs, often called departmental LANs. The primary competitors of micro-based LANs are small multiuser computer systems such as AT&T's 3Bx series and other similar machines. Such LANs, and there are a large number on the market, use all conceivable LAN technologies, and IBM has or is planning on producing micro-based LANs using the most available technologies (broadband, baseband, CSMA/CD, token ring, token bus, etc.). These LANs support a smaller number of workstations than is true of the general purpose systems, but they provide a far larger number of services for the end-user. A micro-based LAN revolves around a file server that provides a central repository of programs, data, and services such as electronic mail. The advantage of such a system over a small multiuser system is that processing is distributed out to the workstations although it provides access to more centrally managed data. Within the network connectivity is often limited, although this can be remedied with gateways and bridges.

GATEWAYS, BRIDGES, AND ROUTERS

The terms *gateway* and *bridge* are not used with great precision in discussions of networks and once were used interchangeably. More recently, however, *gateway* has come to designate the hardware and software necessary to make two technologically different networks communicate with one another. *Bridge* is often used to connote the hardware and software necessary for two networks using the same or similar technology to communicate. Please note, however, that the use of different media (baseband coax, broadband coax, twisted pair, fiber optic, etc.) may not be sufficient to cause the network architecture to be altered. Ethernet, for example, can operate over several different media, on both baseband and broadband systems. Consequently, the device used to move from one Ethernet to another is usually called a bridge. Moving from Ethernet, however, to an SNA wide area network requires a gateway. Gateways and bridges are necessary because in many organizational situations it is not yet possible to design and implement a single, general purpose network, yet it is often necessary to provide workstation–to–workstation communications, ideally without having to go through a central computer system. Into this diverse networking environment gateways and bridges have made their debut.

A brief example will suffice to illustrate the problem. Suppose an organization develops several departmental micro-based local area networks using some standard such as Ethernet, token ring, broadband, or a combination of these technologies. Some standardization can be brought about by using common networking software, such as that from Novell or some other company. That same organization may also have a general purpose LAN, or some other asynchronous RS-232-C network as well as an IBM SNA synchronous system. If the user of a local workstation must also communicate with the central mainframe computer, or multiple computers, on the more general asynchronos and synchronous networks, the problem then becomes one of providing asynchronous and SNA gateways between the departmental LANs and the wider systems. In a similar vein, suppose that an organization has a broadband "backbone" network, but must let two or more departmental LANs communicate with one another. If the departmental LANs use Ethernet (baseband) technology, for example, it is then necessary to provide Ethernet-to-broadband-to-Ethernet gateways. On the other hand, bridge technology might be used if the departmental LANs were both broadband based.

Access to Other Networks

Part of the issue in the micro–to–mainframe connection is the interface between two or more networks. At this writing that usually means between two LANs or between a LAN and a Wide Area Network. In the future it is likely to include the ability to connect to a Metropolitan Area Network as well. When moving data between or among networks there will almost always be the need for either a bridge or a gateway and either device can considerably increase the cost of the connection. Alternatively, when moving between selected LANs, bridging may be both simple and inexpensive.

Moving from One LAN to Another

The network operating system or other networking software can make moving from one PC LAN to another either simple or complicated. Novell has solved the problem—at least from a user's perspective—with the least pain. If we have two (or more) Novell networks, using different technologies [PC Network (broadband), Token Ring, and Ethernet, for example], each of those networks can share a single file server with the simple expedient of placing an appropriate adapter card of each LAN in the server. The three networks can then use a common addressing sequence and it will appear to the user that all users are on the same network. If the broadband PC Network is configured to run over a campus CATV system, then it can be the link for a large number of departmental networks across the campus. Since a Novell system will support multiple file servers, a rather large and complex micro-based LAN can be structured. If a gateway to a corporate network exists on one of the LANs, then all can potentially share the same gateway, although that may not always be desirable. Figure 4.1 illustrates how this arrangement might work. In this scheme of things, the file server doubles as a bridge or gateway.

Moving from a LAN to a WAN

Up to a point a network of LANs might be sufficient for many organizations. If the organization is large enough, however, to require servicing several thou-

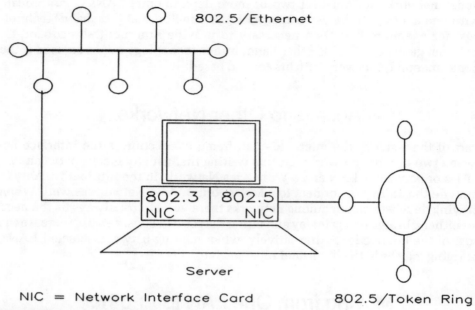

NIC = Network Interface Card

Figure 4.1 Interconnected LANs
NOTE: NIC denotes Network Interface Card.

sand potential users, LAN technology will not currently do the job. While relatively large LANs can be structured by connecting a number of departmental LANs, the upper limit for the number of concurrent users will likely be in the 1,000 to 1,500 range. The practical limit, considering response time and throughput, may be considerably less. With several thousand users, therefore, other networking technologies will also have to be used, and these are most likely to be, in the United States, IBM's SNA (or possibly BSC) or DEC's DECnet. Gateways and bridges will, therefore, be required to make this interconnection happen.

Several companies have bridges and gateways available that can tie Ethernets (802.3) into both VAXs and IBM mainframes and provide appropriate terminal emulation on both. Among the more complete examples of such hybrid networks and the equipment necessary for them are networking systems from DEC, Bridge Communications, and Ungermann-Bass. With the approach promoted by Bridge Communications, for example, it is possible to have a network integrated by Ethernet, but which ties into both DECnet and IBM SNA networks. If a user has only a DEC terminal he or she can access a VAX or access an IBM mainframe with 3270 emulation. A 3x78 user on an SNA network can also tie into either system and when connected to the VAX will be able to have the 3x78 emulate a DEC VT100. An illustrative network is depicted in Figure 4.2.

MAC Level Bridges: 802.1—Internetworking

Almost everyone that deals professionally with networks assumes that people working on LANs will have the need, sooner or later, to communicate with end systems on other networks (LANs, WANs, MANs, etc.). The authors of the IEEE Draft Standard 802.1 (Draft E, July 1, 1987, unapproved) have also made that assumption. An important component of 802.1 will, therefore, be the discussion of internetworking for 802 LANs. To provide full connectivity, therefore, it is important that the methodology of connecting a LAN to another network be explored. The effort is being made to provide standards for the connection of LANs to WANs, such as an X.25 packet-switched network or to other LANs.

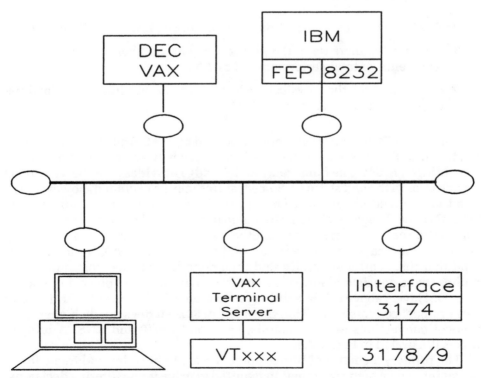

Figure 4.2   LAN as a Network Crossover Strategy

The methods of interconnection are designed to be largely independent of the type of LAN being considered.

Two general categories of internetworking methodologies have been described: an approach based on media access control bridges,[1] and one resident in the OSI Network Layer. In this section we will deal with MAC bridges. A MAC bridge is a device that processes protocols in the MAC sublayer and is transparent to LLC and higher layer protocols. MAC sublayer information controls any forwarding decisions. An interworking unit (IWU) is a device that processes OSI Network Layer protocols operating directly above the LLC sublayer. In this scheme forwarding decisions are based on Network Layer addresses. IEEE 802 Local Area Networks of all kinds, in particular, may be connected together with MAC bridges.

As will be seen in subsequent chapters, each individual LAN has its own independent MAC. The Bridged Local Area Network allows the interconnection of stations attached to separate LANs as if they were attached to a single LAN. Because of MAC, Bridge operates below the MAC service boundary and is transparent to protocols operating above that boundary. A Bridged Local Area Network may provide for:

▼ The interconnection of stations attached to 802 LANs of different types;

▼ An effective increase in the physical extent, number of permissible attachments, or total performance of a LAN;

▼ Partitioning of the physical LAN support for administrative, maintenance, or security reasons.

Separate IEEE 802 LANs are interconnected by MAC Bridges in the manner illustrated in Figure 4.3 by providing frame relay between the separate MACs of the bridged LANs. The frame relay in the Bridge provides MAC Service to the Service User in the end stations. Some features may be excluded, however, due to individual medium access technologies. Given a Bridge that connects two 802 LANs, the Bridge receives a data frame from one and reformats the frame to conform to the requirements of the other. Thus, an end-user on a token ring could communicate directly with an end-user on a CSMA/CD bus. Bear in mind that this is all more easily said than done since actual communication implies that a consistent network operating environment is present operating in the OSI layers above the data link layer. In other words, the MAC Bridge only does protocol conversions within the scope of 802—it does not do higher layer protocol conversions as, for example, between TCP/IP and XNS. A bridged LAN is illustrated in Figure 4.4.

The primary elements of Bridge operation are frame relay and frame filtering, maintenance of the information required to make frame filtering decisions, and management of the frame filtering and associated information. The Bridge

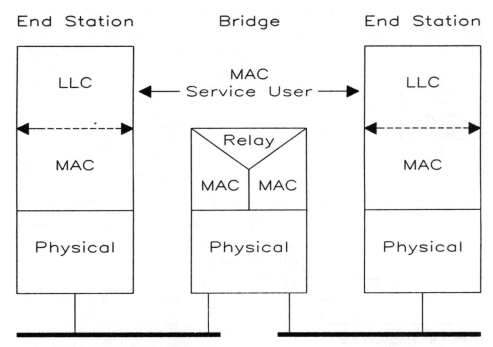

Figure 4.3 MAC Level Bridging
SOURCE: Based on IEEE P802.1, Part D, Revision C, August 1987,*MAC Bridges,* unapproved draft published for comment only, reprinted here by permission of the IEEE. All rights reserved by The Institute of Electrical and Electronics Engineers, Inc., p. 16.

relays individual MAC frames between the separate MACs of the bridged LANs connected to the ports of the Bridge. The order of the frames received on one port and transmitted on another is preserved. The filtering function operates to prevent duplication of frames and to suppress unnecessary LAN traffic. The Bridge must have sufficient intelligence to use and maintain explicit configuration of static filtering information, automatic learning of dynamic filtering information through the observation of traffic, aging out of filtering information that has been automatically learned, and calculation and configuration of the Bridged Local Area Network topology.

Interoperability with OSI

In Chapter 2 we saw that the interconnection of OSI standard networks generally takes place through the Network Layer by use of a relay system. Figure 4.5 (in Chapter 2, Figure 2.5) is reproduced here for the sake of clarity. A message

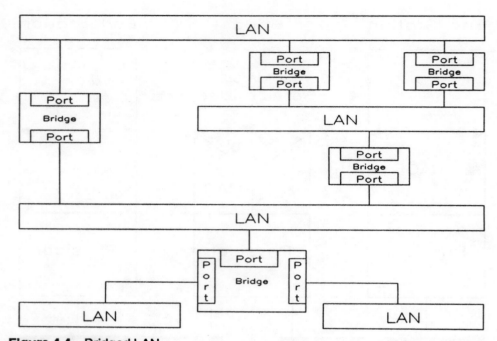

Figure 4.4   Bridged LAN
SOURCE: Based on IEEE P802.1, Part D, Revision C, August 1987, *MAC Bridges,* unapproved draft published for comment only, reprinted here by permission of the IEEE. All rights reserved by The Institute of Electrical and Electronics Engineers, Inc., p. 28.

moves from one Open System network to another Open System network through peer Network Layers. Consequently, in a manner similar to MAC bridges, it is the logic rather than the hardware of the network that is being interconnected. The term used in many of the standards documents is "relay system" since the relay may operate as a bridge, gateway, or router, depending on the situation. The point is, however, that while a MAC level bridge requires the networks being linked to be 802 standard LANs, an OSI relay system can interconnect LANs/MANs/WANs in any combination. Consequently the concept is broader than that of the MAC Level Bridge.

Internetworking with TCP/IP

It may be worthwhile to follow the flow of a typical communication through the Internet.[2] If you have not yet read Chapter 3, it will be helpful to at least review the section on TCP/IP for this section to make sense (also note Figure 4.6). First, there are several levels of addressing required:

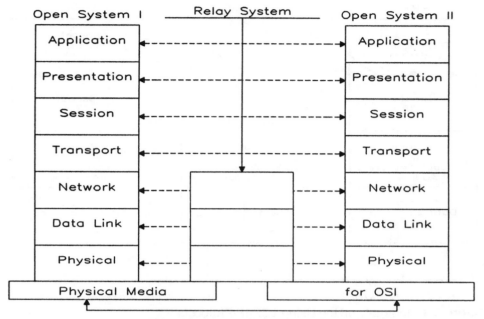

Figure 4.5   Communication Involving Relay Open Systems
SOURCE: International Telegraph and Telephone Consultative Committee (CCITT), Rec-
ommendation X.200, Reference Model of Open Systems Interconnection for
CCITT Applications, Fascicle VIII.5–Rec. X.200 (1984), p. 27.

▼ Application port addresses;

▼ A global network address (managed by IP); and

▼ Local network addresses.

If Network 1 is an IEEE 802.3 network, for example, the "local" network address
is the standard 802.3 address. If Network 2 is an X.25 network, then the "local"
network address is an X.25 address. Gateway X is attached to each network
through specific Network Access Protocols (NAPs) specific to the networks
being joined together. With a standard TCP/IP gateway, the gateway would also
include IP so that messages can be routed to the appropriate global address. We
should note at this point that if the two networks were IEEE 802 standard networks, then it would be possible to use an 802.1 MAC Level Bridge rather than a
TCP/IP gateway. For internetworking to take place, IP must be able to route according to the global Internet address specific to each node. The interface between TCP and the user accessing an Internet application is through port addresses on the host node. The combination of port and global network address
uniquely identifies a process within an environment of multiple networks and

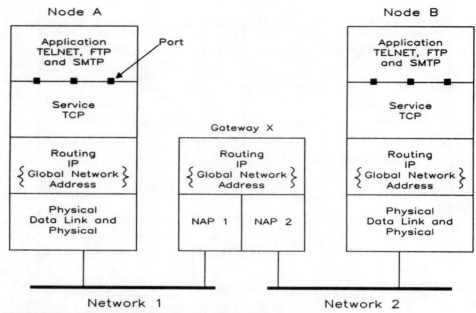

Figure 4.6   Internetworking Using TCP/IP Protocols

multiple hosts. The three-level address—network, host/node, and port—is called a *socket*. The approach to routing or gateways in TCP/IP is, like the OSI model, at a higher level than is true of MAC bridges (Figure 4.6).

TERMINAL EMULATION

When a LAN is connected to a minicomputer or mainframe computer system through gateways or bridges, an important aspect of the service the communications server must offer the PC is terminal emulation. After all, the micro-based workstation, when connected through the LAN to the mainframe, will be functioning essentially as a terminal. In an IBM networking environment this means providing 3x78/79 emulation, while in a DEC network it means using a VT100 protocol. It also means that a complete system will offer some means for file transfer from the mainframe to the micro. Both the terminal emulation and file transfer can be made rather straightforward if the user organization conforms to either IBM or DEC (or some other consistent) standards. Some difficulties can ensue when it is either necessary or desirable to mix approaches to the micro–to–mainframe connection. DEC has provided for attachment of its Ethernets to the IBM world by making an Ethernet attached SNA gateway. With the introduction by IBM of the 9370 Minicomputer and the 8232 channel attached LAN controller with both Ethernet and Token Ring communications,

IBM now, at least, has a small computer that could be made to operate as a gateway to DEC Ethernets. Other approaches are also possible.

Bridge Communications and Ungermann-Bass are both marketing LAN systems (802.3 CSMA/CD) that allow interconnection of IBM, DEC, and other computer products into an integrated network, providing for both 3270 and VT100 emulations. Bridge Communications handles this problem from an Ethernet backbone using standard DEC Ethernet interfaces on VAXs. On the IBM side, Bridge offers an Ethernet controller that attaches to the serial ports of an IBM mainframe's front-end procession (FEP) on the host side. On the user's end an Ethernet controller is provided that will attach a 3274 cluster controller to the Ethernet backbone, thus allowing 3x78/79 terminal users to have access to the IBM host over the Ethernet. The really interesting thing about this scheme is that if the 3x78/79 user must access a VAX on the network, the various Bridge devices provide VT100 emulation to the 3270 terminals, while if a normal DEC user, with a VT100 compatible terminal or PC needs to access the IBM host, Bridge will provide 3270 emulation to that device. Thus all users can have access to all host systems, obtaining the appropriate terminal emulation. This approach is achieved by terminal protocol conversions to the VT100 (ANSI) standard and back again.

IBM NETWORKING STRATEGIES

Notwithstanding the phenomenal success of the IBM PC family of microcomputers, IBM remains primarily a mainframe computer manufacturer. The key to IBM's strategies for micros does not lie in the PC product line *per se*. Rather, IBM's strategic goals are centered in its System Network Architecture. SNA is not a communications protocol. It is an information processing architecture that includes the communications vehicle and the application support for providing data processing services. SNA has evolved from a terminal-oriented architecture of the mid-1970s to a multicomputer distributed processing network. The advent of the PC provided IBM with part of the means to make distributed processing, down to the end-user, a reality. Through Advanced Program-to-Program Communications (APPC or LU 6.2) IBM and others will develop PC software that integrates the PC into the mainframe world.

IBM LANs

LANs are clearly recognized in the IBM scheme of things through the introduction of the PC Network (broadband CSMA/CD) and the Token Ring Network (802.5 compatible). Although many commentators have prophesied the demise of the PC Network because of the clear emphasis of IBM on the Token Ring, the fact that some users will wish to use broadband, and the introduction of software products from IBM that allow intercommunication of the PC Network and the Token Ring, the survival of the PC Network has been assured into at least the near future. Furthermore, both systems make use of NETBIOS, thus assuring long-term compatibility. IBM's LANs will be important to IBM in its overall office automation strategy, but within an SNA framework. Existing minicomputer products such as the System/36 (and perhaps the System/38) will be integrated as well. The clearest effort in this area, however, was the introduction of the 9370, a small multiuser minicomputer competitive with DEC's MicroVAX capable of direct attachment to either the Token Ring or to Ethernet.[3] Notwithstanding the obvious strategic importance of LANs in IBM's scheme of things, they are still concerned with mainframes and have produced products to enhance the micro–to–mainframe link. An example is the Enhanced Connectivity Facilities products.

Enhanced Connectivity Facilities (ECF)

The ECF constitute a set of related mainframe and micro software products designed primarily to provide a PC/MS DOS interface to IBM mainframe data when the PC is connected to IBM's Time Sharing Option (TSO) under MVS or when connected to VM/CMS. Access to ECF services is through either a 3270 communications adapter in the PC that allows emulation of a 3x78 display station, or an IBM LAN operating through a gateway in an SNA environment. One of the IBM 3270-Personal Computers (AT or XT) can also be used. In the PC or PS/2 one or more of the following adapter cards is required:

▼ SDLC Communications Adapter for host connected standalone or gateway.

▼ IBM Personal Computer 3x78/79 Emulation adapter for host connected standalone or gateway.

▼ IBM Token Ring Adapter for network station and gateway.

▼ IBM Personal Computer Network Adapter for network station and gateway.

On the host end the IBM mainframe must run either MVS/XA with TSO/E with the MVS/XA feature or VM/SP. Additional required TSO enhancements include ACF/VTAM and the Interactive System Productivity Facility (ISPF). In addition, if data are to be extracted from DATABASE 2, and/or DL/I databases, then these must be present along with the DXT facility for ECF. For those not familiar with IBM MVS systems, suffice it to say that this would be a fully loaded system which many mainframe environments do not support. It is also a very expensive environment in terms of both CPU cycles and cost. If the host environment is VM, then VM/SP Release 4 must be running along with ACF/VTAM and ISPF for CMS. For DXT, SQL/DS must also be available. The PC software is distributed with ECF and is downloaded from the host. As a consequence, the IBM 3270-PC File Transfer Program for MVS or VM (depending on the operating environment) is also required.

The ECF system consists of software for both the host and the PC called the ECF Servers (host) and Requesters (PC) programs. The functions of the ECF Servers/Requesters programs include host database access, DXT, virtual disks, virtual files, and virtual print capabilities. Each of these will be described.

Host Database Access.   This describes data access from DATABASE 2 and SQL/DS through dynamic or predefined requests. The user is prompted through a full-screen display in developing an SQL language query. The query results can be stored in host files, transferred to a microcomputer, or copied directly to a virtual disk. Host results of the inquiries are sequential files containing the extracted host data. All the functions of file transfer are available to the user at query time.

DXT.   This section describes data extraction from mainframe databases using DXT as the host interface. The IBM PC Requesters program provides an interface for a user to list and select one of these requests for batch execution. Users may extract data using DXT jobs from DL/I and Fast Path databases, from VSAM and SAM files, and from DATABASE 2 and SQL/DS databases. The results of the DXT extraction jobs are sequential files stored at the host in DXT Integration Exchange Format (IXF) in machine form. Users can directly use these results as virtual files or copy them to the personal computer.

Virtual Disk.   As with other products for use with IBM or DEC host computers, the ECF, IBM virtual disk allows the user to use host system disk space as if it were an IBM personal computer fixed disk. File access on the PC is through a DOS device driver interface. The data are stored on the host in MS/PC DOS format without translations. This obviously gives the user access to a very large amount of disk space. The virtual disk will work with most DOS commands such as COPY.

Virtual File.   While Virtual Disk allows the host to be used as if it was part of the PC, Virtual File allows a view of host files from a MS/PC DOS environment. The Virtual File facility takes care of the EBCDIC to ASCII translation when a host file is being used by a microcomputer application program. The data reside on the host but this allows concurrent access to the same data by both micro and host applications. The primary use of the Virtual File, is therefore, to allow the sharing of host data between mainframe applications and the

PC. CMS files are supported in the VM environment and sequential datasets (including partitioned datasets) in the MVS environment. Most DOS utilities will work with such files, including the DOS COPY command.

Virtual Print.   This feature allows the PC to use host printers as if they were PC attached printers. It provides emulation for the various IBM PC printers, doing protocol conversion to IBM 1403 (high speed impact printer) or 3800 (very-high-speed laser printer) data streams. Thus a PC application program, such as a word processor, could be installed to drive something like an IBM Graphics Printer but actually output to a 3800 laser printer on the host machine.

We have noted other software of this general sort, but IBM's is without doubt the most expensive. Consequently, it may not be available at your computing center. In mid 1987 there was a one-time charge of $10,200 to $40,800, depending on the number of users, plus a monthly charge of $850 for the CMS Server or $1,350 for the TSO/E servers. This is clearly an expensive option.

IBM's Impact on Microcomputer LANs

A recurrent theme of this book is the impact of IBM on the entire computer and communications industry. The ubiquitous presence of IBM is not necessarily good for the industry, but it is certainly a fact of life. In the early 1980s IBM made some noise about future developments of local area networks and suggested that they would ultimately introduce four (depending on how one counts LANs). The four were a broadband system, a token ring, a token bus, and LAN services operating in the context of a new 3274 terminal controller. In 1984 IBM introduced its first LAN product, the broadband PC Network manufactured for them by Sytek, Inc., of Mountain View, California. A year or so later, in 1985, the IBM Token Ring Network, using technology developed by Texas Instruments, was announced. The 3174 cluster controller (the replacement of the 3274) can also attach to a Token Ring LAN and IBM now supports the Manufacturing Automation Protocol (MAP, see Chapter 5) using 802.4 (Token Bus). It should be noted that during this period IBM also acquired Rolm, a manufacturer of PBXs and other telephone system equipment. Clearly IBM is attempting to preempt the market.

As with the LAN hardware business, there is considerable competition with LAN software. It is not at all clear that IBM's network software will or can become the standard. Clearly the LAN software distributed for the PC Network will function best in a very small, homogeneous office environment. If essentially the same software is provided for the token ring, the same limitations will exist. In many respects other networking software that will run on the same hardware—Novell's NetWare, for example—has a better, more functional architecture. It has the added advantage that it will run on many kinds of non-IBM hardware as well on those devices with IBM's imprimatur.[4]

DEC NETWORKING STRATEGIES

DEC, like IBM, has developed its own networking architecture called the Digital Network Architecture. LANs within a DEC environment are ultimately a part of DNA. The LAN technology DEC adopted was Ethernet and has been one of the long-term—along with Xerox—supporters of CSMA/CD. Unlike IBM, however, DEC has made Ethernet into an intrinsic part of its configuration of high-performance super-minis and new VAX mainframe-powered VAX systems. If an organization today buys a VAX, it is almost impossible to configure the installation without, at least, a small Ethernet. Convenient terminal access is through an Ethernet attached terminal server, for example. If DEC users must communicate with an IBM mainframe, they must use an SNA gateway which is also Ethernet attached. This approach is depicted in Figure 4.7.

An important deviation from past DEC policies is extensive support for interconnection to IBM networks and facilities. When DEC first announced its original microcomputer, the DEC Rainbow, it was not IBM PC compatible. It was also badly marketed and late in coming to the market. Consequently, the

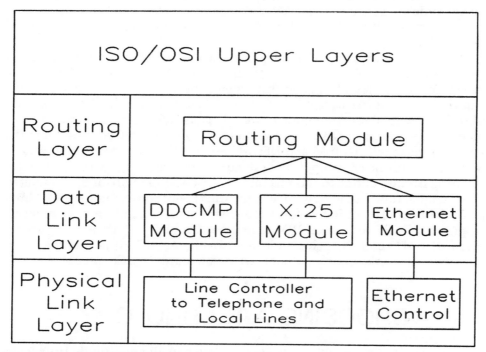

Figure 4.7   DEC's DNA Strategy

Rainbow never sold well. The result of that reversal was that as DEC's networking strategy matured, there has been a migration toward support of the IBM PC family and, in 1986 an announcement was made to produce an IBM compatible PC, though more for system network conformity than as an effort to compete with IBM PCs. At the same time DEC was producing a gateway to SNA and providing support of IBM's DISOSS (a mainframe office automation product) through DEC's own office automation software, All-in-One. At the same time DEC is intent on providing integration through DNA.

OTHER LAN STRATEGIES

There are other vendors that have integrated LAN strategies. We have already mentioned Bridge Communications and Ungermann-Bass. We would be remiss not to mention much larger manufacturers such as AT&T and Wang. Through the mid-1980s AT&T thrashed around for an approach that would provide them with a competitive edge over IBM. At this writing they had not clearly found that system. Essentially AT&T's LAN networking strategy revolves around StarLAN. StarLAN is a twisted-pair based, one and ten megabits, 802.3 conforming CSMA/CD LAN. AT&T's earlier efforts to promote its Integrated Services Network (ISN) far outstripped its ability to provide integrated networking.

Wang has tended to do its integration within an IBM networking framework, although Wang has been a long-time supporter of broadband as a standard transport system. It is clear that Wang's approach can handle both Wang and IBM products in a compatible fashion. It is not as clear that Wang can handle other vendors' products equally well. Because of their roles in the marketplace, the two vendors with which compatibility is likely to be required in the next few years will be IBM and DEC—these are clearly the major players in large-scale multiuser computing systems. In the corporate world, notwithstanding Apple's efforts to sell Macintoshs for desktop publishing and related office automation products, without providing major software support for integration into the mainframe–to–micro distributed computing environment, Apple will likely remain on IBM's sidelines. Apple's impact is being recognized by LAN vendors such as Banyan, Novell, and 3COM in that they now support MAC workstations in their LAN architectures (see Chapter 5).

CHOOSING A TECHNOLOGY

In most organizational environments the choice of an appropriate LAN technology is not a value-free technical decision. The first question should always be: "What problems do I wish to solve with the LAN?" An answer to this should be as comprehensive as possible or no solution will be especially cost-effective. In particular, "I" may not know what all the problems are. Part of the problem identification must, of course, deal with the geographical attributes of the system.

If we need only to provide a LAN for a single office on a single floor, then almost any technology will work, although some will afford better services than others. If, however, we have to contend with a multibuilding campus environment, then few of the baseband systems will suffice. Even in a single, large building, when the actual lengths of cable trays and wiring paths are calculated, it may be found that baseband distances are inadequate, and conduit systems never even approximate the path of a bird between buildings.

A second major issue that must be faced concerns the devices to be attached to the LAN. Is there control over the acquisition of those devices or is an attempt being made to provide connectivity to a random selection of digital devices? Third, are mainframe computers as well as micros and terminals to be connected to the LAN? Fourth, at what speed do we need to communicate? Fifth, are server mechanisms, such as those for file sharing, associated with systems such as Ethernet, required? These, and related issues, form the basis for the decision on the appropriate LAN. Finally, of course, the issue of cost must be confronted, although it is extremely difficult to get more than a very general picture of the true cost of any large system.

The requirement for auxiliary services, such as voice or video, may also influence the decision. If high-quality, large-volume, fast-scan video is required, then either a PBX or a baseband system is appropriate. The only alternative is broadband. If it is necessary to link the data system with a fully connective, telephone-type voice communications system, then only a PBX may suffice.

Finally, management in a large organization is most easily sold on a LAN if the individuals involved can be convinced that a new and esoteric technology is not being foisted on them. None of the widely selling LAN systems use esoteric technologies. It is particularly vexing when explaining the use of CATV for people to see CATV as an esoteric system. CATV technology is a mature technology, even though it is rapidly developing. Many people are still not acquainted with two-way cable, and the fact that CATV is most frequently used by the entertainment industry implies that it might be frivolous.

When the questions posed here have been answered, it will be possible to at least stipulate the broad outlines of the system. Should it be broadband, baseband, or PBX? And we should not overlook the possibility of using some baseband systems connected together with a broadband or PBX system, assuming the appropriate gateways are available.

REFERENCES

1. *IEEE Project 802 Local and Metropolitan Area Network Standards, Draft IEEE Standard 802.1, Overview, Interworking, and Network Management,* "MAC Bridges, Revision C," August 1987, unapproved draft published for comment only (New York: The Institute of Electrical and Electronics Engineers, Inc., 1988).

2. This example is based on William Stallings et al., *Handbook of Computer-Communications Standards,* Vol. 3, "Department of Defense (DOD) Protocol Standards" (New York: Macmillan Publishing Company, 1988), pp. 6–9. Some of the detail on TCP/IP is also based on Stallings et al. in this source.

3. For further information on SNA and its importance, see Thomas W. Madron, *Micro-Mainframe Connection* (Indianapolis, IN: Howard W. Sams, 1987).

4. Thomas W. Madron, "IBM's Token Ring Network," *ComputerWorld,* 1985.

CHAPTER 5

LANs: NETWORK OPERATING SYSTEMS

A Network Operating System (NOS) is the software necessary to integrate the many components of a network into a single system to which an end-user may have access. A NOS manages the services necessary to ensure that the end-user has error-free access to network resources. Additionally, a NOS will normally provide a user interface that is supposed to reduce the trials and tribulations of the using the network. Within the context of the NOS, applications, such as an electronic mail system, can be written which allow virtual circuits (sometimes called "virtual connections") among network entities to be established without direct human intervention.

Under the best of circumstances the end-user should not even know that a network exists. If he or she wishes to do something simple, like copy a file from one place to another, it should be possible to use something like the MS/DOS copy command and simply type: COPY c:mydata.dat p:yourdata.dat. If this was a copy command on a local PC it says, copy a file called "mydata.dat" on my local drive c: to a file called "yourdata.dat" on your remote drive p:. In a well organized network it should not be necessary for drive p: to be local—it should be capable of being defined anywhere on the network. "Anywhere" means just that—on a file server, another micro, a mini, or a mainframe—any intelligent device connected to the network.

If drive p: is on another workstation or server on a LAN, then transfer of a file should be reasonably rapid. If, however, drive p: is defined as being a node on a WAN, a MAN, or a remote LAN, then additional routing steps would be necessary and it would take a little longer. The point is that it should be automatic and governed by the NOS. The alternative is something like using the telephone system. If we want to transfer a file between two computers linked by dial-up modems it is first necessary to access the remote system by dialing its address (telephone number), connecting with it, logging on to it, and then manually initiating some sort of file transfer protocol to do the transfer. This implies that the basic function of any NOS is to manage network addressing—provide the end-user the fundamental capacity to establish a communications link from one node to another.

In Chapters 7, 8, and 9 we will consider the LAN mechanisms necessary to put data out on a physical link. In those chapters we will deal specifically with the IEEE 802.3 (CSMA/CD [Ethernet]), 802.4 (token bus), and 802.5 (token ring) standards which exist at the Physical and Data Line layers of the OSI model. Those standards, and any associated hardware and software that have been produced, only provide the basic capabilities for LANs, however. By themselves, those standards would be much like a telephone system without either a telephone book or an instrument with which to dial a number.

In this chapter we will discuss five network operating systems which provide many of the services necessary for satisfactory use by end-users. The NOSs we will review are the Manufacturing Automation Protocol, IBM's LAN software, Banyan's VINES, Novell's NetWare, and 3COM's 3+ Open. We begin by looking at MAP since it is a non-proprietary system explicitly designed using OSI protocols throughout the full seven-layer OSI model. MAP gives us an opportunity to understand how the OSI model can be applied. It also provides us with a completely standard system by which to measure and understand the others. Following the discussion of MAP we will turn briefly to IBM's NOS primarily because IBM also has a major impact on the strategies of the other providers of NOSs.

Before proceding further a brief comment on the use of the terms *proprietary* and *open system* is in order. *Proprietary* is often applied to software when it is not only owned by a single company, but also when the internal workings of the software are unpublished. In this book *open system* has most frequently been used in conjunction with OSI or other national or international standards because systems based on those standards *must* conform to certain known and publicly understood criteria. In the LAN marketplace success seems to dictate a certain openness by vendors. In the cases of both IBM and Novell, for example, they have often gone out of their way to "open" their systems so that third-party vendors could produce software in conformance to their networks. Consequently, in this chapter, the use of the term *proprietary* does not mean "closed." It simply means single ownership. Effectively, are the copyrights and patents (if any) publicly owned or are they privately owned? To the extent that the term *open system* is used in this chapter, I will continue to employ it in the context of national and international standards. Let it be noted, therefore, that the four vendors discussed in this chapter have, by and large, made any proprietary protocols publicly available and they are, in this sense, "open."

Banyan, Novell, and 3COM are discussed because they are among the most comprehensive NOSs available and because Novell, in particular, is the dominant NOS in the marketplace. Because of IBM's role in the market it will become apparent that other manufacturers, such as Banyan, Novell, and 3COM, must accommodate themselves to IBM's approach to networking, whatever its merits. While it is difficult to assess precise market share, a number of market research firms have attempted to do so. During early 1989 the estimates for Novell ranged from 35 percent to 70 percent, for IBM from 14 percent to about 16 percent, and for 3COM from about 6 percent to about 10 percent. Most agreed that Banyan had about 3 or 4 percent of the market. Beyond that, different studies reported various listings of vendors. All agreed that Novell was number one, IBM number two, and 3COM number three. The results of two such reports may be seen in Figure 5.1.

One major caveat should be noted when reading the results of such reports. The way in which a question is asked in order to obtain the number of LANs in a particular organization can influence the count and this is becoming more complicated as NOS vendors move into the arena of enterprise-wide networking. The question can be stated in terms of the "number of LANs," or in terms of the "number of servers." Asking for the number of servers will cover both standalone LANs and those which are interconnected in an enterprise-wide network. Asking only for the number of LANs may bias the answer in favor of the stand-alones even when the enterprise-wide system is more complex and represents a larger number of servers. This kind of issue is common to all survey research so this note is simply an admonition to take market reseach results with a "grain of salt."

In Figure 5.1(a) the percentages reported are based on the total number of different LANs (106) listed by 100 companies. The sample may or may not be representative of anything and people could report more than one LAN, hence the fact that there were more LANs than companies.[1] Figure 5.1(b) was based on a survey of 2,500 respondents across the United States in medium and large size companies.[2] They were asked what NOSs they thought their companies would be buying during the next year. The percentages are based on those responses. If the data in Figure 5.1(a) are representative, they represent an estimate of market share. The data in Figure 5.1(b) represent expected buying patterns, again, assuming that the sample was representative of something. At the beginning of 1989 Novell possessed twice the market share of IBM and 3.5 times the market share of 3COM [see Figure 5.1(a)]. Moreover, for those companies planning on buying LAN NOSs in 1989, Novell far outstripped IBM and 3COM together by more than 3.5 times.

It must be stressed that this chapter does not represent a catalog of NOSs available. The five that have been selected for review are important either be-

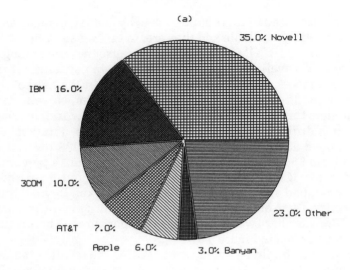

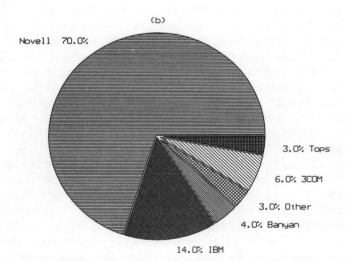

Figure 5.1   (a) LAN Market Share (% of Installed LANs in 1989)
(b) Business Planning to Buy NOSs, 1989 (% of 2,000 Users)

SOURCE: (a) Adapted from Business Research Group as quoted by *ComputerWorld,* February 20, 1989, p. 114. Copyright ©1989 by CW Publishing Inc., Framingham, MA 01701—reprinted from *ComputerWorld* by permission of the publisher.
(b) Computer Intelligence as quoted by *ComputerWorld,* February 13, 1989, p. 59. Copyright ©1989 by CW Publishing Inc., Framingham, MA 01701—reprinted from *ComputerWorld* by permission of the publisher.

cause of the architecture involved (MAP) or their place in the marketplace. Nor does this discussion constitute an endorsement of any of the systems. Before describing each NOS, however, we need to take a brief look at some underlying concepts and products and try to understand where they exist in the scheme of local area networking.

LAN CONCEPTS AND PRODUCTS

Part of the difficulty in discussing LAN operating environments is that a number of different approaches have developed which have the same or similar functions. The use of the OSI Reference Model is one attempt to help bring some conceptual order to an understanding of LANs. Unfortunately that understanding is sometimes more apparent than real in that non-standard products and services are often difficult to equate to the seven-layer OSI model and in any event are not now and probably never will be part of that model. An example is the role and function of NETBIOS, one of IBM's program interfaces to LANs.

The NOS Protocol Stack

Manufacturers of LAN NOS software were, by the end of the 1980s, responding to two major trend setters: IBM and the international standards movement. We should note that IBM was also responding to the standards movement. In Figure 5.2 an attempt has been made to present several of IBM's LAN software configurations, because two important elements of these options, NETBIOS and APPC/PC, have pushed other NOS vendors to respond with similar support and products. In addition to the DOS offerings, IBM's most recent offering (as this was written), the OS/2 LAN Server, is also outlined. NETBIOS is described below and APPC was described in Chapter 3, so suffice it to say at this point that they both occupy about the same position when compared to the OSI model.

The depiction of the IBM offerings in Figure 5.2 illustrates the difficulty in using the OSI framework as a model for a functional understanding of networks. The PC LAN Program, for example, provides selected functions which encompass the range of layers from logical link control (LLC) through the Presentation Layer. Yet not all the functions implied by the OSI Model are implemented by IBM's software. Moreover, it appears that both NETBIOS and APPC occupy somewhat different layer equivalents in the OS/2 and DOS environments. Note that NETBIOS and APPC interface directly to the 802.2 LLC. These issues lead various writers, vendors, and even people within IBM to make var-

OSI	MAP	IBM OS/2	IBM DOS[1]	Banyan[2]	Banyan[2]	Novell	3COM
Application	ACSE, FTAM, MMS, Directory Services	Application / LAN Server Core Services	Application	VINES Appl.	OSI Appl. See MAP	Application	Application
Presentation	ISO 8822/8823	LAN Server Core Services / Requester (SMBs) OS/2	NET-BIOS / APPC	Vines Socket or UNIX System V Transport Layer Interface (TLI)	ISO Presen-tation	Netware APPC NETBIOS TLI Named Pipes	3+Open Named Pipes, APPC/PC NETBIOS
Session	ISO 8326/8327	NET-BIOS / APPC	NET-BIOS / APPC	Vines Socket or UNIX System V Transport Layer Interface (TLI)	ISO Session	Netware APPC NETBIOS TLI Named Pipes	3+Open Named Pipes, APPC/PC NETBIOS
Transport	ISO 8072/8073	NET-BIOS / APPC		ISO 8072/8073		OSI TCP/IP IPX/SPX IBM SNA NETBEUI ATP	OSI TCP/IP XNS NETBEUI ATP
Network	ISO 8348/8473	NETBIOS and APPC Interface Directly to 802.2 LLC		ISO 8473 9542	X.25	OSI TCP/IP IPX/SPX IBM SNA NETBEUI ATP	OSI TCP/IP XNS NETBEUI ATP
Data Link	IEEE 802.2 LLC / IEEE 802.4 MAC	802.2 LLC 802.5 MAC 802.3 MAC PC Network		802.2 802.3 802.5	LAPB	Open Data Link Interface	Varied Data Link Interfaces
Physical	IEEE 802.4 Broadband or Carrierband	802.3, 802.5 Broadband Other		802.3 802.5	X.21	Physical	Physical

Figure 5.2 LAN NOS Protocol Comparisons

NOTES: 1. IBM also provides TCP/IP services under DOS—see Figure 5.7.

2. Banyan also provides TCP/IP services as well as MAC support through AppleTalk—see Figure 5.6.

ied interpretations. Nevertheless, it is still useful in understanding a potpourri of protocol stacks to attempt the OSI comparison.

The approaches to integrated networking by Banyan, Novell, and 3COM are summarized in Figure 5.2, as well. The architectures presented in this chapter were, at the time of writing, still under development so some changes in detail may take place. All three, however, are clearly supporting OSI in one fashion or another and both Novell and 3COM were explicitly supporting (or planning to support) various IBM protocols. A result of the importance placed on TCP/IP protocols by the U.S. Government and by higher education has forced all four vendors to provide Internet support.

Figure 5.2 represents an attempt to illustrate some of the variety possible in configuring a LAN operating environment by comparing MAP, IBM, Banyan, Novell, and 3COM with the OSI Reference Model. Table 5.1 provides an expansion of the acronyms used in Figure 5.2. The information presented in Figure 5.2 is based on materials furnished by the various vendors, but because much of what those vendors are doing is trying to respond to all major trends in the marketplace, it is not always possible to precisely equate their systems with OSI. Moreover, various writers interpret layer equivalences in somewhat different manners. In any event, it is clear that the MAP specification is clear and

Table 5.1   Directory of Acronyms

Acronym	Source	Name or Phase
ACSE	ISO	Association Control Service Element
AFP	Apple	Apple File Protocol
API	...	Application Programmer Interface
APPC	IBM	Advanced Program-to-Program Communication
ATP	Apple	AppleTalk Protocol
CCITT	...	International Telegraph and Telephone Consultative Committee
CMIS	OSI	Common Management Information System
CMIP	OSI	Common Management Information Protocol
DCE	...	Data Circuit-Terminating Equipment
DTE	...	Data Terminal Equipment
FTAM	ISO	File Transfer Access and Management
GOSIP	US Govt.	Government Open Systems Interconnection Profile
IBM	IBM	International Business Machines
IEEE	IEEE	The Institute of Electrical and Electronics Engineers, Inc.
IPX	Novell	Internet Packet Exchange
ISO	...	International Organization for Standardization
LAPB	CCITT/ISO	Link Access Procedures (X.25)
LLC	IEEE/ISO	Logical Link Control
LU x.x	IBM	Logical Unit
MAC	IEEE/ISO	Media Access Control
MAP	G.M.	Manufacturing Automation Protocol
MMS	MAP	Manufacturing Messaging Specification
NCP	Novell	NetWare Core Protocol
NETBEUI	IBM	NETBIOS Extended User Interface
NETBIOS	IBM	NETwork Basic Input Output System
NFS	Sun/Unix	Network File System
OSI	...	Open Systems Interconnection (ISO)
SMB	IBM	Server Message Block
SNA	IBM	System Network Architecture
SPX	Novell	Sequenced Packet Exchange
TCP/IP	U.S. DOD	Transmission Control Protocol/Internet Protocol
TLI	AT&T	UNIX System V Transport Layer
X.21	CCITT/ISO	Interface between DTE and DCE for synchronous operation on public data networks
X.25	CCITT/ISO	Interface between DTE and DCE for terminals operating in packet mode on public data networks
X.400	CCITT/ISO	Message Handling service
X.500	CCITT/ISO	The Directory (OSI Directory Services)
XNS	Xerox	Xerox Network System

uncluttered with respect to OSI, while both Novell and 3COM are attempting to provide a variety of options from at least the Data Link Layer through the Session Layer. Banyan has the clearest commitment to the OSI model of the four private sector vendors. In the first edition of this book I made the point that these vendors should migrate to standard protocols and which they seem to be doing. A somewhat different strategy might be for them to specify a completely OSI compliant system up through the Session Layer, retaining only the Presentation Layer and value-added applications as their primary contributions. The latter appears to be the approach being used by Banyan.

Several additional points should be noted concerning Figure 5.2. In depicting the IBM NOSs, I have shown a kind of "no man's land" for the Network Layer for the OS/2 LAN Server and for the Transport and Network Layers for the PC LAN Support Program. The reason for this is that the IBM NOSs are primarily single-route LANs. Consequently, the routing functions associated with the Network Layer are not necessary and IBM's LAN software does not directly provide those functions in the sense characterized by the OSI Network Layer or by TCP/IP's IP Layer. Some routing is actually necessary in IBM's framework, but it is handled through LAN Manager and Source Routing bridges. The *preferred route* is determined by either of two dynamic route discovery processes: *All*-routes broadcast route determination and *Single*-route broadcast route determination.

Pipes are also explicitly mentioned with respect to 3COM's 3+ Open. While not specifically illustrated, they are also implicit in IBM's OS/2 LAN Server, are supported by Novell's NetWare/286 and NetWare/386, and are similar in function to Banyan's Sockets. In general, *pipes* are software developers' tools for easily creating communications routines in software without having to explicitly control and issue commands to the communications hardware. The *named pipes* noted in the discussions below are Unix-like interprocess communications functions that simplify the programming of distributed applications.[3]

Although it is not clearly illustrated in Figure 5.2, NETBIOS is being used by many independent software developers to interface network applications to the network since it offers an informally standardized applications interface. The consequence of this is that some vendors, such as 3COM, explicitly use and support NETBIOS, while others, like Novell, emulate selected NETBIOS functions. This means that many applications will work equally well on both networks or on others providing NETBIOS support. In the long run it would probably be good for vendors to support one or more of the OSI protocols at the appropriate level for the same purpose. The reason I say this is that the OSI standard protocols are likely to be the ones that will win out in the long run. Part of such a protocol suite would likley include, for example, the IEEE/ANSI 802.2 Logical Link Control which IBM currently provides in partial replacement of NETBIOS. The fact that NETBIOS is not a standard and that it does not seem to fit into the long-term strategy being put into place by IBM would seem to be a reason to qualify its use. On the other hand, it is sometimes argued that NETBIOS has taken on a life of its own in the marketplace and if that proves to be true, it may retain a significant future.

The Physical Layer for several of the NOSs has been left somewhat hazy and they all attempt to support more than one technology. Both Banyan and Novell support at least Ethernet, Token Ring, and ARCnet with occasional support for others. 3COM supports both Ethernet and Token Ring. One recent study indicated that 34 percent of LAN nodes in 1988 were Ethernet, 17 percent ARCnet, 10.5 percent Token Ring, and 38.5 percent a variety of other proprietary systems. These figures can be seen in Figure 5.3. Throughout the 1990s we should anticipate that there will be a growth in Ethernet and Token Ring LANs resulting in the capture of a much larger market share. This conclusion is based on an assumption that growth in the marketplace will come largely in LANs based on international standards. Proprietary LANs are likely to decline most rapidly and if ARCnet systems continue to be priced well below Ethernet and Token Ring hardware, it too is likely to survive.

There are some important philosophical differences among the five NOSs discussed in this chapter and these should be kept in mind. MAP was developed in response to specific manufacturing networking needs. It is not designed to replace wide area networks nor does it purport to be a total networking solution. Since it is self-consciously designed within the framework of OSI, however, real MAP networks should have the potential capacity to interact

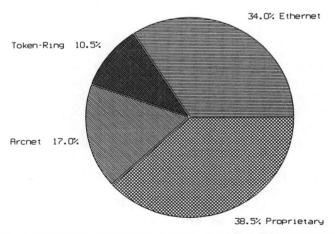

Figure 5.3   LAN Distribution by Physical Layer Protocol (% PC LAN Nodes, 1988)
SOURCE: *ComputerWorld*, May 29, 1989, p. 1. Copyright ©1989 by CW Publishing Inc., Framingham, MA 01701—reprinted from *ComputerWorld* by permission of the publisher.

with other OSI standard networks with a peer-to-peer relationship for selected activities provided a specific MAP conformable network has access to some global OSI network. An important element of making this work revolves around the use of OSI standard addressing and directory services (X.500). In contrast to this by-product of specifying an OSI standard network, is IBM's perspective which views LANs primarily as standalone work-group entities, or as nodes in an SNA networking environment. The LAN's NOS in IBM's networks can become, however, the organizing operating environment for distributed systems in the campus environment that coexist with SNA and are integrated with NetView. NetView is IBM's distributed network management tool.

Servers and the NOS

In addition, there are a number of services that the NOS must support in order to provide the rationale for a LAN installation in the first place. These services include electronic mail, file transfer, security, central database maintenance, and a host of collective office automation utilities such as calendaring, word processing, and similar activities. In order to accomplish these activities NOSs typically use one or more file servers, depending on the size (in terms of connected users) of the LAN. The file servers are usually high-performance PCs running under some operating system that allows multiple activities to take place concurrently. Two approaches have been taken by NOS manufacturers:

▼ Develop a proprietary operating environment, or

▼ Use an existing operating system.

Keep in mind that when we speak of the NOS, we are speaking only of the operating environment running on the server(s). So long as the manufacturer provides the appropriate software, *any* operating system can be used on PCs or workstations on the LAN. This is the reason why some LAN NOSs support such disparate systems as IBM PCs, MACs, Unix machines, DEC VAXs running under VMS, IBM mainframes running under VM or MVS. The most notable example of such an operating environment is TCP/IP.

When IBM got into the LAN business it based its PC LAN Program on PC/MS DOS and this led to a lower level of performance than was true of Novell or 3COM systems. One reason for this is that DOS is a single-tasking single-user system that was pressed into use in a multitasking multiuser environment. Both Novell and 3COM, as a result, produced proprietary operating systems. Since the advent of OS/2, however, IBM, Microsoft, 3COM, and others are moving to an OS/2 platform for their NOSs revolving around the LAN Manager developed by Microsoft. IBM's version of LAN Manager, called LAN

Server, is part of OS/2 Extended Edition and provides an appropriate LAN operating environment. Both IBM's and 3COM's version of the LAN Manager have been tailored to the specific requirements demanded by IBM and 3COM, respectively.

By way of contrast, Banyan Systems early settled on the use of Unix as the foundation for their NOS and have developed in that direction. The advantage of Unix is that it has been around for a long time and there are many more applications that can be easily ported to the LAN environment, although OS/2 based systems should catch up. It is unclear, however, as to which multitasking operating environment—Unix or OS/2—will win the competition of the most appropriate operating system for high-performance PCs and workstations. In contrast to server-based systems such as those produced by IBM, Banyan, Novell, and 3COM, OSI systems such as MAP do not require a server in order to operate. This is also true of TCP/IP networks although a form of server can be configured in such a system.

One further caveat might be noted. In order for a NOS manufacturer to maintain a competitive advantage it must provide a means for third party vendors of value-added products to be able to work with the NOS. This is accomplished by all four of the vendors described in this chapter through Application Program(mer) Interfaces (APIs). APIs provide a systematic means for an independent programmer to access the communications facilities of the NOS and the network the NOS supports. One of the reasons why most manufacturers of LAN NOSs provide support for NETBIOS (see below) is that the NETBIOS APIs are widely used, thus maximizing the number of third party programs that may be used with any particular NOS. This issue is critically important for the development of any server-based applications such as database systems, electronic mail facilities, and the like.

Connectivity Issues

In order to be competitive the two perspectives just set forth have provided both some problems and opportunities for manufacturers such as Banyan, Novell, and 3COM. Each of these companies (and most other manufacturers of LANs) started out with proprietary concerns and were targeted *only* at standalone work-group networking environments. It has become clear to all three, however, that many, if not most, organizations require something substantially broader than standalone PC networks. Those organizations require either that the work-group LANs be interfaced to larger networks which may be OSI standard networks, SNA networks, DECnet networks, or TCP/IP networks, or that the Banyan, Novell, and 3COM networks be capable of being generalized sufficiently to become the NOS standard for the entire organization including micros, minis, and mainframes as well as a diverse set of LANs.

Architectures and Protocols

Specifically, from Figure 5.2 it may be seen that there are at least three network architectures that must be able to be linked to any particular NOS:

▼ IBM's SNA (particularly APPC [LU 6.2])

▼ TCP/IP

▼ Comprehensive OSI systems

This means, in effect, that these vendors must either provide multiple networking methodologies in order to interconnect their LANs to the larger organization, or they must produce a network architecture that might itself serve as the organizing NOS for the entire organization's network. As may easily be seen from Figure 5.2, Novell and 3COM seem to have gone the former route, while Banyan seems to be headed in the latter direction. These issues will be discussed in greater detail within the context of each NOS. Much of what will be discussed concerning these systems are the apparent corporate strategies for future growth rather than the "nitty gritty" of currently available products which, in any event, will have changed by the time this volume is in production.

In addition to the network architectures mentioned above, other protocol or protocol-like issues are of importance:

▼ NETBIOS and NETBEUI

▼ Multiple Data Link and Physical Layer technologies including but not limited to the IEEE 802 standards

▼ AppleTalk Protocol (ATP)

▼ X.25-based systems

NETBIOS (described in a later section) is an IBM product but it has been widely copied and emulated. It is not technically a protocol but it does specify the way in which application designers can gain access to the LAN. It has become so ubiquitous that many incorrectly call it a *standard*. Subsequent chapters (7, 8, and 9) will deal, in detail, with the three primary IEEE 802 standards: CSMA/CD, Token Bus, and Token Ring. While we will not deal in any detail with ATP or X.25, suffice it to say that some method of communicating with Apple Macintoshes is probably a competitive necessity and X.25 is rapidly becoming a major base for wide area networks.

Connectivity and Interoperability

The file server is often used as a communications server for the purpose of linking into WANs or to other LANs. Assuming that the system is designed to support multiple Data Link and Physical Layer protocols and techniques, it is also desirable that the server be able to communicate concurrently with multiple Network Interface Cards based on various technologies, thus possibly making the server itself into a bridge or gateway. The connectivity issues are complicated and require some planning and thinking before implementing a connectivity scheme. Moreover, the concepts of *connectivity* and *interoperability* imply somewhat different approaches to the problem. Of the four commercial products we are discussing, all offer connectivity services in one fashion or another.

The easiest, although often not very integrated method of connectivity is through gateways to other networks. These may or may not be "user transparent," but they are a quick, if often dirty way to get the job done. When networks are interoperable, in addition to being connected, users and processes on one network have full access to the services provided by the other network. Thus, a SNA LAN gateway that makes some LAN appear to an IBM mainframe as a 3270 Display System cluster merely turns the workstations on the LAN into relatively dumb terminal emulators. The older 3270 Display System is referenced here because many vendors other than IBM still emulate some model of the 3274 Cluster Controller. This has been replaced by IBM with the 3174 Cluster Controller which can support some LAN functions. The 3174 Cluster Controller device or emulation turns the network station into a Distributed Function Terminal (DFT) providing access to an IBM host computer system. This process may be expanded, however, to include APPC (LU 6.2), applications at each end of the connection that can interact with one another as peers. In this sense, then, LAN activities are at least somewhat interoperable with SNA activities although the two networks are still not fully interoperable. This is a result of the fact that a LAN's NOS in an IBM environment relies on NETBIOS while SNA is based on Logical Unit to Logical Unit sessions. When the LAN network station operates as a DFT emulator the NETBIOS is replaced by SNA functions of which APPC is one example.

From an end-user's perspective the best way of dealing with networks is to not know they are in existence. That level of transparency is not yet to be found, however. The next best thing is to provide connectivity in a reasonably smooth way requiring a minimum of user intervention. An example might be useful. In a typical DEC VAX environment, for example, the VAX is usually front-ended with an Ethernet and users gain access to the VAX through the Ethernet either through directly attached PCs or through PCs or terminals coming in through terminal servers. In either event, the protocols running on the Ethernet will normally be those supported by DECnet.

If we wish to attach some other random LAN to this system, there is typically the requirement for a gateway that performs protocol conversion from whatever the LAN is using (assuming it is not running the same DECnet protocol) to the DECnet protocols. The random LAN then simply appears as another terminal server to the front-end Ethernet. An alternative method is to give up DECnet protocols entirely and use something in common to both the Ethernet front-end and to the random LAN. One such possibility is TCP/IP. Another possibility is for a LAN vendor to write software for the VAX such that a third-party NOS, such as Novell, becomes the protocol suite of choice. I mention Novell because this is precisely what it has done. With the use of gateways, the attached device or network is simply that: an attached device or network that we have somehow made available. Through more global integration of the attached device or network, however, the full range of network services becomes available all the way through to the host VAX.

The reason why the ideas behind the standards movement are so powerful is that with the adoption of standards comes the promise of integrated networks much like that I have just described. It is currently possible, for example, to set up an 802.3 (or Ethernet) LAN to which are attached an IBM mainframe, a DEC VAX, and a multitude of PCs from various vendors and to have them able to directly access one another with TCP/IP applications such as FTP (File Transfer Protocol), SMTP (Simple Mail Transfer Protocol), or Telnet (Virtual Terminals). With the coming of fully specified OSI networks, TCP/IP systems will migrate to OSI and connectivity and interoperability will be a reality.

NETBIOS and NETBEUI

The NETwork Basic Input Output System (NETBIOS) was introduced at the same time IBM announced the PC Network in 1984. The network microcode is the foundation for program control of the IBM LANs and resides in ROM on the Adapter Card, on diskette, or on the PC's motherboard. NETBIOS, now distributed as a memory resident program, is a complete replacement for the original ROM versions. The memory resident version of NETBIOS appeared about the same time as the Token Ring Network and appeared as a program named NETBEUI.COM, an acronym for NETBIOS Extended User Interface.[4] Other manufacturers, as we shall see, have adopted NETBIOS as a supported interface and sometimes do not support the extensions. In fact, a proposed NETBIOS to TCP/IP standard specifically recommends against the use of the extensions.[5] As Figure 5.1 illustrates, when compared to the OSI reference model, NETBIOS performs functions at approximately the session and presentation layers. The function of NETBIOS is fourfold:

▼ To provide the ability to create a session and interchange information with another user (name) on the network;

▼ To send and receive peer-to-peer or broadcast information on the network;

▼ To define multiple-user names within a node;

▼ To determine network adapter status and control.

Earlier versions of NETBIOS supported up to 32 peer-to-peer sessions on each adapter card although the newest release of NETBIOS (provided via the IBM LAN Support Program Version 1.1) will maintain a maximum of 254 sessions. NETBIOS is to be distinguished from DOS 3.1 (and later) network function calls under interrupt 21H, and from the PC LAN Programs or OS/2 LAN Server, that organize network service functions.

Generally speaking, NETBIOS is a gateway that allows programmers to write code that can communicate in a systematic fashion with network devices. NETBIOS does not provide protocols so much as a systematic means for providing network services that application programs may need. When DOS was extended in Version 3.1 the network system calls then provided under interrupt 21H provided all suppliers of network software the capability to standardize at least some of the access to LAN hardware. Most manufacturers of LAN software have announced or implemented support of NETBIOS for IBM LANs.

Although the hardware for a local area network is fundamental to its operation, it is only half of what is needed. The other half is the network software that actually organizes the network both from a system and user perspective. As with the LAN hardware business, so too with LAN software there is considerable competition. Many of the improvements to LAN software in recent years has been a result of that competition. The PC LAN Support Program, for example, will function best in a very small, homogeneous office environment. At least, in part, for this reason IBM developed the OS/2 LAN Server software which is its NOS offering for distributed processing (see below). In many respects other networking software that will run on the same hardware—Novell's NetWare, for example—has had a better, more functional architecture. It has the added advantage that it will run on many kinds of non-IBM hardware as well on those devices with IBM's imprimatur. Some LAN software components, such as NETBIOS, is supported by most LAN NOSs as a function of competitive pressures.[6]

LANS AND "REAL" OPEN SYSTEMS: MAP

The Manufacturing Automation Protocol is not itself a "standard." Nor is it a protocol. Rather, it is a systematic exploration or specification of the way in which OSI standards can be integrated into a real open system network. Like most generalizations, the foregoing statement is a bit too glib. There are three areas where MAP extends OSI for the particular needs of manufacturing: the Manufacturing Message Protocol, Directory Services, and Network Management. The MAP standards documents present MAP requirements OSI layer-by-layer and we will follow that organization in this chapter. Because of the richness of OSI protocols (or potential protocols) no two real open systems (MAP and TOP, for example) will use the OSI building blocks in the same manner, but at some layers the two should be interoperable when interoperability is needed and desired.[7] Unlike the other NOSs discussed in this chapter, MAP is not a product *per se*, but is intended to guide developers producing real MAP products and networks. IBM, for example, has a MAP conforming offering (MAP 2.1) as will many other vendors. The discussion of MAP, therefore, revolves around what is required in order for a network to be MAP conformable.

MAP specifications are "intended to define a Local Area Network for terminals, computing resources, and programmable devices within a plant or complex," while allowing for the interconnection "of multiple LAN's and for connection to Wide Area Networks or digital PBX's for long distance communications." In one sense MAP constitutes a complete LAN network operating system (NOS) since it fully elaborates an integrated networking methodology that specifies as its primary Physical and Data Link Layers the IEEE 802.4 (token bus) standards. On the other hand, since MAP is specified very self-consciously as an OSI standard network, MAP networks will be able to be easily interoperable with other real open systems, thus having the potential for making any given MAP network part of a global networking community.

The driving force behind MAP was the need for compatibility of communications to integrate factory floor devices by using existing or emerging national, international, and industry standards. The MAP specification indicates for each layer of the OSI Reference Model the appropriate standards necessary to achieve the goals set forth. The physical topology used by MAP—carrierband and broadband token bus—will be discussed in Chapter 8. MAP protocol selections for the ISO/OSI layers are:

Layer 7 — ISO ACSE, FTAM, MMS, and Directory Services

Layer 6 — ISO Presentation Kernel (ISO 8822 & 8823)

Layer 5 — ISO Session Kernel (ISO 8326 & 8327)

Layer 4 — Transport Class 4 (ISO 8072 & 8073)

Layer 3 — ISO Connectionless Network Protocol (ISO 8348 & 8473)

Layer 2 — IEEE 802.2 Class 1/Class 3 and IEEE 802.4 MAC (see Chapter 4 [LLC] and Chapters 7, 8, and 9 [MAC])

Layer 1 — IEEE 802.4 Broadband or IEEE 802.4 Phase Coherent Carrierband (see Chapter 8)

MAP recognizes five distinct classifications of communications capability: MAP end systems, MAP intermediate systems, MAP/EPA systems, MINIMAP systems, and MAP bridges. While this chapter will deal primarily with MAP end systems, the others will be briefly described. In each case conformance with MAP specifications is a combination of the use of required protocols, strongly recommended protocols, and optional though strongly recommended protocols. A MAP end system must support:

▼ The MAP end-system agent capabilities of the network management protocol;

▼ The ISO Association Control Service Element (ACSE) protocol;

▼ The kernel functional unit of the ISO Presentation protocol;

▼ The kernel functional unit of the ISO Session protocol with duplex operation;

▼ The ISO Class IV Transport protocol;

▼ The ISO Connectionless Network protocol;

▼ The End System (ES) capability of the ISO End System to Intermediate System (ES/IS) routing exchange protocol;

▼ The IEEE 802.2 (ISO 8802/2) LLC type 1 protocol (connectionless service); and

▼ Either the IEEE 802.4 10 Mb/s Broadband or the IEEE 802.4 5 Mb/s Carrierband protocol.

Other end-system protocol requirements include at least one additional application layer protocol—a Private Application Service Element (ASE)—to be used in the absence of a MAP specified protocol in order to meet some specific application communication need. In addition, the MAP end system must support either ISO FTAM or ISO MMS and most will support both. The normal MAP end system will also require at least the minimal Directory User Agent capability of the directory service protocol. All these elements of End System Protocol Requirements are illustrated in Figure 5.4. Although Figure 5.4 portrays a full MAP system, the other four MAP system options represent essen-

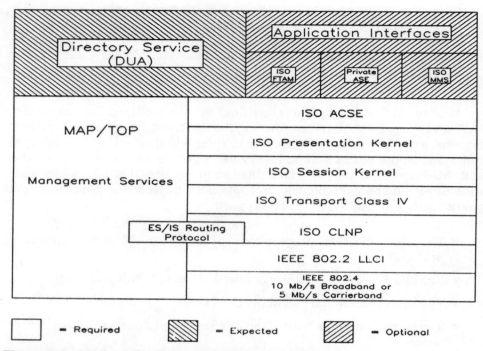

Figure 5.4 MAP 3.0 End System (ES) Requirements
SOURCE: MAP 3.0 Implementation Release, June 23, 1987, p. C2-2.3. ©Copyright 1987
by General Motors Corporation. All rights reserved.

tially subsets of the full model designed for environments not requiring the full end system.

The MAP specification designates specific ISO standards as the basic for manufacturing automation for each layer in the full seven-layer OSI Reference Model as well as the way in which those standards are to be used. Each layer provides services to the next higher layer involving the transfer of two types of information: data and control. While the object of the protocols is to reliably transfer data, the control information is the basis for layer services. The data transferred from layer to layer are generally done so transparently, although it may be reformatted in the Presentation Layer. As outgoing data are passed from layer to layer, additional control information is added similar to the various headers added in the TCP and IP environment. Thus the "data" at an (n)-layer consists of the data *and* control information from the (n + 1)-layer. Therefore, as the outgoing data are passed from an (n)-layer to an (n − 1)-layer, the size increases. As the incoming data are passed from an (n)-layer to an (n + 1)-layer, control information is successively stripped away. This process is illustrated in Figure 5.5.

BANYAN VINES

As we have already noted, manufacturers of NOSs confront not only the need to provide high-quality communications among personal computers and workstations in a work-group LAN, but must also be able to link their LANs to other LANs, minis, and mainframes connected in a much broader network. Banyan Systems, Inc. has developed its VIrtual NEtwork System (VINES) to meet these demands. Like IBM, Banyan early recognized the need for a multitasking operating system to act as a platform for its NOS. Rather than writing its own, as did Novell, or adopting a new and untried system such as OS/2, Banyan adopted Unix V as its platform.

Unlike IBM, Novell, and 3COM, Banyan supports essentially a single version of VINES (currently Version 3.1 with 4.0 announced) that runs on several different platforms acting as servers. VINES/286 and VINES/386 run on a wide

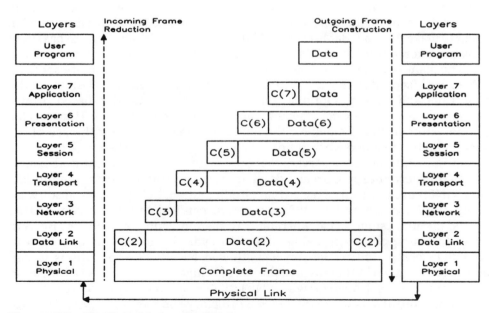

Figure 5.5 Nesting of Layer Protocols
NOTES: C(N), Layer N control information.
         Data(N), Layer N Cumutative data.
SOURCE: MAP 3.0 Implementation Release, June 22, 1987, p. C3-2.5. ©Copyright by General Motors Corporation. All rights reserved.

variety of personal computers using the Intel 80286 and 80386 microprocessors, respectively. Until 1989 Banyan also sold three different integrated servers with VINES closely coupled to the hardware: DeskTop Server (VINES/DTS); Banyan Network Server (VINES/BNS); and Corporate Network Server (VINES/CNS). The first two, based on Motorola's 68,000 cpu, have been discontinued. CNS is a 80386-based machine. Since the base for VINES is Unix System V, the actual platform hardware is irrelevant except for performance issues. Any server can have multiple network interface cards installed using the same or different protocols. With additional optional software, VINES servers can also act as TCP/IP bridges.[8]

The advantage of using a full-blown operating system, such as Unix, as the base for the NOS is versatility. The advantage of writing a dedicated NOS tailored to the problems of networking is speed and performance. In general it is easier to add new functionality to the NOS when it is based on a complete operating system than when it is severely tailored. A potential disadvantage of a tailored system is that every new function may require another server where with a general purpose multitasking operating system such as Unix (or OS/2) the server can be expanded with relatively lower effort and cost. Since a LAN is not only a multitasking environment but also a multiuser system, a multitasking (like OS/2) and multiuser (as is Unix) operating system makes a good deal of sense. Because Unix is a widely used OS, there are also many applications that can be easily linked in order to make them available under LAN operating conditions. Banyan has spent time and effort optimizing Unix for performance and file integrity.

The standard VINES services are extensive: StreetTalk (directory service); VANGuard (security); file and printer services; Time service; NETBIOS emulation; Chat and backup. Optional services include workstation-based printer services; mail; network management; and communications. The Time service is interesting in that a clock for the network is maintained for the use of the server and the attached workstations. The service is versatile enough to handle synchronization between servers that may be located in different time zones, taking into account standard and daylight times. For interprocess communication VINES uses a proprietary virtual circuit system. For purposes of software compatibility, however, NETBIOS calls are recognized, but are converted to the virtual circuit system. Local workstations, therefore, do not need NETBIOS in order to use applications using NETBIOS calls. By using this approach to NETBIOS compatibility Banyan has allowed NETBIOS applications to run across large networks that involve the use of bridges and gateways as well as on local departmental LANs (for which NETBIOS was originally developed).

At the core of VINES is StreetTalk, a directory and naming service that provides access to files, applications, printers, host gateways, users, servers, resources, and communications. StreetTalk is a globally distributed directory system supported on every server in a VINES network. It is StreetTalk that makes the network reasonably transparent to the user since the product integrates all services and users. This allows users to see network resources as virtual extensions of their local workstations. A StreetTalk name consists of three parts: Item@Group@Organization. That this scheme is similar to that adopted by MAP[9] is apparently no coincidence.

The MAP scheme is based on the international CCITT standard, X.500. As the VINES profile in Figure 5.2 makes clear, Banyan has a fundamental commitment to move to OSI standards through the transport layer and to support higher layer OSI standards as well. Like X.500 all network entities (resources) are defined as objects in a distributed directory. According to Banyan, StreetTalk is compatible with X.500 to the extent that StreetTalk has equivalents to most of the directory operations defined in X.500. The strategic objective of Banyan is to make the necessary alterations to StreetTalk so that it will be capable of interoperating with any other X.500 defined entities.

The other service of significance for this discussion is communications. The communications services provided by Banyan are impressive and encompass a well thought-out view of how people in organizations work. The following communications services are available:

▼ PC Dial-in to the VINES network

▼ Asynchronous terminal emulation and file transfer

▼ IBM mainframe 3270 communications (SNA and Bisynch)

▼ TCP/IP Support

▼ Server-to-Server Communications

▼ OSI Support (including X.25/X.29)

▼ Token-Ring bridge support

At the lowest level of connectivity is the provision for allowing dial access to the VINES LAN itself. The optional dial access service allows a dial-in user to have full access to all VINES services available locally. Except for being slower, dial access to a VINES network is no different than using a locally attached network PC. For accessing asynchronous services outside the LAN, the asynchronous terminal emulation and file transfer option is available. This option allows a PC to emulate a (DEC) VT100, VT52, and as many as 40 other terminal types. File transfer is provide via the Kermit File Transfer protocol. An asynchronous computer (a DEC VAX, for example) can be accessed via dial-up or through leased lines and a programmatic interface enables program-to-program communications between PCs and host computers. If the computer to be accessed is an IBM mainframe, then the VINES IBM 3270/SNA software option provides the linkage by allowing any VINES attached PC to access 3270/SNA host applications, perform send/receive file transfer, and to receive host printouts on local PC printers. This is accomplished by an emulator running on the VINES server to make the VINES network appear to the IBM host as a 3270 cluster. The emulator provides an emulation for both the IBM 3274 Model X1C and 3174 with Token Ring cluster controllers for access to the host and for the user PCs emulations of 3x78 Model 2, 3x79 Models 2A and 2B display stations as well as 3287 Models 1 and 2 printers.

For internetworking an extensive set of TCP/IP tools is available.[10] VINES supports TCP/IP routing on the server, FTP, Telnet, RLOGIN (Remote Login), and SMTP on connected PCs, and TCP/IP Server-to-Server (see below) functions. The TCP/IP routing option provides the following services:

▼ Allows the VINES server to act as an IP router;

▼ Encapsulates TCP/IP packets for travel across a VINES network.

The routing option enables VINES servers to route IP traffic via Ethernet, Token Ring, StarLan, and ProNET-10 LANs. For an incoming TCP/IP packet destined for an address on the VINES network the routing option encapsulates the TCP/IP packet in a VINES packet. If that destination is another server equipped with the TCP/IP routing option, with the final destination being another TCP/IP external node, then the software strips the VINES header and sends it on its way to the foreign TCP/IP host or gateway. On the user's PC access to TCP is obtained by a "hotkey" toggle between VINES and TCP/IP applications. Using a version of FTP Inc.'s PC/TCP, VINES provides FTP, Telnet, SMTP, subnetting and routing, and IBM 3270 and DEC VT100/220 terminal emulations. VINES and TCP/IP traffic can share the same physical network. Two versions of PC/TCP are available: TCP120 and TCP121. TCP120 operates over all VINES support LANs, allowing TCP/IP traffic from PC/TCP applications to travel across a VINES network and then out to a foreign host. TCP121 uses only VINES support Ethernet LANs and is used for traffic running directly across a TCP/IP network to a TCP/IP host rather than across a VINES network. TCP120 works in conjunction with the TCP/IP routing option.

Through the VINES Server-to-Server services it would be possible for a large organization to create a very large WAN using, in effect, VINES as the organizing network. Basically, the Server-to-Server options provide a means for linking VINES LANs located in diverse locations. Since StreetTalk is distributed across all the VINES servers in the network—thus allowing users to find appropriate resources anywhere on the larger network—this has the effect of creating a single, virtual network no matter how far flung. There are essentially four options:

▼ LAN Server-to-Server is one option that allows multiple servers to communicate over a variety of LANs including Ethernet, Token Ring, IBM PC Net, ProNET-10, ARCnet, VistaLAN, StarLan, and OMNINET-1B.

▼ TCP/IP Server-to-Server provides a means for using existing TCP/IP networks to pass VINES packets and thereby act as the linkage between the VINES servers. In this case the VINES packet is encapsulated in an IP packet and sent out the TCP/IP network. At the receiving end the IP and TCP headers are removed and the VINES packet continues on its way. This could be particularly useful for government agencies or some institutions of higher education.

▼ WAN Server-to-Server supports multiple communications lines using leased lines operating up to 64 Kb/s using synchronous modems, or public switched telephone networks using asynchronous modems.

▼ X.25 Server-to-Server makes is possible to connect various VINES servers through Public or Private Data Networks such as Telenet or the PDNs being established by various Bell Operating Companies (BOCs). The X.25 software provides support for up to 128 virtual circuits and supports leased lines to the PDN with speeds up to 64 Kb/s using the synchronous modems standard for X.25.

The last piece of the communication services is the OSI strategy recently announced by Banyan. It is this strategy that is outlined Figure 5.2 and expanded in Figure 5.6, since it will become the base for VINES in the 1990s. Basically what Banyan seems to be doing is migrating VINES to an OSI network

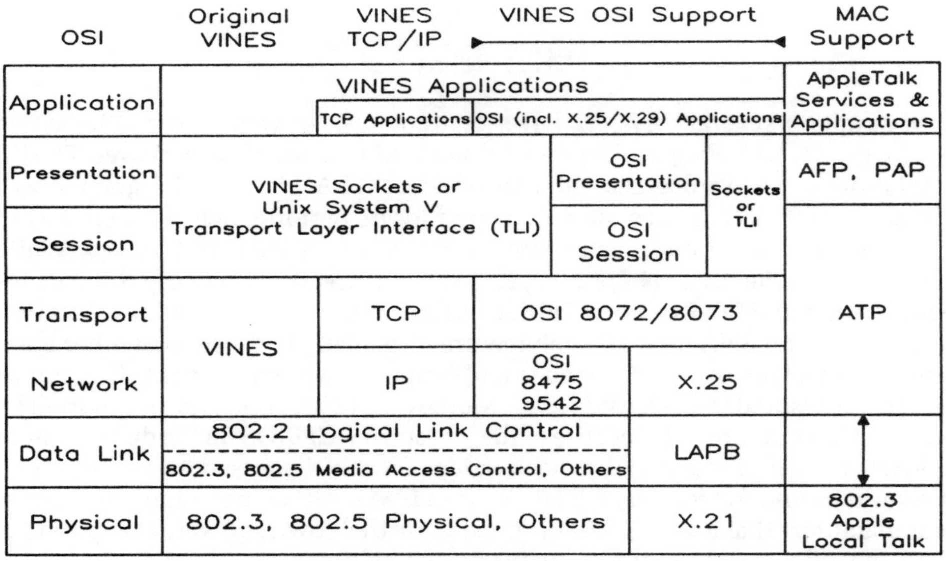

OSI	Original VINES	VINES TCP/IP	VINES OSI Support →	←		MAC Support
Application	VINES Applications					AppleTalk Services & Applications
		TCP Applications	OSI (incl. X.25/X.29) Applications			
Presentation	VINES Sockets or Unix System V Transport Layer Interface (TLI)		OSI Presentation	Sockets or TLI		AFP, PAP
Session			OSI Session			
Transport	VINES	TCP	OSI 8072/8073			ATP
Network		IP	OSI 8475 9542	X.25		
Data Link	802.2 Logical Link Control			LAPB		↑
	802.3, 802.5 Media Access Control, Others					
Physical	802.3, 802.5 Physical, Others			X.21		802.3 Apple Local Talk ↓

Figure 5.6   Banyan VINES Protocol Stacks

platform from the OSI Transport Layer on down. Clearly, until the world moves more-or-less entirely to OSI standards, it will still be necessary to support other network solutions, particularly including TCP/IP until the migration is complete from TCP/IP to OSI. While the Banyan position paper, *Open Systems Interconnect (OSI) Direction Paper* (1989), seems to suggest that it will eventually replace its own protocols with OSI protocols at Layers 1 (Physical) through 4 (Transport) and that VINES applications will coexist with OSI applications at the upper three layers of the OSI model, VINES, TCP/IP, and OSI/ISO transport protocols will continue to exist in parallel for some time into the future. We have already noted that Banyan intends to make StreetTalk fully compatible with X.500 directory services and this means that future VINES networks will be able to have full interoperability with other OSI compliant networks. This approach to the future of networking is interesting in that so far as I know, only Banyan has explicitly stated its strategic direction in terms of OSI standards.

Banyan supports the use of a wide range of technologies at the Physical Layer and, as a result, cannot maintain only a standards-based approach to that layer, or to the media access control sublayer of the Data Link Layer. Specifically, VINES supports ARCnet, Ethernet (and 802.3), David Systems, Inc., IBM PC Network, Omninet-1B, ProNet-10, StarLan (and 802.3 1BASE5), Token-Ring (and 802.5), and VistLAN network interface cards (NICs). Banyan's strategy, although this is not clearly spelled out in its documents, seems to be to use the 802.2 Logical Link Control (LLC) sublayer specification as the general-purpose interface to higher layer protocols.

IBM LANS

IBM supports several Physical Layer technologies as well as essentially two NOSs: the *PC LAN Program* Version 1.3 and the OS/2-based *LAN Server*. The PC LAN Program is an enhancement of the earlier PC LAN Support Program. It was based on PC/DOS and was often criticized for its performance although recent improvements have improved performance and extended its services. While IBM supports the PC LAN Program, its strategic direction is clearly directed toward the use of OS/2 Extended Edition as the platform for integrating LANs into its more general SNA network architecture. Especially because most other manufacturers feel the need to respond to and support IBM developments it is important to understand the two IBM NOSs. Moreover, some services are supported by both NOSs, some are not. Because of the impact of NETBIOS on the development of LAN operating systems, it has been independently discussed, above, although it should be understood that NETBIOS is an IBM product, not a standard. Other manufacturers that use "NETBIOS" must write their own software that provides the same functionality provided by IBM's NETBIOS.

The PC LAN Program provides a common support package for all IBM LAN technologies [Token Ring, PC Network (broadband and baseband), Ethernet] running under PC DOS. It uses IEEE 802.2 Logical Link Control standards thereby supporting the OSI data link layer. It also supports the SNA data link layer which is becoming more consistent with OSI and it provides the base for APPC/PC and NETBIOS. It should be noted that the PC LAN Program requires as least DOS 3.3. Like most LAN NOSs the PC LAN Program makes communication among users available through file copy and message services and allows users to share hardware resources. It will support up to 254 active stations per server. OS/2 Extended Edition adds the functionality of the LAN Support Program to the operating system itself extending support through the use of a complete communications subsystem, support for all IBM LANs, and LAN interfaces such as IEEE 802.2, NETBIOS, and LU 6.2 (APPC). From Figure 5.7 the place of the LAN Support Program may be seen. NETBIOS and APPC/PC, to name only two, are options that can be taken at installation time. It is also clear that the OS/2 LAN Server is much more comprehensive in its architecture.

As might be anticipated, IBM does not support a very wide range of NICs. Rather, it supports only its own approved set of NICs which include the IBM PC Network (broadband and baseband), Token Ring, and at this writing Ungermann-Bass's Ethernet cards. This obviously makes it possible to use IBM software products on the most commonly used systems (other than ARCnet). Unlike both Banyan and Novell (see below), both of which are making efforts to be all things to all LANs, IBM's strategy is narrower and largely confined to the support of its own strategic products and services although it clearly wants to be a major player in the LAN arena. Its support for Ethernet (and 802.3) has, however, been brought about by the pressure of the marketplace. As may be seen from Figure 5.7 is to use 802 standards at the Physical and Data Link Layers, although this is tempered by the fact that the PC Network (broadband/baseband) has never become a standard and must use proprietary protocols under the LLC sublayer.

IBM's PC LAN Program

The NETwork Basic Input Output System was introduced at the same time IBM announced the original broadband PC Network in 1984. Its purpose was to support the PC Network Program, the ancestor of the current PC LAN Program, IBM's DOS-based NOS. The PC LAN Program is a minimum NOS that supports file and communications servers as well as the variety of network adapter cards now marketed by IBM. Even with the introduction of the OS/2-based LAN Server, the PC LAN Program continues to be enhanced. At this writing the newest feature was *Extended Services*.

Extended Services is based on the concept of a *Domain*. A *Domain* is a collection of servers on a LAN that appear to the network user as a single system.

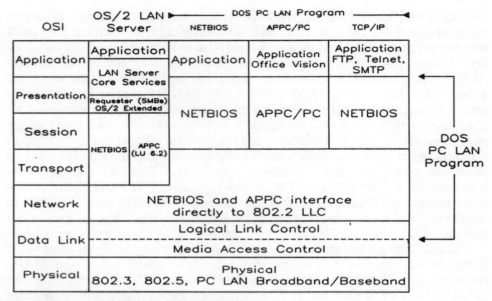

Figure 5.7   IBM LAN Configuration Options

The Domain is managed by a master server called a Domain Controller. In a distributed computing environment it is likely that users will have a variety of needs not all of which will be provided by a single server. The Domain furnishes the mechanism to deliver network resources to selected users determined at log-on time. Multiple Domains may reside on a single LAN. The Domain is part of IBM's strategic direction for distributed LAN environments and helps integrate the PC LAN Program into the broader LAN concepts represented by LAN Service and OS/2 Extended Edition.

With Version 1.32 of the PC LAN Program a DOS user is offered either Base Services or Extended Services. Base Services provides simple resources sharing and network functions. The Base Services may be tailored to maximize memory available to applications at a connected microcomputer. Extended Services allow the user to obtain messaging, peer communications, resource sharing, 3270 terminal emulation, remote dial-in, asynchronous terminal emulation, or requester (see below) to server relationships on either a DOS or OS/2 server. The requster-to-server relationship differs from a client-to-server system in that server-to-server transactions are expected. Multiple servers in a Domain provide a single system image to the user. Extended Services allow network stations to be configured as menu-driven workstations.

The first LAN supported by IBM was the broadband version of its PC Network, originally produced under contract with Sytek, Inc. The second LAN from IBM was the Token Ring and was and is clearly the strategic LAN product from IBM. Subsequently, however, IBM expanded the PC Network line to include a baseband version, and has expanded its LAN support to include Ethernet and the "IBM Industrial Network," which is IBM's implementation of MAP. Throughout much of the 1980s IBM attempted to ignore Ethernet and found it could not do so. Consequently, by 1989, it had started to integrate Ethernet into virtually all its networking and was marketing an Ethernet adapter card made by Ungermann-Bass. Today the major emphasis is on Token Ring and Ethernet with continued support of both flavors of the PC Network. We will describe IBM's Token Ring in a bit more detail in Chapter 9 since it is an implementation of IEEE 802.5.

OS/2 LAN Server

Although *LAN Manager* is the generic version of the OS/2-based NOS (developed by Microsoft) IBM has produced a hardware specific version called *LAN Server*. The various versions of LAN Manager that will eventually be remarketed by many NOS vendors should be able to interoperate with one another and with LAN Server. IBM's version, like the others, is an OS/2 application, but IBM's OS/2 Extended Edition requires an IBM brand name 80286 or 80386 (or 80486) computer in order to run. As has already been noted, OS/2 is required only on the server, however. PCs and workstations on the network may be any combination of DOS and OS/2 systems whether IBM or not. In the IBM scheme—and different from the generic version of LAN Manager—the LAN Requestor (see Figure 5.7) is integrated with a communications manager and a database manager in OS/2 Extended Edition.[11]

Of some importance for this discussion is the point that the Communications Manager is designed to provide a common application interface for OS/2 users with the wide variety of communications devices used in SNA networks: asynch, the 3270 display system, LANs, APPC, and so forth. It is through the Communications Manager that the relationship between an OS/2 workstation and an IBM 370 architecture mainframe or an AS400 minicomputer will take place in an integrated network environment. One of the key elements in the LAN Server (and LAN Manager) is the use of the server-message-block (SMB) file-system protocol. The SMB is part of the Requester (IBM OS/2 Extended Edition) or Redirector (Microsoft OS/2). The requester is essentially an interprocess/intertask communications (IPC) mechanism that handles service requests and replies between the users (clients) and the server. Requests for service come from a client through the client-server protocol to the server. This may be seen in the flow diagram in Figure 5.8. As will be seen, other IPCs, in addition to SMBs, have been developed by other manufacturers. In particular, those supported by other NOSs include the Apple File Protocol (AFP), the

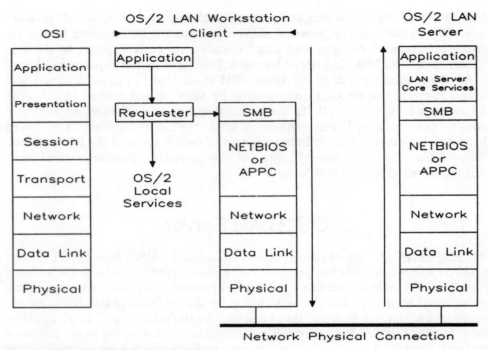

Figure 5.8   Client Request to Server
NOTE: SMB denotes Server Messenger Block.

NetWare Core Protocol (NCP) from Novell, and Sun Microsystems' Network File System (NFS) which has emerged as the standard for servicing Unix clients.

Perhaps the key difference between the PC LAN Program and the OS/2 LAN Server is the support for *distributed* processing applications across a wide-ranging network inherent in OS/2 Extended Edition. Where the PC LAN Program and its predecessor, the PC LAN Support Program, were designed essentially for the support of standalone LANs (notwithstanding gateways and bridges to wider networking), the OS/2 LAN Server is clearly integrated into IBM's overall strategy of distributed processing.

NOVELL NETWARE

For its strategic position in the LAN arena in the 1990s Novell has developed what it calls NetWare Open Systems—its architecture for "providing a comprehensive platform for network computing."[12] NetWare Open Systems consists primarily of two broad products, NetWare 386 and Portable NetWare. Both developments, arising out of Novell's experience since the early 1980s in providing NOSs for work-group LANs, recognize that LANs do not exist in an organizational or technological vacuum. The term they have applied to the new reliance on networking is "network computing." Network computing recognizes that what organizations want and need is a means for integrating LANs and WANs in an easily used network environment. NetWare is actually a family of products that includes ELS (Entry Level System) NetWare (I and II) which provides a single server solution for stand-alone LANs; Advanced NetWare and SFT (System Fault Tolerant) NetWare designed for workgroup computing with SFT providing fault tolerant redundancy; and NetWare 386 and Portable NetWare, the strategic Novell products for the 1990s.

Portable NetWare represents a substantial departure for Novell in that it is designed to allow the porting of server functions to a wide variety of operating systems and machines. We have already noted the fact that Novell, alone among the four commercial systems discussed in this chapter, selected an aggressively proprietary approach to the network operating system. They have made NetWare documentation widely available so that developers are able to write applications that will run well on Novell networks, but they have been able to optimize their NOS by making it perform only those functions necessary in a shared network environment. The result has been that in virtually all published performance evaluations Novell comes out on top, although it appears that Banyan's VINES 4.0 has closed that gap.[13]

What has been recognized, however, especially in the "network computing" or enterprise-wide network milieu, is that it is often desirable to have some other platform act as the host—a platform that need not be dedicated to being merely a file server. In fact, at the time of this writing, NetWare had been running for several months on a DEC VAX VMS platform and Novell had contracted with Phaser Systems under an OEM agreement for Phaser to port NetWare to both IBM's VM and MVS operating systems. Banyan, Novell, and 3COM all have developed strategies that dictate the expansion of their NOSs to the point where they can provide the network integration for enterprise-wide computing. The competitive advantage of being able to port NetWare to large-scale machine cannot be overlooked in the context of the competition to be the network integrator of choice for large organizations.

One of the key elements in the success of any NOS that purports to provide enterprise-wide networking across a variety of network components is a global directory service. Novell plans to implement distributed directory services based on several protocols including X.500, Apple's Name Binding Protocol, Sun Microsystems Yellow Pages (for NFS support), the TCP/IP Domain Name Service, and continued support for the NetWare Directory (Bindery/Service Advertising Protocol). The latter is a single-server protocol that is inappropriate for use in a widely distributed network. Novell's objective is to allow a user on some foreign system to access the Novell network services with the local directory service and protocols and to allow a Novell network user to access a foreign network service using the appropriate Novell directory services. This obviously requires directory gateways that allow protocol conversion and mutual support.

We have already seen how MAP and Banyan's VINES have targeted the CCITT directory standard X.500 as the fundamental yardstick for directory services. X.500 is a distributed directory protocol that allows "transparent" access to network services regardless where they reside. Such a directory system must, of course, be used in conjunction with an appropriate Network Layer protocol allowing for full routing around the network. A single-route network NOS, such as IBM's OS/2 LAN Server, and by inference at least, Microsoft's OS/2 LAN Manager, lack such capabilities. When we review 3COM's 3+ Open we will see another approach to handling this issue.

There are basically three components of the NetWare 386 system: NetWare Services (including 386 NetWare Loadable Modules); NetWare 386 real-time, multitasking, system; and the NetWare File System. The NetWare Services have been written in portable C code and it is this part of the NetWare system called "Portable NetWare." When Novell or an OEM takes the portable C code to another machine or operating system, it is implemented as an application of the native operating system (VMS, VM, MVS, etc.). It is possible, therefore, to port NetWare to Unix, OS/2, or other similar systems as well as to proprietary operating systems. Although Novell officers continue to defend the proprietary, single-purpose operating-system approach in the industry press, clearly the corporation's strategy has recognized a need to extend NetWare services to machines where single purpose operating systems are clearly inappropriate. It should be noted that the term "proprietary" is used here to indicate only that the Novell operating environment is a product of Novell. It is "open" in that Novell has made it and its documentation generally accessible in an aggressive fashion. For this reason Novell insists that "NetWare is more open than *any* other NOS" (private communication).

If we think in terms of the OSI Model, Novell has chosen to provide interoperability services in the Transport and Network Layers. This approach is illustrated most clearly in Figure 5.9. In its original manifestation, NetWare used (and uses) proprietary Transport and Network protocols based, historically, on Xerox's XNS protocols. At the Network Layer the Internet Packet Exchange (IPX) handles addressing and routing issues while the Sequenced Packet Exchange (SPX) seems to control the establishment of virtual circuits. What Novell proposes to do to handle internetworking is for some circumstances to replace SPX and IPX with TCP and IP, or OSI Transport and OSI Network protocols, or IBM SNA's APPC and whatever it may need, if anything, at the Network Layer. For all other layers of the model, Novell intends to use its own protocols although at the Application Layer it does expect to support standard TCP/IP

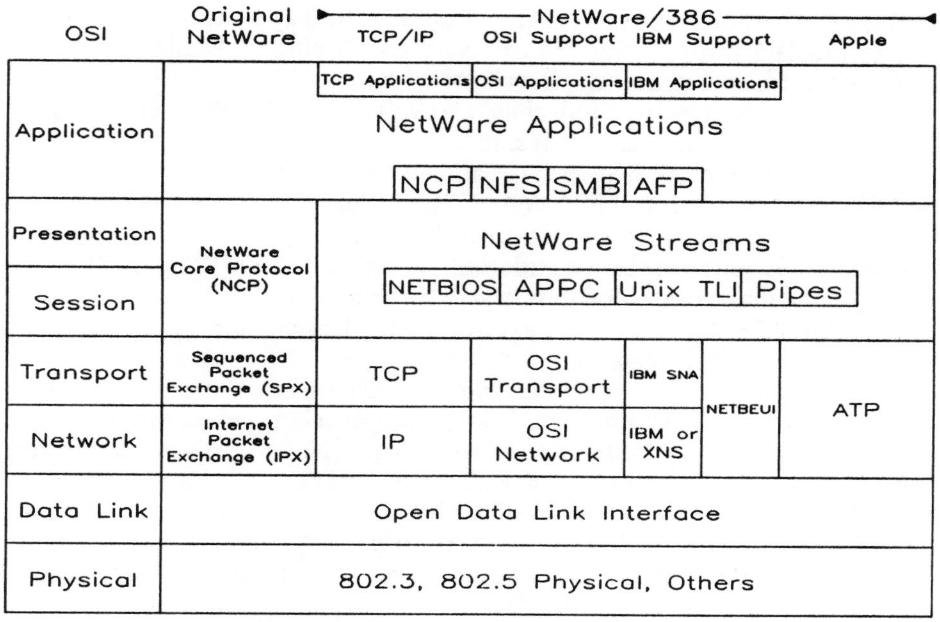

OSI	Original NetWare	TCP/IP	NetWare/386 OSI Support	IBM Support	Apple
Application	NetWare Core Protocol (NCP)	TCP Applications / NetWare Applications / NCP NFS SMB AFP	OSI Applications	IBM Applications	
Presentation		NetWare Streams			
Session		NETBIOS APPC Unix TLI Pipes			
Transport	Sequenced Packet Exchange (SPX)	TCP	OSI Transport	IBM SNA	NETBEUI	ATP
Network	Internet Packet Exchange (IPX)	IP	OSI Network	IBM or XNS		
Data Link	Open Data Link Interface				
Physical	802.3, 802.5 Physical, Others				

Figure 5.9   Novell NetWare Protocol Stacks

and OSI applications. Even though the discussions are vague the same presumption should also be made for use of APPC or there would be no point in supporting it.

At the Data Link and Physical Layers Novell has opted for a very different approach to physical technologies and support of NICs than either Banyan or IBM. The latter, to the extent possible, are relying heavily on 802 standards at the lower layers. In contrast, Novell has specified, in concert with Apple, its own Open Data Link Interface (ODLI) to handle the chores of getting information off the physical link and to the upper protocol layers. They have made the ODLI public so that third-party developers can easily write code to interface at that level, but it is still a proprietary development. At least one impetus for this approach must have been the fact that Novell arguably supports many more NICs (about 90, including those supported by the others discussed in this chapter) than any other NOS manufacturer. The by-product of this is that if a manufacturer of NICs wants them to be compatible with Novell, that manufacturer need only write a software driver to the ODLI specifications and it becomes NetWare compatible. This approach should also make it easier for Novell (and others) to produce Novell compatible bridges and gateways allowing the interconnection of LANs with differing technologies to be integrated into a network that appears as a single, large LAN.

Communications between the transport layer and applications are handled in NetWare/386 through the use of "NetWare Streams." While in a "pure" NetWare environment not all the various IPCs and Client/Server protocols noted in Figure 5.9 are required, they are available for NetWare compatibility with software and workstations designed essentially for other systems. In particular, the support of AFP, SMB, NCP, and NFS allow Macintosh Workstations, OS/2 EE with LAN Requester, NetWare Clients, and Unix NFS Workstations to all be part of a single NetWare/386 LAN. While it is true that emulation of all these protocols will require considerable effort on the part of Novell to stay abreast of changes as they occur, it is also true that support for these protocols provides Novell a high degree of flexibility extending beyond some of the other NOSs described in this chapter.

Access to other networks from a Novell LAN are often supported through the use of gateways—technologies usually supported on independent communications servers. The proliferation of servers on a Novell LAN is a by-product of the single-purpose nature of Novell's proprietary NOS which, unlike the Unix-based system of Banyan or the OS/2 based systems of IBM and 3COM, can accommodate multiple concurrent tasks running in the main file server. At this writing, however, it was unclear as to how well such additional services will run under OS/2-based environments.

3COM 3+ OPEN

3COM's 3+ Open is a NOS based on the OS/2 LAN Manager developed by Microsoft. As such, 3+ Open is generically related to IBM's OS/2 LAN Server since LAN Manager is the core of IBM's product. To a far greater extent than Banyan or Novell, 3COM seems to be resting its strategy for the 1990s squarely on IBM compatibility. 3COM is clearly betting on the prospect that IBM will catch up with and surpass Novell in the highly competitive marketplace. Like IBM 3COM has restructured its operating system platform to rest squarely on OS/2. This has all the advantages and disadvantages previously noted. There are two versions of 3+ Open: LAN Manager Advanced System and LAN Manager Entry System. For comparative purpose we will confine our analysis to LAN Manager Advanced System.[14]

Unlike Banyan which already has implemented a distributed directory service, and Novell, which has announced its intention to provide a distributed directory service, 3COM provides directory services for an enterprise-wide network through a Network Control Server (NCS). In a distributed network linked by bridges and gateways the NCS is a required addition necessary for network management. The difference between 3COM's approach on the one hand and that of Banyan and Novell on the other hand, is that the NCS provides a single point of failure for the network. If the NCS goes down, the extended network is down. With distributed directory services, however, the directory is distributed across all servers on the network, thus ensuring that no single point of failure exists (at least for this function).

In Figure 5.10 an effort has been made to depict the 3+ Open network architecture. Like both Banyan and Novell an objective of 3COM is to support TCP/IP, OSI protocols, IBM protocols (such as APPC and through gateways, other SNA networking), as well as aggressive support for the Apple Macintosh. Except for the Apple support, all others require the use of either NETBIOS or NETBEUI. A comparison of Figures 5.10 and 5.7 will reveal that 3COM's support of IBM LAN structures differs from that of IBM, particularly in the requirement for the use of NETBEUI and NETBIOS. This dependence on NETBIOS may prove to be a problem in the future. Although NETBIOS is widely used in PC-based LANs, it is unclear that it forms a part of IBM's long-term strategy regarding LANs and the only reason it has been widely used was that it originated with IBM. In other words, it is not a standard. With the IBM LANs NETBIOS can be wholly replaced with APPC which is clearly the strategic product for IBM. Because NETBIOS is not a standard, it can be changed or extended at will by IBM and this was done when NETBEUI was issued. The "standard" NETBIOS, therefore, is the one originally designed for the original PC Network.

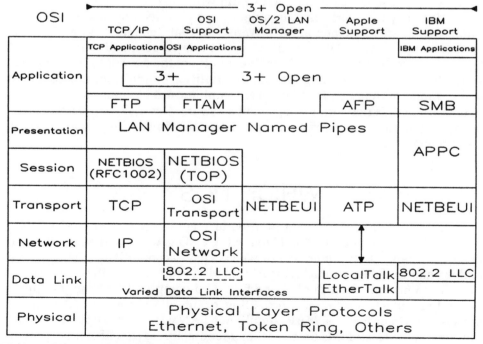

Figure 5.10   3+ Open Network Architecture

On the other hand, this dependence on NETBIOS is a characteristic of Microsoft's implementation of LAN Manager and is not unique to 3COM. Consequently, as more vendors come to support LAN Manager it may be that NETBIOS will take on a life of its own, even more so than is the case today.

At the Data Link Layer the protocols used by 3COM seem less well defined than is true of Banyan, IBM, or Novell. Banyan and IBM seem headed toward the support of the IEEE LLC and MAC sublayers which are OSI compliant. Novell, as we have noted, has developed its own consistent Open Data-Link Interface specification. In contrast, 3COM uses a variety of data link interfaces and seems somewhat unclear about its future use of the 802.2 LLC. X.25 is supported through the use of a gateway and in this respect 3COM has a strategy much more similar to Novell than to either Banyan or IBM. IBM's support of X.25, by the way, is through its front end processors (FEPs) on its mainframes rather than through its LANs.

3COM's IBM consistency strategy is interesting in that it may prove to be both a benefit and a drawback. In some respects IBM and Novell are not direct competitors although in specific situations they may become so. On the other hand, by becoming so IBM compatible, 3COM may place itself in the situation in which it is always in competition with IBM, particularly in large IBM mainframe environments. On the whole it is likely that in such a competitive situation it would lose more often than it would win. This aggressive policy of IBM emulation may be clearly seen in a document produced by 3COM which explicitly compares 3+ Open and NetWare.[15] In that document, in a feature by feature comparison, 3COM submits five IBM-related points illustrating that 3+ Open is better than NetWare. These five points are the only ones listed under a subsection entitled "Multivendor Compatibility." In addition, the document makes much of the need for IBM SAA compliance. As a final point we might note that 3COM's network management software, NetMAP, and its NCS, have been structured to be consistent with IBM's NetView, a large-scale network management facility.

WHICH NOS?

Since this book is not designed to provide specific product advice, no judgment will be made as to the "best" of the LAN NOSs we have discussed. I will, however, attempt to summarize how well we have accomplished the objectives of this chapter. The Manufacturing Automation Protocol (MAP) was presented in order to provide a sense of how a fully OSI compliant LAN might appear. Several manufacturers are now providing, or intend to provide, MAP compliant systems. In order to be MAP compliant a LAN will have to operate through the specific OSI standards listed earlier. Manufacturers can, of course, provide additional value-added services, but they must include the minimum MAP protocol stack in order to be MAP compliant. A more generalized LAN could also be structured using OSI standards and, in the long run, this is probably the direction that LAN manufacturers should go. Within the OSI framework there is still considerable latitude for adding value-added services and features, but if all or most LAN manufacturers became OSI compliant, interoperability would become a more complete reality.

An attempt has been made in Table 5.2 to compare Banyan, IBM, Novell, and 3COM LANs on several features that are of particular importance to the connectivity issues discussed in this book. A close inspection of that table will reveal that the features offered by Banyan, Novell, and 3COM, while distributed somewhat differently, are very competitive although Banyan and Novell seem to have a few features beyond those offered by 3COM. But the three are very similar and as they compete more aggressively with one another will continue to converge in the features they offer. It is clear, however, that the number of features offered by IBM are not as extensive. In fact, with one way of counting the features listed, IBM offers only about half as many as the others. That this difference in the number of features exists between IBM and the others is not accidental, nor can it be dismissed as a misperception of the market by IBM.

IBM, since its introduction of the PC in 1981, has had an enormous impact on the microcomputer market, and by extension, on the LAN market. IBM's strategy in support of LANs, and especially its development of the OS/2 LAN Server (as well as OS/2 itself), is not structured so much around grabbing all it can from Novell or others so much as it is designed to support IBM's overall networking strategy in the context of SNA. Whatever else IBM is or will become, it is still a manufacturer oriented toward the large mainframe market. SNA was developed to support that market. Many of the features listed in Table 5.2 do not appear in IBM's LAN NOS for the simple reason that those functions are supported elsewhere in the global SNA framework. Since Novell was certainly the industry leader at the end of the 1980s they are the target for any other vendor of LANs. It is probably true, however, that IBM is not overwhelmingly interested in many of the installations in which NetWare is found, although they would certainly sell LANs to anyone who "came over the transom." It is in IBM mainframe and minicomputer (AS400) shops, however, where IBM will be very aggressive competitors of Novell. Since IBM also offers (or will offer) a MAP compliant network, they may also be able to insert their other LAN offerings in environments that would, under other circumstances, have gone to other vendors.

In a very real sense, however, IBM seems to be limiting its potential growth as a LAN vendor. This is best illustrated by the fact that unlike most of its other PC-based software, the OS/2 LAN Server *requires* IBM's proprietary version of OS/2 Extended Edition. And in order to run, OS/2 Extended Edition requires the use of an IBM PS/2 as a hardware platform. If this proves to be the case, it

Table 5.2   NOS Comparisons

Feature	Banyan VINES	IBM LAN Serv.	Novel NetWr/386	3COM 3+ Open
Server Oper. System	Unix	OS/2 EE.	Prop.	OS/2
NOS[a]	VINES 4.x	LAN Serv.	NetW./386	LAN Mgr.
User Oper. System	MS DOS, OS/2, MacIntosh, Unix	PC DOS, OS/2	MS DOS, OS/2, MacIntosh	MS DOS, OS/2, MacIntosh
Server CPU	80386, 68000	80286, 80386	80386, Others	80286, 80386
Dedicated Server[b]	Yes	Either	Yes	Either
Distributed Directory Service (X.500)	Yes	No	Yes	Partial
NETBIOS/NETBEUI Sup.	Yes	Yes	Yes	Yes
Links to OS/2	Yes	Yes	Yes	Yes
Links to MacIntosh	Yes	No	Yes	Yes
Share PC Printers	Yes	No	No	No
Dial-Access Login	Yes	No	Yes	Yes
Security[c]	7	2	4	4
Performance[d]	4	2	4	4
Comprehensive OSI Strategy	Yes	No	No	No
TPC/IP Support	Yes	No	Yes	Yes
Fault Tolerance	No	No	Yes	No
Connections per File Server[e]	No Limit	254	250	254
Mainframe Connect.	DEC, IBM	IBM, ?[f]	DEC, IBM	DEC, IBM
SQL Database Appl.	Yes	Yes	Yes	Yes

[a] Only the NOSs that point the strategic directions of the companies are listed.

[b] The issue of whether or not a server can also be used as a workstation is somewhat misleading. In any LAN it is dangerous and inappropriate to try to use the file server as a workstation regardless of whether the NOS allows such use.

[c] Based on a count of how many security features out of a total of seven were supported at this writing as listed in Robert Lauriston, "Seven Top LANs," *PC World*, Vol. 7, No. 6., June 1989, p. 90.

[d] Based on summaries of performance tests conducted by National Software testing Laboratories and reported in Lauriston, in footnote c and in Reference 19(a), pp. 91–96. 4 = Excellent; 3 = Good; 2 = Fair; 1 = Poor.

[e] The actual connections per file server is a function of how the file server is to be used. If it will be used for frequent accesses to a database by a large number of users, performance may dictate as few as 15 or 20 maximum users, for example.

[f] ? denotes potentially possible.

could also pose problems for vendors, such as 3COM, who have opted for a very aggressive strategy of IBM compatibility since their primary competitor then becomes IBM rather than Novell. In the IBM-compatible marketplace, whether for mainframes, PCs, or LANs, there is only one reason to buy non-IBM equipment and software: price and value-added services. If, in all other ways, the product looks like an IBM product and works like an IBM product, then the issue resolves itself to price providing that the consumer does not need any other value-added service offered by the competitor.

In the context of national and international networking trends, it appears that Banyan has the most aggressive strategy for OSI compliance and others have commented that Banyan already offers the most extensive TCP/IP support.[16] While this issue is already very important in the context of U.S. Federal Government and University LAN acquisitions, it will become even more important during the 1990s. Moreover, because of the increasingly rapid movement toward economic union in western Europe—a primary motivation for the standards movement—any LAN vendor that has an aggressive OSI compliant strategy will likely do well in European sales. IBM seems to be moving more rapidly in these directions than either Novell or 3COM.

Part of the problem faced by Banyan, Novell, 3COM and others, but not by IBM, is that they must try to integrate a great many different technologies through their NOS software. IBM doesn't have to do it because of its own more narrow strategic interests in supporting its own networking architecture. These issues are illustrated "drivers" used by the several manufacturers to access Network Interface Cards. IBM has clearly opted for the use of IEEE 802 MAC and LLC specifications as the means for communicating between network hardware and upper protocol layers. Even when using NICs that are proprietary it is possible for a manufacturer to provide a MAC that operates with a standard LLC and this is essentially the approach used by IBM to handle its PC Network cards. IBM's Token Ring and its support of 802.3 (Ethernet) is accomplished within the 802 standards. It would appear that this is the general direction being taken by Banyan, as well. This approach makes eminent sense since when LLC delivers data to upper layers of a protocol stack, the interface is well defined and can be used even if the upper layers are not OSI compliant. It has the distinct advantage of placing these LANs in the mainstream of the standards movement.

The alternative is to adopt one or the other of the specifications developed by Microsoft and Novell/Apple.[17] Microsoft first published its Network Driver Interface (NDI) specification in 1988 while Novell/Apple unveiled a similar specification, the Open Data-Link Interface, in 1989. The ODLI was described earlier in this chapter and I assume that 3COM will adopt the Microsoft specification since it was structured to perform well within the context of LAN Manager. Both specifications deliver data to the upper layer protocols and are supposed to be independent of those protocols, thus allowing upper layers to consist of varying protocol stacks. Because LAN Manager is being adopted by a number of LAN vendors, illustrated by 3COM's 3+ Open, and because of the market penetration by Novell, manufacturers of NICs are likely to write drivers to both these specifications. In point of fact, NDI probably rests on top of the 802 MAC sublayer, substituting for LLC. I say this because NDI has been optimized for use with 802.3 and 802.5. An ARCnet vendor, for example, could use NDI but would, according to Petrosky, "have to make the data frames from the ARCnet card look like 802.3 or 802.5 frames."[18] This is unlikely to take place, of course, since ARCnet already has its own frame structure and which would have to be encapsulated in something else. For a discussion of the 802.3 and 802.5 frames, see Chapters 7 and 9, respectively. Notwithstanding this discussion of NDI and ODLI, we might seriously ask, Why not simply use an 802 MAC or one that emulates an 802 MAC along with 802.2 LLC rather than some new set of protocols or specifications?

In completing this discussion of NOSs it is perhaps appropriate to make a brief comment on the performance of the various systems discussed. On independent tests of relative performance, Novell typically does best, followed by Banyan, followed by 3COM, with LAN Server frequently last not only in fields of four but also in fields of more.[19] These tests were made on the vendors' newer, higher-performance systems. As indicated in Table 5.2, however, summary estimates of performance would normally suggest that Banyan, Novell, and 3COM products all do very well and are competitive with one another. In comparison, IBM's products do not perform nearly as well. Part of the reason for this difference is probably the point made earlier: IBM has structured its LANs to work within the framework of SNA in connection with its own mainframes and minicomputers. In that environment the performance of the LAN with respect to its own file server has considerably less importance. Moreover, IBM has historically tended to correct performance problems of its software by producing new hardware rather than by directly optimizing (beyond a minimum level) the software. In the more competitive LAN market, however, IBM may be pushed to improve the performance of its LAN software in order to maintain a competitive advantage.

IBM's general position is that 802.3 (Ethernet) will reach the end of its product cycle as a large-scale network technology sometime in the 1990s. Even though most LAN technologies are fast by modem standards, with increasing demands for bandwidth as a by-product of the increasing use of image processing and other related user needs, most extant LANs are too slow to handle the volume of traffic we can expect in the near future. Consequently, both 802.3 and 802.5 (Token Ring, even at 16 Mb/s) will be replaced by faster systems in 100 Mb/s and faster range. Candidates for the faster LANs are FDDI, 802.6 systems, and perhaps very high speed ISDN services now being developed. It is probably true that by 1995 a LAN running less than 100 Mb/s will be considered slow. In this faster LAN environment it is likely that those NOSs that have been engineered to make maximum use of international standard protocol stacks will have an advantage over those that are tied to proprietary schemes. This is probably true because those faster LANs will be structured in the context of the international standards movement.

The standards issue will affect third-party manufacturers of network application software, as well. From the discussions of this chapter it is clear that NETBIOS is heavily relied upon to provide the connection between the Data Link layer and the very highest layers in LAN NOSs. Elsewhere[20] we have noted suggestions for linking NETBIOS to TCP/IP. In order to do that the developers of the recommendations suggested that the "standard" version of NETBIOS had to be the original version written for IBM's PC Network (broadband). Earlier in this chapter we noted, however, that several enhancements have been made to NETBIOS by IBM. The point is that NETBIOS is *not* a standard and IBM can change it at will. This is an example of an "open" (that is, publicly documented) procedure, but one that is subject to change at the will or whim of its owner. The reliance of manufacturers on privately owned, nonstandard definitions for network access may impede movement to newer technologies in the 1990s.

Can LAN NOSs provide a common user interface (CUI) to a wide range of networking and connectivity? The answer given by Banyan, Novell, and 3COM to this question would surely be "yes." While not all the elements of the products described in this chapter were available at this writing, it was clear that the directions were set. In IBM's case it is not their objective to make the LAN the primary centerpiece of their networking systems. Certainly the LANs described in this chapter, as well as others on the market, are potentially capable of integrating enterprise-wide networks into a single, more-or-less consistent distributed network.

REFERENCES

1. The study was conducted by the Business Research Group and reported in *ComputerWorld*, Vol. 23, No. 7, February 20, 1989, p. 114. The percentages reported by *ComputerWorld* are different than those reported in Figure 5.1(a). Because the multiple-choice question allowed respondents to make more than one choice, the percentages reported by *ComputerWorld* represented the percentage of responses based on the number of respondents (100). I recalculated the percentages based on the number of installed LANs (106) because, in my view, the number of LANs was more germane than the number of companies interviewed.

2. In contrast to the methodology represented in Figure 5.1(a), the data in Figure 5.1(b) are based on interviews with about 2,500 users at medium

and large U.S. Business sites by Computer Intelligence and reported by *ComputerWorld*, Vol. 23, No. 6, February 13, 1989, p. 59. The base for the percentages is the number of sites represented by the 2,500 respondents when asked what LAN operating systems their company was anticipating buying.

3. Note the discussion in Dennis Linnell, "The OS/2 Puzzle Takes Shape," *PC Tech Journal*, Vol. 7, No. 2, February 1989, p. 48.

4. W. David Schwaderer, *C Programmer's Guide to NETBIOS* (Indianapolis, in: Howard W. Sams & Company, 1988), p. 8.

5. NETBIOS Working Group, Internet RFC 1001 (March, 1987), p. 14. See also, RFC 1002 (March 1987).

6. For a recent and easily available treatment of NETBIOS, see Brett Glass, "Understanding NETBIOS," *Byte*, Vol. 14, No. 1, January 1989, pp. 301–306.

7. Unless otherwise noted, detailed information regarding MAP 3.0 is taken from *General Motors Manufacturing Automation Protocol: A Communications Network Protocol for Open System Interconnection*, Version 3.0 (Warren, MI: General Motors, 1987), Vols. 1 and 2.

8. Review articles on VINES have been consistently positive. See, for example, the following: Jane Morrissey, "Users Cite Improved Security, Performance in Latest VINES," *PC Week*, Vol. 5, No. 17, April 26, 1988; Winn L. Rosch, "Two Routes Lead to Operating System Goal," *PC Week*, Vol. 5, No. 32, August 8, 1988; Chet Schuyler, "VINES Tools Give Banyan a Unix Advantage in Server-Based Apps," *PC Week*, April 24, 1989; and William Wong, "Banyan's VINES 3.0," *LAN Technology*, February 1989.

9. For a more detailed explanation of MAP, see Thomas W. Madron, *LANS: Applications of IEEE/ANSI 802 Standards* (New York: John Wiley & Sons, 1989), Chapter 9. For naming services, see especially, pp. 212–214.

10. For a reasonably complete discussion of TCP/IP see Madron, Ibid., Chapter 10.

11. During 1989 a number of articles started appearing describing aspects of the OS/2 LAN Server. Note the following: Frank J. Derfler, "IBM LAN Manager Implementation: IBM Frills, for IBM Equipment Only," *PC Magazine*, Vol. 8, No. 5, March 14, 1989, pp. 33ff; Dennis Linnell, "The OS/2 Puzzle Takes Shape," *PC Tech Journal*, Vol. 7, No. 2, February 1989, pp. 44ff; Ken Thurber, "OS/2 Hits the Networks," *Byte*, Vol. 14, No. 1, January 1989, pp. 285ff. Note also the related article by Dennis Linnell, "Cooperative Communications," *PC Tech Journal*, Vol. 7, No. 2, February 1989, pp. 52ff, which describes the OS/2 communications manager. While LAN

Manager and LAN Server are, in principle, interoperable, some problems hae been identified. See, for example, Ed Dowgiallo, "Can We Talk?" *LAN Technology*, Vol. 5, No. 9, September 1989, pp. 46ff.

12. *NetWare Open Systems Technical Overview* (Provo, UT: Novell, Inc., 1989), p. 1.

13. A report in the October 16, 1989, issue of *PC Week*, p. 5, indicated that in tests commissioned by that publication, VINES 4.0 outperformed Netware.

14. For an early review of 3COM's system, see Frank J. Derfler, Jr., "3COM's 3+ Open LAN Manager," *PC Magazine*, Vol. 8, No. 4, February 28, 1989, pp. 177–180.

15. *3+ Open and NetWare: Product Comparison* (Santa Clara, CA: 3COM Corporation, 1988).

16. Scott Sharkey, Gregory A. Pruden, Gregory S. Boyd, and Ira S. Hertzoff, "TCP/IP Provides Passage to Foreign LANs," *LAN Technology*, Vol. 5, No. 4, April 1989, pp. 23–28.

17. M. Petrosky, "Driver Specifications Open the Door to Running Concurrent Protocols," *LAN Technology*, Vol. 5, No. 4, April 1989, pp. 44–45.

18. Ibid., p. 45.

19. See, for example, (a) Robert Lauriston, "Seven Top LANs: A Hard Look at Ease of Use," *PC World*, Vol. 7, No. 6, June 1989, pp. 88ff; see especially, the summary performance test results on p. 92. See also, (b) Steve Apiki, Stanford Diehl, and Rick Grehan, "Battle of the Network Stars," *Byte*, Vol. 14, No. 7, July 1989, pp. 154ff, especially pp. 168 and 169. These tests, while not identical, generally confirm one another although Apiki, Diehl, and Grehan did not test Banyan's VINES.

20. See particulary the discussion of the Internet recommendations, RFC1001 and RFC1002, for linking NETBIOS to TCP/IP in Thomas W. Madron, *LANS: Applications of IEEE/ANSI 802 Standards* (New York: John Wiley & Sons, 1989), Chapter 10.

DESIGNING A MICROCOMPUTER-BASED LOCAL AREA NETWORK

Y ou are responsible for "designing" your LAN. I don't mean that you, personally, must design your LAN in the most basic technological sense, but I do mean that you are responsible for the logical design of the system. In classical data-processing terms, you are responsible for doing the systems analysis that will result in a clear statement of your intended objectives for your use of the LAN. Unfortunately, even some information processing professionals fail to recognize this need. Once stated, those objectives can be turned into a set of hardware and software specifications which will allow you to actually bid or buy a LAN. Cost, of course, will likely be a factor in your purchasing decision, but it is often difficult to get a firm grasp in this area. In this chapter we will focus on some of the issues that affect the design and implementation of a local area network.

DEFINING THE OBJECTIVES FOR THE LAN

In Chapter 1 some of the general reasons for acquiring a LAN were presented. There we identified at least three reasons why some people want LANs: the desire for independence in computing, the need for departmental computing, and the need for connectivity, both intra-departmental connectivity and inter-departmental connectivity. Later we also identified the growing need for office automation as another primary reason for LANs. Before we proceed further, however, we need to make more explicit the planning issues involved in determining what kind of LAN we will need.

In practice, at the beginning of a LAN project, design criteria are (or will become) a combination of organizational and technical issues. There are no set design criteria, and new criteria should be assembled for each project. A list of criteria is important, however, to ensure that a network vendor can meet or exceed the requirements. Perhaps the term "design criteria" is too formal and austere although the concerns that follow are likely to be important in many situations.[1]

Organizational Objectives

A realistic analysis should always begin with your known needs. It is a truism, however, that once you install a LAN you will think of things to do with it far beyond what you initially intended. On the other hand, there are probably some things you *must* accomplish with the LAN, and those things should be the basis of your list of organizational objectives. You will, in fact, wish to answer some of the more explicit questions asked in this section.

What Do You Want to Accomplish?

What kind of a system is implied by what you wish to accomplish? For example, traditional office automation applications imply different needs than a LAN used for process control in a laboratory or on a production line. Process control typically requires a deterministic rather than a probabilistic system. To bring that into specific focus, an IEEE 802.5 Token Ring is a deterministic system, while an 802.3 Ethernet—because it uses CSMA/CD as an access method (see Chapter 7)—is a probabilistic system. This example is an obvious one, but others may be implied by other aspects of your needs and objectives.

Expansion

Can the system meet future expansion requirements and, if so, until when? The issue of expansion has several components. How easy and economical is it to extend the cable to locations not wired initially? How large can the LAN—in terms of number of connections, number of concurrent users, and length of cable—grow? Am I dependent on a single vendor to supply compatible hardware? The last question is of some importance in that if a decision is made to acquire a system from a small manufacturer, you do not want to replace the entire LAN if that manufacturer ceases production.

Security

How much security is required? "None" is most likely the wrong answer. While it is true that you may not need heavy security, just to protect the users of your system from mistakes of others, you will need some security. Typical file and server access is through user IDs and passwords. In most offices this approach is probably sufficient. If, however, the data you are acquiring and keeping are at all sensitive, then you may need to use encryption techniques for the files on your file server or even an encryption method that will prevent, or slow down, unauthorized access to your cabling system. If the reasons you are installing a LAN are at all important to you and your organization, then some attention to security features is required, and if your data is important, then you will need to give consideration to security issues. It is also necessary to be aware, however, that security decisions are usually a compromise between the cost of security, including increasing the complexity of the use of the system, and ensuring that the integrity of the data is maintained.

Existing Resources

One issue that is sometimes missed when planning a LAN is whether resources are already available that would make the installation easier or less costly. In fact, one of IBM's marketing techniques for its Token Ring Network is to suggest that existing twisted pair (telephone) wiring might be used instead of having to rewire with coaxial cable or something else. AT&T salespeople, too, in selling StarLan suggest the same thing. I have noted elsewhere that the ability to use existing twisted pair wiring may be more fiction than fact.[2] There are a number of reasons why this may be the case. First, the ownership of the wiring may be in doubt. Second, old telephone wire is usually so poorly documented that it is cheaper to rewire than to follow and rework the wiring. Third, as Kathy Chin, writing in *Communication Week,* has pointed out, most of the wiring is unshielded, which means that it may not be able to support a LAN at all, or it may be able to support only a very small LAN.[3] Fourth, whatever twisted pair may be available, it may not be in sufficiently good condition to use.

If your organization has an existing cable television system, a happier solution might be to use a broadband LAN that runs on standard CATV. If the cable is a two-way video system, you may be on the road with very little additional wiring expense. If it is a one-way cable system, it may be possible to be re-engineered in a cost-effective manner. LANs that use broadband are manufactured or marketed by several companies, including IBM, Ungermann-Bass, Allen-Bradley, TRW, and Sytek, Inc. With all of these systems, it is possible to put together small, self-contained LANs, or to use an existing general purpose two-way CATV system. Sytek, Allen-Bradley, and Ungermann-Bass, among others, also sell high-quality commercial-grade components (such as frequency translators) to support large configurations on standard CATV. Sytek and IBM also sell small system components that cannot be used on a general broadband system. Other manufacturers, such as LanTel, also produce commercial grade components for IBM/Sytek broadband networks.

Some organizations, of course, will already have rigid LAN standards that a department may be required to conform to. Even in the most bureaucratized of companies, however, people discover methods for avoiding conformity rules. Nevertheless, if one or more LAN technologies are already supported, even if your organization has no rigid standards, it may be wise to take advantage of whatever support is available. That may range from assistance in configuring a system to full management of the LAN. This can save an individual department an enormous amount of time, effort, and, possibly, money. A related possibility is that even in the absence of organizational standards, other departments may have already faced the decisions you are facing, or your department may wish to have a bridge between your LAN and another departmental LAN. In either event, you may be able to capitalize on the experience of other departments or, in the case of needing a bridge, you may wish to conform to what another department has already done in order to minimize the cost of inter-LAN communications. You may also be able to rely on the other department for support and advice.

Connectivity

Connectivity in a LAN is the ability of any device attached to the distribution system to establish a session with any other device. Connectivity is an exceedingly important concept in the design of local area networks. Among the questions that should be asked when designing a LAN are: How many devices do you plan to connect in both the short and long term? How many different devices can be connected? Can devices from various vendors be connected? Are bridges and gateways to other similar LANs and/or other networks available at reasonable cost? With a microcomputer-based LAN, the first level of connectivity is with other people and workstations in your own department or office. The second level might be with other similar LANs, and the third level with LANs of other technologies or with a mainframe system. Some of the ways connectivity can be achieved have been reviewed in Chapter 5.

Reliability

A typical LAN has several components: cabling, network interface cards, which are placed within the various devices on the network, and one or more devices used as servers. In a micro-based LAN, all the devices are likely to be personal computers of one kind or another. In a more general-purpose LAN, the devices may be minicomputers, micros, or special purpose devices. The issue at hand is, how reliable the system is. No LAN will be 100 percent reliable, but it can be structured—for a price—to be more or less so. The cabling system itself will likely be the most reliable part of a LAN. In a broadband system, for example, with both passive and active devices, the passive devices have mean time between failures (MTBF) of 30 years or more. The active devices (amplifiers) have lengthy MTBFs. In an Ethernet, where most devices on the cable are passive (transceivers), the MTBFs will be high.

The workstations and servers are another matter. The only way to ensure an effective availability of near 100 percent is to use redundant devices. For workstations, that is not usually considered necessary, although it might be useful to maintain a spare system for those periods when a workstation needs maintenance. The servers, however, can be single points of failure in a LAN, and other precautions may be desirable. One possibility is a system of fault tolerant operation for the file-serving function. A fault tolerant architecture typically requires a fully redundant device that contains a completely redundant database. When updates are made to one copy of the database, they are also made to the second copy as well. One database is always an exact image of the other. Consequently, since the system functions with only a single database, either file server can be out at any one time and all operations can continue. This ensures that you will no longer have a single point of failure in the file server. Not all LAN software supports fault tolerance, although Novell's Netware now does. Obviously the cost of the file server(s) doubles if fault tolerance is required. We should hasten to add, however, that most LANs do not, in practice, require such an absolute level of reliability. The point I am trying to make is that if the cost of downtime is sufficiently high, then redundancy is an appropriate approach to the insurance of operation.

The last item to be considered as a reliability issue, although it is one over which the buyer has the least control, is, how reliable is the data transfer system—is it proprietary or does it conform to published standards? Such standards as those of the IEEE 802 Committee define the methods for ensuring that data get from one point to another on the LAN reliably. Data are typically organized into packets. Part of the packet is some form of checksum calculated on the remainder of the packet. When a packet is received, the checksum is recalculated. If there is a difference, then a retransmission of the packet is requested. We will discuss this issue at greater length in subsequent chapters. Suffice to say that the techniques used in standard LANs do the task well. It is also probably safe to say that proprietary systems also generally do a good job.

Performance

Certainly one of the issues which the designer should be concerned with is the performance of the LAN. Unfortunately there is little hard evidence that can be adduced that would categorically demonstrate that one technology—in a live situation—can actually outperform another. There are laboratory tests that can demonstrate categorically the fastest system, but actual performance in a production system is a byproduct of how it is being used. Moreover, for most contemporary LAN technologies, performance is limited more by the speed of the hard disks on the file server and similar performance characteristics than by the speed of data transfer on the cable.

Part of the answer to issues of performance also relates to the practical matter of how the LAN must be used. Different technologies have different strengths and weaknesses. For example, the performance of a bus-structured CSMA/CD LAN is largely independent of the total number of devices attached to it, while a token ring architecture can degrade simply as a by-product of the number of attached devices. Conversely, with a token ring performance is relatively constant regardless of whether two or many of the nodes are concurrently active, while a CSMA/CD system will degrade as the number of concurrent users increases. If you are designing a LAN for a large number of occasional users, the case can therefore be made for a CSMA/CD system. Alternatively, if you are designing a small- to moderate-sized LAN for a lot of intensive users, then a token ring will likely perform better. It is possible to argue that for small systems with moderate use—and I'm purposely not defining these quantities at this point—almost any of the common LAN technologies will perform satisfactorily. An important question to answer is, therefore, how many concurrent users can be using the system vs. how many total devices can be connected to the system, still providing good response times?

Other Features and Facilities

Because many LAN technologies are capable of being used either for multiple independent LANs or for purposes beyond the traditional scope of data communications, some organizations will find it useful to consider other uses of the wiring system when planning a LAN. Perhaps the best example is the single cable broadband system since it also allows the use of standard video to coexist with data transmission. In other words, should the system be able to carry information other than data (video, voice, and so forth), and if so, what? If a fairly large system is being designed, spread across a very large building or several buildings of an industrial complex or university campus, then broadband may be the best choice. A related question is: Can the system support a variety of computer hardware and software vendors and products? As we have already noted, it is advantageous to be able to buy equipment and software from multiple vendors for the support of your LAN. Some technologies have large numbers of vendors, while others do not, although conditions are changing frequently. A number of manufacturers produce Ethernet hardware products that can be mixed on the same network. There are many components of a broadband system that can be acquired from various manufacturers. Conversely, token ring networks, at this writing, were not widely supported, although this is probably changing even as you read this book.

LANs that *integrate* video, voice, and data communications are being developed at this very moment, and several are in various stages of development or testing.[4] These systems are called Integrated Local Area Networks (ILANs). Unfortunately, these technologies were not, at this writing, commercially available, and probably will not be until sometime in the 1990s. Broadband systems, using standard cable television technology (CATV), come closest to providing such integration at reasonable prices in the current marketplace. A two-way CATV system can support both data and full motion video today as well as limited voice communications at reasonable cost. Various digital techniques for encoding video, voice, and data are being developed that will use fiber-optic backbones for integrated services.

Cost

It is impractical to publish relative costs and expenses in establishing a LAN. There are several reasons why this is true. Pricing is *very* volatile and is, in general, declining; pricing tends to be subject to negotiation—no one pays list prices; costs are closely related to use objectives; and costs tend to be closely related to installation specific problems and opportunities. The only way to get precisely comparative costs is to have alternative systems completely engineered for a particular installation so that you will have all the data necessary for full cost analysis. It goes almost without saying that this involves data which are sometimes difficult to obtain. There are, however, some items that should be remembered when trying to cost out systems, and this section deals with those issues.

Wiring Installation and Maintenance

Of interest to everyone is, how much does it cost? Yet nowhere is there more incomplete and inadequate information than in the cost analysis of LANs. One commonly heard contention, even though it lacks a large measure of reality, is that systems based on twisted pair copper wire are less expensive than those based on coaxial cable. For small micro-based LANs located in a single office, wiring costs are not likely to be of great importance, regardless of what is chosen. For large systems, however, the cost of installation and maintenance can become a major concern. One of the major problems of large systems is that various sizes of the same family of wire may have to be used for trunklines, building wiring, and drop cables, and they may all have different installation implications as well as basic costs per foot. Installation costs will also vary depending on building design and architecture. The size of the system will also determine whether devices, like amplifiers, line extenders, external transceivers, repeaters, or other devices, are necessary; and because these devices must be considered part of the cost of "wiring" the system, the cost of wiring tends to be very installation specific.

There is one issue I would like to lay to rest—at least temporarily. Salespersons for various vendors will claim that one form of wiring is less expensive than another, and therefore better for wiring LANs. Nowhere is this more true than in the distinction between "twisted pair" copper wire and coaxial cable. Generally speaking, fiber-optic cable is the most expensive of the cable followed by shielded twisted-pair copper pair. The shielded twisted pair is what must be used in a quality LAN, even a small one, that uses twisted pair as its medium. RG 59 is coaxial cable used for CATV drop cable, RG 58 is thin-wire Ethernet cable, RG 62 is the coax used to connect 3x7x display stations in an IBM network with a 3274 cluster controller, and #24 twisted is standard telephone (two pair) wire. The three forms of coax listed are usually about the same price, while #24 twisted pair is the least expensive. Obviously if telephone wire could be used, that is the least expensive. For data communications, however, telephone wire should not be used except for the smallest LANs and even then external electrical interferences might cause problems.

Interface Devices

Interface devices are those items that allow a connection to be made to the wiring system or physical medium. Such devices may be boards that are placed inside a workstation or server, they may be standalone components that support workstations through standard serial communications, or they may be devices—such as Ethernet transceivers—that are required to physically connect an Ethernet board to the backbone. Transceivers may be integrated on the boards that are placed inside PCs, or they may be standalone devices. Ring-oriented systems typically require a "wiring center," where the ring is actually located in a single small cabinet with wiring stretching out in a star-like configuration from the wiring center. The average cost per workstation is the total of all devices needed to make a specific system operational divided by the number of devices to be supported.

Workstations and Servers

The workstations and servers on the network will, of course, be a major component in the cost considerations of a LAN, although it must be stressed that workstations may already be available as standalone units or doing terminal emulation into a mini or mainframe computer system. Consequently, you may not wish to include workstations as part of a LAN cost analysis. There is a large difference in cost between high performance super-micros, such as Sun Workstations, MicroVAXs, Apollo Workstations, and the like, and personal computer workstations. Moreover, the use of super-micro workstations will likely require higher performance servers than will a PC-based LAN. The amount of data to be processed will determine the amount of disk storage required on the file server and the kind and quantity of interconnectivity with other networks will determine the number and kind of communications servers. Some LANs will allow servers to be used concurrently as workstations, but that practice should be avoided. Remember that if a server is turned off, or rebooted, all transactions involving that server will be lost. Using a server concurrently as a workstation decreases the stability of the LAN. There are clear cost differentials comparing the use of an IBM PC/XT (or compatible), an IBM PC/AT (or compatible), or a super-micro (such as a MicroVAX) as servers, although part of the decision as to what kind of server to use must be based on performance as well as cost considerations.

Network Software

A set of devices and wiring is ultimately made into a usable network through the software that comprises the network operating environment. The cost of the software varies from vendor to vendor and is usually associated with the number and variety of servers, not the number of workstations. Some software is vendor specific, such as IBM's PC Local Area Network Program used for IBM's PC-based networks, while others, such as Novell's Netware, run on a wide variety of hardware capitalizing on wide variety networking standards, including Ethernet, broadband, Token Ring, and others. In an organization that may use more than one technology, a common user interface can successfully be established through the use of software like Novell's, thus simplifying user support. On the other hand, if standardization takes place with a single technology, the vendor's proprietary software might be most appropriate. It should be noted, however, that the network software affects performance, and different software may provide different features and facilities, especially in value-added features and ease of use. Depending on the way in which the software is priced, it is sometime difficult to equate costs. While Novell has a single charge per file server, others may charge by the workstation.

Expansion and Maintenance

What does it cost to expand and maintain the LAN? Expansion costs will likely be a function primarily of the media technology used and the extensiveness of the initial wiring of a backbone or other general-purpose wiring scheme. In addition to adding another node, there will be the requirement of an additional network interface device. Proper planning of the wiring system at the front end can minimize the hookup costs at the back end. A little savings at the beginning can often result in higher expenditures when expansion becomes necessary. Regardless of your current thinking, expansion will take place. In networking this is almost a law of nature.

Maintenance is even tougher to nail down. On a large network, maintenance costs are apt to run about the same as other high-technology equipment: 5 to 10 percent per year of the total value of the system. With small systems, however, where all the wiring is contained in a small, environmentally secure area, maintenance costs are apt to be very low. In a small system, the system manager may be able to do the maintenance to the physical medium by simply using spare parts and use depot or on-site maintenance for workstations and servers (with the possible use of spares). With a large system, however, it may be necessary to hire technicians to take care of the network or to write a maintenance contract with appropriate vendors. For a small system, proper sparing of components may be the most satisfactory approach, but with a large system some combination of sparing and maintenance contract or personnel may be required.

Management

Regardless of what LAN vendors may tell you, LANs must have some management, and even a small LAN must have someone designated as a LAN system manager. This means that some proportion of someone's time will be required to keep the system functional and up-to-date. With a small LAN this may be simply an add-on responsibility for someone already in the office. For a large LAN it may mean hiring additional personnel for that purpose. Some funds must be set aside for training the LAN system manager. The amount of time that individual must spend is then dependent on a number of factors, but must include the following:

▼ Assignment of user IDs and passwords

▼ Troubleshooting

▼ User training

▼ Software installation and maintenance

In a small office LAN, the person chosen for system manager need not necessarily be a highly technical person, but must be capable of being trained to understand each of the issues mentioned above. Without making provision for a system manager, the users are not likely to be satisfied with the system in the long run. In some larger organizations, systems management for many departmental LANs may be provided by a central organization, either with or without additional charges.

Economies of Scale

Not all of the cost analysis should be concerned with ongoing expenditures. There are some economies of scale that can be realized in the use of LANs that can result in cost savings, and these should be plugged into any cost analysis. Since you will probably be using a print serving function (usually associated with the file server), your department may be able to make do with far fewer printers than if all the PCs in the department were standalone units. Access costs to mainframes might also be reduced through the use of a common communications server or gateway. Users' time may be saved by not having to transport data by hand or by being able to communicate more immediately and effectively though electronic mail functions. In a specific office environment, there may be other cost savings as well, and these should be taken into consideration.

In any event, when values or answers can be given to each of these items, then you will have the specifications available to buy a LAN. You will also have thought through the enterprise in a sufficiently systematic fashion to ensure that you will use the system well, even at the beginning. A word of caution, however. It is possible to immobilize yourself by overdoing the analysis, since there are a large number of LAN vendors and competing marketing hypes. It is important to be able to cut off the analysis and make the purchase. If you are careful in defining your goals, you will find that several technologies will probably be able to meet them. You will also likely find a number of equally cost-effective solutions. In the end you must make a judgment based on your own informed preferences.

THE VARIETY OF LAN OPTIONS

One of the major impediments facing a potential LAN purchaser is the wide variety of hardware, media, and software technologies available. Table 6.1 lists more than 100 LAN suppliers and, as can be seen, a number of manufacturers have more than one LAN. Not all the LAN varieties of even single vendors are reported in Table 6.1. By the mid-1980s there were well over 100 LAN manufacturers.[5] By the early 1990s, although some vendors had failed, there were still about the same number of competitors. There is a major difference that has occurred since the mid-1980s, however. In 1987 when the first edition of this book was written, most LANs on the market used proprietary protocols. An inspection of Table 6.1 will easily reveal that today most LAN manufacturers have moved or are moving to the use and support of international standard protocols. Another major shift is the dramatic increase in the number of manufacturers offering fiber-optic-based products. Note that Table 6.1 is drawn from a number of sources and will undoubtedly be out of date by the time you read this. It was developed primarily to provide a perspective on the variety in the marketplace. The attempt has been made to classify LANs by topology, whether broadband or baseband, and access method.

The LAN topology issue is further confused when it is recognized that some systems, like IBM's Token Ring Network is a logical and electrical ring although it is usually wired in a Star configuration. The ring is contained in a small device called a Multiple Station Access Unit (8228) that supports up to eight devices. Larger LANs are constructed by daisy-chaining the 8228s. As a practical wiring matter, therefore, the Token Ring must be wired as a star topology or as multiple stars with eight devices per star. There are, in fact, several other LANs that pose similar problems, as well as those that are literally of a star topology, both physically and logically. The two most common methods of access management (how a device gets access to the medium) are token passing and carrier sense multiple access with collision detection (SCMA/CD). There are other techniques, but these are the most widely used. Token passing and CSMA/CD are both implemented in different parts of the IEEE 802 standards. Finally, there are a variety of networks for which gateways are commonly needed, and the need for each of these must be understood.

Hardware Technology

In most LANs, Layers 1 (Physical Link) and 2 (Data Link) are implemented to a large extent in hardware with whatever software is needed to operate at those levels available in ROM. For PC-based networks the typical configuration is a card that is inserted inside the microcomputer. In addition, circuitry is available for access to the computer's bus for the transfer of data from other components of the micro to the network. If a modem or transceiver is required, it is often implemented on the board as well. There is a card for token rings, for Ethernets, broadband systems, and so forth. Bridges and gateways are sometimes implemented by simply placing two LAN boards side-by-side in a PC running under a program that does protocol translation from one system to the other, including address translation. In addition to the board that is placed in each workstation and in each server, there is the wiring or physical medium over which the LAN operates. It may be necessary to have other components than simple wiring operating as part of the wiring system. Broadband systems will need a head-end translator and possibly one or more amplifiers. Ethernets will need transceivers and possibly repeaters. StarLans and IBM's Token Ring

Table 6.1 Local Area Networks Summary

Manufacturer	Product	Top. SRBT	Type BrBa	Acc CTO	Speed (Mb/s)	Max Len	802 Std
ADEVCO	LAN-ROVER	--*-	- *	*--	NA	.9	P
Allen-Bradley	Lan/I	--*-	* -	-*-	2.5	12.1	P
Allen-Bradley	Lan/III	--EW	* *	*--	10.0	16.1	3/7
Allen-Bradley	Lan/PC	--*-	* -	-*-	2.5	12.1	P/7
Allen-Bradley	VistaMAP	--*-	* -	-*-	10.0	NoLm	4/7
Altos	ENET	--*-	- *	*--	10.1	3.0	3
Altos Computers	WorkNet II	--*-	- *	--*	1.4	1.4	P
Apollo Computers	Other	-**-	- *	**-.	Std	Std	3/4/5
Apple	LocalTalk	--*-	- *	--*	.2	.3	P
Apple	EtherTalk	--*-	- *	*--	10.0	.5	3
Applitek	UniLAN	--EW	- *	*--.	10.0	32.2	3
Applitek	UniLAN	--EW	* -	*--	10.0	32.2	4/7
Artel	FiberWay	-*--	- *	-*-	100.0	NA	P
AST Research	AST-Ethernet	--*-	- *	*--	10.0	2.4	3
AST Research	AST-EtherNode	--*-	- *	*--	10.0	2.4	3
AT&T	StarLAN	W-E-	- *	*--	1.0	1.2	3
AT&T	StarLAN-10	W-E-	- *	*--	10.0	.1	3
Autocontrol	AC Soft/Net	--*-	- *	--*	1.0	4.3	P
Banyan	VINES	***-	* *	**-.	10.0	NoLm	3/4/5
Bell & Howell	Image Research	--*-	- *	*--	10.0	1.0	3
B-KOMP	The Net-Worker	---*	- *	-*-	2.5	81.2	P
Braegen	ELAN System	--*-	- *	--*	1.5	3.1	P
Charles River	UniverseNet	--*-	- *	*--	10.0	2.5	3
Chipcom	Ethermodem III	--*-	* *	*--	10.0	4.0	3
Codenoll Tech.	Codenet	*---	- *	*--	10.0	4.5	3
Complexx Systems	XLAN	--*-	- *	--*	1.0	2.5	P
Computer Auto.	SyFAnet	--*-	* -	--*	3.0	.9	P
Concord Data	Token/Net	--*-	* -	-*-	5.0	32.5	P
Contel Info Sys.	ContelNet	****	* *	**-.	<=100.0	4.0	+3/5/FDDI
Convergent Tech	Ethernet	--*-	- *	*--	10.0	.5	3
Convergent Tech	RS-422	*---	- *	*--	2.0	.5	P
Corvus	OmniNet/1/4	--*-	- *	--*	1/4.0	1.2	P
Data General	Xodiac	--*-	- *	-*-	2.0	1.6	P
Datapoint	ARCNet	--EW	- *	-*-	2.5	6.5	P
DEC	Ethernet	--*-	- *	*--	10.0	2.5	E/3
Digital Microsys	HiNet	--*-	- *	--*	.5	2.2	P
DSC Nestar Systems	PLAN Series	**E-	- *	***	4.0	10.0	3/4/5
Fox Research	10-Net	--*-	- *	--*	10.0	3.0	P
Excelan	Ethernet	--*-	- *	*--	10.0	2.5	3
FiberCom	WhisperNet	-*--	- *	*--	10.0	8.0	3
Fibronics	System Finex	-*--	- *	-*-	100.0	64.0	FDDI
Gateway Comm	G/NET	-**-	- *	**-	10.0	2.5	3/5/P
Gould	MODWAY	--*-	* *	-*-	1.5	4.6	P
Hewlett-Packard	OfficeShare	*-*-	* *	*--	10.0	2.5	3
Honeywell Bull	Net. Micro.	****	* *	**-	10.0	2.5	3/5

(Continued)

Table 6.1   (*Continued*)

Manufacturer	Product	Top. SRBT	Type BrBa	Acc CTO	Speed (Mb/s)	Max Len	802 Std
IBM	PC Network	--*-	* -	*--	2.0	.6#	P
IBM	PC Network	W-E-	- *	*--	1.0	.5	P
IBM	Token Ring	WE--	- *	-*-	4.0	NA	5
IBM	Token Ring	WE--	- *	-*-	16.0	NA	-
IDEAAssociates	IDEAnet	--*-	- *	*--	.8	.3	P
IDEAAssociates	IDEAshare	*---	- *	--*	.2	>.1	P
IDS	INTELL. B-650	--*-	- *	*--	NA	1.2	P
Intel	OpenNet	***-	* *	**-	10.0	2.5	3/4/5
Invisible Software	Invisible Net.	--*-	- *	--O	1.8	.6	P
LANEX	LAN Products	--*-	* *	*--	10.0	16.1	3
M/A-COM Linkabit	IDX3000	*---	* -	--*	1.5	5.5	P
Magnolia Microsys	MAGNet	--*-	- *	-*-	NA	.3	P
Micom-Interlan	Ethernet	--*-	- *	*--	10.0	2.5	3
Motorola	Ethernet	--*-	- *	*--	10.0	2.5	3
NBI	NBI Net	--*-	- *	*--	10.0	2.5	3
NCR	Tower	-**-	- *	**-	10.0	2.5	3/5
NEC	ViaNet	--*-	- *	--*	1.0	NA	P
Novell	Netware	*E*-	- *	***	10.0	6.9	3/4/5/P
Orchid Technology	PCnet	--*-	- *	*--	1.0	2.2	P
Prime Computer	RingNet/LAN300	-**-	- *	**-	10.0	2.5	3/P
Proteon	ProNET-4/10	WE--	- *	-*-	10.0	?	5/P
Proteon	ProNET-80	*---	- *	-*-	80.0	50.0	P
Pure Data	ARCnet LAN	---*	- *	-*-	2.5	6.1	ARCNet
Quadram	Quadnet VI	--*-	- *	*--	1.4	2.1	3/P
Quadram	Quadnet IX	W-E-	- *	-*-	10.0	NA	5
Quadram	QuadStar	*-*-	- *	**-	10.0	.5	3/ARC
Racore	LANpac I	-*--	- *	-*-	2.0	.3	P
Racore	LANpac II	--*-	* -	--*	16.0	3.0	P
Racore	LANpac 802.5	---*	- *	-*-	4.0	.1	5
Radio Shack/Tandy	Network 4	--*-	- *	*--	1.0	.3	P
Santa Clara	PC NET	--*-	- *	*--	1.0	2.2	P
Santa Clara	SCS Network	--*-	- *	*--	1.0	2.2	P
Siecor	Fiber Token	---*	- *	-*-	16.0	2.5	5?
Siecor	Fiber Ether	--*-	- *	*--	10.0	4.0	3?
Software Link	LANLINK	**-*	- -	--*	.1	.3	P
Standard Data	StandardNET	--*-	- *	-*-	3.0	.9	P
Standard Microsys	ARCnet	--E-	- *	-*-	2.5	3.5	P
Star Technologies	STAR*NET	-*--	- *	-*-	2.5	4.9	P
Sun Microsystems	Open Sys. Net.	--*-	* *	**-	10.0	2.5	3/4
Syntax	VAX/VMS Ether	--*-	- *	*--	10.0	2.5	E
SynOptics	LattisNet	*---	- *	*--	10.0	4.0	3?
Sytek	System 2000	--*-	* -	*--	.1	50.0	7
Sytek	System 3000	--*-	* -	*--	.1	50.0	7
Sytek	System 6000	--*-	* -	*--	2.0	5.0	3
Sytek	System 8000	*-**	* *	**-	10.0	38.6	3/4?
Sytek	PC Network	--*-	* -	*--	2.0	8.1	P

(*Continued*)

Table 6.1   (*Continued*)

Manufacturer	Product	Top. SRBT	Type BrBa	Acc CTO	Speed (Mb/s)	Max Len	802 Std
Tangent Tech	ThinkLink	*---	- *	-*-	1.2	1.8	P
TCL	Ethernet	--*-	- *	*--	10.0	...	3
Tecmar	ELAN	--*-	- *	*--	10.0	2.5	E
10NET/DCA	10NET LAN	*-*-	- *	*--	1.0	.6	3
10NET/DCA	10NET Ether.	--*-	- *	*--	10.0	4.0	3
10NET/DCA	10NET Fiber	*---	- *	*--	10.0	1.0	3?
3COM	3+Share	-***	* *	**-	10.0	1.0+	3/5
Tiara	ARCnet	*--*	- *	-*-	2.5	6.1	P
Tiara	Ethernet	--*-	- *	*--	10.0	.8	3
Tienet	TIENET	--*-	- *	*--	10.0	8.1	E/P
TRW	Concept 2000	****	* *	**-	10.0	16.0	3/7/P
Ungermann-Bass	NET/ONE	*-**	* *	**-	10.0	6.0	3/5/7
Ungermann-Bass	MAP/ONE	--*-	- *	-*-	10.0	NA	4
Vitalink	802.3	*-**	- *	*--	1.4	.3	3
VLSI Networks	1553-NET	--*-	- *	*--	3.0	2.4	P
Wang	WangNet	--**	* -	*--	10.0	12.9	3?
Waterloo	PORT	-*-*	- *	-*-	4.0	6.4	4/5
Watlan	WATSTAR/pc	-*--	- *	-*-	10.0	NoLm	5?
Western Digital	StarLAN	*---	- *	*--	1.0	4.9	3
XCOMP	XNet	--*-	- *	*--	2.5	3.0	P
Xerox	XC 24	--*-	- *	*--	10.0	2.7	3
Xerox	XC 80	--*-	- *	*--	10.0	2.4	3
Xyplex	XYPLEX System	--*-	- *	*--	1.0	13.0	P
Zenith Data Sys.	Z-LAN	*-**	* *	*--	10.0	48.7	3/7?
Zilog	Ethernet	--*-	- *	*--	10.0	1.5	E/3
Zilog	System 8000	--*-	- *	*--	10.0	.7	E/P

NOTES: Not all LANs being manufactured are listed. It is probably not possible to compile such a list. Standard product references should be used when searching for LANs at a particular point in time. It is also possible that some of the companies or products listed are no longer in business. A major source, available in some libraries is *DataPro*, particularly their series on Data Communications. This publication and others like it are updated monthly or quarterly and should be consulted when a major project is contemplated.

Topology: Abbreviated "Top."; classified as S, R, B, or T, meaning Star, Ring, Bus, or Tree, respectively. Sometimes a system is designed as an electrical (or physical) bus, ring, or star, but will be designed to be wired as something else, usually a star. Thus, rather than simply flagging the appropriate topology, an "E" (electrical) and "W" (wiring) will be used.

Type: Broadband (Br) or Baseband (Ba).

Access Method (Acc): classified as C, T, or O for CSMA/CD, Token Passing, or Other, respectively.

Speed is measured in Megabits per second (Mb/s).

Maximum Length is measured in kilometers.

NA means Not Available to the author at the time of writing.

NoLm mean No Limit on length.

A question mark (?) on the right means that while the vendor generally follows the stipulated standard (see below), there has been some non-standard implementation.

Table 6.1   (*Continued*)

802 Std was an attempt to classify the various LANs as 802.3, 802.4, or 802.5. In 1987 when the first edition of *Local Area Networks: The Second Generation* was written, most LANs on the market were proprietary. This (1989) has shifted in favor of standard (IEEE) based LANs, mostly 802.3. P = Proprietary (not a standard). E = Ethernet. Otherwise, a number represents the specific standards. Anything flagged as E will likely have been changed to 802.3 standard by the time you read this. Other CSMA/CD systems will also likely be changed to standard implementations. 7=802.7 broadband recommendations (not actually a standard).

Some vendors (Tandy/Radio Shack is a good example) may currently have some network under their own name but also sell a wide range of other vendors networks. A number of vendors have more than one network. Examples are 3COM, Sytek, Novell, and others. Sometimes those networks are listed separately, sometimes they are summarized on a single line. This depends on the complexity and variety of the LANs and how they have reported both to standard sources and to this author.

SOURCES: Sources consulted included the reference works listed below, computer industry magazines and journals, and vendor information. Refer to the following references for vendor addresses and phone numbers:

Data Sources: Hardware—Data Communications, 4th Quarter 1986 (New York: Ziff-Davis, 1986), pp. I–30ff.

DataPro—Data Communications, December 1988, C11-010-230, Delran, NJ 08075. Telephone: 800-328-2776 (most recent source as of 12/1/89).

will need wiring centers or wiring closets, patch panels, and other accoutrements of twisted-pair wiring schemes. In the case of Token Ring, it will also be necessary to have one or more Multiple Station Access Units. Most broadband and Ethernet systems are more or less "pure" examples of distributed bus topologies where no central point exists. Finally, the system will require one or more servers to provide file and print serving functions as well as other communications functions if that is required. Once you have the hardware assembled, however, you still do not have a LAN.

Network Operating Environment (Software)

In order to be effectively used, the hardware must be bound together through a software-based network operating environment. Sometimes called a network operating system, the integrating software has characteristics often associated with an operating system, yet it clearly must work in association with more traditional operating systems already functioning on various components of the LAN. Thus, part of the network operating environment is a network "shell" that runs on a workstation and screens each application's request to see if it must have access to a server, or whether the local DOS can handle it. Before IBM entered the LAN market in 1984, manufacturers of LAN software devised their own hardware and software methods for dealing with this problem. With the introduction by IBM of its broadband PC Network in 1984 and the Token Ring later in 1985, a new complication/simplification (depending on your point of view) was introduced: NETBIOS. Moreover, in the PC world, Microsoft also introduced some standardization through PC/MS DOS by adding some network specific system calls to DOS 3.1 and expanding it in 3.2 and 3.3. These issues are discussed in detail in Chapter 5.

Media

The discussion of network media is divisible into at least two major segments: the transport technology (broadband or baseband) and the physical medium defined for use with the transport technology. In this section we will look at both these attributes of LANs and attempt to refine an understanding of what they are and why they are important. In earlier chapters we have mentioned broadband and baseband in a somewhat passing fashion, as we have components of the physical medium. In this section we will flesh out the discussion.

Broadband, Baseband, and Telephony

Although there are a number of architectures currently being marketed claiming to be the last word in LANs, for a LAN capable of spanning the floors of a large high-rise or the many buildings of a campus facility, only two contenders are technologically feasible: broadband and telephony. Baseband systems are available for more restricted circumstances and for medium-sized buildings. The reason for drawing this conclusion is that baseband systems are typically limited and do not normally extend beyond about two kilometers. Baseband and broadband are frequently contrasted with one another, while telephone technology represents a considerably different concept.

Broadband LANs.   Broadband systems transmit data, voice, and video signals through the use of cable television (CATV) technology and components. It is a communications medium using a channel having a bandwidth characterized by high data transmission rates. Like telephone technology, CATV is a general-purpose technology that can be used by, but is not restricted to, LANs. The CATV system can be constructed with off-the-shelf components using a mature technology. See the Appendix for more detail.

Baseband LANs.   Baseband systems, in contrast to broadband, may use any physical cable (coax, twisted pair, etc.), but the signal on the cable is unmodulated. Broadband systems typically subdivide the frequency spectrum, not only by standard television channels, but also within channels through some multiplexing scheme (either time division or frequency division or both). Baseband systems, however, do not subdivide the bandwidth and use a wide bandwidth to provide high data rates. The high data rates are required since essentially only one transmission can occupy the cable at any one time. In order to maintain decent throughput, therefore, signals must travel very fast.

Access to a baseband system such as Ethernet is accomplished not through a modem but through a transceiver. The transceiver simply transmits the signal received from the device to which it is attached. The data are formed into frames or packets that consist of a source address, a destination address, and a small quantity of user data. Since baseband systems are designed only for local area networks, somewhat more work has been done with providing office automation products and server mechanisms than is the case with broadband or telephonic systems (although WangNet, a broadband system, has some servers available, and other manufacturers have announced or are developing such servers). On the other hand, voice and video products are generally unavailable for baseband systems.

Although Ethernet through 1983 received the lion's share of the baseband publicity, serious investigation was being given to Datapoint's ARCnet technology, a token passing bus scheme. By mid-1983 it was also apparent that IBM was working on a token passing baseband local area network.

The Telephonic LAN.

In the data communications area, the term "telephonic LAN" is used in this book to describe the LAN products based on telephone technology. Specifically, telephonic LANs are structured around an Electronic Private Automatic Branch eXchange (EPABX) or a Private Automatic Branch eXchange (PABX), different names for the same technology. The acronyms, EPABX and PABX, will be used interchangeably. An EPABX-based LAN uses a star topology, and of all the LAN products available, is virtually the only system using a star, following the method in which telephone systems are organized. Since an EPABX is basically a private telephone system, now available from a number of vendors, an EPABX may encompass both standard voice communications as well as data, although fast-scan television is unavailable.

The modern EPABX is a digital device with extensive redundancy to ensure minimum downtime. Following the telephone model, however, it is fundamentally a switching device. Companies manufacturing EPABXs for data and voice traffic include some of the traditional telephone systems (as well as new ones, such as Rolm) as well as companies that previously sold data switches as a means of managing the ports on large mainframe computers. In mid-1983 AT&T was floating proposals (although with no product) for a "centralized bus" LAN topology that was little more than a repackaged EPABX using a traditional star. This became AT&T's Information Systems Network (ISN).

While the EPABX will provide connectivity equivalent to a broadband LAN, the EPABX approach tends to be slower than either broadband or baseband. With some EPABX systems modems are required, although as digital devices, the newer systems can handle connections not involving modems for direct transmission of digital data. Under normal operating conditions, however, data rates are often limited to around 2400 b/s for asynchronous data as compared with 9600 b/s or 19,200 b/s for broadband and baseband systems, although AT&T's ISN can match the higher data rates. Then, too, although the process of making connections can be automatic, addressing of devices is done in precisely the same manner a telephone call is made and that can take a number of seconds to complete.

MAKING THE CHOICE

The term "design" has been used in this chapter more in a systems context than in an engineering sense. That is, we have focused on why an organization might wish to have a LAN rather than on the technical "nitty-gritty" of specifying hardware and software. The reason for this chapter's emphasis is that it is difficult and perhaps impossible to begin thinking about an appropriate technology without some sense of what is to be accomplished with that technology. For a small standalone microcomputer-based LAN (fewer than 10 or 20 stations, for example), almost any LAN technology will work for you and probably work pretty well. If, on the other hand, the limits of possible expansion are relatively large, and if the geographical area to be covered is more than one office suite, and if connectivity with one or more minicomputers, mainframes, and/or wide area networks is necessary, then the technology can become very important.

The importance of the technology does not rest entirely on technical issues such as throughput, although those issues can be fundamental to making your LAN work well. In addition there are the practical issues of whether the components necessary to meet the defined needs are readily available now or, if not now, sometime in the predictable future. If multiple communications applications are to be supported (data, video, and voice, for example), what technology will do the job now rather than at some ill-defined future time? If we have defined some user interface needs, can they be met with all technologies or only a few? By addressing the issues raised in this chapter, you will be able to make a decision with a relatively high degree of confidence once the systemic limits to the problem are carefully described. In the chapters that follow, we will take a closer look at several of the technical issues in considerably greater detail than we have thus far. Specifically, we will look at the micro–to–mainframe link and how a LAN can solve that problem. Then we will look at the three primary IEEE standards (802.3, 802.4, and 802.5) in sufficient detail to provide a solid understanding of what those standards say about the LAN attributes they describe. The discussion will be rounded out with an examination of the management issues involved in any sized LAN and finally come to some conclusions concerning the latest generation of LANs and what they can do for you.

REFERENCES

1. Another version of this list may be found in Thomas W. Madron, *Local Area Networks in Large Organizations* (Hasbrouck Heights, NJ: Hayden Book Co., 1984), pp. 36 and 37.

2. Thomas W. Madron, "IBM's Token Ring," *ComputerWorld,* October 22, 1985.

3. Kathy Chin, "Twisted, Twisted Little Star, Users Wonder What You Are," *Communications Week,* December 8, 1986, pp. 1, 25, and 29.

4. See, for example, the following: J. O. Limb and C. Flores, "Description of Fastnet—A Unidirectional Local Area Communications Network," *The Bell System Technical Journal,* Vol. 61, No. 7, September 1981, pp. 1413–1440; J. W. Mark, T. D. Todd, and J. A. Field, "Welnet: Architectural Design and Implementation," *Journal of Telecommunications Networks,* Vol. 1, No. 3, 1982, pp. 225–237; F. A. Tobagi, F. Borgonovo, and L. Fratta, "Expressnet: A High-Performance Integrated Services Local Area Network," *IEEE Journal on Selected Areas in Communications,* Vol. SAC-1, No. 5, November 1983, pp. 898–913; and Chong-Wei Tseng and Bor Uei Chen, "D-Net. A New Scheme for High Data Rate Optical Local Area Networks," *Proceeding of the Global Telecommunications Conference,* Miami Beach, Florida, November 30–December 2, 1982, pp. E1.2.1–E1.2.7.

5. *Data Sources: Hardware—Data Communications,* Vol. 6, No. 2, 4th Quarter 1986, pp. I30–I33.

6. Art Krumrey, "NetWare in Control," *PC Tech Journal,* Vol. 3. No. 11, November 1985, pp. 103–119.

CHAPTER 7

ANSI/IEEE STD 802.3—CSMA/CD

This chapter introduces and defines the IEEE 802.3 CSMA/CD (Carrier Sense Multiple Access/Collision Detection) standard; examines where Ethernet, DECnet, and StarLan fit into that standard; examines where 802.3 fits into the overall IEEE 802 standards and international standards; and dicusses why these issues are of any consequence. It will first be instructive to understand why anyone is implementing them. Even IBM is beginning to support 802.3— the first time it has provided support to a networking technology it has not developed. The 802.3, 802.4, 802.5, and 802.6 standards each specify the appropriate MAC sublayer and the Physical Layer. The relationship of 802.3 to other IEEE standards and to the OSI Reference Model may be seen in Figure 7.1.

802.3 MEDIA ACCESS CONTROL

MAC is that part of a data station that supports the various MAC functions that reside just below the LLC sublayer. The MAC procedures include framing/deframing data-units, performing error checking, and acquiring the right to use the underlying physical medium.

802.3 PHYSICAL LAYER

The Physical Layer includes Physical Layer signaling and the physical attachment to the medium. The media used are not usually part of the standards but

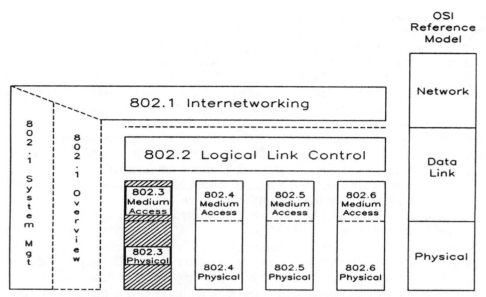

Figure 7.1 Relationship of IEEE Standards and the OSI Reference Model
SOURCE: Based on IEEE P802.1, Draft E, July 1, 1987, *Overview, Internetworking, and Systems Management*, unapproved draft published for comment only, by permission of the IEEE. All rights reserved by The Institute of Electrical and Electronics Engineers, Inc., p. 7.

are described by standards documents because they impinge on the physical attachment. Consequently, in addition to describing signaling and attachment, this chapter will also dicuss the various media currently in use for 802.3 including coax, broadband, twisted pair, and fiber-optic technologies.

IMPLEMENTATION OF AN 802.3 LAN

In order to implement an 802.3 LAN, a number of implementation issues must be confronted. For example, how will the building or the campus actually be wired? Who will do the wiring? In addition, there are the usual management issues involved in what it takes to keep an 802.3 network running smoothly. For example, how shall another connection be ordered? How is the network to be maintained? How will network security be handled?

The media hype centering on IBM's Token Ring Network since 1986 may have led casual observers to conclude that it was the only LAN left on the market. However, when an organization starts evaluating LANs, it will discover that a quick and easy solution to LAN selection is impossible. Of the 802 standard networks, the most widely deployed and supported system is certainly 802.3 (Ethernet). Ethernet is alive and well and will continue to play a major role in local area networking for many years into the future. (Note that the term *Ethernet* was coined and trade-marked by Xerox and is not used in the 802.3 standard, apart from references to work by Xerox. In fact, the earlier versions of Ethernet are not compatible with the 802.3 standard. As remarked elsewhere, in popular parlance, "Ethernet" and "802.3" are currently used to connote an 802.3 standard CSMA/CD network— we will follow that usage here.) There were actually two Ethernet specifications (I and II) prior to the adoption of 802.3. Ethernet I was the original. Ethernet II was the definition that became 802.3—they are essentially the same. Ethernet I devices will not work with 802.3 standard equipment and systems, although many manufacturers produce equipment designed to work with both systems.

The 802.3 standard is being used with increasing frequency. It has been adopted by Boeing's Technical Office Protocol (TOP). General Motors Corp.'s Manufacturers Automation Protocol (MAP) and Boeing's Technical Office Protocol (TOP) are on their way to becoming industry standards, judging from the reactions of computer integrated manufacturing (CIM) equipment vendors. MAP was originally designed around a broadband token passing protocol based on IEEE 802.4 standards (see Chapter 8), while TOP is an Ethernet-based baseband specification incorporating IEEE 802.3 standards. Both are looked upon as the protocols of the future, with CAD/CAM, computer-aided engineering, and production equipment computerized control manufacturers seen as the first of many manufacturing areas in which they will be found.[1]

By 1987 the IEEE 802 Committee on LAN standards had considered and approved several additions to the 802.3 standard.[2] The 802.3 Subcommittee appears to be trying to standardize all possible combinations of transmission media and data rates that might use CSMA/CD.[3] Supplements to the original standard were published in 1988 on the following additions:

▼ ANSI/IEEE 802.3a–1988, Medium Attachment Unit and Baseband Medium Specifications, Type 10BASE2

▼ ANSI/IEEE 802.3b–1988, Broadband Medium Attachment Unit and Broadband Medium Specifications, Type 10BROAD36

▼ ANSI/IEEE 802.3c–1988, Repeater Unit for 10 Mb/s Baseband Networks

▼ ANSI/IEEE 802.3e–1988, Physical Signaling, Medium Attachment, and Baseband Medium Specifications, Type 1BASE5

These included both twisted-pair baseband (802.3e, StarLan) and broadband systems (802.3b). Shortly after the publication of the original 802.3 standard in 1983, the ISO ruled in support of the IEEE 802 LAN standards for Ethernet

CSMA/CD and token bus networks. This standard provides for multivendor environments in organizations by enabling the interconnection of equipment from different vendors. This ruling was a key victory for Ethernet supporters and continues to be important to its growth. IBM withheld support for the 802.3 standard in preference for token ring networks.[4] In 1986, however, IBM introduced the 9370 office minicomputer, which uses both Ethernet and Token Ring support; and in 1988, IBM introduced the 8232 LAN controller, which can channel-attach either a token ring or 802.3 LAN to a System 370 architecture mainframe (4381, 3090, etc.). It is now possible to front-end a computer complex consisting of mainframes, minicomputers, and microcomputers with an 802.3 network using some higher-layer protocols, such as TCP/IP, to integrate the various machines.

Although the developing standards were met with widespread approval by the mid-1980s, it was too early to conclude that standards for LANs were sufficiently well-established to allow communications managers to make intelligent, informed decisions about their LAN interconnection strategies.[5] By the end of the decade, however, the standards were becoming well entrenched and inconnection strategies were taking on greater clarity. Such decisions are not purely technical in any large organization, but rather include some political decisions made at some level of the company. Also, in most large organizations, a single LAN solution is not very likely. This has led to the demand for network interconnection equipment and standards. In Europe, particularly, this has led to developments of system-independent networks, although in the United States, companies like Novell have made significant strides in this direction as well. An example of European strategies is OpenNET, a hardware/software concept that provides a means of connecting various microcomputer types with different operating systems into common local networks.[6]

One of the reasons why there cannot often be a single LAN solution in a company revolves around the use to which the LAN is to be put. There is an important reason why MAP developers have concentrated on a token bus system while TOPS designers have focused in on 802.3 standards. CSMA/CD systems allow media access to a station in a probabilistic fashion. Token passing schemes, on the other hand, are deterministic systems. MAP is a manufacturing system to be used for (among other reasons) process control. Process control systems must have known—determined—access times, whereas office systems can be built on probabilistic models. Bus topologies, in both cases, allow large but not necessarily known numbers of nodes that can easily be changed or enlarged. As was seen in greater detail in Chapter 8, a token bus system essentially provides a logical ring with the capacity to add or delete stations easily. With CSMA/CD systems, the total number of stations (up to some large upper limit) can be easily varied by connecting or disconnecting a node. Token rings, by way of contrast, have the deterministic qualities of a token bus but can present configuration problems in some environments.

A research installation in government, industry, or higher education, for example, may need a LAN for office automation and another for process control in laboratories. These may need to be interfaced to a Digital Equipment Corporation VAX superminicomputer (which uses Ethernet as a standard LAN environment). The VAX, in turn, may front-end a supercomputer or may be connected to a large IBM mainframe through an SNA gateway (or more directly via an 802.3 LAN). If the office automation LAN is 802.3-compatible, then it may run directly on the Ethernet-connecting components of the VAX system; but for direct access, the token passing system used for process control must be "gatewayed" to the Ethernet, preferably in a transparent or *seamless* fashion. Clearly, the demand is growing for integrated open networks.[7] A means of identifying each implementation is with a simple, three-field type notation for the Physical Layer,

<data rate in Mb/s>< medium type><max segment
length (*100 m)>.

The IEEE 802.3–1985 standard, for example, defined a 10 Mb/s baseband system with a maximum segment length of 500 meters. This is identified as "TYPE 10BASE5." This notation will occasionally be used in this discussion.

A DETAILED LOOK AT 802.3[8]

In general, the 802 family of standards deals with the Physical and Data Link Layers as defined by the ISO/OSI Reference Model. The relationship of the ISO/OSI model to the 802 standards may be seen in Figure 7.1. 802.3 specifies a bus using CSMA/CD as the access method. Initial work on the technologies standardized in 802.3 was conducted by Xerox and later in cooperation with Intel and DEC. Xerox holds patents that appear to cover the access mechanism defined by 802.3, although Xerox grants licenses under its patents on reasonable and nondiscriminatory terms. Although most of the 802.3 standard conforms to ISO standard 8802/3, some portions of the IEEE documents are not part of the ISO specification. In particular, those elements referencing United States national standards and recommendations and guidelines for safety are not included in the ISO documents. The first edition of 802.3 (IEEE Std 802.3–1985) defined a 10 Mb/s baseband implementation of the Physical Layer.

Overview

Chapter 2 provides an overview of CSMA/CD and 802.3; a short review at this point will prove useful. Carrier Sense Multiple Access with Collision Detection (CSMA/CD) is a media access method that allows two or more stations to share a common bus transmission medium. A transmitting station waits or defers transmission until a quiet period occurs on the medium. When a quiet period occurs, a message is sent in bit-serial form. When a collision occurs because two or more stations have sent messages at the same time, each transmitting station intentionally sends a few additional bytes to ensure that other stations recognize that a collision has taken place. A transmitting station remains quiet for a random amount of time (called *backoff*) after a collision occurs before transmitting again. This prevents the two (or more) stations from repeating collisions. The 802.3 standard is intended to encompass several media types and techniques for signal rates from 1 to 20 Mb/s.The standard provides a network design architecture that emphasizes the logical divisions of the system and how they work together rather than emphasizing actual components, their packaging, and their interconnection.

By segregating medium-dependent aspects of the Physical Layer, the IEEE standard allows the LLC and the MAC sublayers to support a variety of transmission media. Because implementation is the ultimate aim of the standards, however, the critical issue in implementation interfacing is compatibility. Two compatibility interfaces are defined in the Physical Layer: the Medium Dependent Interface (MDI) and the Attachment Unit Interface (AUI). To communicate in a compatible manner, all stations must adhere to the exact specification of physical media signals as defined, as well as to the procedures that define the correct behavior of the station.

Because most stations will be located at some distance from the trunk cable (in the 10 Mb/s baseband implementation, a 50 Ohm coaxial cable), a small amount of circuitry exists in the Medium Attachment Unit (MAU). This device is normally called a transceiver for baseband Ethernets. The majority of the hardware and all software is placed within the station. It is this hardware and software that operationally defines the AUI as a secondary compatibility interface. The standard does not demand conformance with the AUI, but conformance is recommended, because it allows maximum flexibility in intermixing MAUs and stations. With standard baseband 10 Mb/s Ethernets, this advice has generally been followed. Thus, hardware—and some software—from various manufacturers can be mixed in the same network and will communicate with one another. Type 1BASE5 (StarLan) implementations, however, have sometimes failed to follow this advice; therefore, several of the StarLan implementations cannot be intermixed.

The designs of the interfaces between layers are well defined and provide several services. The interaction between the MAC and LLC sublayers requires facilities for transmitting and receiving frames and status information for use by higher-level error recovery procedures. Signals for framing (carrier sense, transmit initiation) and contention resolution (collision detection), facilities for passing a pair of serial bit streams (transmit, receive) between two layers, and a wait function for timing are contained in the interface between the MAC sublayer and the Physical Layer. Other interfaces are needed to provide higher-level network management functions. IEEE Std 802.3–1985 was intended for commercial and light industrial applications—not for home or heavy industrial environments. While CSMA/CD might be used for home or heavy industry, those applications areas were not originally addressed.

Media Access Control (MAC)

MAC is that part of a data station that supports the medium access control functions that reside just below the LLC sublayer. MAC functions include various services, frame structure, and a MAC method. Each of these functions will be described and discussed in the following sections.

Service Specifications.   One of the primary functions of the MAC sublayer is to provide services to the LLC. These services allow the local LLC sublayer entity to exchange LLC data-units with peer LLC sublayer entities. This provides a means of successfully transfering data and/or control information from one location to another location. The three basic services with corresponding service primitives are MA_DATA.request, MA_DATA.confirm, and MA_DATA.indication. The request primitive is passed from the (N)-layer to the (N − 1)-layer to request that a service be initiated. The indication primitive is passed from the (N − 1)-layer to the (N)-layer to indicate an internal N − 1 event that is significant to layer. The confirm primitive is passed from the (N − 1)-layer to the (N)-layer to convey the results of the associated previous service request.

The MA_DATA.request defines the transfer of data from a local LLC sublayer entity to a single peer LLC entity (or multiple peer LLC entities, in the case of group addresses). The three elements of the MA_DATA.request primitive are destination address (DA), service data-unit (SDU), and service class.

Each of these elements may be thought of as parameters that specify one or more things.

The DA parameter provides either an individual or group address and will contain sufficient information to create the DA field as the MAC sublayer is assembling a frame. The SDU parameter specifies the MAC service data-unit to be transmitted by the MAC sublayer entity. Sufficient information will be included to determine the length of the SDU. The service class indicates the quality of service requested by the LLC or higher layers, although with CSMA/CD, only a single quality of service is provided regardless of the service class requested.

The LLC sublayer entity generates the MA_DATA.request whenever data is to be transferred to a peer LLC entity. The request may be generated as a response to a request from higher layers of protocol or from data generated internally to the LLC sublayer. When the MAC sublayer entity receives the request, the MAC entity appends all MAC-specific fields to the frame being assembled, which is then passed to lower layers of protocol for transmission to the peer MAC sublayer entity.

The function of the MA_DATA.confirm primitive is to provide an appropriate response to the LLC sublayer MA_DATA.request. The response signals either success or failure of the the request. A single parameter—transmission status—passes status information back to the local requesting LLC sublayer entity. Sufficient information is made available to the LLC sublayer by the MA_DATA.confirm for LLC to associate the response with the appropriate request. Because the MAC sublayer services requests in a first-in–first-out manner, the association may be a simple matter of following the order of responses.

Transfer of data from the MAC to the LLC sublayers is defined by the MA_DATA.indication primitive. It consists of four elements or parameters, as follows: destination address (DA), source address (SA), service data-unit (SDU), and reception status.

The MA_DATA.indication is generated by the MAC sublayer to the LLC sublayer to indicate the reception of a frame from lower layers. These frames are reported only if they are valid, received without error, and their DA stipulates the local MAC. The destination address is taken from the DA field of the incoming frame. So that a response can be given, the source address must also be passed for a subsequent transmission. The SDU parameter defines the MAC service data-unit as it was received. Finally, the reception status parameter is used to pass status information to the peer LLC entity.

MAC Frame Structure.

In a LAN, data are transmitted in a highly structured format. This format is the frame or packet structure. In the earlier days of LAN development, the entities were often referred to as packets following other data communications conventions. In the IEEE standards, these units are called "frames." A frame structure is required so that appropriate information for designating destination and source nodes, as well as error-correcting information, is sent and received. The frame is defined by the use of octets. An octet is a bit-oriented element that consists of eight contiguous binary bits. This is similar to the definition of a byte, but the term *byte* has a more restricted meaning. Figure 7.2 illustrates the eight fields of a frame. Of these eight fields, all are of fixed length except the LLC data and PAD fields. The actual sizes are determined by any integer number of octets between the minimum and maximum values determined by the specific implementation of the CSMA/CD Media Access mechanism. The maximum frame size is 1518 octets and the minimum is 64 octets.

The various fields of the frame are defined as follows:

1. Preamble. This is a seven-octet field used to allow the physical signal-

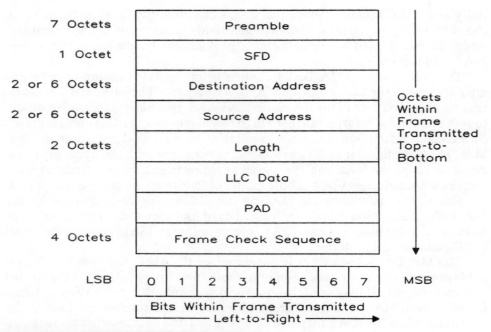

Figure 7.2   CSMA/CD MAC Frame Format
SOURCE: Reprinted from ANSI/IEEE Std 802.3–1985, *Carrier Sense Multiple Access with Collision Detection (CSMA/CD) Access Method and Physical Layer Specifications,* ©1985 by The Institute of Electrical and Electronics Engineers, Inc., by permission of the IEEE. All rights reserved by The Institute of Electrical and Electronics Engineers, Inc., p. 24.

ing (PLS) circuitry to reach its ready-state synchronization with the received frame timing.

2. Start Frame Delimiter (SFD).   This is a fixed sequence of bits that indicates the start of the frame: 10101011.

3. Address Fields.   Each MAC frame must contain two address fields: destination and source, in that order (Who is the frame for and where did it come from?). Each address field must contain either 16 or 48 bits, although at any given time the lengths of both fields must be the same. The support of either or both fields is an implementation decision.

The first bit (LSB) is used in the DA as an address type designation to distinguish between individual and group addresses (for multicasting or broadcasting messages). In the SA, the first bit is reserved and set to zero. For 48-bit addresses, the second bit is used to distinguish between locally or globally administered addresses. Each octet is transmitted least significant bit (LSB) first. See Figure 7.3 for address field formats.

4. Length. This is a two-octet field whose value indicates the number of LLC data octets in the data field. If the number is less than the minimum required for proper operation, a PAD field (simply a sequence of octets) will be added to the data field. The length field is transmitted and received with the high-order octet first.

5. Data and PAD fields. The data field contains a sequence of n octets. Full data transparency is provided so that any arbitrary sequence of octet values may occur. Because a minimum frame size is required, a data field of less than some minimum length (depending on the specific implementation) may require padding with the PAD field. The length field contains the size (n) of the data field. The length of the PAD for LLC data n octets long is (in bits)

maxvalue(0, minFrameSize -
(8*n+2*addressSize+48))

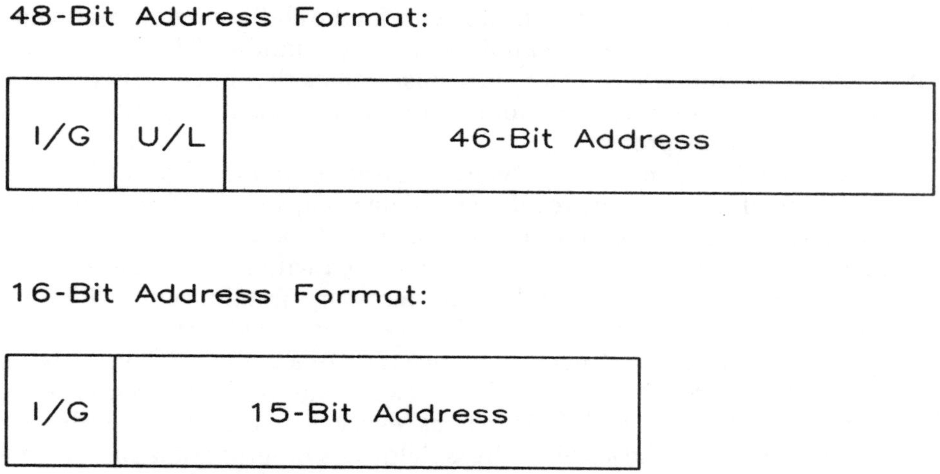

48-Bit Address Format:

I/G	U/L	46-Bit Address

16-Bit Address Format:

I/G	15-Bit Address

Figure 7.3: 802.3 Address Field Format
NOTES: I/G = 0, individual address; I/G = 1, group address; U/L = 0, globally administered address; U/L = 1, locally admistered address.
SOURCE: Reprinted from ANSI/IEEE Std 802.3–1985, *Carrier Sense Multiple Access with Collision Detection (CSMA/CD) Access Method and Physical Layer Specifications*, ©1985 by The Institute of Electrical and Electronics Engineers, Inc., by permission of the IEEE. All rights reserved by The Institute of Electrical and Electronics Engineers, Inc., p. 25.

The maximum possible size of the LLC data field in octets is:

maxFrameSize - (2 * addressSize + 48) / 8.

6. Frame Check Sequence. The FCS field contains a four-octet (32 bit) cyclic redundancy check value. The transmit and receive algorithms generate CRC values which are compared.

A frame is invalid when it meets at least one of the following conditions: the frame length is inconsistent with the length field; it is not an integral number of octets in length; and/or the bits of the incoming frame do not generate a CRC value identical to the one received. Invalid MAC frames are not transmitted to the LLC and the occurrence of invalid frames may be communicated to network management.

Aspects of the handling of frames are implementation-dependent. It may be of value to look at a specific implementation—here, DEC's implementation of Ethernet—before leaving the discussion of the MAC frame structure.

The frame format is flexible, particularly with respect to source and destination addresses, which may be either 16 or 48 bits in length. Manufacturers are free to use either the 16- or 48-bit format or to support both (although this is not required by the standard). Developers are also free to link the frame to higher-level protocols; DEC does so. Thus, many manufacturers use the same equipment, possibly over the same cable, without the ability for devices on networks defined by protocol to communicate with one another. The higher-level protocols may include file transfer protocols such as the Xerox Network System (XNS), Transmission Control Protocol/Internet Protocol (TCP/IP), X.25, or an appropriate DECnet protocol.

The Ethernet Data Link has one type of message or frame. The construction and processing of frames is the result of the data encapsulation function of the Data Link Layer. The subfunctions of framing include addressing and error detection. No explicit framing information is required with Ethernet because the access method (CSMA/CD) provides the necessary framing cues. Two addresses—for source and destination stations—are provided. Error detection is accomplished with a Frame Check Sequence (FCS)—a 32-bit CRC. In a Digital Network Architecture (DNA, Phase IV) network environment composed of DDCMP media, Ethernets, and X.25 systems, every node has a unique address. This requires the use of the 48-bit address field. The Ethernet Data Link Frame format, as used by DEC, is illustrated in Figure 7.4.

The implementation flexibility provided within the 802.3 standard is clearest in the definition of the source and destination addresses. As noted above, the address fields may be either 16 bits or 48 bits. The 48-bit field allows a specific Ethernet node to have a unique address across all interconnected Ethernets or other networks. In DNA (Phase IV), each Ethernet node has a 16-bit node address. If that node is also a DNA node, then the 16-bit address is prefixed by a 32-bit

6 Octets	Destination
6 Octets	Source
2 Octets	Type
46<=N<=1500 Octets	Data
4 Octets	FCS

Figure 7.4   DEC Ethernet Data Link Frame Format
NOTES: Destination: The destination data link address is one of three types: physical, multicast, or broadcast.
Source: The source data link address always contains the physical address of the station transmitting a frame.
Type: The type field is reserved for use by higher-layer protocols to identify the higher-level protocol associated with a frame.
Data: The data field contains higher-level protocol data with full transparency. The minimum length of the data field ensures that all frames occupy the channel long enough for reliable collision detection.
FCS: The frame check sequence contains the CRC-32 polynomial check on the rest of the frame.
SOURCE: *DECnet: Digital Network Architecture, General Description,* Document No. AA–N149-TC (Maynard, MA: Digital Equipment Corporation, 1982), p. 2.12.

address that is assigned to DNA nodes. DNA addresses are, therefore, unique over a single DNA network, which may include multiple Ethernets, DDCMP links, and X.25 links. Associated with this capability is the Type field, which identifies any higher-level protocols associated with the frame. Type values are assigned to the DNA routing protocol and to the DNA Maintenance Operation protocols. In the 802.3 standard, the field that DEC labels "Type" is actually defined as a length field stipulating the length of the data field. Note also that, for DEC, the error control functions necessary for reliable communications are provided by the Network Services Protocol (NSP) in a DNA environment.[9]

MAC Method.   A more detailed functional treatment of the CSMA/CD MAC sublayer is useful for a better understanding of MAC operators. CSMA/CD is applicable to a number of different broadcast media, and the 802.3 standard defines a medium-independent facility within the MAC sublayer. That facility is built on the medium-dependent physical facility provided by the Physical Layer. It is this medium-independence of the MAC sublayer that has allowed expansion of the standard from the original baseband, 10 Mb/s, coaxial cable system, to include broadband and twisted-pair baseband. The LLC sublayer and the MAC sublayer together provide the same function as that described in the OSI Reference Model for the Data Link Layer alone.

A Data Link control procedure generally at least includes data encapsulation (transmit and receive) and media access management functions. Even though the concept of a direct physical link between two network nodes does not apply to a broadcast network, the Data Link functions, transmit and receive, must be performed. In an 802.3 standard LAN, this is a task of the MAC sublayer. Data encapsulation includes framing, addressing, and error detection. Media access management involves both medium allocation (collision avoidance) and contention resolution (collision handling).

An interface between the MAC sublayer and the Physical Layer is provided by the Physical Layer Signaling (PLS) component of the Physical Layer. This allows the serial transmission of bits onto the physical medium. Inside the MAC sublayer, transmit and receive frame operations are independent of one another. An originating station may receive a frame from elsewhere and pass it to the LLC sublayer. The ability to deal with transmission and reception independently can be implemented within the MAC sublayer or with full duplex operations of lower layers.

Normal operation of an 802.3 system assumes transmission and reception without contention from the MAC sublayer that is communicating upward to the LLC to obtain information that should be transmitted or to pass received data. The MAC sublayer also communicates downward with the PLS, either to provide a bit stream to be physically transmitted or to listen for a carrier sense signal sent by PLS to MAC. The process of putting a frame on the physical medium is governed by the Transmit Access Management component of MAC. Somewhat analogously, when the Receive Media Access Management component of MAC senses a carrier, it collects bits from PLS as long as the carrier sense signal remains on, then passes the received frame to Receive Data Decapsulation for processing. Checking for invalid frames is accomplished at this point. If a frame passes all tests, then the DA, SA, and the LLC data-unit are passed to the LLC sublayer, along with an appropriate status code.

Clearly, two or more stations can transmit at the same time, thus creating contention problems. When transmissions from two or more stations overlap, the contention is called a collision. There is a *collision window*—a period of time from the start of transmission to the time the transmitted signal has propagated to all stations on the CSMA/CD medium. Once the collision window has passed, all other stations should notice the signal, due to carrier sense. The time to acquire the medium is a function of the round-trip propagation time of the Physical Layer including the PLS, the Physical Medium Attachment (PMA), and the physical medium. It is this that limits the total length of a CSMA/CD physical medium and dictates minimum frame lengths.

Except for the special case of collisions, selected error conditions are reported by MAC to LLC, but error recovery is not a function of MAC. Error recovery mechanisms may be provided by LLC or by higher layers. Occasional collisions are regarded as a normal part of the media access management procedure.

Discarding of a fragment caused by a collision is not, therefore, reported as an error to LLC. Collision recovery is handled by the transmitting CSMA/CD MAC sublayer. After detecting a collision, the MAC sublayer will retry the transmission until it is successful, or until it reaches some maximum number of attempts. The scheduling of retransmissions is determined by a randomization process called *truncated binary exponential backoff.* At the end of a jam (to enforce the collision), the CSMA/CD MAC sublayer delays before attempting to retransmit the frame.

The delay used by MAC is an integer multiple of slotTime. The slotTime parameter is a unit of time for collision handling. It is implementation-dependent, but for a 10 Mb/s implementation (type 10BASE5), the value is 512 bit times. This also determines the minimum frame length, which must be at least one slotTime (512 bits) in length. The number of slotTimes to delay is chosen as a uniformly distributed random integer r in the range

$$0 <= r <= 2^k$$

where

$$k = \min (n, 10).$$

If all attempts fail, then this event is reported as an error. The algorithm used to generate r must be chosen to minimize the correlation between the numbers generated by any two stations at any given time.

The CSMA/CD Access Method functional capabilities can be summarized as follows[10]:

1. For frame transmission

    a. Accepts data from the LLC sublayer and constructs a frame

    b. Presents a bit-serial data stream to the Physical Layer for transmission on the medium (Note: Assumes data passed from the LLC sublayer are octet multiples)

2. For frame reception

    a. Receives a bit-serial data stream from the Physical Layer

    b. Presents the LLC sublayer with frames that are either broadcast frames or directly addressed to the local station

    c. Discards or passes to network management all frames not addressed to the receiving station

3. Defers transmission of a bit-serial stream whenever the physical medium is busy

4. Appends proper FCS value to outgoing frames and verifies full octet boundary alignment

5. Checks incoming frames for transmission errors by way of FCS and verifies octet boundary alignment

6. Delays transmission of frame bit stream for specified interframe gap period

7. Halts transmission when collision is detected

8. Schedules retransmission after a collision until a specified retry limit is reached

9. Enforces collision to ensure propagation throughout network by sending jam message

10. Discards received transmissions that are less than a minimum length

11. Appends preamble, Start Frame Delimiter, DA, SA, length count, and FCS to all frames and inserts pad field for frames whose LLC data length is less than a minimum value

12. Removes preamble, Start Frame Delimiters, DA, SA, length count, FCS, and pad field (if necessary) from received frames

Physical Layer Signaling (PLS) and Attachment

The Physical Layer consists of three components: PLS, Attachment Unit Interface (AUI), and Physical Medium Attachment (PMI). Some of the services provided by PLS include the peer-to-peer (station-to-station) and sublayer-to-sublayer categories of primitives. For peer-to-peer communications, there are three functions: PLS_DATA.request, PLS_DATA.confirm, and PLS_DATA.indication. PLS_DATA.request defines the transfer of data from the MAC sublayer to the local PLS entity. PLS_DATA.confirm has local significance and provides a response to the MAC sublayer PLS_DATA.request. PLS_DATA.indicate defines the transfer of data from the PLS sublayer to the MAC sublayer. For sublayer-to-sublayer communications, the functions PLS_CARRIER.indication and PLS_SIGNAL.indication are performed. The first transmits the status of the activity on the physical medium from the PLS sublayer to the MAC sublayer. The second transfers the status of the Physical Layer signal quality from the PLS sublayer to the MAC sublayer.

The AUI, normally contained in the station, has the following characteristics: it must support one or more of the defined data rates; it must be capable of driving up to 50 meters of cable; it must permit the Data Terminal Equipment (DTE) to test the AUI, AUI cable, Medium Attachment Unit (MAU), and the medium itself; and it must support MAUs for baseband coax, broadband coax, and baseband fiber. The AUI consists of the cable, connectors, and transmission circuitry used to interconnect the PLS and MAU. The MAU is formally defined as the portion of the Physical Layer between the Medium Dependent Interface (MDI) and AUI that interconnects the trunk coaxial cable to the branch cable and contains the electronics which send, receive, and manage the encoded signals impressed on, and recovered from, the trunk coaxial cable. The MDI is the mechanical and electrical interface between the trunk cable medium and the MAU. In a normal baseband, coaxial, microcomputer-based system, most of the AUI and MAU circuitry is contained on a card that is physically placed in the PC.

The original Ethernet topology used so-called "thick" Ethernet cable for the trunk system. Each Ethernet trunk segment can be only 500 meters in length. The largest baseband system can extend over a total length of 2.5 kilometers or five segments. Each segment is tied together with a repeater, which is a device used to extend the length, topology, or interconnectivity of the physical medium beyond that which is imposed by a single segment, up to the maximum end-to-end trunk transmission line length. Repeaters restore signal amplitude, waveform, and timing applied to normal data and collision signals. The trunk cable is about 10 mm in diameter, either yellow or orange (depending on the coating) with dark (usually blue) markings at 2.5 meter intervals. MAUs connected to the trunk system must be spaced at a minimum interval of 2.5 meters but no more than 100 MAUs may occupy 500 meter segment. A repeater occupies a MAU position on the cable and must be counted in that 100 MAU limit. A transceiver usually contains the physical connection to the trunk cable and the MAU circuitry. The maximum length of the cable connecting the MAU and the AUI is 50 meters. A typical two-segment baseband coax Ethernet (10BASE5) is depicted in Figure 7.5.

Broadband and Other 802.3 Implementations

In 1985, an 802.3-compatible broadband standard, type 10BROAD36, was approved. The latest revision to it was published in 1988. Since that time, the other implementations noted at the beginning of this chapter have been approved. Some of the new standards that expand the basic Ethernet definition are quite benefical. In particular, these additional implementations are designed to implement the CSMA/CD standard on a less expensive baseband coaxial medium, a twisted pair medium (StarLan), and on fiber-optic cable. The following sections consider each of these in turn.

Ethernet on Broadband.   The IEEE broadband standard and products re-

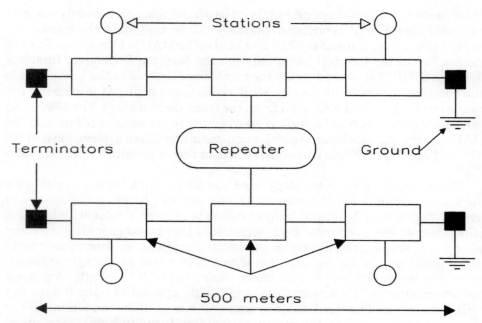

Figure 7.5 Baseband Coax Ethernet

cently developed allow users of Ethernet LANs to change easily between baseband and broadband channels through a device that allows Ethernet controllers to access broadband media. A radio frequency transceiver that modulates the Ethernet signals and puts them on one channel of a multichannel network is described by the IEEE 802 specification; this provides an easy upgrade for users of baseband Ethernet networks. Although the modems and the network cable must be replaced, the same connectors and attachment cables can be used because Ethernet protocol instructions reside on the controller boards in the node computers.[11]

For two-way operation on a U.S. standard CATV system, one or more low-end channels must be used for transmission, and one or more high-end channels must be used for reception. This scheme can also be implemented on a dual-cable system where one cable is used for transmission and the other for reception. This approach is more costly to install and maintain, but it has the advantage of providing added bandwidth. Commercial cable systems are usually single-cable sub-split systems, whereas dedicated systems in large organizations are normally mid-split systems, although this will likely change to high-split as equipment becomes available.

The IEEE 802.3 broadband standard provides for both single- and dual-cable systems. A single-cable system requires, at the headend of the system, a frequency translator that upconverts a transmitted signal on a low-end channel and repropagates it on a high-end channel for reception. The 802.3 broadband standard requires the use of three forward (receiving) channels and three reverse (transmitting) channels for a bandwidth of 18 MHz in each direction (because each standard channel is 6 MHz in width). Although there will be a total bandwidth of 300 or 400 MHz on a standard CATV system, if the system is heavily used, it may be quite difficult to extract 36 MHz for use of Ethernet. Some manufacturers are, therefore, offering somewhat nonstandard implementations that take only 12 or 24 MHz. Typically, this means that the 10 Mb/s data rate is compromised or that some nonstandard protocol conversion is used. With current technology, it is not possible to get the full 10 Mb/s on a single pair of 6 MHz channels. As some analysts have noted, broadband promises bigger, better Ethernets that use controllers now installed in many computers.[12]

Local networks vary widely in the cost of their embedded plant. Broadband networks tend to be more complex and costly to plan, install, and maintain than baseband Ethernet. Even so, there are compelling reasons for a company to implement Ethernet in a broadband network. A draft standard based on DEC's proposal was distributed to the committee in June 1984 and adopted in mid-1985. It defines techniques for implementing 10 Mb/s carrier sense multiple access with collision detection (CSMA/CD) on broadband coaxial cable. A final version was published in 1988.[13] Broadband networks are coming of age. Broadband technology has been used since the late 1960s to provide inexpensive and reliable transmission systems around large industrial sites. Today, an increasing number of universities and other large organizations are using broadband systems because of their flexibility, large bandwidth, and the ability to provide video and voice services as well as data communications.

When implementing Ethernet on broadband, one objective was to make it as compatible as possible with existing baseband systems. The way to do that was to design a broadband MAU or transceiver that would allow the attachment of existing AUI and related circuitry, through a standard AUI cable, to the transceiver. The broadband transceiver (MAU) is more intelligent than its baseband cousin, for it must perform some protocol conversion before placing the signal on the cable through a modulator. Rather than the Differential Manchester encoding scheme used by the baseband system, NRZ encoding is used on the broadband cable. The frame is modified to include a postamble that helps detect the end-of-frame. The preamble is also modified to allow for scrambling of the signal.

On a single-cable system, the offset between outbound and inbound frequencies is either 156.25 or 192.25 MHz. The former corresponds to earlier usage in sub- and mid-split systems. The latter is preferred for high-split systems but works equally well with mid-split. The broadband standard generally followed recommendations by DEC, although DEC's original implementation used a 156.25 MHz offset, while 192.25 is preferred today. IBM, when it announced its broadband PC Network, placed its outbound channel in the middle of the 18 MHz outbound allocation preferred by DEC; this can cause problems for some organizations. The standard provided for several different options for allocating frequencies, and these may be seen in Table 7.1.

Broadband offers a number of opportunities to many organizations. If a university or industrial campus already has a CATV system or wishes to build one, it may be used as an interbuilding backbone system for linking baseband Ethernets. Although the broadband transceivers cost a good bit more than those for baseband systems, baseband Ethernets can be linked together through broadband. Furthermore, broadband allows a more extended trunk system. Finally, the total cost of a broadband system may be shared by the many different services capable of being transmitted on the broadband medium.

Thin Wire (ANSI/IEEE 802.3a1988–10BASE2).

The IEEE 802.3 LAN Subcommittee made 10BASE2 (sometimes referred to as "Cheapernet" or "Thinnet") the first standard low-cost LAN. Cheapernet, a smaller and less expensive version of the 802.3 standard, uses thinner cable than Ethernet and accommodates 30 nodes per segment of cable at a maximum distance of 200 meters between nodes without a repeater. Companies that have already announced support for Cheapernet include National Semiconductor Corp., Hewlett-Packard, and International Computers Ltd.[14] Essentially a smaller version of the 802.3 network, Cheapernet trades off cable span and the number of

Table 7.1   Frequency Allocations for Transmit and Receive Band
(Frequencies in MHz)

TRANSMITTER	RECEIVER	
Transmit Band	Translation 156.25 MHz Receive Band	Translation 192.25 MHz Receive Band
35.75–53.75	192–210	228–246
41.75–59.75	198–216	234–252
47.75–65.75	204–222	240–258
*53.75–71.75	210–228	246–264
59.75–77.75	216–234	252–270
65.75–83.75	222–240	258–276

NOTES: 1. Some of these optional bands are overlapping.
2. An asterisk (*) denotes the preferred frequency allocation.

stations to obtain lower cost and easier installation. It uses RG-58 coaxial cable.[15]

National Semiconductor has a chip-implementing Cheapernet; other hardware manufacturers are developing their implementations. An alternative Ethernet, even less costly, is StarLan, which was proposed by AT&T and is being developed by NCR, Wang, Intel, and others.[16] The 10BASE2 Chip set has the transceiver electronics in the data terminal equipment, along with the interface electronics. This cabling technique eliminates the extra drop cable of an Ethernet set. However, it places certain limits on the Cheapernet version that do not apply to the traditional Ethernet configurations. The components of the Cheapernet interface include the DP8390 network interface controller, the DP8391 serial network interface, and the DP8392 coaxial transceiver interface. These components use IEEE 802.3 protocol.[17] Some PC boards now on the market (those produced by 3COM are good examples) provide both a Thinnet (i.e., Cheapernet) and a standard Ethernet connection.

StarLan (ANSI/IEEE 802.3e–1988—1BASE5).

The quest for a low cost 802.3-compatible network has resulted in an addition to the standard that follows AT&T's StarLan specification. It could become the standard low-cost departmental network for clusters of 25 or fewer personal computers. The objectives of the StarLan specification considered by the IEEE include the use of telephone-type wiring and low-cost equipment and cabling; easy installation, reconfiguration, and service; interconnection of independently developed stations and hubs; and fairness. The network is a low-cost 1 Mb/s Carrier Sense for Multiple Access with Collision Detection (CSMA/CD) network that is based on twisted-pair wiring. It uses the same basic scheme as that which is used by Ethernet and is available in two basic configurations: daisy chaining, which is less expensive and suitable for up to ten personal computers; and a configuration resembling a star, which gave the network its name and which can be used to connect as many as 100 personal computers up to 800 feet from the hub. The specification includes the use of twisted-pair wiring. With the AT&T implementation, the interconnection of up to 1,000 personal computers and up to five levels of hubs is possible.[18]

The development of the StarLan standard opened the market to manufacturers of chips, boards, and LANs for the design and production of products based on the planned specifications: Many companies have developed products tied to the standards. Over 12 companies, AT&T being the most prominent, have introduced or will introduce products for the StarLan network, thus establishing a new and inexpensive alternative to standard Ethernet and the underdeveloped token ring network.[19] Some of the board products already on the market are not yet capable of being intermixed in the same physical network.[20] A 10 Mb/s twisted pair version is also under development and may provide enhanced throughput at a relatively low cost.

10 Mb/s Twisted Pair (10BASE-T). In addition to 1BASE5, the 10BASE-T, 10 Mb/s, twisted-pair, 100 meter expansion of the 1BASE5 standard was close to adoption as this was written and will likely become a standard in 1990 or 1991. Both the 1BASE5 and 10BASE-T proposals are based on AT&T's StarLan expansions of the general 802.3 CSMA/CD standard. The 10 Mb/s specification will operate over a twisted-pair transmission system up to 100 meters in length without the use of a repeater. 10BASE-T supports network configurations using the CSMA/CD access method defined in the ISO 8802-3:1989 (ANSI/IEEE 802.3–1988). The 10BASE-T supplement to IEEE Std 802.3 is designed to provide a simple, inexpensive, and flexible means of attaching devices to the local network medium, which, in this case, may be existing telephone wiring within a building. Until 10BASE-T, the only way in which inexpensive telephone-type wiring could be used was with the relatively low-speed (1 Mb/s) StarLan-based system. The most general objective of the specification is to provide the physical means for communications between local area network data link entities.

A 10BASE-T network may be a component in a larger, mixed-media 802.3 network. Both as a standalone system and as part of a mixed-media network certain constraints operate. For networks extending beyond 100 meters, the 100 meter segments must be attached to one another with repeaters and repeater sets are required for such interconnections. A path between nodes may consist of up to five segments and four repeater sets. When such a network is configured, up to three of the segments may be coax (such as the original 10BASE5) and the remainder must be link segments. If the links between segments are fiber, the fiber link segments may not exceed 500 meters. If a smaller network path is used, up to three repeater sets and four segments, then the length of connecting fiber segments may be as long as 1000 meters.

Fiber-Optic Ethernets. The original concept of Ethernet version 2.0 and IEEE 802.3 CSMA/CD Layer 1 and Layer 2 protocols (Physical and Data Link Layers, respectively) restricted fiber optics to connecting remote half-repeaters (devices that attach widely dispersed Ethernet segments). There are, however, a growing number of Ethernet/802.3 data communication equipment manufacturers who have chosen to ignore this aspect of the specification and to offer other types of fiber-optic Ethernet interconnect methods.[21] A few manufacturers offer 802.3-compatible fiber-optic backbones. Although such systems are available, and it may be necessary to use such a system in electrically noisy areas, they are not 802.3 standard networks. Should the 802.3 Committee someday recommend a fiber-optic Physical Layer standard, current offerings may or may not be compatible. On the other hand, if it is possible to connect an Ethernet controller (AUI) through a standard MAU cable to a fiber-optic transceiver, everything but the backbone would remain standard.

One such optical bus network typifies this situation. In 1986, S.L.

Storozan of American Photonics, Inc., described a U-shaped bus configuration to facilitate two-way communication between any pair of transceivers that are passively tapped to the bus with an optical T-coupler. The network employs the CSMA/CD of IEEE 802.3 for medium access control. The network, consisting of an optical bus, passively tapped transceiver control units, and other optical devices, has two types of user ports. A high-speed port offers up to 10 Mb/s throughput for workstations with communication interfaces conforming to IEEE 802.3, which seem to be increasingly gaining in market position. The other port supports lower-speed terminals such as those of personal computers with RS-232-C interfaces, because their popularity is considered to be equally important.[22] A growing number of manufacturers are making equipment available for the use of fiber as a "backbone" for interconnecting 802.3 LANs.

An alternative configuration is illustrated by Fibernet II. E.G. Rawson described in 1985 the experimental system as a fiber-optic LAN having an active star configuration. It is plug-compatible with the 10 Mb/s coaxial-cable Ethernet LAN at its transceiver cable interface. Ethernet requires the detection of packet collisions; this function is implemented in Fibernet II at the active star node. Collision presence is signaled to the host transceivers with a unique in-band optical signal. Fibernet II features improved electromagnetic immunity, absence of signal radiation from cables, freedom from ground-loop currents due to ground potential differences between remote sites, new network topology options, and a growth path to future broadband services. Fibernet II has been implemented as an experimental system at the Xerox Palo Alto Research Center. Fibernet II can apparently support a network diameter of over 4.0 km, in contrast to the coax Ethernet, which is limited to 2.5 km.[23]

CONFORMANCE TO 802.3

The 802.3 standards are very flexible and allow for a wide variety of implementations. Problems can arise in designing a CSMA/CD LAN for a real company or other organization. On a broadband LAN, for example, there may not be 36 MHz of bandwidth available for use by Ethernet. Consequently, it may be desirable to use products that implement a somewhat compatible 802.3 system by putting the signal out on two 12 MHz channels or by slowing down the data rate (say to 5 Mb/s) and using only a single channel pair. In an industrial environment or other electrically or environmentally dirty area, fiber-optic cable may be the only way to implement a reliable system.

Examples of an Ethernet used primarily for microcomputers are the products produced by 3COM. 3COM claims that it can exceed standard service levels in several areas. The problem with a nonstandard implementation is that users may find that products from another manufacturer may not work on a

LAN if the standards are not followed with some care and accuracy. Conversely, local conditions may require some deviation from the standard to have any service at all. The LAN designer and systems analyst must take all these issues into account when structuring a LAN for a particular environment.

THE FUTURE OF 802.3 LANS

IBM withheld support for the 802.3 standard in preference for Token Ring Networks. To this very day IBM tends to downplay the importance of 802.3 and some of its officials have very recently been quoted as saying that 802.3 will fade away during the 1990s in favor of Token Ring. A result of IBM's perspective was an observation in 1986 by Lynn Haber, associate editor of *Mini Micro Systems*, that "one is moved to question Ethernet's viability, now that IBM has revealed its strategy [Token Ring LAN]."[24] Even as Haber was writing in 1986, however, IBM introduced the 9370 office minicomputer with both Ethernet and Token Ring support, and in 1988 the 8232 LAN controller that can channel attach either a token ring or 802.3 LAN to a System 370 architecture mainframe (4381, 3090, and so on). It is now possible to front-end a computer complex consisting of mainframes, minis, and micros with an 802.3 network using some higher-layer protocols, such as TCP/IP, to integrate the various machines. Notwithstanding IBM's problems with 802.3, there are a number of reasons to believe that it will contiue to be a major LAN contender throughout the 1990s.

First and foremost is that a very large number of Ethernet LANs have been constructed. As early as 1986 it was estimated that more than 30,000 Ethernet LANs had been installed, supported by more than 100 vendors, including giants like DEC. IBM's recent, though grudging support for Ethernet/802.3 reveals a view at IBM that Ethernet is here to stay—at least for awhile. In addition to the apparent market for 802.3, continued development of 802.3 standards has meant that vendors can respond to buyers' needs within the framework of national and international standards. Moreover, as was discussed in Chapter 6, more and more manufacturers are climbing on the 802.3 bandwagon and producing complete LANs based on these standards. A final summary of the standards as they appeared at the beginning of 1990 may be found in Table 7.2.

A second set of developments, already mentioned, is also giving 802.3 Ethernets a boost. The continuing development and widening support for the Technical Office Protocol (TOP) and the Manufacturing Automation Protocol (MAP) provide strong support for both Ethernet and token bus LANs. TOP and MAP are compatible protocols located in Layers 3, 4, 5 (Network, Transport, and Session Layers), 6, and parts of 7. They diverge in Layer 7 (the Application Layer) and in Layers 1 and 2 (Physical and Data Link Layers). At Layer 7, TOP specifies application protocols that address the problems of the technical and office user, whereas MAP deals with factory floor environments. Germane to

Table 7.2 IEEE 802.3 Summary

	10BASE5[a]	10BASE2	10BROAD36	1BASE5	10BASE-T[b]
Bandwidth (Mb/s)	10	10	10	1	10
Media	coax[c]	coax[d]	coax[e]	twisted	twisted
Distance (km)	.5	.2	3.6	.5	.1
Topology	Bus	Bus	Bus	Star[f]	Star[f]

NOTES:
[a] 10BASE5 is the "normal" 802.3 standard originally patterned after Ethernet. 10BASE2 is more restricted in distance but uses less expensive components. 10BROAD36 is the 802.3 broadband standard. 1BASE5 is the CSMA/CD system modeled on AT&T's original StarLAN and 10BASE-T is a high-speed expansion of 10BASE1. The latter two use twisted-pair, unshielded, copper wire ("telephone" wire).
[b] Proposed, not adopted, as of this writing.
[c] So-called "thick" coax with a 50 Ohm impedance, 9.525 mm (.4 inches) in diameter.
[d] Sometimes called "cheapernet" or "thinnet" 10BASE2 uses 50 Ohm coax 4.8 mm (.2 inches) in diameter (RG58).
[e] Uses standard CATV components and cable with a 75 Ohm impedence in various sizes.
[f] Although wired as a star configuration, any CSMA/CD system is logically and conceptually a bus.

this discussion is the fact that TOP originally specified 802.3 10BASE5 for Layers 1 and 2, although the TOP task force was also considering 10BROAD36 (broadband), 10BASE2 (Cheapernet), and 1BASE5 (StarLan) as viable alternatives. They were also considering the possible use of an 802.5 token ring. The point is that TOP is clearly wedded to Ethernet in some form.[25]

REFERENCES

1. S. Zipper, "CIM Gear Firms Move to Automation Stds," *Electronic News*, Vol. 31, No. 1575, November 11, 1985, p. 52. See also, Anon., "An Important Advance in Local Networks," *EDP Analyzer*, Vol. 22, No. 9, September 1984, pp. 13–14; J. Dix, "Users to Demonstrate Pioneer Network At Detroit Show," *ComputerWorld*, Vol. 19, No. 28, July 15, 1985, p. 10; P. Cleaveland, "Local Area Networks for Industrial Control: Standardized LANs Are Spreading, but Others Will Remain," *I & CS*, Vol. 57, No. 8, August 1984, pp. 31–37 (4 pages).

2. Technical Committee on Computer Communications of the IEEE Computer Society, *IEEE Standards for Local Area Networks: Supplements to Carrier Sense Multiple Access with Collision Detection (CSMA/CD) Access Method and Physical Layer Specifications* (New York: The Institute

of Electrical and Electronics Engineers, Inc., 1987). This publication covers ANSI/IEEE 802.3a–1988, Type 10BASE2; ANSI/IEEE 802.3b–1988, Type 10BROAD36; ANSI/IEEE 802.3c–1988, Repeater Unit for 10 Mb/s Baseband Networks; and ANSI/IEEE 802.3e–1988, Type 1BASE5.

3. E. E. Mier, "Proliferating Permutations of the Ethernet 'Standard,'" *Data Communications*, Vol. 13, No. 14, December 1984, pp. 48 and 50+.

4. T. Huggins, "ISO Puts the Ball in Suppliers' Court," *Computing (U.K.)*, October 13, 1983, p. 16.

5. M. Edwards, "LAN Standards Give Telecom Managers Strategies for Making Informed Interconnection Decisions," *Communication News (USA)*, Vol. 23, No. 9, September 1986, pp. 48–57.

6. H. Friedberg, "OpenNET-key to a System Independent Network," *Elektron. Inc. (Germany)*, Vol. 16, No. 5, 1985, pp.78, 80, and 85.

7. See, for example, the following commentaries: N. Mokhoff, "Demand Grows for Integrated Open Networks," *Computer Design*, Vol. 24, No. 11, September 1, 1985, pp. 51–61 (11 pages); N. Mokhoff, "LANs Team up to Widen the Network Connection," *Computer Design*, Vol. 24, No. 2, February 1985, pp. 99–102 and 104+ (13 pages); D. Way and S. Bal, "Getting a Handle on the Elusive Local Network Marketplace," *Data Communications*, Vol. 14, No. 9, August 1985, pp. 195–198 and 201+.

8. The material in this section is taken, except where noted, from Technical Committee on Compiuter Communications of the IEEE Computer Society, *IEEE Standards for Local Area Networks: Carrier Sense Multiple Access with Collision Detection (CSMA/CD) Access Method and Physical Layer Specifications* (New York: The Institute of Electrical Electronics Engineers, Inc., 1985).

9. See *Digital's Networks: An Architecture with a Future* (Maynard, MA: Digital Equipment Corporation), p. 27. While this is a good overview of DEC networking, most of the technical information in this section is taken from *DECnet: Digital Network Architecture*, General Description, Document No. AA-N149A-TC (Maynard, MA: Digital Equipment Corporation, 1982), pp. 2.2ff. Note that this discussion follows the DEC literature and not the 802.3 standard. There are some discrepancies between the two and this is a discussion of the DEC implementation, not of the 802.3 standard.

10. The summary is quoted verbatim from IEEE Std 802.3–1985, p. 32.

11. Menachem E. Abraham, "Running Ethernet Modems over Broadband Cable," *Data Communications*, Vol. 15, No. 5, May 1986, p. 199(8).

12. See Abraham, Ref. 11, pp. 199–212.

13. The latest version is ANSI/IEEE Std. 802.3a–1988, Type 10BROAD36.

14. P. A. Hunter, "Cheapernet LAN Expected to Get IEEE Nod," *Information Systems News*, No. 128, November 12, 1984, pp. 42 and 45.

15. A. B. Raderman and R. W. Flakes, "Video and Voice Communications Join Ethernet on Broadband Cable,"*Data Communications*, Vol. 14, No. 3, March 1985, pp. 293–303.

16. P. Hunter, "Cheaper Ethernet Due," *ComputerWeekly*, No. 933, October 18, 1984, p. 6.

17. "Chip Set Points to Lower Costs in Ethernet Cabling," *Computer Design*, Vol. 23, No. 14, December 1984, p. 160.

18. Jeffry Beeler, "StarLan Clears Highest Hurdle in Gaining IEEE Approval," *ComputerWorld*, Vol. 20, No. 47, November 24, 1986, p. 7(1); see also, David Churbuck, "StarLan is a Low Cost, Departmental Network," *PC Week*, Vol. 3, No. 35, September 2, 1986, p. 110(2). For an evaluation of StarLan see Frank J. Derfler, Jr., "Making Connections: AT&T's StarLan," *PC Magazine,* Vol. 5, No. 22, December 23, 1986, p. 223ff.

19. Eric Sack, "Vote on StarLan Awaited," *MIS Week*, Vol. 7, No. 30, July 28, 1986, p. 1(2).

20. Sack, Ref. 19, p. 1.

21. S. L. Storozum, "Fiber Optic Ethernet Design Tradeoffs," Electro/86 and Mini/Micro Northeast, Conference Record 13/3/1-9 1986, 13–15 May 1986, Boston, MA (Los Angeles, CA: Electron. Conventions Manage., 1986).

22. T. Akiba, A. Okada, S. Suzuki, and O. Takahashi, "Optical Bus Network Using Ethernet and Higher Level Protocol LSIs," IEEE Global Telecommunications Conference, GLOBECOM '84 Conference Record. 'Communications in the Information Age,' 26–29 November 1984, Atlanta, GA, Vol. 3, pp. 1335–1339. See also, for another suggestion, R. P. Kelley, J. R. Jones, V. J. Bratt, and P. W. Pate, "Transceiver Design and Implementation Experience in an Ethernet-Compatible Fiber Optic Local Area Network," Proceedings of the IEEE INFOCOM '84, 9–12 April 1984, San Francisco, CA, pp. 2–7.

23. E. G. Rawson, "The Fibernet II Ethernet-compatible Fiber Optic LAN," *J. Lightwave Technol. (USA)*, Vol. LT-3, No. 3, June 1985, pp. 496–501.

24. Lynn Haber, "DECnet Survives in the LANscape," *Mini Micro World*, Vol. 19, No. 4, March 1986, p. D1.

25. Wendy Rauch-Hindin, "Revamped MAP and TOP Mean Business," *Mini Micro World*, Vol. 19, No. 13, November 1986.

ANSI/IEEE STD 802.4—TOKEN PASSING BUS

Media Access Control and the Physical Layer characteristics of 802.3 (see Chapter 7) and 802.4 standards are quite different. 802.3 is primarily a baseband (although broadband is defined) CSMA/CD system, where as 802.4 is primarily a broadband token passing bus scheme. These differences are very important for the applications that are appropriate for their use. The relationship of 802.4 to the other IEEE standards and to the OSI Reference Model is depicted in Figure 8.1.

A broadband option is specified in the IEEE 802.3 standard and is the primary option in the IEEE 802.4 standard. A brief overview of broadband technology can by found in the Appendix. In the 802.4 standard, three different broadband options are specified, including an option that is based on standard commercial CATV technology. In addition to a discussion of the 802.4 MAC sublayer and the Physical Layer, this chapter deals more extensively than others with CATV-oriented options. A familiarity with the material in the Appendix will be useful for the discussions in this chapter.

Token passing, which was originally used for ring topologies, became available in 1983 on general purpose (rather than proprietary) systems using bus structures. A token simply designates the location "of the poll on a distributed polling list."[1] More explicitly, within the context of IEEE Std 802.4–1985, a token is a specialized frame that regulates the right of access.[2] Each network device must be polled, and as that polling is done, each station has an opportunity to transmit. Thus, there can be no collisions. Polling need not take place in

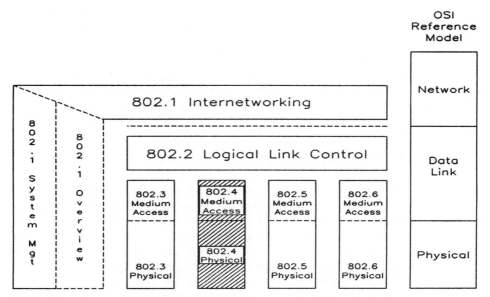

Figure 8.1   Relationship of IEEE Standards and the OSI Reference Model
SOURCE: Based on IEEE P802.1, Draft E, July 1, 1987, *Overview, Internetworking, and Systems Management*, unapproved draft published for comment only, by permission of the IEEE. All rights reserved by The Institute for Electrical and Electronics Engineers, Inc., p. 7.

a centralized fashion because each station can pass the token on following a transmission. Because there is no collision detection (and there are no collisions), the behavior of a token passing system may be accurately calculated. A token passing scheme relies on all devices being serially polled, which implies its own set of problems. This chapter will examine the token bus standards described in the ANSI/IEEE Std 802.4–1985.[3]

In 1983, 3M announced a broadband bus topology LAN using token passing; so did Token/Net from Concord Data Systems. The 3M system used the ARCNET chip set from Datapoint, a proprietary token bus network available since the 1970s. Because ARCNET predates the development of token bus standards, systems based on ARCNET face some inconsistencies with the bulk of the data communications industry, as do other token bus schemes that were developed before the promulgation of the IEEE 802.4 token bus standard.

A token bus system is often described as a logical ring, because some or all nodes on a token bus LAN must be logically addressed as a ring. Just as CSMA/CD can result in lower throughput under conditions where large numbers of collisions occur, so too can token passing schemes degenerate under heavy loads measured by the number of connections on the system; this is because the token must pass every node in either the physical or logical ring before returning to any given connection. The IEEE 802.4 standard has been adopted by General Motors and others in the development of the Manufacturing Automation Protocol (MAP) as the standard MAP access method. MAP has already been discussed in Chapter 5. A token passing scheme was adopted for MAP because process control systems require a deterministic network rather than a probabilistic system. That is, access to the medium must be predictable.

A DETAILED LOOK AT 802.4

The IEEE Std 802.4–1985 document presents a LAN standard that deals with all elements of the token passing bus access method and its associated physical signaling and media technologies. The access function coordinates the use of the shared medium among the attached stations. Shared media can be categorized into broadcast and sequential types. The document deals exclusively with the broadcast type. On a broadcast medium, every station may receive all signals transmitted. Media of the broadcast type are usually configured as a physical bus. IEEE Std 802.4–1985 has been developed to achieve compatible interconnection of stations by way of a LAN using the token passing bus access method. This standard specifies the electrical and physical characteristics of the transmission medium, the electrical signaling method used, the frame formats transmitted, the actions of a station upon receipt of a data frame, and the services provided at the conceptual interface between the MAC sublayer and the LLC sublayer above it.

Introduction and Overview

The primary characteristics of the token access method can be stated as follows:

1. A token controls the right of access to the physical medium—momentary control over the medium is exercised by the station holding the token

2. As the token is passed from station to station by stations residing on the medium, a logical ring is formed

3. A data transfer phase and a token transfer phase constitute steady state operation

4. Ring maintenance functions such as ring initialization, lost token recovery, new station addition to the logical ring, and general housekeep-

ing of the logical ring take place within each station. As a consequence, ring maintenance functions are replicated among all the token using stations on the ring.

Broadcast and *sequential* are the two major categories into which shared media can generally be classified. The 802.4 standard, because it defines a bus structure, specifies a broadcast system. On such a system, every station may receive all signals transmitted—as happens with CSMA/CD LANs. Although this is a broadcast-type LAN, the token access method is always logically sequential. This characteristic is illustrated in Figure 8.2. During normal steady-state operation, the right to access the medium passes from station to station. The physical connectivity may be unrelated to the order of the logical ring. In Figure 8.2, for example, stations A and D can receive frames, although they cannot initiate a transmission because they will never be sent the token.

As with other standards in the IEEE LAN series, the MAC sublayer provides the logic a station needs to gain access to the medium. In the case of the token bus, MAC provides sequential access to the shared bus medium by passing control of the medium from station to station in a logically circular fashion. When the MAC sublayer recognizes and accepts the token from the predecessor station, the local MAC has determined the right to access the shared medium. It also determines when the token shall be passed to the successor station.

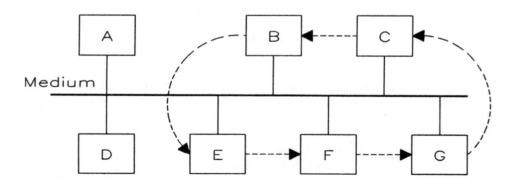

LAN Stations A-G
Logical Ring: Stations B, C, E, F, and G

Figure 8.2 Logical Ring on Physical Bus

Media Access Control (MAC)

There are ten general MAC sublayer functions:

1. Lost token timer
2. Distributed initialization
3. Token holding timer (for multiple classes of service)
4. Limited data buffering
5. Node address recognition
6. Frame encapsulation (including token preparation)
7. FCS generation and checking
8. Valid token recognition
9. New ring member addition
10. Node failure error recovery

In order to perform these functions, the sublayer is partitioned into several asynchronous logical "machines", as illustrated in Figure 8.3. Remember that the MAC sublayer communicates with the higher-level LLC sublayer and with the lower-level Physical Layer (PHY). MAC can either input or output information to both LLC and PHY.

The Interface Machine (IFM) provides communications and buffering between MAC and LLC and between station management and MAC. A variety of services are provided by the IFM. The IFM interprets incoming and outgoing service primitives; it maps the "quality of service" parameters from the LLC to the MAC; it queues service requests; and, perhaps most importantly, it performs the "address recognition" function on received LLC frames, accepting only those addressed to the local station. Central to the functioning of MAC is the Access Control Machine. Among other things, it cooperates with the ACMs of all other stations on the bus in handling the token to control transmission access. The ACM is also responsible for the maintenance of the logical ring, including admission of new stations. The third major function of the ACM is to detect and recover, where possible, from faults and failures in the token bus network.

An incoming bit stream from the Physical Layer is assembled into frames and validated by the Receive Machine (RxM). When validated, the frames are passed to the IFM and the ACM. Assembly and validation is accomplished by recognizing the frame start and frame end delimiters (SD and ED), checking the frame check sequence (FCS), and then validating the frame's structure. Analo-

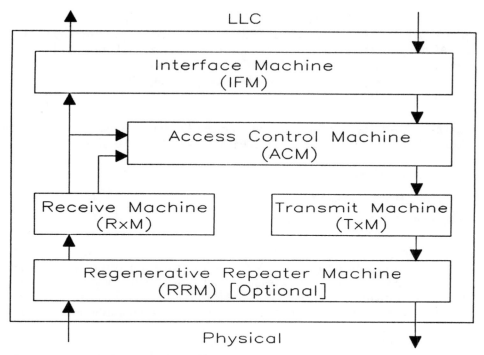

Figure 8.3 MAC Functional Partitions

SOURCE: Based on ANSI/IEEE Std 802.4–1985. Token-Passing Bus Access Method and Physical Layer Specifications, ©1985 by The Institute of Electricial and Electronics Engineers, Inc., by permission of the IEEE. All rights reserved by The Institute of Electrical and Electronics Engineers, Inc., p. 20.

gously, the Transmit Machine (TxM) accepts a frame from the ACM and transmits it in the appropriate format to the Physical Layer. The TxM builds a MAC PDU by prefacing each frame with the required preamble and SD and then appending the FCS and ED. When a Regenerative Repeater Machine (RRM) is present, the operation of the TxM will vary from this description. As noted in Figure 8.3, the RRM is optional and will exist only in special repeater stations—possibly in a broadband or headend remodulator, for example. Both the RxM and TxM may cooperate with the RRM in repeating operations.

Of these five machines, the ACM is clearly the most critical and most complex. It is the key control mechanism for the token bus access method. Both the IFM and RxM support the ACM, although they participate heavily in the operation of the MAC Layer protocol.

Service Specification.   As with 802.3, the 802.4 standard is organized along architectural lines. LLC is described in some detail in Chapter 4. The relationships among LLC, MAC, Physical Layer, and the OSI Reference Model are depicted in Figure 8.4. This section deals with the services provided by MAC to LLC. Although data transfer can be point-to-point or multipoint, either acknowledged or unacknowledged, MAC services provide the means by which LLC entities can exchange MAC service data-units (m_sdu) without an underlying point-to-point connection.

LLC-MAC Service.   As in the 802.3 (see Chapter 7) MAC service specification, in 802.4 there are several service primitives that are defined:

1. MA_DATA.request

2. MA_DATA.indication

3. MA_DATA.confirmation

When an MA_DATA.request primitive is passed to the MAC sublayer, it requests that an m_sdu be sent. An MA_DATA.indication primitive is passed from the MAC sublayer to indicate that an m_sdu has arrived. The MA_DATA.confirmation is sent from MAC to convey the local results of the previous associated MA_DATA.request. All services are mandatory and are required in all implementations.

The MA_DATA.request is the service request primitive for the LLC connectionless data transfer service. The three associated parameters are destina-

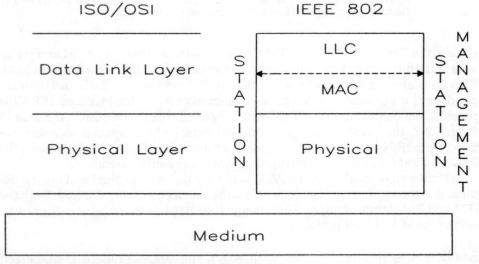

Figure 8.4   IEEE 802/OSI Reference Model

tion_address, m_sdu, and desired_quality. The destination_address specifies either an individual or a group MAC-entity address on the network. The service data-unit to be transmitted by the MAC sublayer is specified by m_sdu, and the desired quality of service is specified by desired_quality. The desired_quality includes both MAC-level priority [with a range of 0 (lowest) to 7 (highest)] and MAC-level delivery confirmation service. This primitive is passed from a LLC sublayer entity to the MAC sublayer to request that the MAC entity compose and transmit the specified frame at the desired quality of service on the LAN. Obviously, receipt of this primitive by MAC causes the attempt to compose and transmit the specified frame.

Four parameters are associated with the MA_DATA.indication service request: destination_address, source_address, m_sdu, and quality. Destination_address and source_address specify the DA and SA fields of a frame, as received by the local MAC entity. The service data-unit received by the local MAC is specified by m_sdu, and the delivered quality of service is delineated by quality. MA_DATA.indication is passed from the MAC sublayer entity to the LLC sublayer entity to announce the arrival of a frame from the Physical Layer. Frames are reported only when they are free of detected errors and the destination_address is that of the local MAC.

Because the function of MA_DATA.confirmation is to provide confirmation for LLC connectionless data transfer, only quality and status parameters are required. The quality parameter specifies the quality of service but, in this case, the service that was actually provided. Status flags the success or failure of the corresponding previous MA_DATA.request. MA_DATA.confirmation is passed from the MAC sublayer entity to the LLC sublayer entity to confirm the success or failure of the service provided for the previous associated LLC data transfer request. When the quality parameter specifies either a request with no response or a response, then this primitive is passed when the requested response frame is received (or when all retries have occurred after a local failure).

Station Management—MAC Services.

In addition to the LLC MAC services, the standard also specifies a set of station management services provided by MAC. Such services are local administrative services between the MAC sublayer and its manager. These services are[4]:

1. Resetting the MAC entity, selecting the MAC entity's MAC address (and implicitly the length of all MAC addresses on the network) and the token passing protocol appropriate for the network (e.g., token bus, token bus repeater), and confirming that the MAC entity can implement that protocol

2. Specifying the values of time and counter preset constants appropriate for the network (e.g., a bus slot_time)

3. Determining whether the MAC entity should be a member of a token passing ring and whether its address appears to be unique to the local network

4. Reading the current values of some of the MAC entity's parameters

5. Notifying the station management entity of relevant changes in the MAC entity's parameters

6. Specifying the set of group addresses that the MAC entity recognizes

7. Providing the means by which station management peer entities can exchange MAC m_sdus without establishing an underlying point_to_point connection

The interactions between MAC and station management are defined in terms of a number of service primitives. A detailed account of the service primitives is available in Part 3 of the standard.

A token passing scheme requires considerable maintenance. The services provided by MAC to and from station management are essential to the management and maintenance of the token bus network. They include logical ring initialization, additions to the logical ring, deletions from the logical ring, and error recovery. Ring initialization takes place when the network is started or after the logical ring has been broken. Sometimes nonparticipating nodes must be granted the opportunity to insert themselves into the ring, and sometimes a station may voluntarily remove itself from the ring. Errors include duplicate addresses (where two stations infer it's their turn), or a broken ring. These maintenance functions are actually consummated by the use of specialized frames which request that various conditions be met.

Frame Formats.   The generic frame format for 802.4 is similar to, yet different than, the frame format for 802.3. The differences can be accounted for by the differing demands of the token bus and the CSMA/CD access methods. Although there is a single generic frame format, which can be found in Figure 8.5, specialized variations of that format are used for various control purposes. All frames sent or received, however, will conform to the general model.c

The differences in the 802.3 and 802.4 protocols begin with the preamble. With 802.3, the preamble is a constant 7 octets long, designed to allow the PLS circuitry to reach its steady-state synchronization, whereas with 802.4, it is a pattern of one or more octets sent to set the receiver's modem clock and level. The maximum number of octets in a frame (the number between the Start Delimiter and the End Delimiter, but exclusive of them) is 8191. A secondary purpose of the preamble is to guarantee a minimum ED to SD time period to allow stations to process the frame previously received. This time shall be at least 2

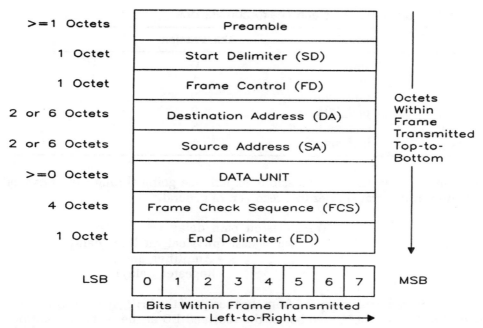

>=1 Octets	Preamble
1 Octet	Start Delimiter (SD)
1 Octet	Frame Control (FD)
2 or 6 Octets	Destination Address (DA)
2 or 6 Octets	Source Address (SA)
>=0 Octets	DATA_UNIT
4 Octets	Frame Check Sequence (FCS)
1 Octet	End Delimiter (ED)

Octets Within Frame Transmitted Top-to-Bottom

LSB   0 1 2 3 4 5 6 7   MSB

Bits Within Frame Transmitted
Left-to-Right

Figure 8.5 Token Bus MAC Frame Format
SOURCE: Based on ANSI/IEEE Std 802.4–1985. *Token-Passing Bus Access Method and Physical Layer Specifications*, ©1985 by The Institute of Electricial and Electronics Engineers, Inc., by permission of the IEEE. All rights reserved by The Institute of Electrical and Electronics Engineers, Inc., p. 42.

μs (microseconds), regardless of the data rate. For example, at a data rate of 1 Mb/s, one octet of preamble is required; at 10 Mb/s, three octets are needed.

Important in understanding elements of the frame formats are several terms (parameters) used to define the frames. The smallest unit of information exchanged between MAC sublayer entities is called a MAC_symbol. A MAC_symbol can be thought of here as a bit with a value of zero (0) or one (1). Physical encoding (PHY_symbol) of the data on the medium can also transmit other MAC_symbols, however, as seen in Table 8.1. The time it takes to send a single MAC_symbol is the MAC_symbol_time, and this varies depending on the data rate for the system. The various MAC_symbol_times may be seen in Table 8.2. A by-product of MAC_symbol_time is Octet_time, which is the time interval required to transmit eight MAC_symbols. The MAC_symbols must be translated into Physical Layer symbols, and these vary with modulation techniques, although they correspond to the waveforms impressed on the physical medium. Transmission_path_delay is the

Table 8.1 MAC_Symbols and Their Abbreviations

Name	Abbreviation
zero	0
one	1
non_data	N
pad_idle	P
silence	S
bad_signal	B

worst-case delay that transmissions experience going through the physical medium from a transmitter to a receiver. In general,

$$\text{Transmission\_path\_delay} = \\ \text{worst\_case (physical\_medium\_delay} \\ + \text{Amplifier\_delay} \\ + \text{Repeater\_delay)}.$$

Station_delay is measured from the receipt of the PHY_symbols that correspond to the last MAC_symbol of the received ED at the receiving station's physical medium interface to the impression of the first immediate_response PHY_symbols onto the physical medium by that station's transmitter. Often a Safety_margin not less than one MAC_symbol_time is required. An important period then becomes Slot_time—the maximum time any station must wait for an immediate_response from another station. Slot_time is measured in octet_times.

$$\text{Slot\_time} = \text{INTEGER (\{ [2 * (Transmission\_path\_delay} \\ + \text{Station\_delay)} \\ + \text{Safety\_margin]} \\ / \text{MAC\_symbol\_time} + 7 \} / 8).$$

Table 8.2: Data Rates and MAC_Symbol_Time

Nominal Data Rate (Mb/s)	Nominal MAC_Symbol_Time (μs)
1	1.0
5	0.2
10	0.1

NOTE: MAC_Symbol_Time is the inverse of the LAN data rate.

Following certain control frames, the MAC protocol provides a Response_window for an immediate_response from another station. That response_window is one slot_time long.

In place of the CSMA/CD Start Frame Delimiter Field, which is one octet in length, are the SD and FC fields, each of which is one octet long. The SD begins the frame and consists of signaling patterns that are always distinguishable from data. The FC determines what class of frame is being sent and is either MAC control, LLC data, station management data, or special purpose data, reserved for future use.

If the transmitted frame is a MAC control frame, then the type of control is specified by bits 3 through 8 of the octet. If the frame is a data frame, then bits 1 and 2 indicate the type of data frame (LLC data, station management data, or special purpose data—from the preceding list); bits 3, 4, and 5 note the MAC action required; and bits 6, 7, and 8 specify the priority. These definitions do not exhaust the bit patterns available, and others may be defined in the future.

The DA and SA fields are defined essentially as they are in 802.3, as is the Frame Check Sequence (see Chapter 7). Addresses are bit strings serving as unique station identifiers or group identifiers. In 802.4, they are used to of order the logical ring. Each MAC address bit string is interpreted as if it were an unsigned integer value sent least-significant bit first. Depending on the bit pattern specified in the FC, the MAC data field can contain one of the following:

1. An LLC PDU used to exchange LLC information between LLC entities

2. A MAC management frame for exchanging MAC management information among MAC entities

3. Some value specific to a MAC control frame

The frame is terminated by the ED, an octet that determines the position of the FCS. The data between the SD and ED must be an integral number of octets, all bits of which are covered by the frame check sequence.

Of great significance to token passing systems are the control structures needed to maintain the ring's integrity, including that special frame, the token. Actually, there are two token frames, the *claim token* and the *use token*. The Claim_token frame may be seen in Figure 8.6 and the Token (use token) frame in Figure 8.7. Information concerning the control structures are passed through the use of the ten special frames, which are identified by the frame control field. The Claim_token is a frame that may have arbitrary values for the data_unit, the length of the data_unit being 0, 2, 4, or 6 times the system's Slot_time as measured in octets (FC=00000000). This frame is sent when the logical ring must be initialized or reinitialized.c

If the successor node fails receipt of a frame, then up to three additional tries are made by sending a Solicit_successor_1 frame (FC=00000001), a

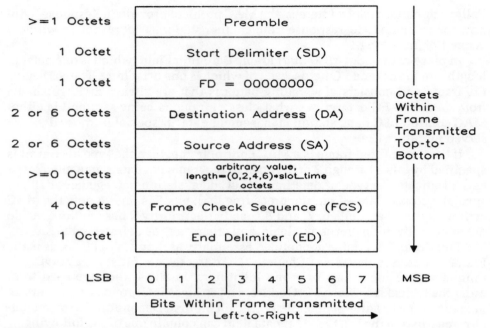

>=1 Octets	Preamble
1 Octet	Start Delimiter (SD)
1 Octet	FD = 00000000
2 or 6 Octets	Destination Address (DA)
2 or 6 Octets	Source Address (SA)
>=0 Octets	arbitrary value, length=(0,2,4,6)•slot_time octets
4 Octets	Frame Check Sequence (FCS)
1 Octet	End Delimiter (ED)

Octets Within Frame Transmitted Top-to-Bottom

LSB | 0 | 1 | 2 | 3 | 4 | 5 | 6 | 7 | MSB

Bits Within Frame Transmitted Left-to-Right

Figure 8.6   Claim_Token Frame Format
SOURCE: Based on ANSI/IEEE Std 802.4–1985. *Token-Passing Bus Access Method and Physical Layer Specifications*, ©1985 by The Institute of Electricial and Electronics Engineers, Inc., by permission of the IEEE. All rights reserved by The Institute of Electrical and Electronics Engineers, Inc., p. 50.

Solicit_successor_2 frame (FC=00000010), and a Who_follows frame (FC=00000011). The first is followed by one response window, the second by two response windows, and the third by three response windows. The response windows give receivers extra time to make the proper address comparisons. Sometimes contention must be resolved with a Resolve_contention frame (FC=00000100), which has a data_unit length of zero but is followed by four response windows. The use token also has a null data_unit and is simply referred to as the Token frame (FC=00001000). The format of the Token frame may be seen in Figure 8.7.

When a station must for some reason drop out of a ring, then a Set_successor frame is sent to the source address from the last frame received. The data_unit field contains the address of the next station in the logical ring, so that the ring can be maintained. The remaining three frames are the LLC data frame, the station management data frame, and the special purpose data frame. All three pass specific kinds of data to receiving stations, rather than users.

The management of a token passing system requires considerably more

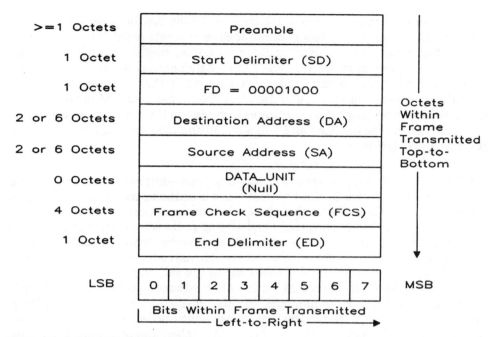

>=1 Octets	Preamble
1 Octet	Start Delimiter (SD)
1 Octet	FD = 00001000
2 or 6 Octets	Destination Address (DA)
2 or 6 Octets	Source Address (SA)
0 Octets	DATA_UNIT (Null)
4 Octets	Frame Check Sequence (FCS)
1 Octet	End Delimiter (ED)

Octets
Within
Frame
Transmitted
Top-to-
Bottom

LSB | 0 | 1 | 2 | 3 | 4 | 5 | 6 | 7 | MSB

Bits Within Frame Transmitted
Left-to-Right →

Figure 8.7 The Token Frame
SOURCE: Based on ANSI/IEEE Std 802.4–1985. *Token-Passing Bus Access Method and Physical Layer Specifications*, ©1985 by The Institute of Electricial and Electronics Engineers, Inc., by permission of the IEEE. All rights reserved by The Institute of Electrical and Electronics Engineers, Inc., p. 51.

overhead than is true of CSMA/CD. Yet, when a logical (or physical) ring has been established, the system will operate in a relatively invariant manner. Timing factors are, therefore, predictable in token passing systems that operate normally. This is why token systems are often referred to as deterministic (rather than probabilistic or stochastic) systems. CSMA/CD, on the other hand, is designed to minimize collisions by backing off transmissions a random amount of time, thus making it probabilistic in nature. In an office environment, the probabilistic character of CSMA/CD doesn't usually matter. In a process-control manufacturing environment, however, this can present serious problems.

Physical Layer and Transmission Medium

As noted previously, with the IEEE LAN standards, the Physical Layer provides the means for connecting to the medium; but the medium is not itself part of the Physical Layer. 802.4 was, however, designed around the use of broadband (radio frequency cable television technology) as the medium. Broadband here refers to high bandwidth data communication systems requiring modulation. Two of the three medium specifications for 802.4, single-channel phase-continuous Frequency Shift Keying (FSK) and single-channel phase-coherent FSK are usually referred to as carrier band systems, rather than broadband. They are modulated systems, however, and therefore are not baseband. Much of the popular debate concerning LANs continues to center on the medium, so this chapter will examine the medium and will also outline the Physical Layer interface service specification.

Overview.
The 802.4 standard was designed—following experience and recommendations from General Motors—as a broadband-based system. In IEEE Std 802.4–1985, three alternative physical medium options were provided, all using 75 Ohm CATV coaxial cable and analog radio frequency signaling. The signaling methods are paired with specific approaches to the installation of the cable plant, in order to provide relatively inexpensive-to-industrial quality systems. Table 8.3 provides a quick overview of the salient characteristics of the specification. An often important feature of broadband systems is the ability to use off-the-shelf CATV components. In this sense all three options qualify as broadband systems, although the first, Phase-continuous FSK, is the most limited and least "standard" in the context of cable television technology. The last, multilevel duobinary amplitude modulation (AM) with Phase Shift Keying (PSK), is also the most versatile in terms of data rates and standardization, using U.S. industry standard two-way cable television design.

As noted in the Appendix, a broadband system operates by modulating a carrier on a 75 Ohm cable. A number of different cable sizes such as RG-6, RG-11, RG-59, and semirigid (0.5 in. to 1.00 in.) are common. Each of these cables has different signal loss characteristics that are calculated into the design of the cable plant and that determine the placement of amplifiers (repeaters in the 802.4 terminology) on the trunk. The most common commercially used connector used to attach a cable to a device is a screw-on F connector, although with the simplest system, Phase-continuous FSK, BNC connectors are specified. Both the Phase-continuous and Phase-coherent FSK systems are single channel, using the cabling system in a manner similar to the baseband Ethernet. No system other than the LAN uses the cable. A by-product of this specification is that nondirectional or omnidirectional taps are used to broadcast all transmissions across the entire cable system in both directions. Obviously, only one signal can be present on the cable at any one time, and this is assured by the token passing protocol. In contrast, the Multilevel Duobinary AM/PSK specification uses standard commercial CATV design and technology.

802.4 Physical Layer Service Specification.
The Physical Layer has two basic functions: to place symbols arriving from the MAC sublayer on the

Table 8.3   802.4 Physical Layer and Medium Summary

Signaling	Data Rate (Mb/s)			Bus	Channel Bandwidth (MHz)			Std
	1	5	10	O/D	1	5	10	
Phase-continuous FSK	Y	N	N	O	N/A	N/A	N/A	N
Phase-coherent FSK	N	Y	Y	O	N/A	N/A	N/A	N
Multilevel Duobinary AM/PSK	Y	Y	Y	D	1.5	6.0	12.0	Y

NOTES: Bus: O=Omnidirectional; D=Directional.
Channel Bandwidth: The entries are in MHz, for each data rate in Mb/s.
Std: Designates whether the specification uses CATV industry standard broadband cable design and channel allocations (Y/N).

physical channel and to accept incoming symbols from the physical channel and pass them on to MAC. MAC can request that a symbol be impressed on the medium, or it can request a specific transmission mode for subsequent data transmissions. The Physical Layer (PHY) can pass an indication and MAC can evaluate the symbol to determine whether it was an end-of-frame. If it was an end-of-frame, then MAC notifies PHY that the next symbol should be either *silence* or the results of a properly transmitted *pad_idle* sequence. These services must be provided to the PHY if it is to meet the specification. In addition to servicing MAC, PHY must also provide some management services provided to the station management functions. These services include

1. Resetting the Physical Layer entity and determining the local area network topology and the Physical Layer entity's role in that LAN

2. Determining the available and current operating modes of the Physical Layer entity and selecting the appropriate operating modes. Choices can include

   a. Transmit and receive channel assignments

   b. Transmitted power level adjustment (per drop cable)

   c. Transmitter output enable/disable (per drop cable)

   d. Received signal source

   e. Signaling mode selection and reporting

   f. Received signal level reporting

Single-channel Phase-continuous FSK.   FSK is a modulation technique whereby information is impressed on a carrier by shifting the frequency of the transmitted signal to one of a small set of frequencies. The term was originally used to denote a type of modulation using two tones (audio frequencies), with one tone representing a one (1) level and the other a zero (0) level. Phase-continuous FSK is a special case of FSK where the translations between signaling frequencies are accomplished by a continuous change of frequency (as opposed to the discontinuous replacement of one frequency by another). It is, therefore, also a form of frequency modulation (FM).

The physical medium is designed as a single-channel FSK coaxial system whereby information is encoded, frequency-modulated onto a carrier, and impressed on the coaxial transmission medium. At any point on the medium, only one information signal may be present. The Physical Layer device is connected to the trunk cable through a very short (350 mm) drop cable that connects to a tee connector on the trunk. The BNC connectors used for this purpose are the same as those used in thin wire Ethernets, although the coaxial cable used in 802.4 is 75 Ohm; Ethernet uses a 50 Ohm coax. Like 802.3, 802.4 specifies the use of Differential Manchester encoding where separate date and clock signals are combined into a single self-synchronizable data stream suitable for transmission on a serial channel.

The communication medium consists of a long unbranched trunk cable that connects to stations by way of the tee connectors. Extensions to a branching trunk can be accomplished through the use of active regenerative repeaters. These are devices used to extend the length, topology, or inter-connectivity of a LAN beyond that which is imposed by the minimum transmit and receive level specifications of the station and the connectivity restrictions of the medium. Regenerative repeaters restore signal amplitude, waveform, and timing. They also prefix enough *pad_idle* symbols to a transmission to compensate for any symbols lost in transmission from the prior station or repeater. In other words, a regenerative repeater connects two or more media segments and repeats anything "heard" on one segment to the other segments. The detailed functional specifications are modeled after the CCITT V Series modem specifications, specifically V.36, although additional detail has been added where necessary.

The value of this specification is that it is relatively inexpensive to install. Extending such a system with repeaters is generally discouraged, although allowed. Network size is a function of both the length of the cable and the number of drops. Because the tee connector is low loss, the drop cables are kept short to limit the shunt capacitance of the cable which can cause a reflection on the trunk]. The total length of a single trunk cable ranges from 1280 meters using RG-59 to 7600 meters using large, semirigid cable (JT4750J). There is no absolute limit to the number of drops, other than physical constraints. The number can rise, but as the number rises, the drop cable length must be minimized. Remember, however, that if the resulting logical ring is very large, throughput will decline, as is true with every ring (logical or physical) system.

Single-channel Phase-coherent FSK.

The purposes of the second specification are similar to the first: to provide ease of installation and services in a wide range of environments; to provide high-network availability; and to facilitate low-cost implementations, as well as low error rates. In addition, however, there was a desire to provide an intermediate system capable of being upgraded to a full, commercial-grade broadband system. Phase-coherent FSK, unlike its phase-continuous cousin, uses only two signaling frequencies that are integrally related to the data rate, and transitions between the two signaling frequencies are made at zero crossings of the carrier waveform.

Unlike the phase-continuous FSK, the phase-coherent FSK system was designed to use CATV-like trunk and drop cable structures permitting the use of components similar to, and in some cases identical with, those mass-produced for the CATV industry. This system is still single-channel and omnidirectional and thus requires the use of nondirectional taps and splitters. All cabling is 75 Ohm, including the drop cable, which has no special length limitations other than those that are a by-product of signal loss. The data rates for the system are much higher than for the phase-continuous FSK specification: 5 or 10 megabits. Connectors to be used are standard F-type connectors common in the CATV industry.

Branching of the trunk can occur using passive splitters that match the impedance of the two segments. The trunk is designed to pass low-frequency AC electrical power, as well as RF. A passive impedance matching tap is used to connect a drop cable to the trunk. The trunk for such a LAN is usually a semi-rigid cable. If planned carefully, the system can be upgraded to full broadband by replacing tap components, adding amplifiers and headend remodulators (translators), and not replacing the cable itself; thus upgrades are less costly. In all RF systems, one point of failure is excessive signal loss, which results in the inability to receive properly without error.

Because in the phase-coherent specification, splitting is allowed with a resulting tree topology, not only the total cable length, but also splitters and taps can add to signal loss. Losses due to components like taps and splitters are explicitly known and must be taken into account when designing the system. Cumulative losses dictate the placement of regenerative repeaters. For example, cascading 96 taps in an unbranched trunk (a 0.5 dB insertion loss for each of 94 taps and 14 dB for the other two taps) consumes the entire dynamic range as specified. Consequently, repeaters may be necessary even when the total cable lengths are relatively short. Drop cable lengths should contribute no more than 1 dB loss (a length of about 30 meters).

Full Broadband Bus.

In addition to the objectives already stated for phase-continuous FSK and phase-coherent FSK systems, IEEE Std 802.4–1985 allowed full scale, commercial-grade broadband systems, in order to to provide a shared medium by some set of totally unrelated applications, such as voice, data, and analog video. Furthermore, there was a subsidiary objective to conserve bandwidth, where possible. While the bandwidth (about 400 MHz) of a CATV system is large, when numerous applications are being run on the system it is easy to run out of spectrum. The use of duobinary AM/PSK was an attempt to meet the latter objective. It is a form of modulation in which data is precoded and signaled as duobinary pulses AM/PSK modulated onto an RF carrier. The PSK component is used in the standard to reduce the RF signal bandwidth, not to carry additional data. Multilevel duobinary AM/PSK uses more than two distinct amplitude levels to represent information. The specification defines a three-level system capable of signaling at one MAC symbol per baud. Remember that the formal definition of *baud* is the time required for an individual signaling event in a digital transmission. With some systems [e.g., Quadrature Amplitude Modulation (QAM)], the bit rate is greater than the symbol or baud rate. The channel allocations suggested for 802.4 are found in Table 8.4.

The specific compatibility considerations built into the specification included the ability for Physical Layer entities to operate on conventional bidirectional (split frequency) CATV-like broadband coaxial cable systems, on similar unidirectional (split cable) systems, or both. The network can, therefore, use standard CATV taps, connectors, amplifiers, power supplies, and coaxial cable. This allows the assignment of different frequency bands for various uses, as illustrated in the example from the University of North Texas described in Chapter 11. This flexibility does, however, have a price—not only in money but also in special system considerations that are not present in single-channel systems. Because bidirectional amplifiers are used to

Table 8.4 North American 6-MHz Mid-split Channels Specified for 802.4 (Frequencies in MHz)

Transmitter	Receiver
Translation 192.25 MHz	
Transmit Band	Receive Band
59.75	252*
65.75*	258*
71.75	264
77.75	270
83.75	276
89.75	282

NOTE: The asterisk (*) denotes overlap with 802.3 specifications.

achieve two-way transmission on a single cable, the Physical Layer entity requires an RF transmitter on the reverse channel and an RF receiver on the forward channel. The amplifiers actually consist of two unidirectional amplifiers [one for the high frequencies (forward), another for the low (reverse)]. At the headend (which does not exist in single-channel systems), the headend translator or remodulator must upconvert the signal from the reverse channel and retransmit it on the forward channel.

The importance of 802.4 and other standards cannot be overestimated. Once a standard is introduced, various manufacturers will rush to produce compatible products. Clearly 802.4 was driven in large part by the need for a LAN standard suitable for the Manufacturing Applications Protocol. Manufacturers are now supporting token bus architecture with chips for general and custom design hardware. Motorola Semiconductor, Gould AMI, Industrial Networking, Inc., and Intel have designed or plan to design new chips. The implementation cost of the IEEE 802.4 token bus standard will be reduced by the production of new chips.[5]

Consider, for example, the MC68824 token bus controller that implements the MAC function for the IEEE 802.4 token bus. The MAC function of a protocol encompasses the most time-critical facilities required in a communications link and represents the major portion of the Data Link Layer of the seven-layer ISO/OSI Reference Model. The VLSI MAC controller reflects both the characteristics of the protocol implemented and the method of system segmentation chosen by the designers to fulfill the requirements of the LAN specification. It interfaces both to a software LLC sublayer and to a Physical Layer.[6] Similarly, Concord Data Systems produces a chip set for its Token/Net LAN, which is 802.4 compatible.

The Token/Net chip set is designed to connect a microprocessor bus to either a carrierband or broadband modem connected to an IEEE 802.4 token bus LAN. The chip set architecture consists of three separate processors: the data chip, the protocol chip, and the DMA chip, connected by a high-performance, byte-wide local bus. The data chip processes serial data for and from the modem, performs framing and error detection functions, converts serial data to parallel or parallel data to serial, and synchronizes the modem data to a common system clock. The protocol chip executes the IEEE 802.4 medium access protocol and performs a portion of the LLC functions, including the immediate response option. The DMA chip provides a connection to an 8- or 16-bit-wide microprocessor bus and supports an efficient data buffer management scheme.[7]

The MAC and LLC protocols can often generate additional development work on systems, even though the physical medium ends up being "nonstandard." An advanced-technology LAN is being developed for military Command, Control, Communications, and Intelligence (C/SUP3/I) or (C^{3}I) systems, for example. In addition to incorporating multilevel security controls, the network uses wavelength-division-multiplexed fiber optics to provide simultaneous transmission of digital, voice, and video traffic at data rates up to 150 Mb/s. Interfaces to heterogeneous serial devices, workstations, and processors are being developed. User services embedded in the network include terminal connection, interprocess communication, file transfer, electronic mail, voice connection and conferencing, video distribution, and circuit switched stream data distribution. The network is designed to meet the U.S. Department of Defense Computer Security Center's A1 multilevel security criteria.[8] The IEEE 802.4 token bus protocol is used for network digital services.

REFERENCES

1. Kenneth C. Mill and Robert H. Douglas, "Local Area Networks: A Comparison of Bus Access Methods," *Digital Design*, June 1983, pp. 125–128.

2. W. Stallings, "A Tutorial on the IEEE 802 Local Network Standard," in R. L. Pickholtz, Eds., *Local Area and Multiple Access Networks* (Rockville, MD: Computer Science Press, 1986), p. 17.

3. Technical Committee on Computer Communications of the IEEE Computer Society, *Token-passing Bus Access Method and Physical Layer Specifications* (New York: The Institute of Electrical and Electronics Engineers, Inc., 1985), 238 pp. Report No.: ANSI/IEEE Std 802.4–1985. Unless otherwise noted, all technical details concerning the standard are taken from this document.

4. This list of services is taken verbatim from Ref. 3, pp. 32–33.

5. H. J. Hindin, "Chip Sets Forge Vital Links for Token Bus Networks," *Computer Design*, Vol. 24, No. 6, June 1985, pp. 69–74 (4 pages).

6. R. A. Dirvin and A. R. Miller, "The MC68824 Token Bus Controller: VLSI for the Factory LAN," *IEEE Micro (USA)*, Vol. 6, No. 3, June 1986, pp. 15–25.

7. M. P. Huth, "A VLSI Chip Set for the IEEE 802.4 Token Bus," Fourth International Conference: Phoenix Conference on Computers and Communications. 1985 Conference Proceedings (Catalog No. 85CH2154-3), pp. 434–438, 20–22 March 1985, Scottsdale, AZ.

8. J. A. Nagaki and A. W. Van Ausdal, "Intergration of Digital, Voice, and Video Data on a Multilevel Secure Fiber Optic Network," 1985 IEEE Military Communications Conference: MILCOM '85, Conference Record (Catalog No. 85CH2202-0), pp. 215–219, Vol. 1, 20–23 October 1985, Boston, MA.

ANSI/IEEE STD 802.5—TOKEN PASSING RING

Because IBM has adopted the token passing ring, the token ring techonlogy has received an enormous amount of publicity. IBM's token ring is based on the ANSI/IEEE 802.5 standard. This chapter will describe the standard and compare the token passing systems of 802.4 and 802.5.

During late 1985 and throughout 1986, following the introduction of the Token Ring Network, it was difficult to pick up a trade journal without seeing an article of some kind concerning IBM's token ring. Prior to its introduction, it had also received considerable attention from media speculators. Presently, 802.5 is the only medium access control protocol specified for a ring topology. The relationship of 802.5 to the 802 family and to the OSI Reference Model is illustrated in Figure 9.1. The adopted version of the ring was an outgrowth of research and development at IBM.[1] The original concept, often referred to as the Newhall Ring (after one of its developers), was proposed in 1969.[2] Like the logical ring of the token bus, the token ring is based on the use of a single token that rotates around the ring. When a station wishes to transmit, it must wait until it receives the token. The receiving station then changes the token from "free" to "busy" and immediately transmits a frame following the busy token.

A DETAILED LOOK AT 802.5

IEEE Std 802.5–1985 is clearly the most superficial of the three primary LAN standards.[3] It is less detailed than 802.3 or 802.4 and leaves open the question

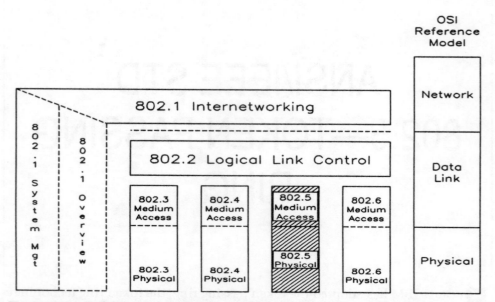

Figure 9.1 Relationship of IEEE Standards and the OSI Reference Model

SOURCE: Based on IEEE P802.1, Draft E< July 1, 1987, *Overview, Internetworking, and Systems Management*, unapproved draft published for comment only, by permission of the IEEE. All rights reserved by The Institute of Electrical and Electronics Engineers, Inc., p. 7.

of suitable media even though it does define a 1 Mb/s and 4 Mb/s, shielded twisted-pair attachment of the station to the medium. There are other anomalies in the 802.5 standard, as well. 802.5 specifies, for example, that each octet of the information filed shall be transmitted most significant bit (MSB) first. This is a reversal of the convention used in 802.3 and 802.4 which specifies transmission least significant bit (LSB) first. Because of this, additional computations are necessary when bridging an 802.5 LAN to an 802.3 or 802.4 network. It is likely that these attributes of the standard are (at least in part) a by-product of IBM's influence on the standard. Consistent with IBM's development of a 16 Mb/s version of the Token Ring, work has progressed on a 16 Mb/s standard. Although the 16 Mb/s version requires some modifications to the standard, particularly at the Physical Layer, the general frame structure of the MAC sublayer remains unchanged. In IBM implementations, however, the size of the frames used will grow from 4,501 octets or bytes to 17,997. The potential for the growth in the size of the frame was part of the original standard as it was published in 1985 since there was no maximum length specified for the information field (see later). The limitation on the information field's size (and thus the size of the entire frame) is limited by the time required to transmit a frame. Consequently, as higher-speed token rings are defined, the frame length may expand.

A token ring LAN is constructed of a set of stations that are serially connected by a transmission medium. All information is transferred serially—bit by bit—from one active station to the next. This is in contrast to either CSMA/CD or token bus systems, which broadcast all data, although only those addressed will acknowledge. In a physical ring, each station usually regenerates and repeats each bit and serves as the means for connecting one or more devices to the ring. The station that currently has access to the medium transfers information to the ring, where it circulates from one station to the next. Stations addressed by the transmission copy the information as it passes. Finally, when the information has traversed the ring, the sending station removes that information from the ring.

When a token passes a station on the medium, that station gains the right to access and transmit its information. Following each information transmission, a token is generated. Conceptually, the token is a symbol of authority that is passed between stations using a token access method to indicate which station is currently in control of the medium. Physically, the token is a control signal consisting of a unique signaling sequence circulating on the medium. That signaling sequence can be thought of as a specialized kind of frame or packet. After transmitting the information frame, the station initiates a new token, thus providing other stations the opportunity to gain access to the ring.

So that a single station cannot monopolize the medium, a token holding timer controls the maximum length of time a station can use or occupy the medium before passing the token. Several classes of service are available with multiple levels of priority. The priority can be assigned independently and dynamically. As in the other LAN standards, error detection and recovery mechanisms are provided to minimize the problems associated with transmission errors or medium transients. In addition, stations may be inserted or deleted from the ring and this must be properly controlled. Because a broken ring can bring the LAN down, a method must be provided for bypassing a station that is deleted either through forethought or malfunction. These issues are diagrammed in Figure 9.2.

As with the 802.3 and 802.4 standards, there are four primary concerns: Logical Link Control, Medium Access Control, the Physical Layer, and the medium itself. Recall that the LLC and MAC are sublayers equivalent to the OSI Layer 2 (Data Link Control), and PHY is equivalent to the OSI Layer 1 (Physical Layer). The medium itself lies outside the Physical Layer. To reiterate, LLC is that part of the Data Link Layer that supports media-independent data link functions and uses the services of the medium access control sublayer to provide services to the Network Layer; MAC is the portion of the IEEE 802 data station that controls and mediates the access to the ring. The Physical Layer is responsible for interfacing with the physical medium. The Physical Layer also

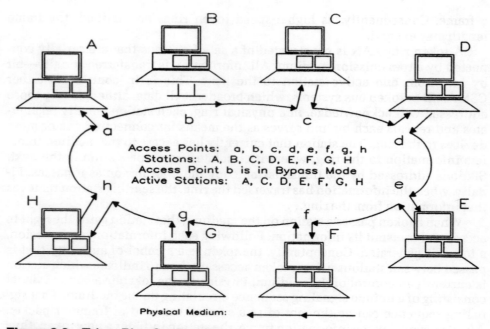

Figure 9.2   Token Ring Configuration
SOURCE: Based on ANSI/IEEE Std 802.5–1985, *Token Ring Access Method and Physical Layer Specification*, ©1985 by The Institute of Electrical and Electronics Engineers, Inc., by permission of the IEEE. All rights reserved by The Institute of Electrical and Electronics Engineers, Inc., p. 24.

detects and generates signals on the medium and converts and processes signals from the medium and from MAC.

Media Access Control (MAC)

Just as access to the physical ring (medium) is controlled by passing a token around the ring, the downstream or receiving station is given the opportunity to transmit when it receives the token. The token is passed when the preceding station initiates a new token after transmission or, if no data transmission is to taken place, it resends the token as received. Information is delivered between peer entities (LLCs or MACs) through the use of protocol data-units (PDUs). There are two recognized PDUs: one is generated by the LLC, the other by Network Management. NMT is the conceptual control element of a station, which interfaces with all the layers of the station and is responsible for the setting and resetting of control parameters, obtaining reports of error conditions, and determining whether the station is connected to or disconnected from the medium.

Upon request for transmission of either type of PDU, MAC prefixes the PDU with the appropriate control information and queues it while waiting for the reception of the token. By modifying the token to a start-of-frame sequence, a station captures it and then appends appropriate control and status fields, address fields, information field, frame-check sequence, and the end-of-frame sequence. The Start-of-Frame Sequence (SFS) consists of a one-octet Starting Delimiter (SD) and a one-octet Access Control (AC). Following the SFS is the substance of the frame: Frame Control (FC), Destination Address (DA), Source Address (SA), Information (INFO), and the Frame-Check Sequence (FCS). When frame transmission begins, the FCS is accumulated and appended to the information field. The transmitting station retains control of the medium until all frames originating at that station are removed from the ring by that station. This prevents frames from continuously circulating on the ring. Throughout this process, MAC must also deal with priority operations.

In general, physical failures are more significant in a ring topology than on a bus. When a hard failure occurs, its cause must be isolated so that recovery can take place. A *failure domain* consists of the following elements:

1. The station reporting the failure, which is called the *beaconing station*

2. The station upstream of the beaconing station (is called the *neighbor*).

3. The ring medium between the beaconing station and its neighbor.

The operation of a failure domain is illustrated in Figure 9.3. If a failure occurred in the domain shown, station G would report it by transmitting beacon MAC frames. Any failure that causes a bit stream interruption in the transmitter side of station F, in the medium between F and G, or in the receiver side of G, will be detected and reported by G using a beacon MAC frame. From the beacon MAC frame(s), all other stations on the ring are notified that the token protocol has been violated, and operations are suspended until the disruption terminates or is removed.

Just as there is an SFS, there is also an EFS (end-of-frame sequence). The EFS is also composed of two octets, each comprising one field: Ending Delimiter (ED) and Frame Status (FS). The FS format may be seen in Figure 9.4. When a ring failure is detected, the current station must know the identity of its upstream neighbor. The process for obtaining this identity is known as Neighbor Notification. Neighbor Notification is based on the A (address-recognized) and C (frame-copied) bits of the FS field. Under normal operation, these bits are transmitted as zeros (0). If a station recognizes the DA of a frame as its own, it sets the A bits to 1 in the passing frame. When a station also copies the frame, then the C bits are also set to 1.

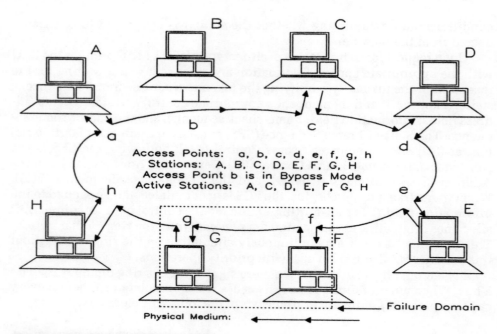

Access Points: a, b, c, d, e, f, g, h
Stations: A, B, C, D, E, F, G, H
Access Point b is in Bypass Mode
Active Stations: A, C, D, E, F, G, H

Figure 9.3 Example Failure Domain
SOURCE: Based on ANSI/IEEE Std 802.5–1985, *Token Ring Access Method and Physical Layer Specification*, ©1985 by The Institute of Electrical and Electronics Engineers, Inc., by permission of the IEEE. All rights reserved by The Institute of Electrical and Electronics Engineers, Inc., p. 44.

Direction of Transmission

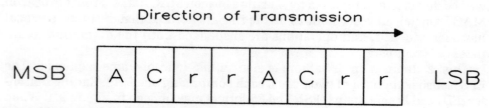

Figure 9.4 Frame Status Field
NOTES: The reserved bits are reserved for future standardization. They are currently (Std 802.5–1985) transmitted as 0's and their values are ignored by the receiver.
(A) address-recognized bits; (C) frame-copied bits; (r) reserved bits.
SOURCE: Based on ANSI/IEEE Std 802.5–1985, *Token Ring Access Method and Physical Layer Specification*, ©1985 by The Institute of Electrical and Electronics Engineers, Inc., by permission of the IEEE. All rights reserved by The Institute of Electrical and Electronics Engineers, Inc., p. 34.

As part of the MAC housekeeping chores, at some point Neighbor Notification will begin by broadcasting the active-monitor-present (AMP) MAC frame. With a broadcast frame, all stations on the ring will recognize that ring as destined for all of them. The first station downstream from the broadcaster will see that the A and C bits of FS are all zeros (0) and will reset the A bits to 1. Subsequent downstream stations will not see all zeros. Stations receiving all zeros regard the frame as having originated from their upstream neighbor. Remember that the station generating the first AMP MAC frame will also remove it. Consequently, this process continues in a daisy-chain fashion until all stations know the identity of their upstream neighbors.

Service Specifications.
MAC provides two-way services to the LLC and to NMT. The services provided by MAC to LLC are designed to allow the local LLC to exchange LLC data-units with peer LLC entities. Several mandatory primitives are defined and required for the LLC sublayer to request services from MAC: MA_DATA.request, MA_DATA.indication, and MA_DATA.confirmation. These are defined in a manner similar to the equivalent service primitives in 802.3 and 802.4. Table 9.1 compares the three standards. 802.3 is clearly the simpler of the three standards with respect to LLC MAC services. Table 9.1 also demonstrates the problem of achieving consistent standards, even in minor tasks like using the same naming and definitional conventions for items that have similar function and meaning.

In both 802.4 and 802.5 standards, network management (NMT) monitors and controls the operation of the MAC sublayer. MAC is required to provide some services to NMT at the boundary between the two. The services involved include the ability to reset MAC and to change MAC operational parameters. When NMT requests MAC to reset, MAC must confirm that the reset has taken place. MAC can also provide a status report to NMT concerning errors or significant status changes. Data may be required by NMT from MAC for these procedures. In network management, there is a major difference between the token protocols and CSMA/CD. In CSMA/CD, no peer management functions are necessary for terminating, initiating, or handling abnormal conditions, because the monitoring of ongoing activities is done by the carrier sense and collision detection mechanisms. IEEE Std 802.3–1985 did not define any local or nodal management activities for the LAN, although the desirability of standards in the area was acknowledged.

Media Access Control Frame Structure.
Two basic formats are used in token rings: tokens and frames. In all illustrations the figures depict the formats of the fields in the sequence they are transmitted on the medium, with the left-most (most significant) bit or symbol transmitted first. This convention contrasts with 802.3 and 802.4, where, in keeping with most microcomputer and minicomputer architectures, the least significant bit is transmitted first.

Table 9.1   Comparison of Service Primitive Parameters

Service Primitive	Parameter	Standard		
		802.3	802.4	802.5
Request	frame_control	no	no	yes
	destination_address	yes	yes	yes
	m_sdu	yes	yes	yes
	service_class	yes	[1]	no
	desired_quality	[1]	yes	no
	requested_service-_class	no	no	yes
Confirm	transmission_status	yes	[2]	yes
	quality	no	yes	[2]
	status	[2]	yes	no
	provided_service-class	no	no	yes
Indication	frame_control	no	no	yes
	destination_address	yes	yes	yes
	source_address	yes	yes	yes
	reception_status	yes	no	no
	m_sdu	no	yes	yes
	quality	no	yes	[3]
	requested_service-class	no	[3]	yes

NOTES: 1. Service_class and desired_quality are both quality-of-service parameters and have similar, if not identical meanings. *_service_class for 802.5 designates the priority of service and is, therefore, conceptually related to service_class and desired quality.
2. Transmission_status and status are defined similarly and provide success or failure indications from MAC to LLC in all three standards. quality and provided_service_class are conceptually related.
3. Note the comments on quality and *_service_class in Notes 2 and 3.

SOURCE: Thomas W. Madron, *Local Area Networks: The Second Generation*, Copyright © 1988 by John Wiley & Sons, Inc., reprinted by permission of John Wiley & Sons, Inc., p. 166.

Protocol conversion, as in bridges and gateways, must take this difference into consideration. The token is the means by which the right to transmit is passed from one station to another. The format of the token may be seen in Figure 9.5. Each field in the token is in turn formatted so that individual bits or sequences of bits have specific meaning. The definition of the fields is identical whether they are in the token or in the frame.

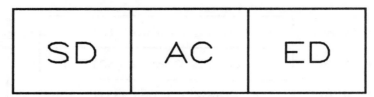

Figure 9.5   Token Format
NOTES: (SD) starting delimiter (1 octet); (AC) access control (1 octet); (ED) ending delimiter (1 octet).
SOURCE: Based on ANSI/IEEE Std 802.5–1985, *Token Ring Access Method and Physical Layer Specification*, ©1985 by The Institute of Electrical and Electronics Engineers, Inc., by permission of the IEEE. All rights reserved by The Institute of Electrical and Electronics Engineers, Inc., p. 27.

MAC and LLC messages are transmitted to the destination station(s) via a frame. The frame format may be seen in Figure 9.6. The portion of the frame actually checked for data integrity is that section over which FCS has coverage. The FCS, as for all the standards, uses a 48-bit cyclic redundancy check (CRC). The starting delimiter is composed of non-data-J, non-data-K, and binary zeros in the format found in Figure 9.7. Recall from Chapter 2 (Figure 2.7) that the 802 standards provide for Differential Manchester coding of data. Whether a signal represents a binary 1 or a binary 0 depends on the polarity of the signal at the time it crosses a bit-symbol boundary—but that polarity has shifted at the mid-point of bit-symbol. By way of contrast, a non-data-J symbol has the same polarity as the preceding symbol, whereas a K symbol has the opposite polarity. There is no mid-bit polarity change with the J and K symbols, as there is with data bits 1 and 0. The SD is, therefore, a unique sequence composed of a combination of J, K, and 0 bit symbols, as described in Figure 9.6.

The Access Control field provides information necessary to allow access to the medium. As seen in Figure 9.8, the priority bits indicate the priority of a token and, therefore, which stations are allowed to use the token. There are eight levels of priority, extending from 000 to 111 (binary). The token bit indicates whether a token (0) or a frame (1) is being received. To prevent either a token with a priority greater than 0 or a frame from continuously circulating on the ring, the monitor bit, when set to 1, flags the condition. The monitor bit is transmitted as a 0 in all frames and tokens, but the *active monitor* may modify the bit. The FC field is depicted in Figure 9. 9. It has frame-type bits and control bits. The frame-type bits specify whether the frame contains a MAC PDU (00) or a LLC PDU (01). Other bit patterns are reserved for future use. If the frame contains a LLC PDU, then the ZZZZZZ bits are designated as rrrYYY, where the rrr bits are reserved and shall be transmitted as zeros (0), and where the YYY bits may carry the priority of the PDU.

Following the FC are the DA and SA addresses. Either 16- or 48-bit ad-

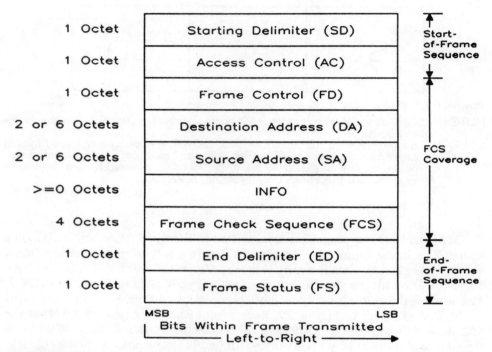

Figure 9.6   Token Ring MAC Frame Format
SOURCE: Based on ANSI/IEEE Std 802.5–1985, *Token Ring Access Method and Physical Layer Specification*, ©1985 by The Institute of Electrical and Electronics Engineers, Inc., by permission of the IEEE. All rights reserved by The Institute of Electrical and Electronics Engineers, Inc., p. 27.

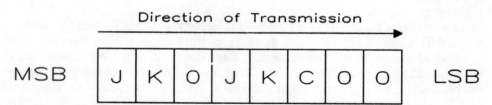

Figure 9.7   Starting Delimiter (SD)
NOTES: (J) non-data-J; (K) non-data-K; (O) binary zero.
SOURCE: Based on ANSI/IEEE Std 802.5–1985, *Token Ring Access Method and Physical Layer Specification*, ©1985 by The Institute of Electrical and Electronics Engineers, Inc., by permission of the IEEE. All rights reserved by The Institute of Electrical and Electronics Engineers, Inc., p. 28.

Direction of Transmission

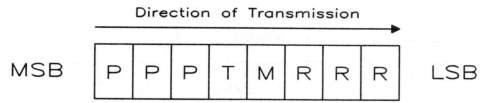

Figure 9.8 Access Control (AC)
NOTES: (P) priority bits; (T) Token bit; (M) monitor bit; (R) reservation bits.
SOURCE: Based on ANSI/IEEE Std 802.5–1985, *Token Ring Access Method and Physical Layer Specification*, ©1985 by The Institute of Electrical and Electronics Engineers, Inc., by permission of the IEEE. All rights reserved by The Institute of Electrical and Electronics Engineers, Inc., p. 28.

dresses may be implemented with formats similar to 802.3 and 802.4 (see Chapters 7 and 8). More complicated than in 802.3 and 802.4 is the information field structure. The information field is, of course, optional. When it is present, the content of the field is termed a *vector*. A vector is the fundamental unit of MAC and NMT information, and only one vector is permitted per MAC frame. The vector contains its length (VL), an identifier (VI) of its function, and zero or more subvectors. This structure may be seen in Figure 9.10. VL is a 16-bit binary number that gives the length in octets of the vector, including the VL subfield. The range of values, in decimal, is 4 <= VL <= 65535 (524,280 bits), because the minimum information field must contain the VL and VI subfields (of two octets each).

The VI is a 2-octet code that identifies the vector, as noted in Table 9.2. If there are data in addition to VL and VI, then vectors require those data to be contained in subvectors. There may be multiple subvectors within a vector.

Direction of Transmission

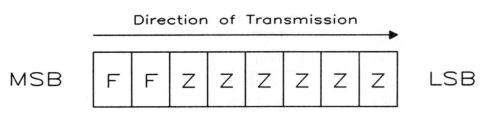

Figure 9.9 Frame Control (FC)
NOTES: (F) frame-type bits; (Z) control bits.
SOURCE: Based on ANSI/IEEE Std 802.5–1985, *Token Ring Access Method and Physical Layer Specification*, ©1985 by The Institute of Electrical and Electronics Engineers, Inc., by permission of the IEEE. All rights reserved by The Institute of Electrical and Electronics Engineers, Inc., p. 29.

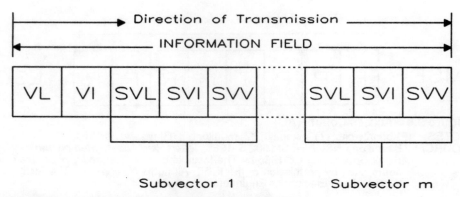

Figure 9.10 MAC Frame Information Field Structure

NOTES: VL (2 octets) is the Vector Length, VI (2 octets) is the Vector Identifier; SVL (1 octet) is the Subvector Length, SVI (1 octet) is the Subvector Identifier, SVV (n octets) is the Subvector Value.

SOURCE: Based on ANSI/IEEE Std 802.5–1985, *Token Ring Access Method and Physical Layer Specification*, ©1985 by The Institute of Electrical and Electronics Engineers, Inc., by permission of the IEEE. All rights reserved by The Institute of Electrical and Electronics Engineers, Inc., p. 32.

SVL is the subvector length, SVI the subvector identifier, and SVV the substantive data carried in the subvector. SVL is an 8-bit binary that gives the length in octets of the subvector. Because an 8-bit binary number cannot delineate more than 256 octets (0-255), and SVL and SVI are each one octet long, an ordinary SVV would seem to have a limit of 254 octets in length. If SVL contains hex FF (255), it means that SVV is longer than 254 and the actual length is included in the next two octets. If SVI = FF, then an expanded identifier is being used and is contained in the next two octets. The subvectors are of two general types: hex 00 through hex 7F designate specific, common strings (to many vectors) of MAC or NMT data and may be standardized to facilitate sharing of data be-

Table 9.2   Vector Identifier (VI) Codes

VI Hex Values	Meaning
0002	Beacon
0003	Claim Token
0004	Purge Mac Frame
0005	Active Monitor Present (AMP)
0006	Standby Monitor Present (SMP)
0007	Duplicate Address Test (DAT)

SOURCE: ANSI/IEEE Std 802.5–1985, pp. 35–38.

tween MAC and NMT. Codes hex 80 through hex FE are for specific, and perhaps temporary, definition. Finally, SVV contains the substantive data to be transmitted. Subvectors themselves may contain other subvectors and other types of vectors.

As the frame is being transmitted, the FCS is accumulated and appended to the frame and is identical to the FCS of 802.3 and 802.4. Two additional octets are then added to the frame: the ED shown in Figure 9.11, and the FS, already discussed and described by Figure 9.4. The ED, like the SD, is a specific bit pattern with special meaning. The J and K bits are defined in the same manner as the ED and SD. The intermediate frame bit (I) takes the value of 0 or 1, to indicate the last or only frame of the transmission (0) or that this is the first or intermediate frame of a multiframe transmission. The E bit is transmitted as 0, but as every station checks tokens and frames for errors, the E bit of tokens and frames that are in error is set to 1. To complete the frame, the FS octet is added to the end of the bit stream being sent. Sometimes it is necessary to abort a transmission; this is done with an Abort Sequence composed of only an SD and an adjacent ED. This sequence may occur anywhere in the bit stream and receiving stations are to be designed to be able to detect the abort sequence under virtually all conditions.

Physical Layer and Media

In keeping with the generally superficial nature of ANSI/IEEE Std 802.5–1985, a total of 14 pages are dedicated to the Physical Layer and medium specifications. The entire standard is a mere 86 pages. The section on Physical Layer and medium specifications for ANSI/IEEE Std 802.4–1985, at 74 pages, is al-

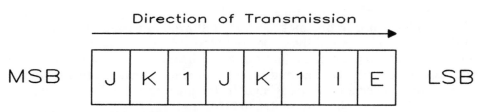

Figure 9.11   Ending Delimiter (ED)
NOTES: (J) non-data-J, (K) non-data-K (1) binary one, (I) intermediate frame bit, (E) error-detected bit.
SOURCE: Based on ANSI/IEEE Std 802.5–1985, *Token Ring Access Method and Physical Layer Specification*, ©1985 by The Institute of Electrical and Electronics Engineers, Inc., by permission of the IEEE. All rights reserved by The Institute of Electrical and Electronics Engineers, Inc., p. 34.

most as long as all of 802.5. The Physical Layer and medium specifications for ANSI/IEEE Std 802.3–1985 are considerably longer, at 107 pages, than the entire 802.5 standard. The merits of a technical standard cannot be judged by the number of pages in the report. Nevertheless, the 802.3 and 802.4 Committees produced detailed documents that would seem to give substantial guidance to manufacturers wishing to implement 802.3 or 802.4 systems, and it may be arguable that the 802.5 Physical Layer is simpler and more easily described than the other two. This holds true for the medium discussions, as well, although an early note in Std 802.5–1985 (p. 19) implies that the consideration of media should not be considered closed: "The definition of suitable media (twisted pair, coaxial cable, and optical fiber) for connecting stations that meet the attachment standard specified herein is a subject for future consideration." In any event, the standard defines a system with alternative data rates of 1 Mb/s or 4 Mb/s. The maximum number of stations specified is about 250.

802.5 Physical Layer Specifications.   The PHY specifications are limited to data symbol encoding and decoding, symbol timing, and reliability. The PHY layer encodes and transmits four basic symbols presented to it by MAC. These symbols are

> 0 = binary zero
>
> 1 = binary one
>
> J = non-data-J
>
> K = non-data-K

The symbols are transmitted to the medium in the form of Differential Manchester-type coding, which operates by generating two line signal elements per symbol. For binary ones and zeros, a signal element of one polarity is transmitted for one-half the duration of the symbol, followed by a contiguous transmission of a signal element of the opposite polarity. The resulting signal has no direct current (DC) component and can easily be inductively or coupled with induction or capacitance. The mid-bit transition also conveys inherent timing information. To decode incoming signals, the algorithm used for encoding is reversed, with the symbols presented to MAC.

One objective of the Physical Layer is to recover the symbol timing information inherent in the transitions between levels of the received signal. It must provide suitable timing at the data signaling rate (1 Mb/s or 4 Mb/s) for internal use and for the transmission of symbols on the ring. In normal operation, one station serves as the active monitor. All other stations on the ring are frequency- and phase-locked to that station. A *latency buffer* is provided by the active monitor to assure minimum latency and phase jitter compensation. *Jitter* is instability in a signal waveform over time due to signal interference.

In order for the token to continuously circulate around the ring, it must have time (expressed in number of bits transmitted) for a signal element to proceed around the entire ring. This phenomenon is called *latency*. The minimum latency period is equal to the time it takes 24 bits to make the circuit, because there are 24 bits in a token. Latency will vary from one system to another. Regardless of the data rate, a delay of at least 24 bits must be provided. The source timing of the ring is also supplied by the active monitor station. The mean data signaling rate is controlled by the active monitor station. Even so, segments of the ring can operate at speeds slightly higher or lower than the "official" timing signals. The cumulative effect of these variations in speed cause variations in the latency of a ring that has been configured with a maximum number of stations.

Physical Layer Services.   The Physical Layer provides services to MAC and to the NMT. The PHY to MAC service allows the local MAC sublayer entity to exchange MAC data-units with peer MAC sublayer entities. All PHY data-units have the duration of one symbol period. Three service primitives are provided for the MAC sublayer to request services from the PHY layer. As with other service primitives, these consist of request, indication, and confirmation. MAC sends a request to PHY every time it has a symbol to output. On receipt of the request, PHY encodes and transmits the symbol. When PHY is ready to service another request, it returns a confirmation to MAC. The indication primitive defines the transfer of data from PHY to MAC and is sent every time PHY decodes a symbol. On receipt of the indication primitive, MAC accepts a symbol from PHY.

The PHY to NMT service is of considerable importance to the operation of the token ring. The first section, "A Detailed Look at 802.5," in this chapter has shown why network management, as defined in 802.5, is of considerable importance to the token ring, but of little practical concern to CSMA/CD. Recall that NMT is the conceptual control element of a station and interfaces all the layers of the station. It sets and resets control parameters, obtains reports of error conditions, and determines if the station should be connected to or disconnected from the medium. The station in this instance is a physical device attached to a shared-medium LAN for the purpose of transmitting and receiving information. A station is identified to the network by a DA. The services provided by PHY to NMT allow the local NMT to control the operation of the PHY Layer.

In order to accomplish this task PHY uses two service primitives: PH_CONTROL.request and PH_STATUS.indication. The request primitive is generated by NMT to request the PHY layer to insert to or remove itself from the ring. This is the most important control function of NMT. Conceptually, the request primitive has one parameter, control_action, which may take on one of two states: INSERT (signal insertion into the ring) or REMOVE (signal removal from the ring). The request is generated whenever NMT requires insertion or deletion. The indication primitive is used by PHY to inform NMT of errors and significant status changes, through the status_report parameter. The physical effect of the request parameter on specific LANs, once the technical details of the standard have been resolved, is often to open or close an electromechanical relay so that the ring includes (relay switch open) or excludes (relay switch closed) the station from the ring.

The Physical Medium: Shielded Twisted Pair.   At the time of its publication, ANSI/IEEE Std 802.5–1985 defined only a single medium, unlike 802.4 or 802.3 (along with its amendments). It specified the functional, electrical, and mechanical characteristics of balanced, baseband, shielded twisted pair attachments to the trunk cable of a token ring.

To connect a station to the trunk cable, a connecting cable is attached through a Medium Interface Connector (MIC) from the station to a Trunk Coupling Unit (TCU). There are, conceptually, two cables: a PHY/MIC cable that runs from the station's Physical Layer to the MIC, and a TCU/MIC cable that runs from the MIC to the TCU. None of this may be apparent in a real LAN. Repeaters, as in other LAN implementations, may be used to extend the length of the trunk line beyond limits imposed by normal signal degradation. The standard recommends the use of two twisted pair shielded cables for connecting the station to the ring. The standard does not, however, recommend a specific trunk cable configuration. The TCU could in principle be twisted pair coaxial cable or fiber-optic cable.

IBM'S TOKEN RING

Perhaps the best way to grasp the 802.5 is to take a look at IBM's Token Ring. There has been a wide variety of commentary on and description of IBM's Token Ring since its introduction in October of 1985.[4] Brookshire and Molta have neatly summarized the LAN. They note that IBM's Token Ring Network conforms to ANSI/IEEE Std 802.5–1985.[5] As its name implies, it uses a ring topology and the token-passing access method. Commonly, microcomputers are connected with shielded or unshielded twisted-pair cable to a wiring concentrator called a multistation access unit (MAU). The original Token Ring operated at 4 Mb/s, with a maximum of 100 meters from the wiring concentrator to a computer and 72 stations using unshielded telephone-type wire. In 1989 that was extended to 16 Mb/s. When shielded twisted pair is used, larger LANs of up to 260 stations can be constructed.[6] The construction of any LAN is always something of a tradeoff between price and performance. One difficulty vendors of Token Ring hardware share in common with IBM is that the list price for a typical network interface card in late 1989 was about $700—approximately twice that of an 802.3 (Ethernet) NIC. Moreover, in the 16 Mb/s version shielded twisted pair is required, driving installation costs up further.

The ability to transmit token ring signals on unshielded wire depends on the quality of the wire, the interconnection methodology, and the signal filtering.[7] Each wiring concentrator supports up to eight stations, and concentrators can be linked together using twisted pair or fiber-optic cable to form extended rings. Although IBM's token ring is still not supported by as many of manufacturers as those that support 802.3, the fact that it is made by IBM will likely lead other manufacturers to support it in the future, and its non-IBM support is gaining ground. The token ring can be connected to IBM's mainframe and minicomputer communications system.

Because in its initial offering of the token ring, IBM chose to use a wiring concentrator, many observers have mistakenly inferred that the system was a logical rather than a physical token ring. The ring exists inside the concentrator rather than running around a room or a building. This simplifies the design and implementation of the TCU and allows the use of traditional point–to–point wiring—with which IBM is familiar. The design also allows, mostly as a marketing ploy, that existing telephone wire might be used. The use of unshielded twisted pair is problematic; in most real systems—at least in large organizations—the probability that existing twisted pair can be used is low. Even though the wiring concentrator connects only eight devices, one of the connections can be used to connect another concentrator, as illustrated in Figure 9.12. An extended ring that ran around a building could, therefore, be put together.Moreover, through the use of bridges, if a broadband or fiber-optic backbone were available in a campus environment, it would be possible to bridge concentrators (or groups of concentrators) across buildings. This approach to wiring and the interconnection of concentrators is consistent with IBM's prior announcement of its cabling system, which includes among other things, shielded twisted pair.

Although there has been widespread praise for the token ring, words of caution have also been expressed. Matt Kramer has remarked that IBM's Token Ring Network does not have adequate network management or internetworking capabilities for extensive wide-area network configurations, according to corporate network managers trying to implement the LAN to connect systems dispersed over a wide area. Though the network is responsive and reliable in office-area configurations, extensive interconnected networks or wide-area networks of token rings cannot be built easily, sometimes due to transmission delays. Network management must be exceedingly careful with a large interconnected token ring network. Many large-network users plan to link their wide-area networks by satellite,

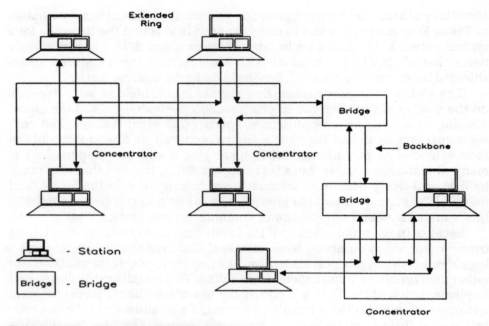

Figure 9.12   Extended IBM Token Ring

which will not require that each large subnetwork be connected to all others. The internetworking strategy of IBM has caused much concern over the bridges that are used to interconnect two token ring networks.[8]

The problems noted by Kramer deal, in part, with the issue of what constitutes a *heavily loaded network*. It is often suggested that in a heavily loaded network, a token ring will perform better than a CSMA/CD system, even when the CSMA/CD system is operating at nominally higher data rates. Recall, however, that we can define *heavily loaded* in different ways. One way is to look at the number of frames being passed over the network—in other words, the traffic load. Another way is to count the number of attached stations—the node load. Because on a token ring every active station must look at and do something with the token and with every frame, the larger the number of connected devices, the worse the response, even if only a few stations are currently using the channel. Conversely, on a bus system, particularly a CSMA/CD bus, the absolute number of stations is irrelevant—what matters is the traffic load. With a small LAN of a few stations, but with a heavy traffic, the token ring may well outperform CSMA/CD. Conversely, with a very large number of nodes, but with low-to-moderate loads (as would be expected in an office automation application), a CSMA/CD system might be expected to outperform a token ring. Other networks with higher speeds or other performance enhancements might deviate from this generalization. Performance is closely tied to how the LAN is to be used.

CONFORMANCE TO AND THE FUTURE OF 802.5

The marketplace and manufacturing milieu for 802.3 (Ethernet) is well established and thriving. The same will likely be true of 802.4 token bus networks in the near future. In both those standards there was a high degree of concern for the interoperability of devices made by different manufacturers, and at least for 802.3 standard devices this is proving to be true. The differences may lie in the fact that 802.3 was originally sponsored by a consortium of manufacturers that had developed Ethernet, although Xerox was its original driving force. 802.4 was pushed by companies who were not computer manufacturers, most notably, General Motors, to support MAP.

802.5, however, was sponsored primarily by IBM. The result of IBM's sponsorship seems to be a standard that is not entirely consistent in its approach with the other standards either in operational details or definitions (which could have been much the same across protocols), and which—at least originally—had a number of holes. By the beginning of 1990 a number of vendors were entering the Token Ring support market although the number of vendors producing Token Ring cards does not approach the array of vendors of 802.3 hardware. IBM is attempting to capitalize on the popularity of TCP/IP among some market segments by producing TCP/IP software for the Token Ring. This will help introduce the Token Ring into some organizations that heretofore have relied exclusively on 802.3. Like 802.3, 802.5 is undergoing revision, most notably in the direction of a 16 Mb/s upgrade, already being manufactured by Texas Instruments and IBM.[9]

There are other token rings than 802.5, although most will be related to that technology as time goes by. The "backbone" mentioned in the discussion of IBM's Token Ring, and briefly illustrated in Figure 9.12 provided an illustration of a possible need for a wider-area higher-speed ring network. Examples of such networks are the emerging 802.6 and FDDI high-speed ring network standards. A fundamental problem with both 802.3 and 802.5, regardless of the debate over which provides superior performance, is that during the 1990s and into the next millenium higher-speed systems will be necessary. Neither 802.3's 10 Mb/s or 802.5's 16 Mb/s are sufficiently fast to handle the demands which will confront LAN developers in the short-term future. With growing demands for transmission of graphics, video, and other high-volume data, backbone technologies, and even technologies linking workstations, will have to be faster than current technology provides. The result is that while 802.3 and 802.5 will likely continue to compete fiercely throughout the 1990s, the developmental impetus will be toward faster LANs.

REFERENCES

1. N. Strole, "A Local Communications Network Based on Interconnected Token-Access Rings: A Tutorial," *IBM Journal of Research and Development*, September 1983; and R. Dixon, N. Strole, and J. Markov, "A Token-Ring Network for Local Data Communications," *IBM Systems Journal*, No. 1, 1983.

2. W. Farmer and E. Hewhall, "An Experimental Distributed Switching System to Handle Bursty Computer Traffic," *Proceedings of the ACM Symposium on Problems in the Optimization of Data Communications*, 1969.

3. Unless otherwise noted, the discussion of the technical aspects of the standard will be taken from Technical Committee Computer Communications of the IEEE Computer Society, *IEEE Standards for Local Area Networks: Token Ring Access Method and Physical Layer Specifications* (New York: The Institute of Electrical and Electronics Engineers, Inc., 1985). This is referred to as ANSI/IEEE Std 802.5–1985. All definitions are taken verbatim from this volume or are very closely paraphrased.

4. See, for example, the following: "Outline of IBM's Token Ring LAN," *Nikkei Electron. (Japan)*, No. 396, 1986, pp. 249–260; P. Baccanello, "Spinning the Token Ring (IBM Token Ring)," *PC: Indep. Guide IBM Pers. Comput. (UK Ed.) (GB)*, Vol. 3, No. 8, August 1986, pp. 46–48; F. X. Dzubeck, "IBM's Token-Ring Strategy," *Adm. Manage.*, Vol. 47, No. 2, February 1986, pp. 16–17; Rob Garretson, "IBM Cannot Satisfy Demand for Token-Ring Adapter Cards," *PC Week*, Vol. 4, No. 4, p. 1(2); D. Hand, "The IBM Token-Ring Network," Networks 86, *Proceedings of the European Computer Communications Conference*, 10–12 June 1986, London, England, pp. 333–334; J. Scott Haugdahl, "IBM Token-Ring Network (The Token-Ring Solution)," *PC Tech Journal*, Vol. 5, No. 1, January 1987, pp. 50–70 (14 pages); C. K. Heaney, "Link Those Micros (in Banks)," *ABA Banking J. (USA)*, Vol. 78, No. 8, August 1986, pp. 45, 48, and 50; Ed Eisenberger, "IBM's Token-Ring-to-Mainframe Blitz," *PC World*, Vol. 4, No. 10, October 1986, pp. 321–333 (7 pages); E. H. Killorin and P. J. Musich, "A User's Guide for Evaluating the IBM Token-Ring," *Telematics & Informatics (GB)*, Vol. 3, No. 2, 1986, pp. 127–131; David S. McMaster, "IBM's Token-Ring: What Are the Alternatives?" *Mini-Micro Systems*, Vol. 19, No. 11, September 1986, pp. 105–116 (7 pages).

5. Robert G. Brookshire and David J. Molta, "Microcomputer Networks for Research and Teaching," A paper presented at the annual meeting of the Southwestern Political Science Association, March 18–21, 1987, Dallas, TX; Frank J. Derfler, Jr., "Making Connections: The IBM Token-Ring Network," *PC Magazine*, Vol. 6, No. 1, 1987, pp. 227–241.

6. Norman C. Strole, "How IBM Addresses LAN Requirements with the Token Ring," *Data Communications*, Vol. 15, No. 2, February 1986, p. 120.

7. Richard J. S. Bates, Lee C. Haas, Robert D. Love, and Franc E. Noel, "The IBM Token Ring Will Handle up to 72 Stations at the Full 4-Mbit/s Data Rate," *Data Communications*, Vol. 15, No. 3, March 1986, p. 279.

8. Matt Kramer, "Token-Ring Has Wide-Area Troubles," *PC Week*, Vol. 4, No. 6, p. C1(2).

9. Note the recent review article on Token Ring by David Greefield, "Into The Ring: Token Ring Gains Speed and Adherents," *LAN Magazine*, September 1989, pp. 134ff.

CHAPTER 10

MANAGING LOCAL AREA NETWORKS

Even the smallest micro-based LANs must be managed! A successful network is one that does not inhibit the use of network resources, regardless of what those resources may be. Perhaps the most overlooked problem in successfully implementing even a small LAN is that every network needs an administrator. In the sense of the term used here, the network "administrator" is the local departmental person responsible for looking after the network. With a small network that may only take 10 or 15 percent of that person's time. For a large network it may take 100 percent of the time of several people. The successful network administrator will organize the functions of the system so that the user doesn't even know it's there.

LANS MUST BE MANAGED

One approach to network management has been presented by IBM's Richard B. Freeman. Freeman has identified six "distinct disciplines associated with managing the components of a network"[1]:

1. Problem determination
2. Performance analysis
3. Problem management

4. Change management

5. Configuration management

6. Operations management

Problem determination, which must be distinguished from maintenance and service procedures, is the process of identifying failures so that appropriate vendor and service organizations can be called. Problem determination should identify what failed, not necessarily why it failed. Network measures of response time and availability is the function of performance analysis. This can include, in a local area network using CSMA/CD protocols, such measures as the number of collisions, as well as a set of data that collectively can be called "traffic."

The reporting, tracking, and resolution of impediments to the user's ability to communicate effectively with a target device is called problem management. Changes in network components must be tracked, reported, and approved through the process of change management. Configuration management requires the creation of a database containing an inventory of the "past, present, and future physical and logical characteristics of network elements."[2] The configuration database would include terminal and port information, and the precise configuration of each network access device (in a broadband system, the configuration of every network RF modem). Finally, operations management deals with the remote manipulation of various network devices. This will include, but not be limited to, support for linking new devices, providing documentation on how to perform certain network functions (such as file transfers from one node to another), and related issues.

The central point to be made is that the management of a network is a "real" management problem (and opportunity), not simply an issue of ensuring that a cable is run from one point to another and that appropriate connectors are soldered to the cable. I suspect that more than one member of upper management has uttered some comment to the effect that "there's not much to network control—go run another cable." To Freeman's list of six elements of network management should be added user support (training and documentation), security, and planning.

A somewhat different attempt to describe "network management" has been suggested by Judith Estrin and Keith Cheney of Bridge Communications.[3] They suggest that network management can be broken into four main categories: installation and configuration, monitoring and control, security and access control, and diagnostics. As Estrin and Cheney note, "Each of these is important in the different stages of local area network installation, operation, and growth."[4] In other words, network management is often used to describe a wide range of behaviors necessary to plan, operate, control access to, and maintain a network. Others have suggested that the management, maintenance, and diagnostic functions are distinctly different from one another in a hierarchical fashion, with management at the top and diagnosis at the bottom; however, all must interact with one another. In this scheme of things, management goes beyond running the LAN, it involves "fitting the LAN into the business."[5] However one defines it, LAN management must take place. Not even a small LAN can get along without it.

ORGANIZING USERS IN A NETWORK

In an unpublished presentation given in June 1981, IBM Communications Specialist Mel Achterberg outlined a number of management issues involved in network control, including the problem of "user interface." The underlying point made by Achterberg was that "an informed user is a happy user or not as unhappy as one who is uninformed."[6] In the rush of enthusiasm that accompanies the installation of a LAN, those most deeply involved with the project may forget that the objective is not the installation of the network, *per se*. Rather, the network is installed to provide useful services for its users. A departmental micro-based LAN, in particular, is usually purchased and installed to provide one or more specific functions. Examples of such functions are the following:

1. Connectivity. This is the ability for users to transfer data back and forth.

2. Access to Expensive Peripherals. This is the old economy of scale argument in a new guise.

3. A Common Database System. Frequently, there will be a need for a commonly accessed database available for common inquiry and updating.

4. Common Software Access. Some software, specifically written for a multiuser environment, may be needed apart from traditional database functions.

5. Value-added Services. These may include electronic mail, calendaring, and similar office-automation projects.

6. Gateways, Bridges, and Communications Servers. If there is need to access other networks, then these may be essential.

All of these services imply the need for user support, including having someone to help resolve problems and the provision of user documentation and training.

Assuming that someone, even by default, will be available to field user problems with the network, that individual must have the documents necessary to diagnose whatever ails the user. If the problem turns out to be user-related (something a user has perpetrated in some fashion or another), then some consultative advice will be required. If the problem is network-related, then the network administrator must be able to either suggest a solution to the user or refer the problem to other appropriate personnel for resolution.[7]

In order to resolve user problems effectively, then, the network administrator must have at his or her disposal at least the following manuals and support documents:

▼ Messages and codes for all operating systems on the network, as well as for all machines: In addition, the messages and codes for major applications should also be available.

▼ Operators' guides for all equipment available to the user: This includes manuals on terminals, network devices, access methods, and any other relevant information.

▼ Problem determination guides for all relevant equipment

▼ Network configuration data are required to determine whether the user has somehow changed, or had changed, parameters on network access equipment: This implies that the user interface will also have the equipment available to check on the current configuration.

The fundamental objective for user interface documentation is to be able to maintain a functioning network at all times. It cannot be accomplished without proper and appropriate documentation. Moreover, a network cannot be said to be functioning if the end-user cannot make use of it in an appropriate and efficient manner. It is the function of the network administrator to ensure that all related support personnel are armed with appropriate information.

Another major set of documentation needed for appropriate network functioning is that supplied to the user. At the very least two types of documentation are required by the user: how to use his or her terminal and how to deal with the network. In addition, sooner or later, the user will need more detailed information on the systems being used, although that may or may not be the task of network management itself. In a local area network a key item of documentation will be the publication of a LAN directory, similar to a telephone directory, in order to support the connectivity implicit in the system.

Although it is possible to simply distribute the entire manual that comes with a terminal and with network devices, that level of detail is probably both inappropriate and dangerous. A properly configured network probably will not make available all capabilities of the system to the average user. Furthermore, the average user will not be interested in all possible details of both terminals and network access. Consequently, the objective should be to provide a minimal level of good documentation, probably in the form of reference cards, that summarizes the major features and facilities of the network. Such documentation might include not only operator instructions but also a user-oriented problem determination guide for any equipment he or she might be using.

If the system is to operate for the benefit of the user, then adequate documentation must be available at all appropriate levels. It is one function of the network administrator to organize affairs of the network so that such documentation is acquired, written, and maintained. After all, documentation is helpful only if it is up-to-date.

MAINTAINING THE NETWORK

Network maintenance consists of fixing outages when they occur, and, more importantly, preventing outages from occurring. To prevent outages maintenance includes such mundane tasks as upgrading network operating system software, testing cables and active components on the cabling system, network interface cards (NICs), and monitoring workload, throughput, and response time. Even after all this even the smallest PC-based LAN will fail sometime. When the LAN does break, it will be necessary to call in all the diagnostic tools you can find. There are several obvious things to check in a LAN when as outage does occur.[8] First, read the relevant parts of all manuals, and be sure you understand the error messages. Then check the NIC, then the drop cable, then the trunk cable, and then the server. If at first you don't succeed, try a binary search, by dividing the network in half and testing the operation of each half (if that is at all feasible, of course), then concentrate on the half that did not work.

There are at least two issues relating to outages: how best to minimize the impact of outages and what do we do when they do happen. When outages occur, the objective should be to get the system back in operation as quickly as possible, but through the use of backup equipment we can also speed recovery time thereby minimizing the impact of the outage. In general, when designing the total system, every effort should be made to reduce the number of single points of failure. Where such single points of failure occur, then if it is economically feasible, backup equipment should be available. Particularly with large LANs, the cable itself is often the most common point of failure. In a small LAN one can probably "walk-the-cable" and visually inspect it. With a large LAN encompassing several miles of cable, visual inspection is not usually a viable alternative. Moreover, many cable problems cannot be identified visually.

Backup Considerations

Although when the LAN was designed an effort was made to avoid single points of failure, it is probably not possible to avoid them all. In broadband systems, using a single cable, a frequency translator is required at the head end of the system. That translator may be the only single point of failure on the network, but it's there. Avoiding failure of the translator can only happen by having at least two, perhaps switched automatically when one goes out. There may be other units that are equally critical—the file server, for example. The term "backup" may also mean protection of data, as well. More will be said of this in the section on security.

In the case of the frequency translator or the file server, either operationally redundant units or spare units will suffice for quick replacement and recovery. In its newest version of its network operating system, Novell makes provision for a redundant file server. In fact, Novell goes further than a simple redundancy in that it is possible to configure a fault-tolerant system. That means that the second file server can be configured as a complete image of the primary server with files that are updated concurrently (and transparent to the users) on both servers. Perhaps the primary problem with redundancy or duplication to minimize outage is the cost associated with such a strategy. Whether the cost is justified is dependent on how critical the networking enterprise is based on a cost/time ratio. If it is less costly to put up with an hour or a day of downtime than to maintain redundant systems, then the strategy should be to get the equipment fixed as quickly as possible, recognizing that some downtime is inevitable. If, on the other hand, the downtime is more costly than maintaining redundant systems, then such systems become critical. In any event, when a component breaks, it should be fixed as quickly as possible.

Managing Outages

It is important in dealing with outages to publicize appropriate expectations before something happens. Thus, we should, *in writing,* set forth those expectations for both users and vendors. This can often be done contractually with vendors, but is more difficult with users. Users are usually not very patient with outages of any variety and tend to vent their ire in very direct ways. Some of the edge of that anger can be ground away by making the normal operating procedure for dealing with problems clear to users.

As with any computing operation, it is important to formalize who will call the appropriate vendors. The best way to control the situation is to designate a single originator for the calls. If the vendor is to return the call, within what time limit? When the vendor does call, what next? Does the owner or the vendor identify the source of the outage? After a component is fixed, who is to contact whom? How will calls be tracked and who will do the tracking? While these issues are not unique to local area networks, when an institution becomes dependent on an integrated communications system any downtime can be not only important but also vital.

It is also important that records be kept on sources of failure since recurrences of the same or similar problems can mean faulty components or faulty design. An error capture document should be structured that will allow network operations to capture error indicators, tests and results, and related data. Intermittent problems are especially troublesome, but data collected over time can, perhaps, assist in tracking such problems. To the extent possible a variety of people within the organization should be trained in communication aids and tests in order to assist in the diagnosis of outages.

In a large organization with many departmental LANs, an in-house communications group may maintain test equipment and have the ability to fix even complex problems. Even if the communications unit does not do its own maintenance, it may be useful to acquire and learn to use some test equipment for problem diagnosis. Diagnostic equipment ranges from relatively simple analog and digital test equipment to sophisticated network controllers and management systems.[9]

MANAGEMENT TOOLS FOR MAINTENANCE AND PERFORMANCE

Closely related to diagnostic testing is the equipment necessary for monitoring performance. The data collected for performance monitoring are also closely related to the more general management function as well as to the planning issues discussed below. Perhaps the primary purpose of monitoring network performance is to provide the data necessary for optimum network configuration. Optimum configuration will provide the greatest throughput of data, and, in a CSMA/CD network, means there will be a relatively low number of packet collisions. In a packet-switched CSMA/CD system, at least, load (channel use) and packet size affect the potential for collisions.

The consequence of load and packet size means that it is necessary to collect data related to packets, characters, sessions, and channels. The data collected can then be used to predict network performance under varying conditions. In a network in which more than one channel is used, it is possible to place services and users specific to those services on the same channel with a bridge across the channels. It is thereby possible to optimize throughput for classes of users, although cross-channel uses will see some degradation. Without the ability to monitor traffic and performance, it is not possible to make the management decisions necessary for network reconfiguration, expansion, or change.

Although there is a dearth of diagnostic hardware and software, there are devices coming to market that can assist the network administrator. Some devices are relatively simple and designed to test for continuity (no breaks) or shorts on the cable. Some of these are standalone devices while others are cards that are placed in PCs, and, when combined with the appropriate software, can provide information concerning collision rates on an Ethernet, or frame inspection on a token ring. A major step beyond simple continuity testing is the creation of devices sometimes called time domain reflectometers that not only tell whether there is a cable break, but can also indicate approximately where the break has occurred. At that level of sophistication, however, the price tag tends to the high side (about $3,000), making it difficult to justify the cost for a small network. For a large network, however, or for an organization with many departmental LANs, such a cost would not be prohibitive.

For broadband systems there are a number of devices available since the technology has been extensively used for a number of years. There are, for example, monitors that can automatically test signal quality from various points on the network. Network monitors are available to collect more detailed data on frames and packets and/or provide more detailed reports on network performance. The range of pricing for monitors varies greatly as does their level of sophistication. Related to monitors are protocol analyzers that can provide a detailed look at protocol behavior and protocols within protocols.

PLANNING

From the comments already made, it is clear that a network of any substantial size is likely to be very dynamic. It is unlikely that there will be a time when it is "fixed" without change, unless, of course, the organization itself is near death. It is important, therefore, to have, as an intrinsic part of the management of the LAN, an ongoing planning function so that both problems and opportunities can be anticipated. One of the primary planning issues is how fast the network can expand.

Although the LAN should be designed with expansion in mind, the rate of expansion will depend on funding, and personnel and product availability. User demand for network services in a dynamic organization will likely outstrip any planned expansion. The need for expansion, change, or reconfiguration will depend on network traffic, throughput, and network availability in appropriate organizational locations. No matter how much planning is done by network managers, users will always make last-minute demands that were unanticipated and may have the funds to underwrite those demands.

In a narrow sense network planning consists of the forecasting of change and expansion through the use of models based on performance data. The planning function must be made an intrinsic part of network management, primarily because few people wish to do it. The planner must use every tool available, and "hard" data, such as usage statistics by computer system terminals, nodes, and total transactions, can be used to model the network and gain some sense of what is happening. Over time such data can provide the basis for extrapolation forecasting. As with most problems of technological forecasting, however, much planning must be based on "soft" data, because what is needed is a handle on new uses and new users. These items—new uses of the network and new users—may be subject only to some technique of subjective forecasting, although if that is accomplished systematically then some knowledge may be gleaned from the planning exercise.

In most organizations the concept of "planning" is given great lip service, but much of what passes for planning in large organizations is only that—lip service. For planning programs to be taken seriously, it is necessary to have not only goal-oriented planning, but implementation planning as well. The alteration of plans on the fly may sometimes be necessary, but planning for its own sake, with little serious effort made to implement those plans, is a worthless, unpleasant, and unduly expensive exercise in futility.

Notwithstanding the negative comments concerning planning, the successful network manager must anticipate the future. The success of that enterprise, whether called "planning" or not, will dictate the success of the network and its management. At the very least the planning process will provide a guide for funding requests, and the data used to support the planning will provide the fundamental building blocks for decision-makers up and down the organizational chain.

NETWORK SECURITY

Since the inception of computer networks, security has been an often discussed topic. While most discussion of network security has been limited to the data-processing community, the discussions sometimes surfaced in the public press. By 1983, however, the issue of computer network security had become the topic of a popular motion picture (*War Games*), and the problem received widespread comment in the popular press. One of the primary objectives of computer networks, and especially of local area networks, is to provide easy and convenient access to computer systems within an organization and that very ease of use can sometimes conflict with security needs. Consequently, as Thomas L. Davidson and Clinton E. White, Jr. have observed, "measures must be taken by the network security system to identify legitimate users of authorized purposes while denying unauthorized access or use of sensitive data."[10]

Davidson and White suggest that we can think of a security system "as a series of concentric circles forming layers of protection around computer data and resources."[10] The outer rings represent the least security and the inner rings the most security. The real difficulty with the concept presented by Davidson and White is that it is too simplistic in light of modern technology. Some similar approach is, however, probably useful in gaining an understanding of the security issue. Rather than concentric circles, we might instead think of security as a series of layers with the topmost layer representing the tightest security, and the bottom layer the least security. This approach is depicted in Figure 10.1.

Since one of the primary objectives of a local area network is connectivity, successful implementation of a highly connective system tends to thwart some methods of security and control. The various layers of security are designed to prevent unauthorized access and herein lies a major issue of security: At what point is the maintenance of security more costly than a security breach? That question must be answered within each individual organization.

Other issues also intrude into the discussion of security. The size of a network may preclude problems of security or may increase those problems. A small LAN, totally contained in a single office, probably has different security

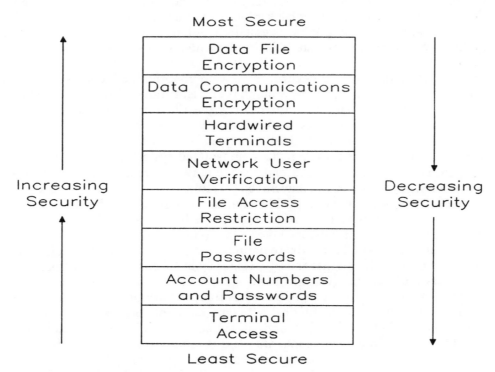

Figure 10.1   Layers of Security

problems than a large LAN spread across a campus environment. In a small LAN, data integrity may be compromised more as a result of inadvertence than of malice, and relatively simple techniques might be appropriate. In a large LAN, encryption or call-back techniques might be needed. With a small LAN it may be possible to control what is attached to a system, but in a large LAN such control may be more difficult. In a large, highly connective system, for example, an individual with a LAN connection may simply plug in a cheap auto answer modem and a new point of semi-public access is created that would be difficult to detect even if rules against such connections were in effect.

Considerable effort has been expended creating encryption systems for data transmission and storage. Those without the key to the encrypted information cannot access the content of the data, although the files themselves might be vulnerable. The integrity of the files can be protected through the use of passwords, but password systems generally are reasonably easy to circumvent.

A better approach would be to isolate sensitive data and its access on "private" concurrent networks using, perhaps, an alternative communications protocol in conjunction with encryption and call-back techniques. A call-back system can often be implemented rather simply and consists of the computer breaking the connection to a user, after the user had properly logged on an application, then calling the user back at one or more authorized terminals from which the application might be accessed. Such hardware systems, supported by the appropriate software, could be implemented in cost-effective ways with many LANs.

How much damage can occur if there were unauthorized disclosure or alteration of sensitive data, and how much is an institution willing to pay to protect the information? These are the critical questions in designing a security system, but it is true, nevertheless, that the only secure computer system is one which is electrically and physically isolated—and if that were the case, it would not be networked. Even in such an isolated system, however, issues of physical security exist. We can make some networks relatively more secure than others, but total security may not be possible.

Security is important and problems of security should be heeded. On the other hand an excessive concern for security will ensure a certain amount of paranoia on the part of network managers. Some security problems exist because some data may be essential to national security, or to the economic well-being of a corporation. Other security issues exist because there are "hackers" (computer enthusiasts given to tinkering) and vandals all around us. Better laws which protect data as legislation has traditionally protected other property might be one way to better deal with computer network security, although such laws are likely to be only marginally effective. The investment individuals and organizations have made, are making, and will make in the future is enormous, however, and security systems aid us in protecting that investment.

There are other unresolved problems with increased security, as well.

First, virtually any security measure, such as those envisioned in Figure 10.1, will have a detrimental impact on performance of the system being secured. Second, almost without fail users will object to security measures since those measures make the network more difficult to use. It was the security procedures traditionally used on large mainframe systems that bothered many users to the point where they insisted on moving to a departmental LAN environment. It is difficult to imagine user-friendly security since security features are designed primarily to keep people out—not make it easier to get in. Yet, as local networks become linked in regional, national, and international networks it behooves corporations and governments to pay attention to security.

NECESSARY TECHNICAL EXPERTISE

What is necessary to be a LAN manager? When implementing departmental micro-based LANs, the person who spearheaded the move to install the LAN is probably most frequently chosen to manage it. His or her job title may not change, and the individual may have little knowledge of data communications, but the enthusiasm that carried the day, combined with difficulties in adding staff, are likely to make the instigator of the LAN the candidate. Sometimes it is the department head, other times simply a person trying to get some assistance to do the job more effectively. In a large organization, the LAN manager will probably be backed up by a corporate communications or office-automation staff. In a small organization the individual may be alone. This implies that perhaps two levels of LAN management are necessary, or at least desirable:

1. Local departmental management as the first line of attack/defense regarding the LAN

2. Corporate management with the resources to do the detailed technical organization necessary to integrate the departmental LAN into broader networks

The departmental LAN manager may do little but wait for a problem, then call the corporate cavalry, or he or she may be expected to do much more, such as integrating the LAN into the daily work of the department, setting up menus to ease the task of using the LAN, or performing many of the management functions outlined in this chapter. In a small organization the LAN manager will certainly be called upon to do these chores. Clearly training can become an important part of the expenses in establishing a LAN. That training can come from many sources. Today manufacturers of equipment and/or network software offer such training courses. In most large cities independent training opportunities are available through specialized courses or at the local college or university. Within very broad limits, the money spent for training is well worth the expense to any organization and should be a standard part of the planning for LAN installation and maintenance. A result of such specialized training is that while the LAN manager may not have started out as a "technical" person, he or she is likely to end up as his or her department's technical representative.

LAN MANAGEMENT IN PERSPECTIVE

Network management will be accomplished well or it will be accomplished poorly—but it will be accomplished. Dealing with a network consists of far more than merely pulling cable and attaching connectors. In all of the activities mentioned in this chapter, there is the underlying demand of the political structure inherent in any organization, and that political structure will either impede or encourage the network and its management. Providing a LAN connection for one user and not for another, or a terminal for one user and not for another, or a "better" terminal for one user and not for another, are activities akin to the patronage systems of old-style party politics.

It is entirely appropriate to think of the distribution of network services as a patronage system since the demands for patronage will often be made by those with the greatest data communications needs. The disadvantage of such a view, however, is that users with legitimate, but not politically forceful, needs may be ignored. Hence, network management may also be likened to old-style precinct captains who not only represented the organization to the voters, but also represented the voters to the organization. This analogy breaks down at a critical point, however, for when the network is operating properly—as it always should—it will be transparent to the user. The user should not know it's there nor should he or she be concerned about the transport mechanism used to get data from one point to another.

It is the responsibility of network management to anticipate needs, not only from those wheels that squeak the loudest, but also of those more silent potential users, and to represent those needs to upper management. In a large organization this need to walk between the demands of contending users or potential ones will never be part of the job description. Yet the success in walking this tightrope will dictate the success of the network itself.

REFERENCES

1. Richard B. Freeman, "Net Management Choices: Sidestream or Mainstream," *Data Communications,* August 1982, pp. 91ff.

2. Freeman, Ref. 1, p. 91.

3. Judith Estrin and Keith Cheney, "Managing Local Area Networks Effectively," *Data Communications*, Vol. 15, No. 1, January 1986, pp. 181–189.

4. Estrin and Cheney, Ref. 3. p. 181.

5. Aaron Brenner, "Theories: Management vs. Maintenance vs. Diagnostics," *LAN: The Local Area Network Magazine*, March 1987, p. 34.

6. Mel Achterberg, IBM Communications Specialist, "Implementation Techniques to Manage Communication Networks," June 11, 1983 (unpublished presentation).

7. Several sections of this chapter follow similar themes I have developed elsewhere, especially the following: Thomas W. Madron, *Local Area Networks in Large Organizations* (Hasbrouck Heights, NJ: Hayden Books, 1983), Chapter 6.

8. Gary Baker, "Doctoring a LAN," *LAN: The Local Area Network Magazine*, March 1987, p. 43.

9. See the review article by Gary Baker, "Tools of the Trade," *LAN: The Local Area Network Magazine*, March 1987, pp. 36–38. Although this is a relatively superficial review article containing several errors, it does give a current perspective on current LAN diagnostic tools. See also, John Seaman, "Controlling Network," *Computer Decisions*, August 1982, p. 144.

10. Thomas L. Davidson and Clinton E. White, Jr., "How to Improve Network Security," *Infosystems*, June 1983, p. 110.

C H A P T E R   1 1

MAKING IT WORK

We cannot say that a local area network will meet the data communications needs for all organizations, but we can say, however, that the values possessed by LANs make them potentially important for most organizations. But there are some important points to remember when designing and installing LANs:

▼ LANs are installed to increase people productivity.

▼ LANs are installed to promote and extend a cooperative work environment for both people and machines.

▼ LANs will not operate themselves—LANs need management.

▼ While both the hardware and software LAN technology is growing and maturing at an impressive rate, a truly integrated system that incorporates micros, minis, and mainframes is not yet available.

▼ LANs are not yet all things to all people.

When a LAN is installed, regardless of its size, we want it to work as advertised. Whether the LAN is designed as a general-purpose information transport system—as is usually the case with large broadband (CATV) projects—or a small specialized network, we are responsible for making it work, and "making it work" is not primarily a technical problem, although technical issues are important. LAN technologies, as they are currently being sold, are well known. Making them work in a technical or engineering sense is also fairly well understood by appropriately trained personnel. On the other hand, if the technical support staff are not well supported by appropriate management commitment, resources will likely not be made available to use the system to its maximum capabilities. In this chapter we will attempt to summarize some of the pitfalls that must be avoided in the installation, implementation, and continuing operation of a LAN.

When deciding to install a LAN, there are at least two ways to approach the problem. First, buy a vendor specific system. By this I mean it is possible to deal with a single manufacturer or manufacturer's representative and use nothing but equipment and software with a single label. Xerox, DEC, IBM, and many others produce and market such LANs. The advantage in this approach is that the vendor (or its representatives) will usually take responsibility for installing and implementing a "turn-key" LAN. The distinct disadvantage is that vendor specific LANs may not be capable of supporting many, if any, products from "third-party" sources. The consequence is that the buyer may not be able to take advantage of new lower cost products, or unusual ones. The ability to support a device is often a function of the network operating system.

The second approach might be to acquire a "generic" LAN. With a generic LAN, even if a systems integrator functions as a purchasing agent for the buyer, the NOS, file server, communications server, network interface cards (NICs), and micros may all come from different manufacturers. The advantages of such an approach, when done carefully, are lower overall cost, more flexibility in the selection of hardware and software, and, as a result, the ability to tailor the system more completely to the specific needs of the buyer. The disadvantages include greater involvement on the part of the buyer in component selection and implementation management in order to better understand the system for long-term management. This conclusion might be disputed by computer stores, systems integrators, and others involved in the selling and installing of LANs, but being forewarned is being forearmed. It is certainly true if you intend to design, install, implement, and manage the LAN yourself.

THE COSTS AND BENEFITS OF A LAN

In the early chapters of this book, we noted many of the reasons for installing a LAN. We can summarize most of those reasons under the term "connectivity." When any node can communicate easily with any other node, then most of the specific objectives can be met; but at what cost and for what benefits? First, it is important to remember, or to understand, that not all costs are monetary, and not all benefits can be resolved into profits. Second, even though many of the costs and benefits are not fiscal in nature, there is little point, from a business perspective, to implement a LAN if that implementation will not provide some competitive advantage to the organization. Third, competitive advantages can be either directly monetary or behavioral in the sense of improving the quantitative and qualitative performance of the members of the organization. By improving the quantitative and qualitative performance of the people that make up the organization, the quality of services or products provided will also improve.

Costs

The costs associated with introducing a LAN to an organization include (but are probably not limited to) the following:

▼ Materials purchases including the acquisition and installation of cabling and associated equipment

▼ Software purchases, including the network operating system, and appropriate multiuser software

▼ Management, including oversight of software installations, adding and subtracting stations, backup, maintenance, and establishing and improving the user interface

▼ Coordination of establishing bridges and gateways to other networks, when necessary, as well as the associated software and equipment costs

▼ Ongoing training of both end-users of the LAN and the personnel used to manage and maintain the network—a never-ending process if there is any turnover at all in your organization

With small LANs all these items may be performed by one person. With a large LAN, a staff may have to be hired to perform these functions, particularly the ongoing functions implied by the need for updating software, management, and training. Because many of these functions are ongoing, and because a LAN will tend to grow, a continuing budget will likely be necessary.

Benefits

In an organization a LAN is the foundation for a system of office automation. The primary benefit an organization can realize from a LAN, therefore, is similar to the benefit a house can derive from a foundation of concrete or stone. It provides a base for constructing a solid system for the technology that can improve the efficiency and effectiveness of a workforce, particularly a white-collar workforce. As we have seen, however, LANs are not only for office automation, they are also available as the base for factory automation as well. The key to either application is *connectivity*. Connectivity allows station-to-station communications to take place which, in turn, make possible:

Direct, immediate communications

Transfer of files

Electronic mail

Multiple concurrent access to a common database

Central filing of organizational data and documents

Concurrent authoring of a single text document using a multiuser word processor

Common organizational calendaring for more efficient scheduling of meetings

Efficient sharing of files for multiple reviews prior to final publication of reports, proposals, and similar documents

Although "imagination" is a bit difficult to quantify, monetary savings or improvements can be placed on many of the other points just listed. Electronic mail is an often used example. The preparation of an internal paper memorandum, dictated to and typed by a secretary, can cost as much as $7.00. The same message, sent electronically, can cost as little as $.03. The filing of documents electronically rather than in paper files can produce similar savings. Common calendaring, when used properly, can save an enormous amount of secretarial time. All of these things collectively may not enable you to fire your secretary, but they may significantly reduce the need for additional clerical personnel. The other items listed tend to help people work more efficiently, thus producing better results more quickly. This means that it may be possible for the same people to produce proposals, letters, documentation, and similar documents with higher quality and greater speed. Furthermore, in many, perhaps most, organizations, the existing personnel will have higher morale as a result of obtaining better tools with which to work. Better use of personnel can provide that competitive advantage we spoke of earlier.

CASE STUDIES IN THE USE OF A LAN

Case studies can sometimes provide good examples of how and how not to implement LANs. The two presented here demonstrate many of the differences between implementations in small and large organizations. The first is a church with about 2,000 members, a full-time staff of six, several part-time staff members, and a few regular, but voluntary, staffers. The total of the regularly scheduled personnel complement was, therefore, about 10, clearly qualifying as a small organization. The second is a large public university with about 22,000 students, 60 departments, and 3,000 faculty and staff, with large central computing facilities as well as departmental computing needs.

Lest businesspeople think these organizations are not comparable to their own organizations let me hasten to point out that they both have problems functionally similar to businesses of comparable size: they deal with personnel issues, payroll, revenue, budget, document composition, database needs, and payment of taxes among others. They, like any business, must use personnel as efficiently as possible, must transmit and receive messages, produce presentations, and in general provide the services any organization must provide. The one single advantage both organizations might have over a business is that internal consulting assistance was available either from existing staff (the university) or from members (the church). Just as businesspeople like to think of their own organizations as unique entities, so too do people in universities and churches. I am willing to argue, however, that when it comes to organizational behavior involving the common problems listed above, organizations are organizations are organizations and they all are constrained to operate in similar ways.

A LAN in a Small Organization

Computers were introduced into the church in the Fall of 1983 when a Texas Instruments Professional Computer (TIPC) was acquired to support two functions: word processing and a church management system called the Local Church Software System (LCSS). LCSS was a relatively complex dBase II application that was being sold to churches in the region. The TIPC was configured with a hard disk, one floppy, and sufficient memory to run LCSS. WordStar was initially chosen as the word processor. The system was acquired during a period of transition from a retiring business manager to a new business manager interested in using computers, although the system was actually purchased before the new business manager was hired. The hardware was configured specifically to be able to run the church management system.

By early 1984 little use had actually been made of the system beyond a significant use of the word-processing capability by the senior pastor. The implementation of LCSS had been relatively hit-or-miss, and the system was still in development when it was purchased. When the new business manager was hired in early 1984, he spent several months evaluating LCSS and the use of the TIPC. When the system was acquired staff expectations were, perhaps, too high. The church staff suffered from the same expectations that business or university people often adopt: that the system will work the first time and forever after and that it will immediately save time and effort. Even though forewarned, they forgot that the learning curve takes time, effort, and frequently money. Moreover, the LCSS software was not fully developed when purchased and was never completely debugged. In fact, by late 1985 the LCSS developers were trying to get out of the business, and it had become apparent that the system would never mature properly. Moreover, it was time consuming to run and terribly inefficient.

As a result of the theft of several typewriters, a Xerox memorywriter, and most of the original software for the TIPC in December 1985, a decision was forced on the church to further computerize or give it up. Although LCSS was not lost through the theft, it was already clear that something else would have to be used for church management. It was also apparent by that time that stronger efforts were necessary to bring automation to the production of the weekly newsletter, the weekly bulletin, and other documents produced by the church. In early 1986 a small task force of computer professionals who were members of the church was organized to re-evaluate the office-automation needs of the church.

The results of that re-evaluation produced a list of critical functions that could be addressed by automation:

▼ Church management system, including:

 Membership

 Stewardship

 Attendance

 Bookkeeping

▼ Printed communications:

 The weekly newsletter

 The weekly worship bulletin

▼ Correspondence, memoranda, and telephone messages

▼ Resource management:

 Facilities scheduling

 Inventory

 Maintenance

 Vehicle scheduling

By 1986 it was clear that a move to the IBM PC standard was advisable to capitalize on the variety of software and support hardware available. It was also clear that more than one PC was needed to replace the stolen typewriters as well as to provide the other functions listed above. Since multiple PCs were to be acquired, it was thought that some economy of scale could be realized if they could access a single high-quality laser printer. To make use of the laser printer, as well as to meet the other needs listed, it was decided to implement a local area network. Multiuser software was evaluated and multiuser Word Perfect chosen as the word-processing system. A church management system was designed and written (using Dataflex) by one of the task force members. Novell's Advanced Netware was chosen for the network operating system. Because of its low cost, Corvus' Omninet was selected as the LAN transport system.

The system was designed to grow, since only three workstations and a file server were acquired as part of the original installation. It was expected that there would be a need for growth in the database as well as increasing demand to provide more workstations. Both needs became apparent almost as soon as the system was implemented. Finally, funds were set aside to provide professional training for the church staff to learn Word Perfect and other elements of the system, including attendance at network training offered by Novell. For cost reasons IBM compatible systems were acquired rather than real IBM PCs. The final configuration was as follows:

▼ PC hardware:

An IBM PC/XT compatible with one megabyte of memory, 37-Mbyte hard disk, one floppy, and a monochrome monitor

Three IBM PC compatible workstations, each with one Mbyte of memory, one floppy drive, and a monochrome monitor

One IBM PC/XT compatible with 10-Mbyte hard disk, one floppy, and color monitor

One Hewlett-Packard LaserJet+ laser printer

One 600-watt uninterruptable power supply for the file server

One 60-Mbyte tape backup unit

▼ Network hardware and software:

Novell Advanced Netware 86

Corvus' Omninet network interface cards for each PC, cable, and connectors

▼ Software:

WordPerfect (networking version)

DataFlex, a database management language to support the church management system

The church management system by now called the "New Generation Church Management System"

PC-DOS 3.1 and miscellaneous other items of software

▼ Training:

Ten hours of instruction for WordPerfect

Ten hours of instruction for the church management system

Fifty hours of general follow-up support and problem-solving after installation for the entire system

Novell's network training was added after the fact for the business manager, since it became apparent that some church staff member required that level of training

Notwithstanding the amount of planning that went into the project, implementation and training was somewhat slower than anticipated but, once installed, the equipment and LAN worked well. As Douglas Chadwick, the business manager has indicated, however, "there have been highs and lows, successes and failures, time well spent and time wasted horribly."[1] Over the entire process perhaps the greatest disappointment was the LCSS software that never came close to living up to expectations. The planning process, according to Chadwick, was "excellent in terms of quality people doing the analysis and planning, support from the lay leadership groups, and staff participation once things got moving." By mid-1986, therefore, the church had a working LAN and was reasonably satisfied with the progress it was making in office automation.

If we could have left the story at this point, we might conclude that the organization and automation lived happily ever after. By the end of 1986, however, it had become clear that more workstations were required, as well as a larger, faster file server. After surveying the IBM compatibles then on the market, a brand other than those originally acquired was purchased, including an AT compatible system and Netware 286. Unfortunately, not all AT compatibles work properly with Netware 286, and the one purchased was never capable of being used by the newer software. Moreover, it had difficulty driving the LaserJet over the network, and there were a series of hardware problems with both the 286 server and the new additional workstations. By the end of the first quarter of 1987, the expansion hardware had been returned to the vendor and arrangements were being made to replace the defective computers with those from another manufacturer. By that time the business manager had also recognized the need for network training.

The point of this narrative is that when implementing a LAN, especially in a small organization dependent on "outside" help and assistance, there will be many ups and downs. Some of the lessons to be learned are as follows:

▼ This case study is a good illustration of the fact that there must be a local LAN manager, regardless of the general technical expertise available for consulting purposes.

▼ While the LAN manager may gain initial experience by default, sooner or later he or she must get more extensive, formal training.

▼ End-user training must be budgeted and scheduled, especially for essential network software and for dealing with the network.

▼ Proper implementation and operation of a LAN requires "people time" as well as proper installation.

▼ LAN hardware and software is not "bulletproof."

▼ The acquisition and implementation of a LAN can become more of an adventure than originally anticipated.

Notwithstanding problems faced, the church just described has a strong commitment to automation, and the staff views the utility of automation positively, if sometimes frustrating. By understanding some of the pitfalls of others, however, it may be possible to avoid similar ones awaiting you.

Deploying LANs in a Large Organization

A second case study that may be of interest deals with a large public university. When it comes to the installation of departmental LANs, the difference between a large business and a university lies only in the possibility that a large business may be able to exercise greater control over the technology to be used. In a university there is often a greater sense of departmental independence than in a business. Neither of these dicta are absolute, however. Even in large businesses that claim to exercise great control over which LANs are implemented, I have seen departmental managers blithely ignore the company standards. Likewise, in universities, I have often seen a considerable measure of standardization, even when formal standardization policies are not in place. Both kinds of organizations face similar problems of technical and political complexity.

With campus-wide networks, either in a university or industrial/business environment, there may be local problems or opportunities that encourage or discourage standardization. In an environment where some networking has been in place for a fairly long period of time, it may not be economically feasible to replace all older networks with a single new campus-wide system. This may result in multiple, overlapping networks even for data communications. Even when that problem does not exist, it is possible, depending on local conditions and modes of organization, to have at least three separate networks, one each for data, voice, and video.

At North Texas State University (NTSU), LANs were implemented on both the campus-wide level and the departmental level. The advantage the university had was that when the campus-wide network was planned and installed no significant amount of networking had been accomplished. What little had been done could be largely ignored. The planning for the campus-wide LAN was begun in 1982, and the fundamental objective was to provide a high degree of connectivity for access to mainframes, minis, terminals and, at that time, relatively few microcomputers. It was clearly understood by the planners, however, that expandability was essential. The absolute need for such a network came about as a byproduct of massive upgrading of the computer system from a single IBM-compatible mainframe and an old HP/2000 minicomputer to one containing at the outset three DEC VAXs, two IBM-compatible mainframes, the HP/2000, and a proposed HP/3000 for library automation. Other systems were also available on the campus, and it was clear that sooner or later they too would be connected. The new IBM-compatible mainframes and the VAXs were to be housed in a new computer-based facility in another building from the old computer room.

The search for a technology took into account all the foregoing issues, as well as the desire to incorporate other communications systems as far as possible. A new telephone system had been installed only a year before, and it was not considered feasible to re-engineer it to incorporate data communications. Concurrently with the planning for data communications, it was clear that those departments concerned with video production and dissemination wished to have a CATV system constructed on the campus but had been unable to gain administrative support. The Computing Center was, therefore, able to capitalize on the need for both video and data communications and proposed that a CATV system be constructed for serving both purposes. The proposal was accepted and the trunk cable system connecting about 60 buildings was installed in 1983. Eight buildings were initially wired and connected to the trunkline at the same time. The Computing Center became the manager of the CATV system.

A Sytek LocalNet/20 was selected as the system of choice for an asynchronous RS-232-C academic campus-wide local area network. Even at this writing virtually the only method available to provide near universal connectivity is through standard asynchronous RS-232-C communications. Ungermann-Bass and 3M were also contenders, but were not able to deliver equipment in the required time framework. In addition, point-to-point radio frequency modems were used to implement a "standard" IBM bisync 3270 display network running over the CATV system, although care was taken to acquire equipment that would be capable of migrating to SNA. Over a period of about four years, the number of CATV outlets in buildings rose from a few hundred in 1983 to about 7,000 in 1987, with users in eight buildings in 1983 to users in almost all buildings in 1987. From any CATV outlet two-way data and video communications could be generated. The campus CATV system was connected to the city CATV network for obtaining and providing video feeds, and to a microwave network (TAGER) that allowed higher education in the Dallas/Ft. Worth Metroplex to provide educational opportunities for private-sector companies. During 1986 a high-speed (T1) data communications system was designed to run over the TAGER microwave network.

By 1986 the widespread distribution of large numbers of microcomputers at NTSU, and the desire for continuing distribution of computing, had led to demands for departmental networks. By default rather than policy the Computing Center became the de facto departmental LAN systems integrator on the campus. It was clear that there was not campus-wide consensus on a single LAN technology, so the Computing Center staff internally agreed to support three hardware systems: the IBM PC Network, Ethernet, and the IBM Token Ring. Several issues were taken into consideration: the need for connectivity to the campus-wide Sytek LAN and to the 3270 Display Network; the need to remain consistent with national, international, and industry standards; and the need for continued use of the CATV backbone. There was also an implied need to meet different departmental requirements. Hardware technologies were also chosen so that a single NOS could be used across all technologies.

The IBM PC Network, originally designed and manufactured by Sytek, was clearly going to be supported by both IBM and Sytek. Moreover, since it was a broadband system it could be run over the entire CATV network, thus allowing departments scattered in several buildings to share a single departmental LAN without bridges or gateways. The existing CATV cable plant could be used with a minimum amount of additional wiring. Use of the general CATV system also allowed concurrent access to the several channels of video programming supported on the system. Sytek had also announced, and then provided, a PC Network to LocalNet/20 bridge/gateway so that a PC with a PC Network NIC could directly access any of the mainframes or minis on the LocalNet/20 LAN as well as its own departmental file server. By using commercial grade head-end translators, it was theoretically possible to connect as many as 1,000 PCs to the PC Network, although if any very large absolute number of sessions were established at any one time it is likely that throughput would be a problem. Network security on multiple file servers was preserved primarily through password protection.

Ethernet was selected as a second technology because of the large number of manufacturers supporting 802.3 standard devices, because of DEC's strategic use of Ethernet, and because of the popularity of Ethernet in higher education generally. Ethernet bridge technology was available at the time to provide interconnection of departmental LANs across the broadband CATV system. Gateways were available to provide access to both asynchronous networks and to 3270 Display Networks. Moreover, in those cases where a higher degree of security was desirable, it was possible to isolate an Ethernet from other networks to a greater extent than was true, at least in principle, with the PC Network. The use of Ethernet had the disadvantage of requiring additional wiring for the connection of devices and did not provide simultaneous access to the CATV system for using video.

Support for IBM's Token Ring came originally as much for public relations reasons as for anything else. It was apparent, because of the amount of publicity IBM was giving to and getting for the product that, at least some university users were going to demand the Token Ring regardless of any real rationale. It was also apparent, however, that the Token Ring was becoming a strategic product for IBM, much the same way the Ethernet had become a strategic product for DEC. An important add-on early announced in the Token Ring's life cycle were gateways to 3270 Display networks, an important issue at NTSU. Like Ethernet the use of Token Ring required additional wiring, and although IBM promised broadband bridges, it was clear that supporting devices would be a while in coming. Even at this writing considerably fewer products were available for the Token Ring than for Ethernet, although that will probably be remedied by both IBM and third-party developers in the future.

Even though organizational politics and other issues demanded the use of more than one hardware technology, the Computing Center was able to convince most people that a single NOS would be desirable. A single software environment was needed so that support problems, including user training, network enhancement, maintenance, and application software acquisitions could be simplified. The only NOS available at that time that would run on all three technologies was Novell's Netware, and it was adopted. Although there are some problems with Netware, not the least of which has been inadequate documentation (although Novell seems to recognize this and is remedying this problem), Netware supports a large array of hardware and application software. Adoption of a common NOS minimized the support problems associated with multiple hardware systems.

NTSU has implemented a number of department LANs. The techniques for managing these networks continue to evolve. By default the technical support staff within the Computing Center, specifically the data communications group, became the default campus-wide systems integrator supported by academic computing (user services) and office automation personnel (also within the Computing Center). One person within the data communications group became the de facto specialist in departmental PC-based LANs. Because of the paucity of personnel support within the Computing Center, and in recognition of many of the issues discussed in this book, the Computing Center insisted that each department that implemented a LAN designate someone as the departmental LAN manager.

It was strongly recommended that the departmental LAN manager take advantage of the training offered by Novell. One advantage of a university environment over a business one is that many times the designated LAN manager was a graduate student, or senior undergraduate, in computer science working part-time for the department. This meant that departments could obtain well-skilled personnel to watch after the network at relatively low cost. The disadvantage of this arrangement is that turnover is apt to be high as students graduate. Many departments, however, opted to slice off some time of existing full-time people to do LAN management, and sometimes this was the department head.

The lessons gleaned from the case study of a LAN implementation in a small organization also apply to a large organization. In addition, there are some lessons essential for a large organization as well:

▼ Departmental or work-group LANs must be interfaced with larger networks, and this must be planned at the outset even when departmental members don't fully understand the need.

▼ A corollary of the foregoing is that the technology is gradually coming into place that, with full connectivity, some largely ignored functions, such as proper backup, will be possible from LANs to mainframes.

▼ LAN management will be a combination of centralized service and distributed oversight.

▼ While training in a small organization may be periodic, it will become continuous in a large organization as many LANs are installed.

▼ Access to central systems is usually as important, and perhaps more important, than access to the departmental file server.

▼ The ability to download corporate information to the departmental file server is usually required.

▼ Interfacing departmental electronic-mail systems and campus-wide mail is not always possible with current software technology (at least not with off-the-shelf technology).

▼ Even with locally available technically skilled people, Murphy's Law will continue to operate: Whatever can go wrong will.

Once the departmental LANs are up and running, however, ideas on what to do with the LANs usually outstrip the ability to implement them. This should be considered a positive rather than negative development because it means that regardless of the problems, user acceptance is high.

LANS AS AIDS TO ORGANIZATION

One of the implied premises on which this book is based is that there is a demand for end-user computing. Historically, those of us that manage large data centers have sometimes tried to stand in the way of the use of micros, and, more recently, the deployment of departmental LANs. Sometimes the deployment of such technology was seen as a threat to the sale of mainframe computer resources, and hence a diminution of the importance of central computing. Such a view, however, is not only short-sighted but is also counter-productive in the sense that the technology of information processing and the demands of end-users are expanding the use of the technology regardless of what central information-processing centers may think.

What we need to do is to understand the role of micros and departmental LANs in the total information-processing picture, then run around in front of the crowd and exercise leadership in the manner in which such systems are to be implemented. It is also clear that in the years to come, the revenues to central computing from the sale of mainframe resources will decrease (relatively, not absolutely) compared to revenues from data communications. The technology, including micros and LANs, is now available to make cost-effective distributed processing a reality. What this does mean is that the role of the central information-processing center is evolving and changing—we are becoming more like the telephone company and less like the electric company.

The onslaught of micros and LANs is also changing the way departments other than the central information-processing center do business as well. The promise, not always fulfilled, is that the technology can assist individuals in doing more work in the same time so that human labor is made more cost-effective. Especially when the technology is used as the base for office automation, the rewards to be reaped are great, although these may be more significant for some operations than for others. Especially in areas of report production and distribution where common access to word processing and the files being processed, departmental databases, and information to be analyzed, perhaps downloaded from central systems, are involved, human productivity can increase greatly.

THE POLITICS OF NETWORKING

Networking, like politics, is often the "art of the possible." The ability to provide network services, is, in virtually all organizations, limited by time, money, and perceptions of the extent to which a specific department is doing "critical" work. Moreover, as we have seen, different people and different departments will have varying ideas about what constitutes the "best" network environments for them. In a more global sense, when it comes to setting standards, it is also clear that standards themselves are a byproduct of compromise and accommodation. I have noted elsewhere that prior to the promulgation of IEEE Std 802.5 (token ring), comments were rife in the trade press claiming that the 802.5 Committee was merely waiting for IBM to tell it what to approve. Although I have not personally tried to verify those claims, and even though they may be more apocryphal than not, it seems apparent from the various additions to the standards, especially 802.3, that many different special interests are being accommodated.

Within an organization, networking strategies are not usually developed by fiat, but rather through a process of discussion that may or may not include true technical evaluations. Consequently, differing needs, differing personal preferences, and differing perspectives on what should be accomplished by networking are all part of the decision-making process. We have, again, the need to compromise among conflicting special interests. When it is recognized that as a practical matter, with many (but not all) LAN implementations almost all available technologies will operate equally well (or equally poorly), then we can more clearly understand LAN decisions as part of an organization's political process. Even the allocation of LAN ports or outlets will, in many organizations, operate more like a patronage system than anything else. Remember the old adage that the "squeaky wheel gets the grease." Another old political truism is that one's friends should be rewarded.

Coalition building is an important part of the functioning of any organization. What this means is that to be effective in a bureaucracy, it is necessary to build good relationships up and down the chain of command. It means, in addition, that good relationships must also be built with those at any point in the organization that can assist you in doing your job. Thus, when a fundamental networking decision is being made, such as what campus-wide transport technology to use, if the task is approached properly, many special interests can be brought together in support of one technology over another. This was implied in the university case study above, when I noted that support was gained from those interested in video communications when it became clear the CATV was also a viable data communications option. This was an example of coalition building within an organization.

Once a truly connective network is in place, along with value-added services, such as electronic mail, it can change the flow of messages between or among people in the organization. So in the long run there continues to be a political impact on the manner in which the organization operates. Especially when additional communications software is put into place, such as computer conferencing systems or bulletin-board systems, new human networks within the organization can arise that probably would never have developed with older, less connective technologies. The telephone must have had a similar impact when it was introduced in organizations, yet the new computer technologies have the potential for more far-reaching realignments of influence.

While I do not wish to overemphasize the role of politics in data networking, I must point out that the behavior of people within an organization is, first and foremost, a form of political behavior. Informal relationships are often more important than chains of command. The objectives are influence, power, prestige, and money, even if for the purpose of doing one's job better; and people seem to instinctively understand one of Machiavelli's dicta: Even when playing politics most assiduously, never admit it—use other terminology, make the process appear to be economics, technology, or something else, but never politics. I note these issues because once highly connective networks like LANs are in place, the potential for a reorganization of the traditional politics may change drastically. And perhaps this aspect of human behavior should also be a part of the planning process when networks are designed. After all, as we have noted, one of the objectives in the implementation of LANs is to alter aspects of human behavior—to make people more productive.

THE FUTURE AND IMPORTANCE OF STANDARDS

Throughout this book we have emphasized "standards." Standards are important because they reflect current thinking about technology, as well as current consensus regarding the technology in question. From the point of view of a consuming organization, standards mean the availability of competing products from several manufacturers followed by presumably lower costs through competition. In the long run it also is likely to mean a greater variety of options for tailoring networks to perform in ways specific to the needs of particular organizations. A mild problem exists in that there are several standards organizations operating both in the United States and internationally, especially in Europe. While many of the standards organizations attempt to cooperate with one another, there is also some competition among them based on differing national political and technical conditions. Then there are the *"de facto"* standards from major corporations. For almost any offering from IBM, someone is likely to call it a *de facto* standard even if few buy it. Thus IBM's SDLC protocol is slightly different than the European HDLC standard. Just bear in mind that while some *de facto* standards may become national or international standards, many (perhaps most) will not.

Notwithstanding the caveats just expressed, standards are important. We have already noted many of the reasons for this. They standardize approaches to networking so that products can be manufactured by many, various products can be interconnected in a standard fashion, and those of us that buy the technologies can have a reasonable chance of knowing and understanding what we get. National and international standards are important for buyers and smaller manufacturers, since those standards make the smaller manufacturers more competitive with the giants. This popularity of standards is growing and will continue to be of growing importance as our world continues to be more inter-dependent. Greater inter-dependence means a greater need for wide-spread data communications, and this means a greater need for standards.

Given the importance of standards, therefore, perhaps the "bottom line" when making a choice of networks is: unless there are other compelling reasons not to, buy systems that explicitly conform to national and/or international standards in preference to systems that do not. I would go even further. If a manufacturer claims that it is providing a "standard" (whatever that is, 802.3, 802.4, or 802.5, for example), write a clause into the purchasing terms and conditions specifying that the equipment must work with other "standard" implementations. And the buyer must beware. An example is the IBM/Sytek PC Network that does, apparently, use an 802.3 standard set of frame protocols, yet the network is not an 802.3 standard network. In fact, the IEEE 802.3 Committee has explicitly refused to place its imprimatur on that technology. Because both IBM and Sytek continue to support the system, however, local conditions may dictate that it is a good local solution, but approach the buying decision with open eyes.

LANS VS. MULTIUSER SYSTEMS

Because this is a book on local area networks, we have not had much to say about multiuser systems except that LANs may serve as an access point to large mainframes or superminis. Especially at the level of departmental computing, however, this issue deserves a bit more thought. In one context I have dealt with LANs in the sense of being simply data transport systems designed to provide peer-to-peer communications. We have, however, also discussed file servers, print servers, and communications servers as part of a complete LAN. Particularly if a LAN is installed for central database access (transaction processing), an alternative to be considered is a small multiuser system. While LANs (with appropriate servers) will not soon, if ever, displace large-scale computing, they compete head-on with departmental-sized systems, such as the DEC Micro-VAX, IBM's 9370, AT&T's 3Bx series, and many others.

Some of the advantages of multiuser systems are:

▼ Single-vendor integration;

▼ Single-vendor maintenance;

▼ Support for larger and faster disk drives, although this is likely to change somewhat as microcomputer technology advances;

▼ Software licensing may be less expensive, although this is not always the case;

▼ Data security is likely easier on a multi-user system;

▼ Systems are available from large, stable, well-known companies with demonstrated expertise;

▼ Since the central processor is usually much more powerful than a standard PC-like device, data-processing capabilities are likely to be more powerful, although this too, is changing.

Some of the disadvantages are:

▼ The multiuser system represents a single point of failure—when the central system is down, all users are down;

▼ Expansion is difficult or impossible;

▼ As with LANs, the larger the number of concurrent users, the slower the response time, but this may be more evident on a multiuser system than on a LAN, since most LAN processing is distributed to each local station;

▼ Although LANs require management, when a department acquires a multiuser system it means that the department is setting up a computing center with most attendant problems.

I have avoided comments on cost for either the list of advantages or disadvantages because cost to an organization is so dependent on local configurations. Some would argue that multiuser systems have a lower cost per user than LANs, but a higher front-end cost. This assertion has little foundation in reality. It depends on how the multiuser system and the LAN are configured. There is cabling cost for both systems. If users are equipped with microcomputers, regardless of the system, no economy is realized at that level. In fact, if microcomputers are used as workstations (rather than dumb terminals), then peer-to-peer connectivity among the micros is likely lost with a multiuser system. In other words, to get a specific cost comparison, it would be necessary to configure a multiuser system and a LAN for a specific department based on meeting the same set of specified needs. In general LANs will give more flexibility, connectivity, and growth potential while, for a small number of users, a multiuser system may provide more power. It may be, of course, that a multiuser system should be combined with a LAN to provide the best computing environment.

LANS VS. EPABXS

A second technology that competes head-on with LANs is the Electronic Private Automatic Branch eXchange (EPABX). When multiuser systems compete with LANs for central-processing needs, especially transaction processing on a central database, EPABXs compete with LANs on grounds of connectivity among devices. EPABXs are the traditional mechanisms for intra-facility communications optimized for telephony. The argument is usually made within an organization that EPABX technology can support both data and voice, although this dual support is often more apparent than real. AT&T, the largest supplier of EPABX technology, attempts to sell such a "combined" voice/data system with its Information Systems Network (ISN) by providing two EPABXs: one for data the other for voice. ISN itself is a data-only EPABX.

LANs and EPABXs have often been distinguished by differences in data rates since EPABXs have traditionally been limited to terminal speeds up to about 19.2 Kb/s. New EPABX technology now allows switching of circuits with data rates up to about 64 Kb/s, although this is still much slower than most LANs. Two issues are important in considering the differences between LANs and EPABXs. With voice communications channel utilization is relatively low, and the average session time is short. With data communications some type of transmission can have 100 percent channel utilization and average session time is much longer (one rule of thumb once was about 30 seconds to 3 minutes for a voice session and 30 minutes for a terminal data session). Both issues limit the value of an EPABX more than a LAN. On the data side, the content of the data also may have a major impact since to fill a screen with characters may take about 16,000 bits, while to fill it with Computer Aided Design Graphics may require 500,000 or more bits. Some LAN technologies would be able to deal with these high data content problems more effectively than would EPABX technology.

Perhaps one of the key differences between EPABXs and LANs is that bandwidth on a LAN is allocated on demand. The manner in which this is done is different for token passing and CSMA/CD schemes, but even for token passing systems when a station is idle it depletes the network capacity very little. With an EPABX, however, whenever there is an active connection between a terminal and some other device, network capacity is depleted absolutely. The amount of network capacity depleted on an EPABX is usually the same as that required for a single digital voice channel. As a result, even if the terminal is connected at 300 b/s, it depletes the EPABX capacity by 128 Kb/s independent of whether data is actually being transmitted.[2]

The advantages of EPABX technology are few. In fact, from my perspective, the only advantage of an EPABX system is that it may support both voice and data applications, although this may come at relatively high cost. The disadvantages, however, are numerous[3]:

▼ Potential connectivity is lower than use of a LAN;

▼ Terminal-based technology with low to moderate data rates;

▼ Relatively long setup times to establish a session;

▼ Limited instantaneous bandwidth availability;

▼ Minimal protocol conversion/emulation capability;

▼ Applications, such as broadcast distribution or resource sharing of print or file servers among PCs or terminals, are poorly supported or nonexistent;

▼ Possesses no intelligence beyond switching;

▼ Does not provide the services that are associated with LANs, thus requiring some central processing system.

I am not enamored of EPABX technology. EPABXs are too costly for departmental systems and cannot serve adequately as a general-purpose transport technology for large (campus-wide) data communications. AT&T, in particular, but also other EPABX manufacturers, are selling many institutions EPABXs for data communications but, in my view, they are doing those institutions a disservice. Today, they are often combining the EPABX technology with a fiber-optic backbone that ultimately requires multiple small EPABXs for a large extended system. This is essentially the approach AT&T uses for ISN. While data rates between EPABXs may be relatively high, the potential bandwidth of the fiber-optic cable is probably under-used, and it still does not have the versatility of large-scale broadband (CATV) systems. With the same number of outlets, the cost for ISN will likely be higher than for a comparable CATV system, and the CATV system can today support a much wider variety of communications. Using EPABX technology as a means for providing data communications technology is probably a mistake.

SOFTWARE ISSUES

When LANs are implemented, one often underfunded expense is the acquisition of appropriate software. Remember how a LAN works when it comes to applications software. The program is read off the file server disk and into the memory of the local workstation. Depending on the configuration of the software, data may be saved either on a local disk or on the file server's disk. Part of the power of a LAN is that processing is distributed while files may be centralized. This characteristic even results in the availability of diskless workstations where all software, including the operating system, is read from the LAN's file server. This has the advantage of lower cost per workstation, but the disadvantage is that the local workstation is unusable without the LAN and the file server (the single point of failure problem we observed with a multiuser system).

The result of this is that one of the first questions asked by a naive department when implementing a LAN is, can we use one copy of WordStar (or some other piece of single user software) from the file server. The technical answer to this question is "yes," the legal (and moral) answer is "no." That is, a program like WordStar can be configured to work from a file server and, depending on the NOS being used, will be able to write files either locally or on the file server's disk. When you buy a piece of single-user software, however, you legally commit yourself, through the license agreement and copyright laws, to use it yourself, usually on only a single microcomputer. When you implement WordStar or something else on a LAN, you are allowing multiple access to the software (prohibited by both licensing and copyright laws) and are, therefore, limiting the revenue to be derived by the manufacturer.

There is at least one technical problem to implementing single-user software in a multiuser environment. When software is written for a multiuser environment, either on a LAN or on a multiuser system, it is written to protect the resulting files or records of the file from being updated, or changed, by being concurrently acted upon by more than one user. This is a problem solved in multiuser systems many years ago. The problem is that if two or more people attempt to update the same record at the same time, the data will become garbled and perhaps the entire file will be lost. Locking is accomplished at least at two levels, and perhaps three: file, record, and, possibly, field. File locking is important when an entire file must be imported, as when a program is loaded. Record locking is needed when a database is being updated. Field locking, while not common on LANs, is a more efficient method of dealing with the same issues as record locking. Some computer language compilers provide for locking services (Microsoft's Quick BASIC, for example), and the network operating system will also provide some of the locking services.

One of the advantages of using a file server is that common files can be used, and possibly updated, by more than one person at a time. Single-user software does not provide the provisions necessary to protect the files in a multiuser environment. One of the primary objectives in using a LAN is to access a common database or allow multiple authors to work on a common report concurrently. In other words, you must invest in multiuser software for use on a LAN. You must budget for it and you must provide the means for updating it when new versions become available. While other uses of the file server (backing up workstation files on the file server disk, for example) do not pose these problems, the integrity of common files must be protected. These issues must be made clear to all users of the LAN or technical, legal, or moral problems may ensue. There probably should be published organizational policies dealing with these problems.

IS ONE TECHNOLOGY ENOUGH? OR, WHAT LAN SHOULD I USE?

As you may have figured out by now, the answer to these questions is neither straightforward nor absolute. Depending on the needs of your organization, you may not even be able to standardize on a single LAN technology—at least not at the present stage of LAN development. You must first ask yourself some questions and perhaps spend some time collecting the answers:

- ▼ How large is the LAN to be at the outset?

    How many stations?

    How large geographically?

    How many concurrent sessions?

- ▼ How large might the LAN grow in one year, two years, or five years?

- ▼ What LAN software applications do you intend to implement immediately?

- ▼ What might users like to do with the LAN in one year, two years, or five years?

- ▼ What value-added services (electronic mail, calendaring, etc.) are needed now, or in one year, two years, or five years?

- ▼ Are auxiliary communications services (voice, video) needed now, or in one year, two years, or five years?

- ▼ Do the primary applications require a deterministic access method (process control, for example) or will a probabilistic system (for office automation, for example) do the job? Alternatively, is some combination needed?

- ▼ Do the throughput requirements demand a high-speed system (10 Mb/s or more) or will a lower speed LAN (5 Mb/s or less) meet the needs?

▼ Is the system a PC-based LAN, or do we need to connect a wide variety of devices (minis, mainframes, terminals, PCs, etc.)?

▼ What are the file server requirements?

▼ What are the bridge and gateway requirements to other networks?

▼ Is there an already installed cabling system that might be used for the LAN?

▼ What are the institutional requirements for the LAN and for connecting the LAN to other networks?

▼ Are there institutional software requirements?

▼ Is there an institutional support staff?

If you want maximum safety, buy from a large manufacturer with a proven track record. If you want maximum flexibility, find some assistance and put the LAN together piece by piece. If you want something in between, find a systems integrator who will design and install a LAN for you. If you choose either of the last two options, choose a system based on national and international standards, if a standard LAN will meet other needs established by your analysis. As a somewhat unsatisfactory conclusion, the answer to what system is the best is that "it depends." It depends on your organization's needs.

REFERENCES

1. Douglas J. Chadwick, "Computer Utilization in a Large Church," a paper delivered at the National Institute in Church Finance and Administration, Candler School of Theology, Emory University, Atlanta, GA, Summer, 1986.

2. "Data Transmission Alternatives: LAN or PBX," *PC Communications* (Delran, NJ: Datapro Research Corporation, formerly Data Decisions, 1985), p. 765:10.

3. See the discussion by Israel Gitman and Benedict J. Occhiogrosso, "LAN vs. PABX," in Raymond L. Pickholtz, ed., *Local Area & Multiple Access Networks* (Rockville, MD: Computer Science Press, 1986), pp. 251–288. See especially, pp. 279ff.

BROADBAND (CATV) TECHNOLOGY AND LANS

Broadband technology is not understood as well as other media by those interested in data communications. Because of the possible role of broadband in 802.3 and 802.4 standard networks, some additional comment seems appropriate. Broadband systems transmit data, voice, and video signals through the use of cable television (CATV) technology and components. It is a communications medium that uses a channel having a bandwidth characterized by high data transmission rates. Like telephone technology, CATV is a general purpose technology which can be used by, but is not restricted to, LANs. The CATV system can be constructed with off-the-shelf components using a mature technology.

BROADBAND OVERVIEW

A broadband network is essentially a bus topology, although, in practice, it is usually a relatively complicated bus. More explicitly, it is a branched directional bus that is termed a "tree." Such a topology combines multiple busses in a hierarchy that contains a central location (headend) and multiple node locations (outlets). Signals flow in two separate paths to establish two-way communications. Transmitted signals are directed toward the headend, while received signals arrive from the headend. These two signals use either separate channels on a single-cable system or two separate cables on a dual-cable system. Various terms are used to characterize and identify the transmit and receive directions.

Transmitted signals going to the headend are referred to as *inbound, up-link, reverse,* or *upstream* signals. Received signals coming from the headend have parallel terms: *outbound, downlink, forward,* and *downstream.* A broadband coaxial cable system can serve as a wide bandwidth communications medium capable of supporting independent and simultaneous applications such as data, video, voice, security, and other similar services.

Any broadband system requires two channels on which data must move. An *outbound* channel is used for traffic leaving the *headend,* and an *inbound* channel is used for traffic directed to the headend. The headend of the system is simply a signal processor that takes an inbound signal and upconverts it to an outbound channel. When a device transmits, it always does so on the inbound channel and receives on an outbound channel. Both channels can reside on a single cable or can, like Wang's broadband system, use two physical cables—one for inbound traffic, the other for outbound traffic.

CATV systems operate with either a 300 MHz or 400 MHz spectrum divided into 39 to 58 television channels of 6 MHz each. The spectrum is organized in a sub-split, mid-split, or high-split system. The *split* refers to the placement of the *guard-band* in the spectrum. The guard-band is a range of frequencies that divides the forward and return channels of the system and is a required dividing line. This organization is illustrated in Figure A.1.

The original CATV systems, and most of those used for commercial television transmission, use a sub-split scheme, because a commercial operator makes money by transmitting entertainment. Consequently, a commercial operator has traditionally wanted the maximum number of outbound channels. In a full two-way environment, however, it is likely that more inbound channels are necessary than are required for normal commercial operations. A high-split system simply provides even more return paths, although in the early 1980s, CATV component manufacturers were not regularly manufacturing or delivering high-split equipment. Even though most commercial operations do not currently have two-way capacity, the conversion to a two-way system is not necessarily expensive. A 400 MHz sub-split system provides four return (inbound) channels and 54 forward (outbound) channels; the mid-split system divides the spectrum into 14 return channels and 38 forward channels.

A broadband system operates by modulating a carrier on a 75 Ohm cable. A number of different cable sizes, such as RG-6, RG-11, RG-59, and semirigid (0.5 in. and 0.75 in.), are common. Each of these cables has different signal loss characteristics that are calculated into the design of the cable plant and determine the placement of amplifiers (*repeaters*, in the 802.4 terminology) on the trunk. The most common commercially used connector to attach a cable to a device is a screw-on F connector, although with the simplest system, Phase-continuous FSK, BNC connectors are specified. When implementing a CATV

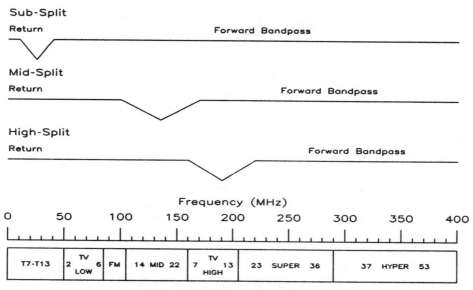

U.S. CATV Channel Assignments

Figure A.1   Single-Cable Frequency Allocations (U.S. CATV Standards)
NOTES: Although all three frequency allocations can be used for single-cable broadband
LANs, the IEEE recommendations are generally consistent with mid- and high-
split schemes, although the 802.7 recommendations modify this a bit. Sub-split is
used primarily for commercial television because it maximizes the number of for-
ward channels.
SOURCE: Based on *Data Communications,* February 1983. Copyright ©1983, McGraw-
Hill, Inc. All rights reserved.

system, the organization of that system affects the selection and spacing of amplifiers on the trunkline and perhaps within buildings. Amplifiers are required
on the system to periodically boost the signal strength along the cable. Amplifiers are unidirectional in dual cable systems and bidirectional in single-cable
systems. Digital signals, in order to make use of CATV, must be converted to
analog signals through the use of a radio frequency modem. Thus, broadband
always uses modulated signals.

Many of the broadband LANs use a CSMA/CD access method similar to
that used by Ethernet, although 802.4 was designed primarily with broadband
in mind. In part, this is undoubtedly because CSMA/CD has typically been
used in a bus-oriented network, while token passing schemes have been the
access method for ring topologies.

The entire sub-, mid-, or high-split CATV spectrum is divided into forward
and reverse channels. Transmission always takes place on the reverse channels
and reception always takes place on the forward channels, in keeping with
video usage in the United States. Thus, all components are directional, because

all transmissions are to the headend or from the headend at separated frequencies. Typically, the trunk or backbone cable, which may be many kilometers long, is structured as a simple bus or, for larger systems, a tree structure, using semirigid cable. Amplifiers are used for maintenance of signal level, although the design should limit the number of cascading (in series) amplifiers.

The IEEE Std 802.4–1985 recommended a communication medium configuration known in the cable industry as a single-cable mid-split configuration. This is also the preferred configuration for IEEE Std 802.3–1985. A high-split configuration would actually provide more reverse channels and thus greater opportunities for two-way communication but, as of 1989, high-split components (e.g., amplifiers) are difficult to come by and more expensive than is true for either sub-split or mid-split configurations. Commercial cable systems typically use a sub-split configuration. The recommended offset of 192.25 MHz between the forward and reverse channels, however, apply equally well to mid- and high-split systems, so that as high-split equipment becomes available, LAN components will not have to be changed.

With current technology, a data rate of 1 Mb/s requires about 1.5 MHz of channel bandwidth; 5 Mb/s requires 6 MHz (standard North American CATV channel); and 10 Mb/s requires 12 MHz. Remember that these bandwidth figures must be doubled, because the same bandwidth is required for both forward and reverse frequencies. Actual frequency recommendations are not a part of the complementary ISO standard, because frequency allocations are a subject for national standardization. Table A.1 lists the preferred pairing for the North American 6 MHz channels using standard North American CATV nomenclature. The frequencies specified are those of the lower band edge. Unfortunately, the preferred channel allocations are also preferred by many other applications, including the 802.3 Ethernet on broadband standard. Consequently, it is likely that manufacturers will produce equipment capable of using other channel allocations than those specified, or that will be frequency-agile so that other applications can truly be used on the broadband medium.

The signal, when transmitted, is sent to the headend remodulator (translator, repeater), which upconverts and retransmits the signal to the receiving channel. This approach is illustrated in Figure A.2. The point is that many different kinds of communications systems can coexist on a standard commercial grade broadband system. At the University of North Texas (UNT), for example (see Chapter 11), the use of the spectrum included six channels of full two-way video, a standard IBM BSC/SNA network using point-to-point RF modems, a very large Sytek LocalNet/20 CSMA/CD LAN, and a large IBM PC network (broadband). Ethernet on broadband was being planned. Although there were no plans for an 802.4 network, that was also possible if the need ever arose.

Because the total bandwidth of contemporary CATV systems is usually 400 MHz, both a large volume and wide variety of communications is possible. It is true that the cost of the initial installation of such a system (UNT connected

Table A.1   North American 6 MHz Mid-split Channels

Reverse Channel	Frequency (MHz)	Forward Channel	Frequency (MHz)
T10	23.75	J	216
T11	29.75	K	222
T12	35.75	L	228
T13	41.75	M	234
T14	47.75	N	240
2′	53.75	O	246
3′	59.75	P	252
4′	65.75	Q	258
4A′	71.75	R	264
5′	77.75	S	270
6′	83.75	T	276
FM1′	89.75	U	282
FM2′	95.75	V	288
FM3′	101.75	W	294

NOTES: The primes (′) indicate that the primed reverse-direction channels are offset from the conventional (commercial CATV) forward direction channels of the same (un-primed) name.

about 60 buildings and in early 1987 had about 7,000 outlets) is not trivial, but the incremental cost of adding some new communications system is minimal. When organizations piecemeal the installation of multiple communications systems, a new wiring plant is usually laid side by side with existing wiring systems. Thus over time the cost of the total wiring plant will equal or exceed a

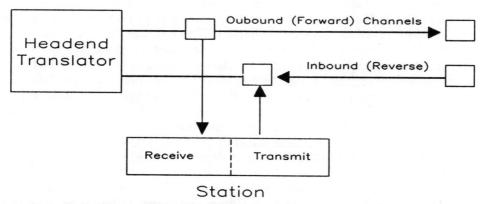

Figure A.2   Broadband Transmission and Reception

commercial grade broadband system without providing the functionality. The cable system just described is called a single-cable design. It is also possible to design a dual-cable system so that transmission takes place on one physical cable and reception on the second physical cable, with appropriate connections made at the headend. This has spectrum advantages but also makes for a much more complicated cable design in a large system.

IEEE 802.7 RECOMMENDATIONS

As a supplement to the other IEEE 802 standards, the IEEE Computer Society has sponsored the IEEE Project 802.7: *Broadband Local Area Network Recommended Practices*. Although only an unapproved draft, published for comment only, was available at the end of 1989,[1] a number of vendors were claiming conformance to 802.7 as may be seen from Table 6.2. Notwithstanding, the draft status of the document at this writing, it, or something very close to it, will have been approved by the time you read this Appendix. The primary purpose of the document is to specify the physical, electrical, and mechanical characteristics of a properly designed IEEE 802.7 broadband medium. The recommendations are consistent with the needs and demands of CATV, MATV, and wide area broadband systems. The specific purpose of the document, however, is to specify the media performance necessary to support IEEE 802.3 and 802.4 video and narrow band services.

The 802.7 recommendation is organized into several sections dealing with medium specifications, medium utilization, documentation, installation guidelines, testing, and maintenance.

An effort was made to make the 802.7 recommendation consistent with existing standards and codes in order to establish consistency within related disciplines. Those standards include appropriate FCC rules and regulations, IEEE 802.3 and 802.4 standards, and recommended practices published by the National Cable Television Association (NCTA). The recommended frequency allocation in 802.7 varies slightly from the standard commercial CATV organization. Without going into excessive detail, for all cable systems the recommendation suggests a 400 MHz bandwidth. For dual-cable the inbound and outbound frequency range suggsted is 54 to 400 MHz; for single-cable, mid-split systems, the suggested inbound frequency is 10 to 108 MHz and outbound is 147 to 400 MHz; and for single-cable, high-split systems, the inbound is 10 to 174 MHz and the outbound is 234 to 400 MHz. The recommended channel assignments for use of 802.3 and 802.4 are referenced in Chapters 7 and 8, respectively.

What the 802.7 recommendation does, essentially, is to summarize the acceptable broadband practices that have developed more or less incrementally over the last 30 years or so. Overall the recommendations are a little tighter than is typical for commercial CATV, although that makes good sense when using a CATV system for LANs. When a vendor suggests that it is using 802.7 recommendations, it means that good broadband practices are being used and that a system built to those specifications will have minimal qualities for providing reliable broadband service.

REFERENCES

1. IEEE Project 802.7: Broadband Local Area Network Recommended Practices, Document Number IEEE-802.7A/D8-89/1, Draft 8.0, June 1989. All rights reserved by The Institute of Electrical and Electronics Engineers, Inc., 1989 (unpublished).

GLOSSARY

Because many of the terms used in this book may be unfamiliar to the more casual reader, a short glossary is provided. The glossary generally follows definitions given in the text and is an expanded version of the glossary found in Thomas W. Madron, *Local Area Networks in Large Organizations* (Hasbrouck Heights, NJ: Hayden Book Company, 1984). When there is some disagreement concerning definition, the following sources have been consulted: the glossary for *EDP Solutions* (Datapro Research Corporation); Kent Porter, *The New American Computer Dictionary* (New York: New American Library, 1983); Master Publishing, Inc., *Dictionary of Electronic Terms* (Dallas, TX: Master Publishing, Inc., 1984); and Master Publishing, Inc., *Dictionary of Microcomputer Terms* (Dallas, TX: Master Publishing, Inc., 1984). Terms used with and relating to IEEE 802 standards have been taken from the appropriate standards documents. While there are several dictionaries of computer terms available, if the dictionary is more than five years old, it may not have many currently used terms in it. Other terms have been taken from the current literature.

amplifier In a broadband system, a device for strengthening the radio frequency signal to a level needed by other devices on the system.

answer modem See *modem*.

ASCII American (National) Standard Code for Information Interchange, X3.4–

1968. A seven-bit-plus parity code established by the American National Standards Institute to achieve compatibility among data services and consisting of 96 displayed upper- and lowercase characters and 32 non-displayed control codes.

Asynchronous transmission A mode of data communications transmission in which time intervals between transmitted characters may be of unequal length. The transmission is controlled by start and stop elements at the beginning and end of each character; hence it is also called start–stop transmission.

Attachment unit interface (AUI) The cable, connectors, and transmission circuitry used to interconnect the physical signaling (PLS) sublayer and MAU.

Bandwidth The range of frequencies assigned to a channel or system. The difference expressed in Hertz between the highest and lowest frequencies of a band.

Baseband (signaling) Transmission of a signal at its original frequencies, that is, unmodulated.

Batch processing A technique in which a number of data transactions are collected over a period of time and aggregated for sequential processing.

Baud A unit of transmission speed equal to the number of discrete conditions or signal events per second. Baud is the same as *bits per second* only if each signal event represents exactly one bit; the two terms are often incorrectly used interchangeably.

Bisynchronous transmission Binary synchronous (bisync) transmission. Data transmission in which synchronization of characters is controlled by timing signals generated at the sending and receiving stations, in contrast to asynchronous transmission.

b/s (bits per second) See *baud*.

BNC-connector A 50 Ohm BNC-series coaxial cable connector of the kind commonly found on RF equipment.

BR The bit-rate of data throughput on the trunk coaxial medium expressed in Hertz.

Branch cable The AUI cable interconnecting the data terminal equipment (DTE) and MAU system components.

Bridge The hardware and software necessary for two networks using the same or similar technology to communicate; more specifically, the hardware and software necessary to link segments of the same or similar networks at the Data Link Layer of the OSI Reference Model; that is, a MAC-level bridge.

Broadband   A communications channel having a bandwidth characterized by high data transmission speeds (10,000 to 500,000 b/s). Often used when describing communications systems based on cable television technology. In the 802 standards, a system whereby information is encoded, modulated onto a carrier, and band-pass filtered or otherwise constrained to occupy only a limited frequency spectrum on the coaxial transmission medium. Many information signals can be present on the medium at the same time without disruption, provided that they all occupy nonoverlapping frequency regions within the cable system's range of frequency transport.

Bus   The organization of electrical paths within a circuit. A specific bus, such as the S-100, provides a standard definition for specific paths.

Carrier sense   The signal provided by the Physical Layer to the access sublayer to indicate that one or more stations are currently transmitting on the trunk cable.

CATV   Community Antenna Television. See *broadband*.

CCITT   Consultative Committee International Telegraph and Telephone. An organization established by the United Nations to develop worldwide standards for communications technology; note, for example, *protocols* to be used by devices exchanging data.

Central processing unit   See *CPU*.

Centralized network   A computer network with a central processing node through which all data and communications flow.

Centronics   A manufacturer of computer printers. Centronics pioneered the use of a parallel interface between printers and computers and that interface, using Centronic standards, is sometimes referred to as a Centronics parallel interface.

Collision   Multiple concurrent transmissions on the cable, resulting in garbled data.

Communications   See also *Data communications*. Transmission of intelligence between points of origin and reception without alteration of sequence or structure of the information content.

Communications network The total network of devices and transmission media (radio, cables, etc.) necessary to transmit and receive intelligence.

Computer conferencing A process for holding group discussions through the use of a computer network.

Computer network One or more computers linked with users or each other via a communications network.

Connectivity In a LAN, the ability of any device attached to the distribution system to establish a session with any other device.

CP/M Control Program for Microcomputers. Manufactured and marketed by Digital Research, Inc.

CPU Central Processing Unit. The "brain" of the general-purpose computer that controls the interpretation and execution of instructions. The CPU does not include interfaces, main memory, or peripherals.

CSMA/CD Carrier Sense Multiple Access with Collision Detection. A network access method for managing collisions of data packets.

Cursor A position indicator frequently employed in video (CRT or VDT) output devices or terminals to indicate a character to be corrected or a position in which data is to be entered.

Database A nonredundant collection of interrelated data items processable by one or more applications.

Data file A collection of related data records organized in a specific manner. In large systems, data files are gradually being replaced by databases in order to limit redundancy and improve reliability and timeliness.

Data communications The transmission and reception of data, often including operations such as coding, decoding, and validation.

Data link An assembly of two or more terminal installations and the interconnecting communications channel operating according to a particular method that permits information to be exchanged.

Data Link Layer The conceptual layer of control or processing logic existing in the hierarchical structure of a station that is responsible for maintaining control of the data link.

Data management system A system that provides the necessary procedures and programs to collect, organize, and maintain data files or databases.

DB-25   A 25-pin connector commonly used in the United States as the connector of choice for the RS-232-C serial interface standard.

Disk (disc) storage   Information recording on continuously rotating magnetic platters. Storage may be either sequential or random access.

Distributed data processing (DDP)   An organization of data processing where both processing and data may be distributed over a number of different machines in one or more locations.

Distributed network   A network configuration in which all node pairs are connected either directly or through redundant paths, through intermediate nodes.

DOS (Disk Operating System)   A general term for the operating system used on computers using disk drives. See also *operating system*.

Download   The ability of a communications device (usually a microcomputer acting as an intelligent terminal) to load data from another device or computer to itself, saving the data on a local disk or tape.

Electronic mail   A system to send messages between or among users of a computer network, and the programs necessary to support such message transfers.

Emulator, terminal   See *Terminal emulator*.

Ethernet   A LAN and its associated protocol developed for (but not limited to) Xerox. Ethernet is a baseband system.

F-connector   a 75 Ohm F-series coaxial cable connector of the kind commonly found on consumer television and video equipment.

Fiber optics   A technology for transmitting information via light waves through a fine filament. Signals are encoded by varying some characteristic of the light waves generated by a low-powered laser. Output is sent through a light-conducting fiber to a receiving device that decodes the signal.

Floppy disks   Magnetic, low-cost, flexible data disks (or diskettes), usually having either 5.25 or 8 in. diameters.

Flow control   A speed-matching technique used in data communications to prevent receiving devices from overflow and loss of data.

FEP (Front-end Processor)   A communications device used for entry into a computer system. The FEP typically provides either or both asynchronous or synchronous ports for the system.

Frame A transmission unit that carries a protocol data-unit (PDU).

Gateway The hardware and software necessary to make two technologically different networks communicate with one another; a gateway provides protocol conversion from one network architecture to another and may, therefore, use all seven layers of the OSI Reference Model.

HDLC Hierarchical Data Link Control. A highly structured set of standards governing the means by which unlike devices can communicate with each other on large data communications networks.

Headend In a broadband LAN or CATV system, the point at which a signal processor upconverts a signal from a low inbound channel to a high outbound channel.

Hertz A unit of frequency equal to one cycle per second. Cycles are referred to as Hertz in honor of the experimenter Heinrich Hertz. Abbreviated as Hz.

High-split In a broadband system, the organization of the spectrum which places the guard-band at about 190 MHz. The mid-split system offers the greatest amount of spectrum for return path channels (14 channels).

IBM International Business Machines. One of the primary manufacturers of computer equipment (usually, though not exclusively, large-scale equipment).

IEEE The Institute of Electrical and Electronics Engineers, Inc.

Impedance In a circuit, the opposition that circuit elements present to the flow of alternating current. The impedance includes both resistance and reactance.

Interactive processing Processing in which transactions are processed one at a time, often eliciting a response from a user before proceeding. An interactive system may be conversational, implying continuous dialog between the user and the system. Cf. *Batch processing.*

Interface A shared boundary between system elements; defined by common physical interconnections, signals, and meanings of interchanged signals.

ISO/OSI International Standards Organization Open Systems Interface. A seven-tiered network model.

Kilohertz One thousand hertz. See *Hertz.*

Line extender In a broadband system, an amplifier that is used to boost signal strength, usually within a building.

LLC See *Logical link control.*

Local area network (LAN) A computer and communications network that covers a limited geographical area, allows every node to communicate with every other node, and does not require a central node or processor.

Logical link control (LLC) That part of a data station which supports the LLC functions of one or more logical links.

Logical record A collection of items independent of their physical environment. Portions of the same logical record may be located in different physical records.

Mainframe computer A large-scale computing system.

Manchester encoding A means by which separate data and clock signals can be combined into a single, self-synchronizable data stream, suitable for transmission on a serial channel.

Manager's workstation A microcomputer containing an integrated package of software designed to improve the productivity of managers. A workstation will usually, though not exclusively, include a word processor, a spreadsheet program, a communications program, and a data manager.

Medium attachment unit (MAU) The portion of the Physical Layer between the MDI and AUI that interconnects the trunk cable to the branch cable and contains the electronics that send, receive, and manage the encoded signals impressed on and recovered from the trunk cable.

Medium dependent interface (MDI) The mechanical and electrical interface between the trunk cable medium and the MAU.

Medium access control (MAC) The portion of the IEEE 802 data station that controls and mediates the access to the medium.

Menu A multiple-choice list of procedures or programs to be executed.

Microcomputer A computer system of limited physical size and, in former times, limited in speed and address capacity. Usually, though not exclusively, a single-user computer.

Microprocessor The CPU of a microcomputer, which contains the logical elements for manipulating data and performing arithmetic or logical operations on it.

Mid-split In a broadband system, the organization of the spectrum that places the guard-band at about 140 MHz. The mid-split system offers a substantial amount of spectrum for return path channels (14 channels).

Minicomputer A computer system, usually a time-sharing system, sometimes faster than microcomputers but not as fast as large mainframe computers.

Modem MODulator/DEModulator. A device that modulates and demodulates signals transmitted over communication facilities. A modem is sometimes called a data set.

Network See *Communications network; Computer network.*

Node Any station, terminal, computer, or other device in a computer network.

Octet A bit-oriented element that consists of eight contiguous binary bits.

Off-the-shelf Production items that are available from current stock and need not be either newly purchased or immediately manufactured. Also relates to computer software or equipment that can be used by customers with little or no adaptation, thereby saving the time and expense of developing their own.

Office automation Refers to efforts to provide automation for common office tasks including word processing, filing, record keeping, and other office chores.

On-line processing A general data processing term concerning access to computers, in which the input data enters the computer directly from the point of origin or in which output data is transmitted directly to where it is used.

Operating system A program that manages the hardware and software environment of a computing system.

Originate-only modem A modem that can originate data communications but cannot answer a call from another device.

Outlet Access point, with an appropriate connector, to a communications medium.

Packet switching A discipline for controlling and moving messages in a large data communications network. Each message is handled as a complete unit containing the addresses of the recipient and the originator.

PBX/PABX Private branch exchange or private automated branch exchange. A switching network for voice or data.

Peer protocol The sequence of message exchanges between two entities in the same layer; it utilizes the services of the underlying layers to effect the successful transfer of data and/or control information from one location to another location.

Peripheral   Computer equipment external to the CPU that performs a wide variety of input and output functions.

Personal computer (PC)   An alternate name for *microcomputer*, suggesting that the computer is to be used for personal and individual work or entertainment.

Physical record   A basic unit of data that is read or written by a single input/output command to the computer.

Program   A set of instructions in a programming language used to define an operation or set of operations to a computer.

Protocol   A formal set of conventions governing the format and relative timing of message exchange in a communications network.

Protocol data-unit (PDU)   The sequence of contiguous octets delivered as a unit from or to the MAC sublayer. A valid LLC PDU is at least 3 octets in length and contains two address fields and a control field. A PDU may or may not include an information field in addition.

RAM   Random Access Memory. Semiconductor memory devices used in the construction of computers. The time required to obtain data is independent of the location.

Reliability   In data communications or computer equipment, the extent to which hardware or software operates in a repeatable manner, often characterized (for hardware) as a low mean-time-between-failures (MTBF).

Remote access   Pertains to communication with a computer by a terminal distant from the computer.

Remote batch terminal (RBT)   A terminal used for entering jobs and data into a computer from a remote site for later batch processing.

Remote job entry (RJE)   Input of a batch job from a remote site and receipt of output via a line printer or other device at a remote site.

Repeater   A device used to extend the length, topology, or interconnectivity of the physical medium beyond that imposed by a single segment, up to the maximum allowable end-to-end trunk transmission line length.

ROM   Read Only Memory. A memory device used in computers that cannot be altered during normal computer use. Normally a semiconductor device .

Router The hardware and software necessary to link two subnetworks of the same network together; more specifically, the hardware and software necessary to link two subnetworks at the Network Layer of the OSI Reference Model.

Session Active connection of one device to another over a communications system, during which interactions do or can occur.

Software A term used to contrast computer programs with the "iron" or hardware of a computer system.

Spectrum A range of wavelengths, usually applied to radio frequencies.

Spreadsheet programs Computer programs that allow data to be entered as elements of a table or matrix with rows and columns and to manipulate the data. Programs widely available on microcomputers are Lotus 1-2-3 and SUPERCALC.

Start-stop transmission See *Asynchronous transmission*.

Station A physical device that may be attached to a shared-medium LAN for the purpose of transmitting and receiving information on that shared medium.

Sub-split In a broadband system, the organization of the spectrum that places the guard-band at about 40 MHz. The sub-split system offers the least amount of spectrum for return path channels (4 channels).

Tap A device that allows an exit from a main line of a communications system.

Teletex One-way transmission of data via a television system.

Terminal A device that allows input and output of data to a computer. The term is most frequently used in conjunction with a device that has a keyboard for data entry and either a printer or a video tube for displaying data.

Terminal emulator A software or software/hardware system for microcomputers that allows the microcomputer to behave like some specified terminal such as a DEC VT100 or an IBM 3278/79.

Text editor A program that provides flexible editing facilities on a computer for the purpose of allowing data entry from a keyboard terminal without regard for the eventual format or medium for publication. With a text editor data (text, copy, etc.) can be edited easily and quickly.

Text formatter A program for reading a data file created with a text editor and transforming the raw file into a neatly formatted listing.

Token The symbol of authority that is passed between stations using a token access method to indicate which station is currently in control of the medium.

Token passing A collision avoidance technique in which each station is polled and must pass the poll along.

Transaction processing A style of data processing in which files are updated and results are generated immediately as a result of data entry.

Trunk cable The trunk (usually coaxial) cable system.

Turn-key system A system in which the manufacturer or distributor takes full responsibility for complete system design and installation and supplies all necessary hardware, software, and documentation.

Twisted pair The two wires of a signaling circuit, twisted around each other to minimize the effects of inductance.

Upload Refers to the ability to send data from an originating terminal (usually a microcomputer) to another computer or terminal.

Videotex A two-way method of communications integrating video and a related communications system.

Winchester disks Hard magnetic disk storage media in sealed containers. Not all sealed disks are Winchester drives.

Word processing The transformation of ideas and information into human communication through the management of procedures, equipment, and personnel. Generally refers to text editing and formatting on a computer.

INDEX